BALLET GUIDE

BACKGROUND, LISTINGS, CREDITS, AND
DESCRIPTIONS OF MORE THAN FIVE HUN-
DRED OF THE WORLD'S MAJOR BALLETS

by *Walter Terry*

ILLUSTRATED WITH PHOTOGRAPHS

DAVID & CHARLES

Newton Abbot   *London*

ISBN 0 7153 6958 X
First published 1976
Second Edition 1979
© Walter Terry 1976

Printed in the United States of America
for David & Charles (Publishers) Limited
Brunel House   Newton Abbot   Devon

For John Ferrone, who was my strict but always encouraging and absolutely essential taskmaster for the 1959 ancestor of this book

Acknowledgments

My gratitude to *Saturday Review/World* magazine for permission to use brief passages and paraphrases from my own reviews that appeared in that publication; to the Dance Collection of the New York Public Library and its curator, Genevieve Oswald, for essential research materials; to Helen Gillespie Atlas, publisher of *Dance News*, for translations from Russian texts providing data that would have been impossible to include without her commanding knowledge of both ballet and the Russian tongue; to Jørgen Heiner, curator of the Library of the Royal Theater, Copenhagen; to Klas Ralf, chief of the Press Department, the Royal Opera, Stockholm; to Maris Liepa, principal dancer of the Bolshoi Ballet, for data on ballet repertory in the Union of Soviet Socialist Republics; to the publicity directors of the many ballet companies whose works are included in this book; and especially to Andrew Wentink, a young writer, dance scholar, and librarian, for invaluable assistance in preparing the essential credits of when (premières), where (places of first performances), and who (initial casts), a task performed with eagerness and exactitude.

Contents

1 *Introduction*
The History of Ballet 1
On Looking at the Ballet 13
19 *Glossary*

27 Abyss	45 Le Baiser de la Fée
27 Actus Tragicus	48 Ballade
28 Adam och Eva	48 Ballet Imperial
28 After Eden	49 Ballet School
28 The Afternoon of a Faun	49 Bartók Concerto
31 The Age of Anxiety	50 Bartók No. 3
32 Agon	50 La Bayadère
33 Aimez-vous Bach?	51 Le Beau Danube
34 Aleko	52 Beauty and the Beast
34 Allegro Brillante	53 The Bedbug
35 L'Amour et Son Amour	53 The Bells
35 Anastasia	54 Bhakti
36 An Evening's Waltzes	54 Les Biches
36 Annabel Lee	55 The Big City
37 Anna Karenina	56 Billy the Kid
37 Apollo	58 Billy Sunday
40 Apparitions	58 Birthday Offering
41 Assembly Ball	59 The Bitter Weird
41 Astarte	59 Black Angel
42 As Time Goes By	60 Black Swan
42 At Midnight	60 Blood Wedding
43 Aureole	60 Bluebeard
43 Aurora's Wedding	62 Bluebird Pas de Deux
44 Bacchanale	63 Bogatyri
44 Badinage	63 Bolero

63   Bolt
64   Le Bourgeois Gentilhomme
64   Bourrée Fantasque
64   La Boutique Fantasque
66   Brahms Quintet
66   Brahms-Schönberg
       Quartet
67   Brahms Variations
67   Brandenburg Nos. 2 and 4
67   The Bronze Horseman
68   Brouillards
68   Bugaku
68   The Cage
70   Cakewalk
71   Camille
72   Cantata
72   Canto Indio
72   Capital of the World
73   Capriccio Espagnol
73   Capriccioso
73   Caprichos
75   Capricorn Concerto
75   Capriol Suite
76   Carmen
78   Carmina Burana
79   Carnaval
80   Catulli Carmina
80   Ceremonials
80   Ceremony
81   Chabriesque
81 · La Chatte
81   Checkmate
82   Chopin Concerto
82   Chopiniana
83   Choral Variations on
       Bach's "Von Himmel
       hoch"

83   Choreartium
84   Choreographic Miniatures
84   Cinderella
86   Cirque de Deux
87   Clarinade
87   Clockwise
87   The Clowns
88   Commedia Balletica
88   Con Amore
90   The Concert
90   Concerto (McLain)
91   Concerto (MacMillan)
91   Concerto Barocco
93   Concerto Grosso
93   La Concurrence
93   Confetti
94   The Consort
94   Constantia
94   Coppélia
98   Le Coq d'Or
99   Le Corsaire
100 Cortège Burlesque
100 Cortège Hongrois
100 Cortège Parisien
101 Cotillon
101 Courante
101 Creation of the World
101 La Croquese de Diamants
102 Cupido
102 Cyrano de Bergerac
103 Dances at a Gathering
103 Dance Symphony
103 Danse Brillante
104 Danses Concertantes
105 Dante Sonata
105 Danza a Quattro
106 Daphnis and Chloë

107	Dark Elegies	127	The Eternal Idol
108	Day on Earth	127	The Eternal Struggle
108	Death and the Maiden	128	Etudes
109	Les Demoiselles de la Nuit	128	Eugene Onegin
109	Designs with Strings	129	Evening Dialogues
109	Devil's Holiday	129	The Exiles
110	Diable à Quatre	130	Façade
110	Dichterliebe	130	Facsimile
110	Dim Lustre	131	Fadetta
111	A Distant Planet	131	Fall River Legend
111	Divertimento	134	Fancy Free
112	Divertimento No. 15	137	Fanfare
113	Donald of the Burthens	138	Fanfarita
113	Donizetti Variations	139	Fantasies
114	Don Juan	139	Far from Denmark
115	Don Quixote	140	Feast of Ashes
116	Double Exposure	140	Field Figures
117	The Dream	140	La Fille Mal Gardée
117	Dream Pictures	143	Filling Station
118	The Duel	145	Firebird
118	Dumbarton Oaks	148	The Flames of Paris
119	Duo Concertant	148	Die Fledermaus
119	Dybbuk	149	Les Fleurs du Mal
120	The Dying Swan	149	Et Folkesagn
120	Early Songs	149	Les Forains
121	Eaters of Darkness	149	The Fountain of
121	Ebony Concerto		Bakhchisarai
122	Echoing of Trumpets	150	Four Bagatelles
122	The Ecstasy of Rita Joe	150	The Four Marys
123	Les Elfes	151	Four Moons
123	Embrace Tiger	151	The Four Temperaments
123	Enigma Variations	152	À la Françaix
124	Episodes	153	Frankie and Johnny
125	Errante	153	Gaîté Parisienne
125	La Esmeralda	155	Gala Performance
126	L'Estro Armonico	157	Gamelan
126	Et Cetera	158	Gartenfest

158 Gayane
158 Gemini (Nebrada)
159 Gemini (Tetley)
159 Ghost Town
160 Giselle
166 Glinkiana
166 The Gods Amused
167 The Gods Go A-Begging
167 The Goldberg Variations
168 The Golden Age
168 Gorda
168 Gounod Symphony
168 Graduation Ball
170 Grand Pas Classique
170 Grand Pas Espagnol
171 Grand Pas–Glazounov
171 Grandstand
171 Graziana
171 The Great American Goof
172 The Green Table
172 The Guests
172 Hamlet
173 Harbinger
173 Harlequinade
174 Harlequinade Pas de Deux
174 The Harvest According
175 Haugtussa
175 The Haunted Ballroom
176 The Heart of the
    Mountains
177 Helen of Troy
178 Las Hermanas
178 Hip and Straight
179 L'Histoire du Soldat
179 Homage au Ballet
179 Homage to the Queen
180 The Hump-Backed Horse

181 The Hundred Kisses
181 Icare
182 Icarus
182 The Ice Maiden
182 Idylle
183 Igrouchka
183 Illuminations
185 The Illusory Fiancé
185 In All Eternity
186 Incubus
186 Intermezzo
186 Interplay
188 In the Night
189 The Invitation
189 Irish Fantasy
189 Ivan the Terrible
190 Ivesiana
191 Jardin aux Lilas
193 Jazz Calendar
194 Le Jazz Hot
194 Jeu de Cartes
195 Le Jeune Homme et la
    Mort
196 Jeux
196 Jewels
197 Jinx
198 Job
198 Joseph the Beautiful
198 Judgment of Paris
199 Jungle
199 Kermessen i Brügge
199 Kettentanz
200 Konservatoriet
200 Labyrinth (Massine)
201 Labyrinth (Butler)
201 The Lady and the Fool
202 Lady from the Sea

202 Lady into Fox
203 Laurencia
203 Legend of Love
203 Leila and Medzhnun
203 Leningrad Symphony
204 The Lesson
205 Liebeslieder Walzer
205 The Limpid Brook
206 Lost Illusions
206 Le Loup
206 Mademoiselle Angot
207 Madrigalesco
207 The Maids
207 La Malinche
208 Manon
209 Marguerite and Armand
209 Les Matelots
210 Meadowlark
210 Medea
211 Meditation
211 Mendelssohn Symphony
211 The Merry Widow
212 The Merry Wives of
       Windsor
212 Messe pour le temps
       present
212 Metamorphoses
212 Metastaseis & Pithoprakta
213 A Midsummer Night's
       Dream
213 Mignon Pas de Deux
214 The Miraculous Mandarin
215 Les Mirages
215 Missa Brevis
215 Miss Julie
216 Monotones
217 Monument for a Dead Boy

217 Monumentum Pro
       Gesualdo
218 Moonreindeer
218 The Moor's Pavane
218 Mother Goose Suite
220 Movements for Piano and
       Orchestra
220 Moves
220 Mozart Concerto
221 Mozartiana
221 Mutations
221 The Mute Wife
222 Mythical Hunters
222 Napoli
224 N.Y. Export, Op. Jazz
225 Night City
225 Night Song
225 Nightwings
226 Nijinsky, Clown of God
226 Les Noces
227 Nomos Alpha
228 The Nutcracker
232 Olympics
233 Ondine
233 On Stage!
234 Opus Lemaître
234 Opus I
235 Opus 65
235 Opus 12
235 Orpheus
238 Out of Lesbos
238 Paganini
238 Paquita
239 Paquita Pas de Deux
239 Parade
240 Paradise Lost
240 Pas de Dix

241 Pas de Quatre
244 Pas des Déesses
245 Pas de Trois (Glinka)
245 Pas de Trois (Minkus)
246 Path of Thunder
246 Les Patineurs
247 Percussion for Six—Men
247 Percussion for Six—Women
247 La Péri
248 Persephone
249 Peter and the Wolf
250 Petrouchka
253 Phèdre
253 Picnic at Tintagel
255 Pictures at an Exhibition
255 The Pied Piper
255 Piège de Lumière
256 Pierrot Lunaire
256 Pillar of Fire
259 Pineapple Poll
260 Poème de l'Exstase
260 Les Présages
261 Prince Igor
262 The Prince of the Pagodas
262 The Prisoner of the
    Caucasus
263 The Prodigal Son
265 The Prospect Before Us
265 Pulcinella
266 Pulcinella Variations
266 Raggedy Ann and Raggedy
    Andy
267 The Rake's Progress
268 Raymonda
268 Raymonda Variations
269 Recital for Cello and Eight
    Dancers

269 The Red Detachment of
    Women
269 The Red Poppy
270 The Rehearsal
270 The Relativity of Icarus
270 Remembrances
271 Les Rendezvous
272 Revenge
272 Reveries
272 Ricercare
273 Rinaldo and Armida
273 The River
273 Road of the Phoebe Snow
274 Rodeo
276 Romance
276 Romeo and Juliet
281 Ropes
281 A Rose for Miss Emily
281 Rose Latulippe
282 La Rose Malade
282 Rouge et Noir
283 Le Sacre du Printemps
284 Sacred Grove on Mount
    Tamalpais
284 Saint Francis
285 Salade
285 Saltarelli
285 Sargasso
286 Scènes du Ballet
286 Scheherazade
288 Scherzo à la Russe
288 Scherzo Fantastique
289 Schubertiade
289 Schubert Variations
289 Scotch Symphony
290 Sea Shadow
290 The Seasons

291   Sebastian
291   Secret Places
292   Sephardic Songs
292   Serenade
294   The Seven Deadly Sins
295   Seventh Symphony
295   Shadowplay
296   The Shakers
296   The Shining People of
         Leonard Cohen
296   The Shore of Hope
297   Shurale
297   Sisyfos
297   Slaughter on Tenth Avenue
298   The Sleeping Beauty
303   Solitaire
304   Some Times
304   Sonata for Eight Easy
         Pieces
304   Song of the Earth
305   La Sonnambula
307   Souvenirs
307   Spartacus
307   Le Spectre de la Rose
308   Square Dance
309   Stars and Stripes
310   The Still Point
311   The Stone Flower
312   Stravinsky Festival
313   A Streetcar Named Desire
314   Street Games
315   Suite en Blanc
315   Suite No. 3
315   Summerspace
316   Swan Lake
323   La Sylphide
328   Les Sylphides

330   Sylvia
332   Sylvia Pas de Deux
333   Symphonic Variations
333   Symphonie Concertante
333   Symphonie Fantastique
334   Symphony in C
335   Symphony in Three
         Movements
335   Tales of Hoffmann
336   Tally-Ho!
337   The Taming of the Shrew
337   Tango Chikane
338   Tarantella
338   Taras Bulba
338   Tatiana
338   Tchaikovsky Pas de Deux
339   Tchaikovsky Suite No. 2
339   Theatre
339   Theme and Variations
340   There Is a Time
341   These Three
341   This Property Is
         Condemned
342   The Three-Cornered Hat
343   The Three Musketeers
343   Three Preludes
343   Three Virgins and a Devil
344   Threnody
345   Til Eulenspiegel
345   Time Out of Mind
345   Time Passed Summer
346   Tommy
346   The Traitor
347   Triad
347   Tribute
347   Trinity
348   Triumph of Death

349 Trois Valses Romantiques
349 The Twelve
349 Two Pigeons
350 Tyl Ulenspiegel
350 Tyrolian Pas de Deux
350 Tzaddik
350 Undertow
352 Unfinished Symphony
352 The Unicorn, the Gorgon,
       and the Manticore
352 Union Pacific
353 Les Vainqueurs
353 Valentine
353 La Valse
355 Valse-Fantaisie
355 Valse Fantaisie (formerly
       Part II of Glinkiana)
355 Variations for Four
356 Variations pour une Porte
       et un Soupir
357 Variations for Tape and
       Choreography
357 La Ventana

358 Villon
358 Violin Concerto
359 Viva Vivaldi!
359 Voluntaries
359 Walpurgis Night
360 Watermill
360 Water Study
361 A Wedding Bouquet
361 Wednesday Class
362 Weewis
362 Western Symphony
363 The Whims of Cupid and
       of the Ballet Master
365 Who Cares?
365 Les Whoops-de-Doo
365 William Tell Variations
366 The Wind in the
       Mountains
366 Windsong
366 The Young Lady and the
       Hooligan
366 Youth

367 *Appendix: London Premieres of American Ballets*
369 *Index*

Illustrations

Following page 106

Le Ballet Comique de la Reine
Lafontaine, the first professional ballerina (Paris Opera Ballet)
Michaël Denard (Paris Opera Ballet)
Lucile Grahn in *La Sylphide*
Fanny Elssler
Pas de Quatre (Grisi, Taglioni, Grahn, Cerrito)
Ulanova coaches Maximova
Danilova in *Swan Lake*
American Indian Ballerinas (Larkin, Tallchief, Hightower, Chouteau)
Baryshnikov in *Le Corsaire*
Adam och Eva (Royal Danish, Alhanko, Segerstrom)
Apollo (American Ballet Theatre, Makarova, Nagy)
Apollo (Norwegian National Ballet, Nureyev, Sindberg, Leahy, Rütter)
Apollo (American Ballet Theatre, Denard)
Astarte (Joffrey Ballet, Zomosa)
Bartok Concerto (National Ballet, Mathe, Burke)
Bayaderka (Leningrad Kirov Ballet)
Bluebeard (Ballet Theatre, Baronova, Golden, Banks, Dolin)
Bourrée Fantasque (New York City Ballet, LeClercq, Robbins)
Capriccio Espagnol (Ballet Russe de Monte Carlo, Danilova, Massine)
Carmen (Royal Danish Ballet, Bruhn, Simone)
Carmina Burana (Pennsylvania Ballet, Fuerstner)
Cinderella (Royal Ballet, Ashton)
The Concert (New York City Ballet)
Daphnis and Chloe (Fokine, Fokina)

Le Diable à Quatre (Netherlands Dance Theater, Sarstadt, Lenaître)

Don Quixote (New York City Ballet, Balanchine)

Don Quixote (Australian Ballet, Nureyev, Aldous)

Don Quixote (Bolshoi Ballet, Maximova, Vasiliev)

The Dream (Royal Ballet, Sibley, Dowell)

Echoing of Trumpets (Royal Swedish Ballet)

Enigma Variations (Royal Ballet, Rencher, Beriosova)

Eugene Onegin (Stuttgart Ballet, Haydée, Madsen, Hanke)

Fall River Legend (American Ballet Theatre, Chase, Young, Wilson)

Fancy Free (Ballet Theatre, Robbins, Kriza, Lang, Reed, Bentley)

Far From Denmark (Royal Danish Ballet, Frishøi, Flindt)

La Fille Mal Gardée (Royal Ballet)

La Fille Mal Gardée (Engraving by Choffart)

La Fille Mal Gardée (Royal Ballet, Nerina, Blair)

Firebird (Royal Swedish Ballet, Lang, Haggbom)

Firebird (Royal Swedish Ballet, Lang)

The Fishermen's Dance (Royal Swedish Ballet, av Paul, Graff)

Four Bagatelles (New York City Ballet, Kirkland, Tomasson)

Giselle (Ballet Theatre, Gollner)

Giselle (American Ballet Theatre, Makarova, Nagy)

Glinkiana (New York City Ballet, Hayden)

The Great American Goof (Ballet Theatre, Golden, Loring)

Hamlet (Bolshoi Ballet, Liepa)

Illuminations (New York City Ballet, LeClercq, Magallanes, Hayden)

Interplay (Ballet Theatre)

Jewels (New York City Ballet, Verdy, Ludlow)

Konservatoriet (Royal Swedish Ballet, Lidström, Graff, Lang)

Le Loup (Royal Danish Ballet, Simone, Flindt)

Following page 234

A Midsummer Night's Dream (New York City Ballet, Villella)

A Midsummer Night's Dream (New York City Ballet, Mitchell)

Monument for a Dead Boy (Harkness Ballet)

Moonreindeer (Royal Danish Ballet, Kehlet, Hønningen, Holm)

Mythical Hunters (Norwegian National Ballet, Rütter)

Napoli (Royal Danish Ballet)

Les Noces (American Ballet Theatre)
Les Noces (Royal Ballet, Mead)
The Nutcracker (National Ballet, Peterson)
The Nutcracker (New York City Ballet)
The Nutcracker (Royal Ballet, Park, Nureyev)
Pas de Quatre (Ballet Russe de Monte Carlo, Markova, Krassovska, Slavenska, Danilova)
Pierrot Lunaire (Tetley)
Pillar of Fire (Ballet Theatre, Lyon, Chase, Kaye)
Poème de l'Extase (Stuttgart, Fonteyn)
Raymonda (Royal Ballet, Fonteyn, Nureyev)
Romeo and Juliet (Royal Danish Ballet, Holme, Kronstam, Vangsaa)
Romeo and Juliet (Bolshoi Ballet, Ulanova, Lapauri)
Romeo and Juliet (Pittsburgh Ballet, Franklin, Ivanov, Filipov)
Romeo and Juliet (Royal Ballet, Park)
Rose Latulippe (Royal Winnipeg Ballet, av Paul, Rutherford)
Sebastian (Harkness Ballet, Aponte)
Serenade (Boston Ballet, Wyckoff, Figueroa, Bauer)
Shadowplay (Royal Ballet, Dowell)
The Sleeping Beauty (Russian Imperial Ballet)
The Song of the Earth (Royal Ballet, Mason, Dowell)
The Song of the Earth (Royal Ballet, Parkinson, Dowell)
Souvenirs (Harkness Ballet)
Spectre de la Rose (Royal Danish Ballet, Kehlet, Ostergard)
A Streetcar Named Desire (Ballet Theatre, Youskevitch)
Swan Lake (Bolshoi Ballet, Fadeyechev, Plisetskaya)
Swan Lake (Royal Ballet, Fonteyn, Nureyev)
Swan Lake (Royal Ballet, Dowell, Sibley)
Swan Lake (Royal Ballet, Mead, Mason, Drew, Lorrayne)
Swan Lake (Royal Swedish Ballet)
The Taming of the Shrew (Stuttgart Ballet, Cragun)
The Taming of the Shrew (Stuttgart Ballet, Madsen, Kiel)
Triad (Royal Ballet, Sibley)
Trinity (Joffrey Ballet)
Triumph of Death (Royal Danish Ballet)
Triumph of Death (Royal Danish Ballet)

Variations Pour une Porte et un Soupir (New York City Ballet, Aroldingen)

Villon (Pennsylvania Ballet, Rodham, Guzman)

Violin Concerto (New York City Ballet, Mazzo)

Walpurgis Night (Bolshoi Ballet, Liepa)

The Whims of Cupid and the Ballet Master (Royal Danish Ballet, Nielsen)

Who Cares (New York City Ballet)

Les Whoops-de-doo (Royal Winnipeg Ballet)

BALLET GUIDE

Introduction

The History of the Ballet

Today ballet is flowering. The nations of the world exchange great companies, a vast array of teachers instruct the young in the hope that from the millions of students another Makarova, another Fonteyn, perhaps a Nijinsky or a Nureyev, will emerge. But ballet has flowered before, ballerinas have been the toast of continents, and masterpieces for the theater of ballet have been created; yet there have been tragic declines. They have come when technique, tricks, surface glitter have replaced adventure, feeling, purpose; when the makers of ballet have forgotten that ballet is part of dance and that dance is an expression of physical, mental, and emotional urgencies, both concrete and abstract, through rhythmic, ordered, dynamic movement. Movement, without expression and urgency, is the skeleton of dance devoid of its living body.

So it is that the dances of early man, or rather his reasons for dancing, are really not very remote from the most elegant and shining way of dance that the Western world has ever devised. And as ballet enters upon a new golden age, the onlooker may well realize that the forces, newly harnessed and imaginatively adapted, of man's ancient dance heritage are responsible in a great degree for the renewal of a vivid theater art. The anguished passion in Antony Tudor's *Pillar of Fire,* the radiant acts of adoration in George Balanchine's *Orpheus,* the disturbing drive of Flemming Flindt's *The Triumph of Death,* or the exuberance of Agnes de Mille's *Rodeo* are all ballet, yet each springs from compulsions as old as man himself, as old and as enduring as dance.

Not every ballet must have a serious message or even a literal

1

meaning. A ballet can be created from the stimulus of music as well as from a narrative plan or a passion for formal grandeur and the endless miracle of design. Whether it is trivial or profound, dramatic or abstract, a ballet can live and communicate life if its choreographer and its executants, the dancers, combine expression with discipline, urgency with form. Today these truths are known, but when ballet first began, trial and error was the rule. There were no true choreographers at first and no professional dancers. Indeed, the initial creators of ballet did not know what they were creating and the word ballet itself had yet to come into being.

It started—this ballet of ours—almost by accident. It started with a dinner party, a rather special affair, a few years before Columbus sailed into the unknown to find a new world.

The sumptuous occasion that Bergonzio di Botta arranged for the Duke of Milan and his bride on their visit to the Italian town of Tortona in 1489 was more of a banquet fête than a true ballet. Yet the ingredients of ballet, as well as of the culinary art, were present in this court spectacle.

Classical figures of gods and heroes, using declamation, song, pantomime, and dancing, paid tribute to the honored guests through a spectacle which, unlike earlier banquet balls in Italy and other lands, had a theme (albeit tenuous) and a cast of characters derived from classical mythology (and not from a group of unrelated sources). The performers were not professionals; rather, were they gifted, or important, members of the household, and the site of the performance resembled not at all the theater with its proscenium arch as we know it today. Still, the elements of a ballet theater were here in this dramatic, rhythmic, organized, and stylized welcome to distinguished guests.

Jason and his Argonauts enacted a scene reflective of their pleasure in the honor bestowed upon the gathering by the Duke's arrival and, before departing, presented him with the Golden Fleece, which, appropriately, turned out to be a lamb, roasted and gilded. Mercury arrived with the calf he had stolen from Admetus; Diana brought a stag; Atalanta, a boar; Isis, birds (cooked in their feathers); Hebe, the nectar of wine; and other figures made their offerings. Servings, recitations, and pantomimes were interspersed with dancing, not ballet in the formal sense, but the social dances of the day. Indeed the word ballet itself comes from *balletti* (derived from the Italian *ballare*, meaning "to dance"), which, until the late sixteenth century, simply indicated the figures used in the court dances of the era.

Throughout Italy the ducal courts lavished time, money, and talent upon these fêtes. Even the genius of Leonardo da Vinci was called upon to contribute designs for a spectacle which, in magnificence, surely shamed the efforts of di Botta. Revivals of ancient Roman plays were also instituted but here again dancing found an outlet in the prologues, interludes, and epilogues which frequently turned out to be more appealing to the audiences than the dramas themselves.

Slowly, the dancing performers of the fêtes and in the plays began to extend the range of action and enhance the patterns of their court dances, infusing them with newly acquired skills and even evolving special movements for primitive, bacchic, or dramatic situations in which the steps of the social dance would not suffice.

Italy, of course, was not alone in this nurturing of pre-ballet spectacle. France fostered the form; the German states glorified the pageant; and the Tudor monarchs celebrated England's rise to power with jousts and ceremonies, pantomime, and ultimately, elaborate masques. But if Italy gave ballet its first impetus, it remained for France to create the first genuine ballet and to assume command of ballet progress, a command which was to endure for almost three centuries.

Catherine de Medici, the Italian-born Queen of France, is known to modern students as a rather ruthless woman, involved in the Saint Bartholomew's Day massacre and in elaborate political activities, dominating her three sons who reigned but briefly while she, as Queen Mother, made her power felt not only throughout the kingdom but also across Europe. Catherine, however, during her docile married life and even after her political ascendancy as Queen Mother, loved dancing and was an expert dancer herself.

The dancing skill of a queen, no matter how celebrated she may be, is hardly sufficient to warrant her inclusion in a history of ballet. But Catherine looms large in the story of ballet because she was a producer, the regal producer of *Le Ballet Comique de la Reine*, a spectacle which boasted a choreographer, cost the French treasury more than three million francs (a tremendous sum in those days), ran for five hours, entertained some ten thousand persons, and stirred up envy throughout the courts of Europe.

The event took place in Paris, October 15, 1581, in the great hall of the palace. In effect, this was an in-the-round presentation, for the royal family sat at one end of the hall, the audience sat or stood around the sides, on raised platforms, in galleries, and the performers used the great expanse of remaining floor as their theater.

Le Ballet Comique de la Reine included declamation, song, instrumental music, mechanical spectacle (Mercury descended in a cloud), and dancing; but all of these elements had been given theatrical unity through the choreography of the Italian-born Balthasar de Beaujoyeulx. Although the production made a tremendous impression and Beaujoyeulx was hailed as a master choreographer, the French court failed to promote the new theatrical genre it had instituted, perhaps because of financial stresses and political unrest. The royal family and the courtiers returned to the simpler fêtes and masquerades of an earlier day and left the development of ballet spectacle to the Italians and, particularly, to the English and their lavish masques.

The French, however, made an enduring contribution to the history of ballet through a book. In 1588 a priest, using the pen name Thoinot Arbeau, wrote a treatise in dialogue form called *Orchésographie*, which not only provided a valuable record of the dance forms and dance music of the sixteenth century (in addition to comments on the dances of ancient times) but also a clear exposition of the evolution of social dance steps into the more stylized and demanding actions of the ballet.

Eighty years after the presentation of *Le Ballet Comique de la Reine*, the French returned in force to guide the course of ballet and to make Paris the Mecca of ballet for the next two centuries. In Elizabethan England the queen herself had encouraged the production of lavish masques and had given the art of dancing a royal boost through her own energetic skills ("Her Majestie rose and dawnced," we are told) as a dancer. The consort and regnant queens who followed Elizabeth also engaged in theatrical dancing but it remained for France's Louis XIV, himself an accomplished dancer, to put ballet in charge of professionals and thus assure its future.

In 1661 the king ordered the establishment of the *Académie Royale de la Danse* in Paris (to be followed subsequently by *l'Académie Royale de la Musique* and the later union of the two). Jean-Baptiste Lully, the celebrated composer (he was also a dancer), was its director and Pierre Beauchamp, a famous dancer at court, became its ballet master and the first to specify in his training the five classical positions of the feet, employed to this day.

Although ladies took part in ballets presented at court, they modestly hesitated about appearing in the theater itself, and young boys, in travesty, assumed female roles. But in 1681, because of the training provided by the *Académie*, the first ballerina, Mlle. Lafontaine, made her appearance in *Le Triomphe de l'Amour*. Not only did Amour triumph but Lafontaine as well, and a new and enduring species of star, the ballerina, came into being.

At the Paris Opéra, Lafontaine was succeeded over the years by an array of glittering ladies: among them the durable and gifted Prévost; La Camargo, who shortened her skirts from floor- to calf-length so that audiences could see the *entrechat*, which she had perfected, and who transformed the female dancer from a gliding creature to an aerial one; Sallé, who let down her hair and discarded costume encumbrances to become a great actress-dancer and the first female choreographer of note; the saucy and pleasure-loving Guimard, who refused to grow old; the nineteenth century's fabled Taglioni, who rose onto the points of her toes and ushered in the ethereal, mystical Romantic Age of Ballet; Taglioni's earthy rival, the sensuous Elssler; their famed colleagues, the Italian Cerrito and the Danish Grahn; and a little Philadelphia girl, Augusta Maywood, the first American to dance as ballerina in the near-sacred Paris Opéra.

The Paris Opéra may have been the official temple of ballet

but the art itself could not be confined by the walls of one theater, by the frontiers of a single nation. In the sixteenth and seventeenth centuries royal and ducal courts of any standing fostered dancing, sometimes as a resplendent social activity, again as a fête or masque or theater presentation. With the eighteenth century the patterns established by France's Royal Academy and the Opéra spread to other European capitals and the art of ballet, Italian-born, French-bred, and basically international in substance, took on the characteristics of the varying cultures which nurtured it. England was quick to foster professional ballet. London managers presented Continental stars to delighted audiences. Sallé, an early favorite, had produced her first choreography (*Pygmalion*) there, and the Romantic Age of Ballet flourished in London as brilliantly as in Paris.

Denmark, with its Royal Danish Ballet and two master choreographers (Galeotti and Bournonville), launched a theater dance tradition that would eventually carry it to international triumphs in the twentieth century. Austria (which produced Elssler), Sweden, Russia, and the Italian states played their roles in the development of a still growing art. America in Colonial times and during the early decades of the nineteenth century was by no means out of the ballet picture; but destiny, the fire and virtuosity of Italian dancers, the directorial and creative skills of the French, and native talent were to make Russia the magical hub of ballet achievement. Indeed, the term "Russian ballet" became for a time almost synonymous with the word ballet itself.

Russia, however, did not invent ballet, although it did establish an Imperial Ballet School early in the eighteenth century and commenced ballet productions not many years thereafter. A century later Russia was turning out accomplished dancers; but for the most part the reins were held by the French, English, Swedes, Italians, and others. Great ballerinas associated with the Paris Opéra traveled to Russia, as they did to other lands, bringing the newest in ballet accomplishments to fascinated audiences. But the ballerina, glamorous as she was, represented a messenger—the creative Camargo and Sallé were rare exceptions—for behind her artistry lay the inventions, codifications, and exploits of ballet masters and choreographers, almost all of them men.

Lully and Beauchamp had been among the first to create for the newly flowering ballet. As performers, Gaetan Vestris (who called himself "God of the Dance") and his son Auguste remained unrivaled from the middle of the eighteenth century into the nineteenth. The great Jean Georges Noverre instituted his choreographic reforms during the Vestris era and, along with the composer Gluck, who gave new direction to the opera, and Garrick, the British acting genius, brought to the ballet his theories of dramatic purpose and meaningful movement as distinct from sheer physical virtuosity or mere spectacle.

Vigano, the inventor of choreodrama; Dauberval, whose ballet *La Fille Mal Gardée* is still performed; Blasis, choreographer and author of *The Code of Terpsichore;* Didelot, a Swedish pupil of Vestris the younger, who became ballet master and chief choreographer for the Russian Imperial Ballet; Coralli, creator of *Giselle;* Philippe Taglioni, father of Marie and choreographer of the history-making *La Sylphide;* Saint-Léon, creator of *Coppélia* and, at one time, ballet master in Russia; Perrot, dancer and co-choreographer of *Giselle*—these were among the great men who not only danced in but made ballets.

For Russia, the most important man of all was Marius Petipa, the Frenchman who came to St. Petersburg in 1847 and remained in command of the Imperial Ballet until his retirement in 1903. Aside from giving Russia and the world a treasury of great ballets —among them, *The Sleeping Beauty, Don Quixote,* portions of *Swan Lake* (all of the celebrated Act III of this four-act classic), and the plan for *The Nutcracker* (he was ill at the time of its staging and his wonderfully gifted and sadly neglected assistant, Ivanov, actually mounted it)—Petipa secured the collaboration of a distinguished composer, Tchaikovsky; trained his charges brilliantly; and advanced the technical range of ballet by exploiting the virtuosic prowess of the Italian Legnani (the first to dance the famous sequence of thirty-two *fouettés* in *Swan Lake*) and the fiery dramatic skills of Italy's Zucchi.

Petipa gave to the Imperial Russian Ballet's native dancers

the choreographic materials with which to work, and Zucchi and Legnani provided them with technical challenges that, at first, they could not match. But then along came Kchessinska to equal Legnani as a virtuoso and to be named Russia's one and only *prima ballerina assoluta;* Preobrajenska, another great dancer; and, as the twentieth century touched the horizon, the shimmering Karsavina and the electrifying Nijinsky, both vital forces in Diaghilev's greatly traveling troupe; Fokine, reformer and master choreographer; and the incomparable Pavlova, who brought ballet to the world.

What was happening in Russia under Petipa, no matter how stirring, was not sufficient to make the ballet world bow to Russian domination. Over the decades the Paris Opera Ballet had retained its eminence not only through its presentations at home but by permitting artists (and sometimes they went without permission) identified with it to go out and extend its luster by performing in other capitals. Russia must do the same, only on a larger scale, and in 1909, it did just that. Paris, ironically enough, was the scene of the Russian triumph.

Serge Diaghilev, art connoisseur and a nondancer with great directorial gifts, gathered together a company of dancers from the Imperial Theater and with the rebellious young Fokine as chief choreographer and Karsavina, Pavlova, Nijinsky, Mordkin, and other luminaries as his stars, opened in Paris in May of 1909, and introduced a new era of ballet to the world.

In this and ensuing seasons in Western Europe, in England (and ultimately in America), the brilliant dancing of the Russians, the vivid and novel ballets by Fokine (*Prince Igor, Scheherazade, Petrouchka, Firebird, Les Sylphides, Le Spectre de la Rose*) and other avant-garde choreographers (Massine, Nijinsky, Nijinska, Balanchine), new musical scores by great contemporary composers, and scenery and costumes designed by the most celebrated painters of the day, made the Diaghilev Ballets Russes the talk of the artistic world. New techniques of dancing and staging, new creativity, new artistic standards had indeed come to change the course of ballet.

For twenty years, until his death in 1929, Diaghilev and his company represented the peak of ballet, unrivaled creatively, rivaled in a popularity only by the adored Pavlova and her own company. Thus, when Diaghilev died and his dictatorial grip on ballet fell lax, not only did his company fall to pieces but the end of international ballet seemed certain.

Two years passed and then the balletic stirrings began. In Monaco some of the scattered dancers were reassembled, new stars were added, some of the Diaghilev repertory restored, and new works by Massine and Balanchine created for a company to be known as the Ballets Russes de Monte Carlo, codirected by René Blum and Col. W. de Basil. Alexandra Danilova was its prima ballerina, with Irina Baronova, Tamara Toumanova, and Tatiana Riabouchinska as the highly publicized "Baby Ballerinas."

Meanwhile, in England there were other ballet stirrings. In 1931 Ninette de Valois, an Irish-born Diaghilev dancer who had founded a ballet school in London in 1926, presented the first all-ballet performance at the Old Vic. The success of the venture convinced the Old Vic director, Lillian Baylis, that ballet could be included along with drama and opera repertories. Ballet in Britain, for the twentieth century, was born as de Valois, Frederick Ashton, and such stars as Alicia Markova led the growth of English ballet from Vic Wells to Sadler's Wells to Royal.

In 1933 the Russian-born American impresario, S. Hurok, took a gamble and brought the Ballet Russe de Monte Carlo (the plurals were dropped after the first seasons) to America, and with its coming ballet became a permanent part of the American theatrical scene.

America, of course, had seen and even produced ballet long before the Ballet Russe de Monte Carlo planted the roots of ballet firmly in the New World.

During Colonial times, dance attractions of various sorts—pantomimes, harlequinades, solo acts—were to be seen on American stages but with the end of the Revolution and the establishment of the Republic, genuine ballet came into its own. A small French invasion took place with French ballet artists and ballet masters guiding the progress of the ballet art in America. The English also participated, as they had before the war, in American theatricals;

but the post-Revolution mood of the new nation made them tolerated rather than welcomed, although they were patronized. Fortunately, America had produced a native ballet artist of considerable gifts, John Durang, customarily referred to as America's first dancer.

Although Durang appeared in classical ballets, in importations from Europe as well as in American ballets and pantomimes (many of them built around patriotic themes), he was most famous for his "Hornpipe," a dance he managed to insert into many productions. If one wonders what a hornpipe was doing in the middle of a ballet, it must be remembered that folk and social dances were frequently integral parts of ballets and that acrobatics, dancing on the tightrope (Durang actually danced his "Hornpipe" on eggs on occasion), and the like constituted accepted dance material.

In the early nineteenth century two child prodigies appeared to give American ballet a special luster. They were Augusta Maywood, who went on to triumphs in Europe, and Mary Ann Lee, the first to dance *Giselle* in America. Julia Turnbull and George Washington Smith were two more Americans who, along with Durang, Maywood, and Lee, helped the American ballet dancer to hold his own in an era that witnessed visits by dancers from abroad, bearing such illustrious family names as Vestris and Taglioni, and by Fanny Elssler in person.

Elssler, arriving for a brief visit, remained for two years and won the admiration of intellectuals, the adoration of the public, and the respect of the Congress of the United States, which went into recess so that its members might attend her Washington performance.

Traveling troupes from Europe continued to flourish during the middle decades of the century and just as interest was waning, ballet received a new impetus with the production of an extravaganza, *The Black Crook* (1866), with Marie Bonfanti and Rita Sangalli as two of its ballerinas. But *The Black Crook*, which ran for two years, and its imitators were not enough to postpone ballet's decline in the American theater. There were sporadic and sometimes distinguished attempts to produce good ballet but nothing much of balletic moment occurred until Anna Pavlova and Mikhail Mordkin electrified an audience at the Metropolitan Opera House in February 1910.

For fifteen years Pavlova, on her frequent tours of the United States, kept the magic of ballet aglow. Momentary bursts of interest in the art were evoked by the occasional appearances of the Diaghilev Ballets Russes, Nijinsky, and other Russian artists.

In England, between the close of the Romantic Age and the great Diaghilev era, ballet kept its chief hold on the public through the ballets at the Empire Theater (1887–1914) and the Alhambra (1871–1914). The Austrian ballerina, Katti Lanner, was the Empire's first ballet mistress and choreographer, and for a decade (1897–1907) Adeline Genée reigned as the undisputed star. In America, the lone Pavlova influence was not augmented by constant Diaghilev seasons—Fokine and other Russian expatriates helped the cause of ballet—so permanence was not achieved until the 1930s had begun. The transplanting of the Monte Carlo to America, the founding of the School of American Ballet (1933) and its associated company, the American Ballet (1934), by Lincoln Kirstein and Edward M. M. Warburg with George Balanchine as the guiding genius, and the forming of Ballet Theatre (now the American Ballet Theatre) in 1939 were the major events in inaugurating a new ballet age for America.

There were, of course, other forces at work. In Philadelphia (a dance-minded city which had produced Durang, Lee, Maywood, and Smith) Catherine Littlefield launched her ballet company, featuring works on American themes as well as the classics (Miss Littlefield produced the first full-length *Sleeping Beauty* to be seen in America). In Chicago, Ruth Page fostered the development of American ballet through her companies and her imaginative forward-looking choreographies. The San Francisco Ballet also had its inception in the early thirties, and in other cities smaller-scale regional ballets came into being.

Still another force, a nonballetic one, was at work creating new interest in the art of dance. This was the so-called modern dance, stemming from Isadora Duncan, and from Ruth St. Denis, Ted Shawn, and their famed Denishawn Dancers, who had brought opulently produced dance programs to every city, and almost every town in America. With Martha Graham, Doris Humphrey, Charles Weidman, Hanya Holm, and Helen Tamiris as its leaders, modern dance had not only established itself as an avant-garde (and indigenous) theater dance form but also had made its powers felt in the world of ballet. Some movements used in modern dance, certain of the principles behind such movements, and the adult themes stressed by modern dance influenced strongly many of ballet's own choreographers.

Even Balanchine himself, a master classicist, was not untouched by modern dance; for although traditional technique provided his genius with the necessary tools of creation, certain of his dramatic ballets showed the influence of modern dance. With England's Antony Tudor and America's Agnes de Mille, Jerome Robbins, and their colleagues, the influence of modern dance has been even more apparent. In Europe, the influence of Duncan was felt by the young Frederick Ashton and the modern dance innovations of Rudolf Von Laban and Massine, Ninette de Valois, and other ballet leaders. Kurt Jooss, with his ballets, represented a middle ground where ballet and modern met.

Year by year ballet sank its roots ever more deeply into American soil. Massine's *Union Pacific*, its title to the contrary, was more Russian than American but there could be no doubts about *Billy the Kid* (Eugene Loring), *Rodeo* (Agnes de Mille), and *Fancy Free* (Jerome Robbins). In addition to these and many other ballets, American flavors penetrated the performing of ballet itself through the vigorous style of American dancers and through the rhythms of new ballet scores composed by American musicians.

The American Ballet and its little sister, the Ballet Caravan, eventually grew into the Ballet Society and ultimately into the world-renowned New York City Ballet. The Ballet Russe de Monte Carlo, in the late 1930s, split into two units, one retaining the parent name and the other naming itself the Original Ballet Russe, since deceased. Ballet Theatre, following its history-making debut in New York in 1940, developed into a company of international stature and built a repertory which became the most varied—traditional classics, contemporary pieces in classical style, Americana, dramatic ballets, comedies, French works, the great ballets of England's Antony Tudor—in the entire field of ballet.

There have been other companies, some large and some little ensembles, some lasting and others temporary, but all have helped to carry American ballet to more and bigger audiences. Some of the choreographers and dancers have taken leaves of absence from their strictly ballet duties to bring ballet into musical comedy, movies, and television. Indeed, the success of de Mille's *Rodeo* swept her into *Oklahoma!* and gave her an opportunity to change the course and elevate the standards of musical comedy dancing. Robbins' *Fancy Free* was expanded into the hit musical *On the Town* and by the mid-1950s the faces of ballerinas, the names of choreographers, and the steps of the ballet had become familiar to television viewers from coast to coast.

The 1930s saw the renaissance of British ballet. Not only did the de Valois efforts serve the interests of the elite, but with World War II the general public. Audiences swelled, government support came for even more than the Sadler's Wells Ballet, new talents emerged (Margot Fonteyn succeeded Markova and new stars were born), Ashton became a world figure in the exclusive circle of master choreographers, and the crown itself recognized the stature of British ballet accomplishments by conferring charters upon, first, the Royal Winnipeg Ballet, and, second, the London-based Royal Ballet.

For the 1960s and 1970s, ballet in Britain, the Commonwealth, in America, in every land and in hundreds of cities, became a resurgent, creative, productive, enormously popular enterprise, indeed the "Liveliest Art."

Catherine de Medici, with her *Ballet Comique de la Reine,* had her moment of absolute ballet supremacy. Today, nearly four hundred years later, the duties and the glories of ballet are shared by the dancers of many nations.

On Looking at the Ballet

There is a difference between seeing and looking. One can see out of the corner of his eye but if he really wants to look at something, he faces it square on and focuses upon it. Dancers illustrate the difference between seeing and looking in two methods of executing multiple turns.

When the ballet dancer does his pirouettes (turns done in place on a single spot) or traveling turns, he uses what is known as "spotting" in order to keep from getting dizzy. He *looks* at an object, light, or spot and holds his gaze upon it while his body begins to turn and when the stretch of the neck has reached its limit (about half a turn), he snaps his head around and refocuses immediately upon the same object. This process is repeated until the turns are completed. Sometimes there are two turns, sometimes thirty-two, as in the long *fouetté* sequence in *The Black Swan.* Some dancers "spot" at two or four selected places instead of one; but the point is they *look* during their spinning travels.

In contrast is the kind of turn in which one *sees* but does not look. Ted Shawn, in dancing his *Whirling Dervish,* did not use spotting because the religious nature of the dance demanded that the turns appear to be the instinctive fulfillment of inner ecstasy rather than a technically maneuvered virtuosic feat. Mr. Shawn explained that he avoided dizziness in this dance of more than two hundred turns by not looking. He saw where he was going but he did not look at any object or point along the route, for a constant shifting of focus would result in a blur and the blur would eventually make the dancer too dizzy to continue.

Fortunately, an audience can sit still (or reasonably so) and concentrate upon the act, or art, of looking. The most elemental accomplishment in looking at a ballet is to discover something pretty, a pretty figure, a pretty costume, a pretty movement, a pretty pattern. Of course, if a ballet is not concerned with prettiness, this limited criterion of looking will be useless. Few ballets these days are built on prettiness, although many of them have pretty aspects. Some are actually concerned with ugliness, tension, despair, such as Balanchine's often macabre *Ivesiana* or Cranko's *Opus One* or Robbins' *Age of Anxiety* or Tudor's impassioned study of frustration, *Pillar of Fire.*

To be content with looking for prettiness in ballet is little different from expecting only prettiness in music, painting, or literature. The "Mona Lisa" is quite pretty in a way but it is more than that. There are pretty turns in Mozart symphonies but these figures are embellishments on great musical fabrics. In dancing also, one should look beyond prettiness.

For the schooled or semischooled or even untutored viewer, there is much to look at, and look for, in ballet. Technical exactitude, for example. One doesn't have to be a trained musician to hear a pianist play wrong notes, a violin scrape, or a singer force a tone; and even if he does not know the names of traditional ballet movements, he can recognize unsteadiness, stiffness, effort, slurring, and sloppy action. Conversely, he can find authority, stylishness, a flowing quality in passages which are obviously intended to be lyrical and brightness in those which are designed for allegro speed.

Ballets with plots introduce character and situation and here one must look for dramatic verity as well as for technical skill and musicality of movement. If a ballerina is dancing the role of a frightened girl, her actions must communicate fear; but if she is a proud princess, every action and gesture must reveal assurance, power. The era and the locale of a ballet will also affect the quality and even the purpose of a movement of dance. A farm girl in the century-old *Giselle,* with its European setting, will move quite differently from a farm girl in Agnes de Mille's roaring, lusty, twentieth-century American *Rodeo.* Some of the basic steps in these two distinctly different ballets may be the same but they are danced differently, colored differently, and the onlooker must look at them differently.

Pamela May, England's fine ballet mime, once pointed out that her very walk, her courtly bows, and her gestures as the ruling Princess in *Swan Lake* are in outline the same but in quality quite different from those of the Queen Consort in *The Sleeping Beauty,* a queen whose husband is master of the realm.

The great Russian-American ballerina, Alexandra Danilova, also notes that a classical movement, such as the arabesque, is never the same twice, that it varies in style and in meaning depending upon the character who is doing it, the musical base, the period, the situation, and where it comes in a phrase of action. The arabesque, then, can simply present the body in a lovely line, perfectly balanced on one foot (or toe) with the other leg extended to its fullest stretch, high in the air or low, or in varying degrees, to the back. But, at times, as when it is used by the Queen of the Swans, it mirrors flight; when the mischievous Swanilda in *Coppélia* darts into arabesque, it manifests exuberance; when Hagar in *Pillar of Fire* rises into arabesque it is almost as if she would escape from the tragedy of earth to a higher and freer realm of air. The meanings are endless and the viewer, to find full enjoyment, should be prepared to look for them.

Finally, there is the complete joy and excitement of looking at the ballet not only with the eyes, not only with the mind, but also with the body. The principle involved is called kinesthetics, perception of movement, and the best way to truly perceive movement is through responses which are reflective of the muscular, neuromuscular, jointal, organic movements of dance. This seems difficult? It is not at all.

When someone is about to take a skid or a fall, the watcher instinctively, although he is perfectly safe himself, attempts to recover balance for the one in danger (empathy). This instinct for reflecting or reacting to (not imitating) the movements of others in our own bodies can be cultivated into a very special kind of esthetic which enables us to share in the immediate action of dance itself. Such a response to movement is easy to nurture because it is instinctive. Those who have studied dancing, those who are athletic have, of course, developed such responses but the sedentary layman needs merely to awake this slumbering instinct.

When the ballerina balances on *pointe,* the onlooker should permit himself to feel the remorseless pull of gravity, should feel a sympathetic tightening of the muscles as body-weights are redistributed to give perfect balance to the figure poised momentarily on a tiny perilous pedestal. When turns are added to such balancing feats, one adds a pulling in of the muscles as they strive to hold close to an orbit. The high swing of a leg invites the sensuous feel of the stretch in our own hip sockets; the lift of the dancer's arms finds an unseen but felt response in the release of our own shoulder muscles; and as the dancer leaps skyward, there is no reason why we should not also fill our lungs with air and find, while sitting in our seats, that our torsos have lifted, almost imperceptibly, upward.

Squirming is not necessary to a true kinesthetic response. But we should permit the force, the beauty, the excitement of action to brush across our bodies and not be content with noting the motions of stage images only with our eyes. For if we respond kinesthetically to a dance itself and by taking part, we know more perfectly what each movement means—whether that meaning is literal, symbolic, fantastic, romantic, or virtuosic, or purely kinetic —and why each such movement was created by the choreographer.

Ballet, of course, has many theatrical forms and, consequently, many types of meaning. The onlooker who expects every movement to have a literal, pantomimic meaning is doomed to confusion, for there are ballets which have no story to tell, no specific characters to present, no situation to reveal. These are abstract ballets, or "pure" dances. But they do have meaning, just as a symphony has meaning, although narrative is absent. The meaning resides in form, pattern, disciplined action and action in space; in developing movement plan, contrasts, the relationships of one body to another.

There are plotless ballets which exploit mood, hint at dramatic situation, project specific emotions but leave their motivations undefined. These are rather like reveries—although they can be and often are enormously exciting or touching—which give visual form to haunting, coquettish, or even tempestuous passages in the accompanying music.

There are ballet episodes, mainly virtuosic, which capitalize on the danger inherent in dancing, and there are those, mainly lyrical, which duplicate the flow of poetry or the lilt of melody with the movements of the dancing body.

Then there are the dramatic ballets—tragedies, comedies, fantasies—in which identified characters advance the plot to its conclusion. Sometimes—and this is particularly true of old-fashioned ballets—rhythmic pantomime is used to tell the story while the actual dancing serves either as interludes to the drama or as a highly stylized extension of the pantomime. In *Swan Lake,* for example, the Swan Queen tells the story of her past through pantomime and explains in pantomimic terms how she can be released from enchantment; but her actual dancing is designed to characterize a swan, a queen, and a girl in love; and in her wholly danced adagio with the Prince who is to save her, romance is clearly projected.

Most contemporary dramatic ballets hold pantomime to a minimum, use it to give flavor to a period piece, or do away with it altogether. When pantomime is absent, outright dancing must do the job of telling story. To a great degree, this has been made possible through the absorbed principles (and many of the movements) of modern dance. It has also been made possible by the effort of choreographers to fuse revelatory gesture and a traditional dance step into a single, meaningful movement; gesture and dancing, instead of alternating, are united into a whole. This is not to say that the great classics of earlier years failed to employ this device on occasion; but the dramatic ballets of today use it almost exclusively.

Thus, in Tudor's *Lilac Garden* or *Pillar of Fire*, in de Mille's *Fall River Legend*, or in Cullberg's *Miss Julie* the drama is danced rather than acted. Balanchine, a great classicist, also dispenses with pantomime and in *Orpheus* uses the eloquence of dance and danced gesture to communicate the full story and the deep emotions of an ancient myth.

The range of ballet is seemingly limitless and the range of the onlooker's enjoyment and appreciation covers an equal span. A performance is a dual project in which those on both sides of the footlights participate. As in radio or television, there is transmission and there is reception and both need to be working equally well if the experience is to prove profitable. Thus, the dancers transmit and the audience receives and this reception must not be passive; for if it is, only half a performance has taken place, only half the magic of the theater has been achieved.

It is not enough to see ballet. One must look at it; and with looking will come understanding, adventure, and a genuine opportunity to share in the vitality, and, occasionally, the illuminating beauty of an ephemeral but ever-living art.

Glossary

ADAGIO A dance in slow tempo. Also, that portion of a classical *pas de deux* in which the ballerina, assisted by her partner, displays her beauty of line and her mastery of flowing, lyrical, and sustained movements.

ALLEGRO A dance sequence in fast tempo.

ARABESQUE A traditional ballet position in which the dancer stands on one leg with the other leg extended behind in a straight line. Positions of the arms may vary and the distance between the free leg and the floor may also vary. In an *arabesque penché*, for example, the body is tilted forward and the free leg extends high into space, sometimes reaching a position vertical to the floor. (See illustrations and cover photograph.)

ATTITUDE A traditional ballet position in which the dancer stands on one leg with the other leg raised behind the body but with bent knee. The pose was inspired by Bologna's famed statue of the god Mercury. If the free leg is extended to the front, instead of to the rear, and adheres to the same spatial design as the movement described above, it may also be referred to as an *attitude*. (See illustrations.)

BALLERINA The term is misused when applied to any female dancer. The *ballerina* is a leading female dancer in a ballet company and if a major company has two or more *ballerinas* on its roster of stars, the principal one may be called a *prima ballerina*. The highest rank, given to the greatest female dancer of a nation and of an era, is *prima ballerina assoluta*, last officially awarded by the Czar of Russia to Mathilde Kchessinskaya (or Kchessinska).

19

BALLET   Derived from the Italian word *ballare,* meaning "to dance."

BALLET D'ACTION   A ballet with a story.

BALLETOMANE   A person devoted to the ballet, a fan, who attends as many performances as possible, is an appreciative and critical viewer, and strives to interest others in the art.

BALLON   A term applicable to the execution of all dance movements in air. The resilience of the dancer and his ability to rise easily off the ground in a jump or leap and to descend lightly.

BATTEMENT   A kick, either high (*grand battement*) or low. In a *battement tendu,* the kick extends only as far as the stretched foot will allow with the tip of the toe remaining on the floor. It may be done in any direction. (See illustrations.)

BATTERIE   The term applied to all movements in which the legs and feet beat together, usually in air (*entrechat, brisé, cabriole,* etc.). In the classroom certain preparatory exercises involving beats are done at the ballet *barre.* The dancer stands on one foot while the free foot accomplishes the beats.

BOURRÉE   See PAS DE BOURRÉE.

BRISÉ   A leg-beat in air. The dancer rises from the floor, beats one leg against the other and lands on both feet in *fifth position.* A *brisé* varies from the *entrechat* in that only one leg does the beating movement, and it varies from the *cabriole* in that the landing is made on both feet.

CABRIOLE   A virtuosic movement in air (usually for male dancers but not exclusively) in which one leg swings out in a high kick and is held at the peak of its extension while the other leg leaves the floor and strikes it in a swift beat or beats. The legs are straight, the feet pointed, and the movement may be done to the front, rear, or side. (See *Brisé.*)

CARACTÈRE   A term used to describe a dancer who performs non-classical character or national dances—such as a czardas or gypsy dance—in a ballet. A *demi-caractère* dancer is one who is called upon to combine character steps with classical action.

CHANGEMENT DE PIEDS   A step in which the dancer jumps from *fifth position,* changes the feet in air and lands in *fifth posi-*

tion but with the position of the feet reversed (if the dancer starts with the right leg in front, he will finish with the right leg in back).

CHOREOGRAPHER The creator of a ballet, the one who invents, selects, and designs the steps and the movements and puts them into rhythmic, geometric, or dramatic sequences which have form, progression, and purpose.

CODA The concluding portion of a *pas de deux* or ballet.

CORPS DE BALLET The chorus or ensemble of a ballet company.

CORYPHÉE A dancing rank which lies between *corps de ballet* dancer and soloist. One who is assigned a few phrases of movement distinct from the actions of the *corps* but who does not perform a complete solo.

DANSE D'ÉCOLE The classic dance, the dance based upon the traditional technique of the classical ballet.

DANSEUR NOBLE A classical male dancer, independent soloist, and partner to the *ballerina*.

DÉVELOPPÉ The gradual unfolding of the leg as it is raised in an extension from the floor. Performed to the front, back, or side. The unfolding action is centered in the knee, which bends as the working leg is withdrawn from the floor and which is straightened when the peak of the extension is achieved.

DIVERTISSEMENT A dance or a series of danced episodes without plot. An entire ballet may be a *divertissement* or the term may apply to the "diverting" interludes in a dramatic ballet.

ÉCHAPPÉ A step in which the dancer's feet move swiftly from a "closed" to "open" position and from soles flat on the floor to *demi-pointe* or, in the case of the female dancer, full *pointe*. Executed from *first* or *fifth positions* to *second position*, either with a jump or with a quick *relevé*.

ELEVATION Aerial action, the ability of the dancer to move as easily in air as on the ground (related to *balloon*).

EN ARRIÈRE To the back.

EN AVANT To the front.

EN DEDANS Inward (toward the body).

EN DEHORS Outward (away from the body).

ENTRECHAT A vertical jump, with the body held in a plumb line, during which the dancer changes the position of his feet several times with a beating of the legs. The number of changes achieved indicate an *entrechat quatre, entrechat six,* etc. (See illustrations.)

ENTRÉE   An entrance, such as the opening passages of a *grand pas de deux* or a suite of dances.

FIVE POSITIONS   The traditional positions of the feet (there are related and numbered positions of the arms also) in ballet. (See illustrations.)

FOUETTÉ   A whipping movement of the working leg which propels the dancer into a turn, into multiple turns, or shifts of direction.

GARGOUILLADE   A movement in air (closely related to the *pas de chat*) in which the knees are drawn up equally high at the climax of the leap while the leading foot describes a circle in space *en dehors* and the other foot moves through a circle *en dedans.* In a loose play on words, dancers sometimes refer to it as "gargling with the feet."

GLISSADE   A smooth, gliding movement starting from *fifth position,* separating into an open-leg position (rather like a leap held to the floor), and returning to *fifth position.*

JETÉ   A leap in which the dancer pushes off the floor with one leg, describes an arc in air, and lands on the other foot. In a *grand jeté,* the dancer seeks the highest elevation possible to him, with the leading leg thrusting out and up as high as the body structure will permit and the propelling leg, once it has left the floor, reaching back to a high extension. Sometimes a near-split may be achieved in a *grand jeté.* (See illustrations.)

LIBRETTO   The story of a ballet or the plot, incident, or theme on which it is based.

MODERN DANCE   A free dance developed concurrently in America and in Central Europe during the twentieth century. Unlike ballet, it has no traditional vocabulary of movement from which dancers and choreographers may draw standard steps. It possesses highly advanced technical skills and methods for classroom training but the dances themselves are composed of freshly invented actions inspired by the music, idea, period, and purpose of the piece.

NOTATION   A script method for writing down the movements of a dance or ballet so they may be revived or reproduced by others capable of reading the script. Methods employing stick figures, sometimes placed on a musical staff and in other cases paired with musical symbols, have been used for several centuries. The most exact form of notation known today is called *Labanotation*. Another contemporary notational method, developed in England, is the *Benesh system*.

PANTOMIME   Imitative movement, usually gestural, by which emotions, character, and the key points in a plot are communicated to an audience. Both realistic and stylized gesture may be used. Among the traditional gestures used in ballet, those indicating Love (the hands are pressed against the heart), or Anger (arms are raised above the head and fists are shaken), may be considered reasonably realistic while Dance (hands circling around each other over the head), and Queen (the index finger touches either side of the brow where a crown might rest), would be looked upon as stylized gestures.

PAS   A danced step or movement. Also used to denote a short dance or dance passage (in this sense, usually used with a modifier, such as *pas seul* or *pas de deux*, etc.).

PAS D'ACTION   Episodes in ballet which advance the plot, introduce dramatic incident, or establish relationships among the characters. A combination of dancing and pantomime.

PAS DE BASQUE   A light, sliding step (name derives from Basque dancing).

PAS DE BOURRÉE   A walking step, usually swift, done on the ball of the foot or, with the female dancer, usually on *pointe*. The dancer may travel in any direction and the steps are customarily so short that the separation between the dancer's legs as she moves is barely discernible.

PAS DE CHAT   A catlike step. From a *plié* in *fifth position*, the dancer leaps into the air, drawing up one leg (with bent knee) and immediately duplicating the action with the other leg so that at the peak of elevation, the toes almost meet in air.

PAS DE DEUX   A dance for two. A classical *grand pas de deux* is performed by a *ballerina* and a *premier danseur* and is divided into an *entrée, adagio,* two *variations,* and *coda.* Also, *pas de trois* (a dance for three), *pas de quatre* (for four), *pas de cinq* (for five), *pas de six* (for six), etc.

PAS DE POISSON   A climactic movement in a phrase of action in which the female dancer hurls herself in the direction of the floor and is caught by her partner as her body bends upward in a fishlike arc. When the male dancer jumps upward and describes a similar arc of the body, the movement may also be described as a *pas de poisson,* although this male movement is actually a form of *soubresaut.* The same body line is described in space at the peak of a *cabriole en arrière.* (See illustrations.)

PIROUETTE   A turn of the body on one foot. Usually, the female does the movement on *pointe;* the male, always on *demi-pointe* (on the ball of the foot). The free leg may be held in any of a number of approved positions—against the ankle of the working leg or higher up along the calf, straight out to the side (*à la seconde, en attitude,* etc.). (See illustrations.)

PLIÉ   A bending of the knees, with the hips, legs, and feet turned outward. A *demi-plié* is a small knee-bend while a *grand-plié* is a deep knee-bend. This is the movement which enables the dancer to spring high into the air and to return to the ground (when a second *plié* is done) lightly, without jarring.

POINTE   The tip of the toe. The female dancer, when she is dancing *sur les pointes* (or, more popularly, on *pointe*) is moving on the tips of her toes and wearing blocked toe slippers which give her added support. Toe dancing, incidentally, is not synonymous with the word *ballet,* for ballet existed long before the *ballerina* rose onto *pointe* and long before the toeslipper was invented. *Pointe* dancing added new physical peril, new movement possibilities, and new beauty to the basic, established technique of ballet.

PORT DE BRAS   The positions and the movements of the arms. (See illustrations.)

RELEVÉ   Rising onto *pointe* or *demi-pointe.*

RÉVÉRENCE   A low, courtly, graceful bow.

ROND DE JAMBE   A rotary movement of the leg either on the floor or in the air (*à terre* or *en l'air*).

SAUTÉ   A jump.

TERRE-À-TERRE   Steps which are done on the ground.

TIGHTS   The skin-tight garment which encases the body from trunk to feet.

TOUR   A turn. A *pirouette* is a *tour* but the term is usually employed with a modifier, such as *tour jeté, tour en l'air,* etc.

TOUR EN L'AIR   One of the most brilliant movements for the male dancer (although it is sometimes executed by the female). From *fifth position* in *demi-plié*, the dancer springs straight up into the air and does a complete turn of the body before landing in the position from which he started. Most male dancers can accomplish a double turn in air, a few can do triples. In a virtuosic sequence, the male dancer may be called upon to execute a whole series of doubles, one right after the other.

TURNOUT   The body position characteristic of ballet, with the legs turned out from the hips at (with professional dancers and advanced students but *not* beginners) a 180-degree angle.

TUTU   The skirt worn by the female ballet dancer. In the romantic style (instituted by Taglioni), it reached almost to the ankle. In the later classic style it has been shortened so the entire leg is revealed, the *tutu* extending out from the hips rather like a huge powder puff.

VARIATION   A solo dance. The same as *pas seul.*

Abyss

Choreography, Stuart Hodes; music, Marga Richter; libretto, after Leonid Andreyev; décor and costumes, André Delfau. First performed by the Harkness Ballet, Cannes, France, February 21, 1965. The ballet was first performed in New York by the same company at the Broadway Theatre, November 3, 1967. A revival by the City Center Joffrey Ballet was first presented March 3, 1971.

This ballet, based on a story by Leonid Andreyev, is cast in modern dance terms although it does contain *tours en l'air*, ballet lifts, and the like. It concerns two young lovers, romantic but not sensual, with the boy honoring the total innocence of the girl. Three rough men enter, separate the sweethearts, carry her off, after ripping off her dress. When she returns, there is no doubt that she has been brutally assaulted. At first the boy is all tenderness and shocked solicitude, but as if violence begets violence, his attraction to her becomes wholly physical, and as the ballet ends, she becomes the dazed victim of another raping.

Lone Isaksen and Erik Bruhn were the lovers in the first performance.

Actus Tragicus

Choreography, Maurice Béjart; music, Johann Sebastian Bach (Cantatas 51 and 106); décor and costumes, Joelle Roustan and Roger Bernard. First performed by Ballet of the Twentieth Century, 1969. The first American performance, by the same company, was at the Brooklyn Academy of Music, January 29, 1971.

Adam och Eva

(Adam and Eve; Eden—Pas de Deux)

> *Choreography, Birgit Cullberg; music, Hilding Rosenberg (Concerto for String Orchestra); scenery and costumes, Per Falk; lighting, Nananne Porcher. First produced by American Ballet Theatre at the 54th Street Theatre, New York, October 4, 1961.*

A passionate and playful view of the world's first couple as they enjoyed themselves in Eden. At the premiere, the roles were danced by Caj Selling and Mariane Orlando. Per Arthur Segerström and Anneli Alhanko were the dancers on the occasion of the Royal Swedish Ballet's 200th anniversary gala, November 7, 1973.

After Eden

> *Choreography, John Butler; music, Lee Hoiby; decor and costumes, Rouben Ter-Arutunian. First performed in New York by the Harkness Ballet, November 9, 1967; first performed by the City Center Joffrey Ballet, March 21, 1972; and by The Pennsylvania Ballet, October 18, 1973.*

There are many ballets and modern dance works based upon the Adam and Eve theme. *After Eden*, although conceived in modern dance terms, was created especially for ballet. As the title suggests, it takes place after the idyllic initial life in Eden and after the Temptation and Fall, concerning itself with the two exiles, their remorse, their shame, their passing anger with each other and their ultimate coming together in necessity and love.

Lawrence Rhodes and Lone Isaksen were its first dancers.

The Afternoon of a Faun

(L'Après-Midi d'un Faune)

> *Choreography, Vaslav Nijinsky; music, Claude Debussy; scenery and costumes, Léon Bakst. First produced by Diaghilev's Ballets Russes, Paris, May 29, 1912. First American perform-*

*ance, same company, New York, January 18, 1916. Entirely
new conception and production with choreography by Jerome
Robbins, music of Debussy, costumes by Irene Sharaff, décor
and lighting by Jean Rosenthal. First performance, New York,
May 14, 1953, New York City Ballet. Also produced by
Jerome Robbins' Ballets: U.S.A. The Robbins version was
staged for the Royal Ballet and first performed by that company, London, December 14, 1971. Another version, choreography by Serge Lifar, was first performed March 18, 1935,
in Paris. This version was revived by the Paris Opera Ballet
and first performed in London in the fall of 1954. The Robbins' version was first presented by the Royal Danish Ballet,
March 12, 1966.*

In the Nijinsky creation, as the curtain rises a faun is seen atop
a little hill washed in warm and golden sunlight. He appears
to be part youth, part animal, for there are tiny horns on his head,
a strange cast to his face and although his upper body is bare (in
early performances, this was covered in the same manner as the
legs), his hips and thighs are marked with the brown patches of
a goatlike creature.

The faun, luxuriating in the sun, plays his flute, eats from a
bunch of grapes, moves lazily. But alertness floods his body as
seven nymphs enter on their way to bathe at a nearby pool.
Slowly, gracefully, he descends from his hill in order to observe
these lovely creatures at closer range. The nymphs, in turn, are
fascinated by this strange boy-animal, but as he leaps playfully
into their midst, they run away.

Curiosity brings them back but the quick dartings, the sensual
gestures of the faun frighten them off again—all but one, a nymph
with more curiosity or greater daring than her sisters. She dances
with him, permits him to touch her, and even suggests that his
savage but strangely delicate movements of courtship are not un-
welcome. But then she also succumbs to fear, and flees, dropping
her scarf behind her. The sad faun retrieves the scarf and, bearing
it in his arms as if it were precious, slowly climbs back to his re-
treat. Kneeling, he presses the scarf to his lips in a kiss; then,

spreading it on the ground, he lets his body sink slowly upon it in gentle amorousness.

Nijinsky, in creating *The Afternoon of a Faun,* departed from all of the ballet traditions of his day. The classical turnout of the limbs, and curved *port de bras* were replaced by sharp two-dimensional designs inspired, presumably, by the figures on an antique Greek vase or frieze. The actions, slow and, of course, highly stylized, were paired with many poses, moments of arrested action which were not so much pauses as they were preparations for motion to come.

Naturally, the ballet caused a great deal of discussion when it was first introduced and minor scandals attended the ballet's closing passage, which many felt to be far too erotic. Modifications in the faun's final gesture were introduced but over the years various interpreters of the role have adapted the movement to suit their individual conceptions, some giving accent to the sad and tender lostness inherent in the closing measures, and others stressing the aspect of sexual substitution.

The choreographer himself was the first and perhaps the greatest interpreter of the Faun. Leonide Massine, also excelling in this role, was the first to dance it in America. Other distinguished male artists who have assumed the leading part include Igor Youskevitch and George Zoritch.

In the Robbins choreography, the mythical faun, the archaic nymphs, the hillside setting have disappeared. The scene is a modern ballet studio, light and airy and unoccupied except for a young man, who lies on the floor. With the inviting notes of the music, he stirs, stretches, glances at his image in the invisible mirror, which, we are directed to believe, spans the width of the stage between performer and audience.

As he tests his body in a series of movements, part gymnastic and part balletic, and poses, he watches himself intently, perhaps marveling at the form of the body, the beauty of moving muscles, perhaps worshiping his danceself. After a few minutes, he subsides again into repose beside the ballet *barre.*

A young girl, dressed in an abbreviated dance practice costume and with her hair loosely falling against her face, enters and takes her position by the *barre*. The boy, moving with the animal celerity and grace of the ancestral faun, sits up and watches this new creature. Her eyes are on the invisible mirror and his eyes turn to it also. They meet, they touch, they dance; but it is their united image which seems to fascinate them as they savor the reflections of their bodies moving from one lovely pose to another. It is a strange courtship conducted in and for a mirror, a courtship which rests entirely on union through dancing.

There is a moment when the personal pull of attraction seems stronger than dance. The boy lifts the girl into his arms and she stretches out her long body as if to touch the horizons. A rapturous shudder races through her, they sink gently to the floor and the boy places a kiss on her cheek. Looking at herself in the mirror, she touches the place where the kiss was planted. Her startled, almost unbelieving expression could be the look of one who has been swiftly but gently ravished. But indeed, it is the union in cool image which has been ravished by the kiss. The special spell, remote but somehow secretly erotic, has been broken. The girl rises to her feet and leaves, and the boy-faun lies down to sleep, undisturbed by his adventure. Or do the images find rebirth in his dreams? Each can only guess as he, the onlooker, would will it.

The roles in the Robbins ballet were created by Francisco Moncion and Tanaquil LeClercq. Jacques d'Amboise and Allegra Kent also became famous interpreters of the roles.

The Age of Anxiety

Choreography, Jerome Robbins; music, Leonard Bernstein (Second Symphony, based upon the poem, "The Age of Anxiety," by W. H. Auden); scenery, Oliver Smith; costumes, Irene Sharaff. First produced by the New York City Ballet, New York, February 26, 1950.

The Age of Anxiety is divided into six scenes—"The Prologue," "The Seven Ages," "The Seven Stages," "The Dirge," "The Masque," "The Epilogue"—and centers around four characters, three men and a girl. They meet as strangers but because each is seeking inner security, faith, and the purpose of life, they are drawn closely together.

Throughout the ballet, except for the recurring leitmotif of the four in conference and in search, a large company of dancers populates the various scenes, representing figures of rushing, heartless society, worshipers of a master, jazz-crazy revelers, masked creatures of fantasy, ordinary passers on the scene, symbols of youth, embodiments of struggle and aspiration.

In the choreography Robbins employed whatever vocabularies of dance movement were needed to give vivid form and choreographic architecture of large scale to the ballet and to communicate the inner passions of the four leading characters.

At the first performance the choreographer himself, Tanaquil LeClercq, Francisco Moncion, and Todd Bolender were the four principals.

Agon

Choreography, George Balanchine; music, Igor Stravinsky. First presented by the New York City Ballet, New York, in a benefit preview, November 27, 1957, and with the formal première taking place December 1. Agon was added to the repertory of the Stuttgart Ballet and first performed by that company, June 6, 1970. A version with totally new choreography by Kenneth MacMillan and decor by Nicholas Georgiadis was first performed by the Royal Ballet, London, August 20, 1958.

Agon, with its specially commissioned score by Stravinsky, is, in all probability, the most complex ballet, both musically and choreographically, of our time. The title comes from the Greek, meaning "contest," and this nonnarrative ballet is just about that. The composer has challenged the choreographer not only with his contemporary treatments of such early dance forms as the *galliard,* the *saraband,* and the *branle,* but also with rhythmic devices almost impossible to count, varying sonorities, tonal witticisms, surprises of all sorts. The choreographer, Balanchine, has met the challenge and passed it and his own challenge on to the dancers, for his movements—classical, free-style, gestural—at times reflect the musical notes, argue with the score, dance lightly upon it, and even comment upon it. The result is a work which, although cool and remote from human feelings, represents an incredible array of movement invention in which the dancers, as representatives of the contest, are pitted against each other in matters of prowess, against the tremendous demands of the choreography, against the complexities of the music.

If the work is storyless and almost mathematical, it is, nonetheless, wholly theatrical, for it celebrates at all times the strength and the skill of the human body, causing it to create miracles of movement on stage. In a *pas de trois* (the *branle*) for two boys and a girl, and in a *pas de deux* for a boy and a girl, the movement invention is not only awesome but enormously exciting. Humor, a kind of muscle humor, occurs again and again as a phrase of action will close with surprise flourish or understatement: a simple sequence might conclude with an unexpected burst of virtuosity; or an elaborate preparation resolve into a tiny gesture.

At the première, principal roles were danced by Melissa Hayden, Diana Adams, Barbara Walczak, Barbara Milberg, Roy Tobias, Jonathan Watts, Arthur Mitchell, and Todd Bolender.

Aimez-vous Bach?

Choreography, Brian Macdonald; music, Johann Sebastian Bach. First performed in America by the Royal Winnipeg Ballet, Boston, July 2, 1964.

Aimez-vous Bach? represents something of a trademark for the Royal Winnipeg Ballet, although it has been performed by other troupes, for it is at once reverent and irreverent, classical and modern. It ranges from pure classical steps through choreographic jibes at Balanchine-style clichés to hot jazz. The characters include an elegant but harried ballet master, a flip jazz interloper, two dedicated young soloists, and a prima ballerina.

Aleko

Choreography, Leonide Massine; music, Peter Ilyich Tchai-kovsky (Trio in A Minor, *orchestrated by Erno Rapee*); *book, Massine and Chagall, based on the Pushkin poem "Gypsies"; scenery and costumes, Marc Chagall. First produced by Ballet Theatre (now the American Ballet Theatre), Mexico City, summer 1942. First New York performance, October 6, 1942.*

This ballet, built upon classical technique, adapted folk-dance forms, and the kind of free-style movement used frequently by Massine in his symphonic ballets, tells the story of Aleko, a city youth who joins a gypsy band and falls in love with Zemphira, daughter of a gypsy chief. At first Aleko's affection is reciprocated by the fiery girl and the two enjoy a passionate relationship.

Soon, however, the fickle Zemphira wearies of the newcomer and turns her amorous interest toward a youth of her own tribe. When Aleko actually discovers her infidelity, he pleads with her, begs her to return; but with her negative reply, he loses his mind. Dreams come to him, visions of classical revenge, and he determines to kill the faithless girl and her lover.

In a wild and impassioned scene, Aleko stabs the gypsy who has won the heart of his beloved and then kills Zemphira. But he himself is not destined to find release in death, for Zemphira's father rules that the most exacting punishment for Aleko will be banishment from the gypsy tribe forever.

The role of Zemphira was created by Alicia Markova. George Skibine was the Aleko in the first presentations and Hugh Laing the Young Gypsy. Alicia Alonso, Nora Kaye, Erik Bruhn, and John Kriza were among later interpreters of the ballet's principal roles.

Allegro Brillante

Choreography, George Balanchine; music, Peter Ilyich Tchai-kovsky (*single movement of the unfinished* Piano Concerto No. 3). *First produced by the New York City Ballet, New York, March 1, 1956. The ballet is also in the repertories of the Boston Ballet, Les Grands Ballets Canadiens, the Pennsylvania Ballet, the Royal Swedish Ballet, and the Stuttgart Ballet.*

Allegro Brillante, for two principals and an ensemble of eight (four girls and four boys), is a pure choreographic exercise without plot, incident, or specific mood. Its point is the exploitation of brilliant classical action through fresh sequences of steps and constantly shifting patterns. The ballerina is accorded some exceptionally difficult movements which display her skills, the *premier danseur* has a pleasant variation of his own and the ensemble passages are both pictorially fetching and kinetically exciting. The dance patterns for the two principals moving together are vivid and require perfect timing, for the perilous and the beautiful are artfully wedded in the choreography.

Maria Tallchief and Nicholas Magallanes were the stars of the first performance.

L'Amour et Son Amour

(Cupid and His Love)

> *Choreography, Jean Babilée; music, César Franck (Psyché); Scenery and costumes, Jean Cocteau. First produced by Les Ballets des Champs-Élysées, Paris, December 13, 1948. First American performance by Ballet Theatre (now the American Ballet Theatre), April 17, 1951.*

The ballet was especially created by the choreographer for himself and for his wife, Nathalie Philippart.

Anastasia

> *Choreography, Kenneth MacMillan; music, Peter Ilyich Tchaikovsky and Bohuslav Martinu; décor and costumes, Barry Kay. First performed by the Royal Ballet, London, July 22, 1971. (A one-act version created for the Berlin Opera Ballet was performed in Berlin, June 25, 1967.)*

This three-act ballet considers the mystery of Anna Anderson, who has long claimed to be the Grand Duchess Anastasia, daughter of the last Czar of Russia, and who has said she escaped from the firing squad at Ekaterinburg, Siberia, when the Imperial Family was murdered. The first act, set in 1914, is a picnic involving members of the Imperial Family. Act II, 1917, is the eve of revolution when a court ball is interrupted by revolutionaries—in this act there is a glimpse of the Czar's favorite dancer, the *prima ballerina assoluta*, Mathilde Kschessinska. The final act is a fantasy involving dreams, nightmares, and fact with Mrs. Anderson and her identity.

In the Royal Ballet production the title role was first danced by Lynn Seymour. The *pas de deux* for Kschessinska and partner had Antoinette Sibley and Anthony Dowell in the initial cast.

An Evening's Waltzes

Choreography, Jerome Robbins; music, Serge Prokofiev; décor and costumes, Rouben Ter-Arutunian. First performed by the New York City Ballet, May 24, 1973.

An airy "dancy" piece in which varying moods are captured through highly imaginative movements and movement sequences.

Patricia McBride and Jean-Pierre Bonnefous, Christine Redpath and Helgi Tomasson, Bart Cook and Sara Leland, were the first to dance it.

Annabel Lee

Choreography, George Skibine; music, Byron Schiffman; décor, André Delfau; book, Skibine, based on the poem by Edgar Allan Poe. First produced, Grand Ballet du Marquis de Cuevas, Deauville, August 28, 1951.

The ballet, holding to the Poe theme and accompanied by a singer, is a romantic tragedy in which two happy lovers are parted by death.

The title part was danced by Marjorie Tallchief.

Anna Karenina

Choreography, Maya Plisetskaya, Natalia Ryzhenko, and Vladimir Smirnov-Golovanov; music, Rodion Shchedrin; book, Boris Lvov-Anokhin (after Leo Tolstoy); decor, Valery Levental, with costumes for Plisetskaya by Pierre Cardin. First performed by the Bolshoi Ballet, June 11, 1972.

The Bolshoi ballerina's first major choreographic effort is this work based upon Tolstoy's famous love story. Highlights of the ballet are a series of *pas de deux*. Plisetskaya herself first danced the title role.

Apollo

(Apollon Musagète)

Choreography, George Balanchine; music and book, Igor Stravinsky; scenery and costumes, André Bauchant. First presented by Diaghilev's Ballets Russes, Paris, June 12, 1928. First American performance by the American Ballet, New York, April 27, 1937, with scenery and costumes by Stewart Chaney. Also added to the repertories of Ballet Theatre (now the American Ballet Theatre), April 25, 1943, the New York City Ballet, November 15, 1951, the Royal Danish Ballet, January 18, 1931, and the San Francisco Ballet. The Stravinsky score had been commissioned by Elizabeth Sprague Coolidge and had had its first presentation at the Library of Congress on April 27, 1928, in a staging (no longer used) by Adolph Bolm. Immediately after this Washington première, the composer turned his work over to Diaghilev and Balanchine. Balanchine's Apollo joined the repertoires of the Ballet Nacional de Cuba in 1960, of the Royal Ballet and the Norwegian National Ballet in 1966, and the Stuttgart Ballet in 1967. It was revived by the American Ballet Theatre and given its first performance January 10, 1974. The ballet is also performed by the Boston Ballet, and was added to the repertory of the Wiener Staatsoper, Vienna, September 10, 1967.

The Apollo of this story is not the complex, often awesome deity of the Greek pantheon but a youth in whom the duties of god-hood are still incipient, a boyish god who discovers his identity with the arts, and becomes the leader of the Muses.

The prologue takes us to an Aegean island. It is night; but a night pierced by a beam of light centering upon the figure of Leto giving birth to Apollo, son of Zeus. She is high on a rock and as her supplicating arms fall and her head drops low, the light upon her disappears and is replaced by one at the base of the rock where the newborn Apollo, wrapped in swaddling clothes, is first seen. He hops awkwardly forward as two handmaidens rush to-ward him, catch him, hearken to his mute wail, and start to un-wind his constricting bonds. But before they have completed their task, the young god, suddenly energized, initiates a mighty spin which frees his body of the swaddling clothes. He stands there, uncertain, lost, until the handmaidens bring him a lute upon which he is destined to make divine music for the world to emulate. To the newborn, the lute is strange; and the handmaidens, standing behind him, instruct him by extending their arms and striking the strings. Soon he copies their gestures and a god of music comes into being.

Following a blackout at the close of the Prologue, the lights come on with brilliant clarity, disclosing Apollo as he plays the lute with great, sweeping circular gestures as if he would draw music from the very air as well as from the instrument itself. Placing the lute upon the ground, he begins to dance, extending the music of the instrument into the instrument of the human body.

Now the Muses enter, Calliope representing poetry; Poly-hymnia, drama or mime; and Terpsichore, dancing. There are greetings and a welcome; and, in a series of pure and lovely move-ment phrases and sculptured tableaux, Apollo guides them toward richer explorations of rhythm, of gesture, of movement, of beauty.

Next, Apollo gives each of the three Muses a symbol of her special art: a tablet for Calliope, a mask for Polyhymnia, a lyre for Terpsichore. In turn the Muses perform their solos. Apollo finds fault with the first two. Calliope's poem, which she has written (gesturally on the palm of her hand) as she concludes her dance, does not quite meet Apollo's demands; and Polyhymnia in her dance has let ecstasy take hold of her and has opened her mouth to speak and declaim, rather than permitting the purity of mime to speak for her.

But Terpsichore dances without flaw and Apollo bestows his hoped-for praise upon her. Then he himself dances, movements which are grand, actions which are simple, steps and gestures perfectly allied to the music. For this is a god who dances. The chosen one, Terpsichore, joins him after his solo and together they move through the partly lyrical, partly playful measures of a *pas de deux*.

The two other Muses return and the four dance joyously as Apollo lifts them aloft or guides them as if he were the master and they the daintily prancing horses in a chariot race. Finally, in token of his love and approval, he rests his head in their hands. Hearing in the music the call of his father, Zeus, Apollo prepares to depart for Olympus. The Muses, sitting on the ground, raise their dancing feet upward into a cone and Apollo touches them. Gently lifting them, he joins them in poses symbolizing unity of the arts and then leads them toward the rock. He starts the ascent toward the home of the gods, and the Muses follow, the four silhouetted in their celestial climb, as Leto, watching her son depart, falls back into the arms of her maidens.

When *Apollo* was first presented, it caused something of a controversy, for although Balanchine's choreography was classical in the purest sense, it was not conventional in its arrangements of traditional steps nor in its relating of gesture with full-scale action. As the years have passed and as many modern influences have penetrated ballet, *Apollo* no longer seems daring but its designs and form retain their freshness and their aptness to the theme. *Apollo*'s first hopping jumps, his wild strumming of the lute, the sudden extension of fingers into a harsh and spreading reach, the wordless mouthings of Apollo and Polyhymnia, and the unusual movement designs and poses of the four once so startling in themselves now clearly reveal their dramatic purpose.

Among the dancers who have performed the role of Apollo are Serge Lifar, Lew Christensen, André Eglevsky, Igor Youskevitch, Michael Penaro, Henning Kronstam, Ivan Nagy, Rudolf Nureyev, and Jacques d'Amboise. Those who have danced the roles of the Muses include Alice Nikitina, Alexandra Danilova, Lubov Tchernicheva, Felia Doubrovska, Vera Zorina, Rosella Hightower, Nora Kaye, Alicia Alonso, Maria Tallchief, Tanaquil LeClercq, Melissa Hayden, Patricia Wilde, Allegra Kent, Cynthia Gregory, Natalia Makarova, Patricia McBride, and Suzanne Farrell.

Apparitions

Choreography, Frederick Ashton; music, Franz Liszt; book, Constant Lambert; scenery and costumes, Cecil Beaton. First presented by the Sadler's Wells Ballet (now the Royal Ballet), London, February 11, 1936. First American performance, same company, New York, October 25, 1949.

This ballet, divided into a Prologue, three scenes, and an Epilogue, treats of a Poet and his fantastic sources of inspiration. (Thematically, it is related to the plot of Hector Berlioz's *Symphonie Fantastique*.)

In the Prologue the Poet is discovered in his study, working intently on a new creation. Obviously the flow of inspiration is inadequate, for he rises and moves about irritably. Suddenly in his darkened windows appear three apparitions: a beautiful woman, a dashing hussar, and a monk. He is attracted instantly to the woman but the visions fade and the Poet returns to his desk believing that inspiration has at last come to him. But he has become so enamored of the girl that work is impossible and he seeks escape in sleep brought on by a potion.

In the following scene, in his dreams, he finds himself at a ball and there he rediscovers the lovely apparition. He dances with her briefly but her interest is directed toward the Hussar and she leaves the Poet. The second scene takes place in a forest and as the dream continues the Poet sees the Monk leading a funeral procession. Fear touches him, and he approaches the bier, tears the obscuring cloth from the dead figure and discovers the body of his beloved.

The third scene carries the dreaming Poet to a cavern where some nameless ceremony is in progress. The woman appears and the Poet is shaken to see her transformed into an ugly, evil creature who seeks to capture him. In terror he faints and the face of the beloved suddenly recaptures its former beauty.

In the Epilogue, the Poet awakes and believing the dream to be an omen of the hopeless life he is destined to lead, kills himself. As his body is borne away, the dream-figure of the beloved returns to mourn.

The two principal roles in *Apparitions* were created by Robert Helpmann and Margot Fonteyn.

Assembly Ball

Choreography and décor, Andrée Howard; music, Georges Bizet (Symphony in C). First presented, London, April 8, 1946. First American performance, San Francisco, December 13, 1951. A Sadler's Wells Theatre Ballet production.

Assembly Ball is a nonnarrative ballet which, however, employs varying moods, hints of romance, touches of comedy. A youthful master of ceremonies, a ballerina, an old man, and an ensemble of boys and girls perform their dances and variations—solos, duets, trios, group figurations—in accord with the musical stimulations and disciplines demanded by each of the score's four movements. The style of the ballet is classical; the mood, spirited and chiefly romantic.

June Brae and Leo Kersley headed the first cast.

Astarte

Choreography, Robert Joffrey; music, composed and played by Crome Syrcus; decor, Thomas Skelton; costumes, Hugh Sharer. First performed by the City Center Joffrey Ballet, New York, September 19, 1967.

Astarte has been described as "the first psychedelic ballet," for it is not unlike a trip within a mind turned into an arena of fantasy by drugs. It is also, technically, a multimedia ballet, for gigantic images in color of the two principals pass before the viewers' eyes in a constant kaleidoscope of sensual portraiture. The live figures, moving with their videotape counterparts, seem tiny by comparison but their oddly detached physical passions are instantly felt by the onlooker. The choreography is an adroit mixture of pictures and people with the projections providing the more spectacular effects. First cast: Maximilian Zomosa and Trinette Singleton.

As Time Goes By

Choreography, Twyla Tharp; music, Franz Josef Haydn (Symphony No. 45 in F-Sharp Minor, third and fourth movements); costumes, Chester Weinberg; lighting, Jennifer Tipton. First performed by the City Center Joffrey Ballet, October 24, 1973.

Twyla Tharp, an avant-garde modern dancer, choreographs both for her own modern dance group and for ballet companies. Frequently her creations reflect the steps and styles, along with the music, of earlier decades in the field of popular entertainment. Unlike some of her other dances, which are set to popular tunes, *As Time Goes By* places its antics along with Haydn's classical measures. The ballet has no story but it suggests passing relationships as its seemingly improvised interweaving of ballet movements with modern dance actions and general antic behavior pass by.

There are no star dancers in the piece, for although there are solo bits, they too are passing.

At Midnight

Choreography, Eliot Feld; music; Gustav Mahler ("Sieben Lieder aus Letzter Zeit"); décor, Leonard Baskin; costumes, Stanley Simmons. First performed by the American Ballet Theatre, New York, December 1, 1967. Eliot Feld's American

Ballet Company performed the ballet at the Festival of Two Worlds, Spoleto, Italy, June 27, 1969. It was added to the repertory of the Royal Swedish Ballet and first performed by that company as Vit Midnatt, *March 1, 1973.*

Feld's *At Midnight* is a ballet about loneliness. The choreographer does not give literal interpretation to the Rückert verses but he mirrors their moods. There are reaching, longing hands probing space for destination but there are also many tactile expressions as hands clasp fleetingly or as bodies brush together, auguring, perhaps only briefly, an end to loneliness.

Bruce Marks headed the first cast, which also featured Eliot Feld, Christine Sarry, Cynthia Gregory, and Terry Orr.

Aureole

Choreography, Paul Taylor; music, George Frederick Handel; lighting, Thomas Skelton. First performed by the Paul Taylor Dance Company, Connecticut College American Dance Festival, New London, Connecticut, August 4, 1962. First performed by the Royal Danish Ballet, May 25, 1968.

Aureole, created as a work for a modern dance company, is now danced by ballet troupes and, in a switch, by a ballet dancer (Nureyev) with a modern dance group. It is a storyless work that captures the lightness of Handel in airy jumps, swift turns and traceries of racing steps, and the dignity of Handel in the forceful torso actions and the broad sweep of arms.

Taylor himself headed the first cast.

Aurora's Wedding

(Also, *Princess Aurora*)
(See also *The Sleeping Beauty*)

Aurora's Wedding or, as it is sometimes called, *Princess Aurora,* is actually the final act of the three-act *The Sleeping Beauty,* choreographed by Marius Petipa with music by Tchaikovsky.

Since the concluding act is composed mainly of *divertissements,* it is frequently produced as an independent short ballet. It contains the famous *Bluebird Pas de Deux* and the *Grand Pas de Deux* for Aurora and her cavalier, as well as national dances, character dances, and the like. Adaptations, deletions, and additions have been made by choreographers engaged to restage the work as a complete ballet.

Because of its glittering background and costumes, its virtuosic classical dances, and its variety of shorter numbers, *Aurora's Wedding* has long enjoyed an enormously popular career separate from the mother creation, *The Sleeping Beauty.* It was presented as a one-act production by the Diaghilev Ballets Russes, May 18, 1922.

Bacchanale

Choreography, Leonide Massine; music, Richard Wagner (Tannhäuser); libretto, scenery, costumes, Salvador Dali. First produced by the Ballet Russe de Monte Carlo, New York, November 9, 1939.

Dali's surrealist ballet was described in a program note at its première as "The First Paranoiac Performance." The work deals with the hallucinations of the mad King Ludwig of Bavaria and includes among its many figures a living umbrella, Lola Montez, women on crutches, Venus, and a masochist and his wife enshrined by scenery and properties (a large broken swan, a mountain, a fiery cloud, stacks of bureau drawers, and a whole corps of umbrellas which pop open simultaneously at the finale).

Obviously, a synopsis of the plot is impossible.

Badinage

(Formerly *Bergensiana*)

Choreography, Fredbjørn Bjørnsson; music, Johan Halvorsen (Bergensiana); costumes, Bjørn Wiinblad. First presented by a unit of the Royal Danish Ballet, Oslo, Norway, June 9, 1957. First presented in America by members of the Royal Danish Ballet at Brooklyn College, New York, June 29, 1957. The same company presented it for the first time in Denmark, October 12, 1957. The Juilliard Dance Ensemble performed the work in New York, for the first time under the title Badinage, *May 6, 1966.*

Le Baiser de la Fée

Choreography, George Balanchine; music and book, Igor Stravinsky; scenery and costumes, Alicia Halicka. First produced by the American Ballet, April 27, 1937, New York. Presented by the Ballet Russe de Monte Carlo, April 10, 1940, New York. Revived, New York City Ballet, November 28, 1950, New York. Earlier presentations took place abroad and among them was a version choreographed by Frederick Ashton for the Sadler's Wells Ballet (now the Royal Ballet). A later version for the Royal Ballet was choreographed by Kenneth Mac-Millan and given its first performance, London, April 12, 1960. A new version of the ballet, a divertissement, was choreographed by George Balanchine for the New York City Ballet's Stravinsky Festival, and first performed by that company, New York, June 21, 1972. Another version was choreographed for the Norwegian National Ballet by Indris Lipkovski, and first performed by that company in 1959.

The ballet, in four scenes (the first, a prologue; the last, an epilogue), is based upon the story by Hans Christian Andersen, "The Ice Maiden." The Stravinsky score was inspired by the music of Tchaikovsky and represents, both musically and dramatically, Stravinsky's tribute to his predecessor. Stravinsky himself notes that the story, in which a fairy places a magical kiss upon a newborn boy, separates him from his mother, and later when he is full-grown claims him forever with a second kiss, could be viewed as an allegory on the life of Tchaikovsky, who had been blessed and claimed by the muse of music.

As the ballet begins, a woman enters a darkening scene bearing a baby in her arms. Snow falls, at first gently and then with increased fury. The mother, buffeted by the winds and the snowflakes which have evolved into grown figures of mystical power and strength, attempts to protect her child but she is overcome and dies. The winds whisk her off and the child is left deserted. The Ice Maiden, a fairy dressed in gleaming white and crowned with shining jewels, is drawn in on a sleigh. Dismissing her attendants, she moves swiftly into the sharp, elegant, and coldly bright measures of a dance, followed by a black-clad form, her shadow, which duplicates all of her actions. The fairy comes upon the babe, lifts it close to her, and places the fateful kiss. Then, moving the child to safer ground, she disappears. Peasants enter, searching. One bears a lantern and the light falls upon the tiny figure in the snow. The men hold the body of one searcher as he reaches out, perhaps over a snow crevice or across a little stream, toward the boy. The child is rescued and the men depart.

The second scene takes place in a Swiss village. Twenty years have gone by and the lost baby is now a man about to be married to the miller's daughter. It is a festive scene; the villagers celebrate the forthcoming marriage with folk dances and with displays of shooting prowess in which, of course, the hero excels. There is a mimed yodeling contest, a duet for the young lovers, and incidental frolic. The celebrants eventually move off and the boy is left alone, deep in thought.

A gypsy enters but the face is that of the Ice Maiden. As the youth sits on the ground, the gypsy grabs his hand and studies his palm, moving it savagely in a circular action. Recognizing him, the gypsy rises to dance a series of wild and beautiful phrases which fascinate the passive young man. He follows her and reaches to embrace her as she flashes across the stage, hair flying, lashing the air with her arms and with rapierlike stabs of her legs. At the close she places her body behind his and, stretching her arm across his shoulder, points in the direction he is to go. Then propelling him forward, she forces him away from his village.

The third scene takes place in a mill where preparations for the wedding ceremony are under way. In the rough-hewn and gaily decorated room, village girls, friends of the Bride, dance. The Bride herself, dressed all in white, joins them and they admire her wedding dress. She leaves briefly as her friends resume their dancing and upon her return they depart. She looks out the window for the expected Bridegroom, but as he comes in, searching for her, she moves to another window. For a time they move back to back, not seeing each other as they turn, ironically, in the wrong directions.

At last they find each other and a gentle love duet follows, each having solo passages expressing joy. But while the Bride is dancing, the shadow of the Ice Maiden appears fleetingly and frightens the young girl. Now the villagers rejoin the lovers and ensemble dances begin. The Bride and the Bridegroom dance happily but the girls throw the veil over the Bride's head and lead her off. The boy is left alone for a moment and then his veiled Bride returns. But something has changed. He moves toward her as if he were hypnotized. He embraces her and they move together until the Bride places part of her veil over his head. He throws it back, revealing the Ice Maiden. He presses his head close to her, she touches him, and leads him away.

In the Epilogue, the Bride enters the empty room but as she searches vainly for her betrothed, the back wall of the room seems to disappear and she sees high in the sky the Ice Maiden, holding out her arms to the youth who climbs desperately through space to reach her and her magical embrace. The sorrowing, watching Bride bids her groom good-bye as the curtain falls.

The final tableau of *Le Baiser de la Fée* has been reworked many times, using various lighting effects and assisting properties; but the choreographer has never fully obtained an effect which is magical and, at the same time, easily viewed from all seats in a theater.

At the first performance in New York, the principal roles were danced by Gisella Caccialanza as the Bride; William Dollar as the Bridegroom; and Kathryn Mullowney as the Fairy. Other well-known interpreters have included Alexandra Danilova and Tanaquil LeClercq (the Bride); André Eglevsky, Frederic Franklin,

Nicholas Magallanes (the Bridegroom); Mia Slavenska and Maria Tallchief (the Fairy).

Ballade

Choreography, Jerome Robbins; music, Claude Debussy (flute solo, Syrinx, and Six Antique Epigraphs, orchestrated by Ernest Ansermet); scenery and costumes, Boris Aronson. First produced by the New York City Ballet, New York, February 14, 1952.

Ballet Imperial

Choreography, George Balanchine; music, Peter Ilyich Tchaikovsky (Piano Concerto No. 2); scenery and costumes, Mstislav Doboujinsky. First produced by the American Ballet, New York, May 27, 1941. Presented by the Ballet Russe de Monte Carlo, Chicago, 1944, and New York, February 20, 1945. Also staged for the Sadler's Wells Ballet (now the Royal Ballet), London, April 5, 1950, with new scenery and costumes by Eugene Berman. The ballet is also in the repertory of the Australian Ballet, and La Scala Opera Ballet, Milan, Italy. The New York City Ballet production was completely revised with new decor and costumes by Karinska and retitled Tchaikovsky Concerto No. 2. It was first performed in its revised form, January 12, 1973.

This classical ballet in three movements—"Allegro Brillante," "Andante non Troppo," "Allegro con Fuoco"—is a tribute to Marius Petipa, the great nineteenth-century ballet master, just as *Le Baiser de la Fée* represents Stravinsky's tribute to Tchaikovsky. However, in *Ballet Imperial*, the choreographer does not attempt to recreate the story ballets for which Petipa was renowned, nor does he employ the miming passages common to nineteenth-century ballets. Rather does he seek to recapture Petipa's classical style and flavor in movements perhaps more elaborate than many Petipa knew, but based on the same traditional actions, and through hints of gesture incorporated into the dancing itself. The ballerina, in the first Balanchine version, is conceived as a true queen of dance, imperious but gracious and always elegant. The cavalier is the suitor, eager but restrained, impeccable in manner, the polished worshiper of imperial beauty. The assisting female soloist and the corps are present to augment the wonders of the ballerina's actions, to frame her motions, to act, in a sense, as courtiers.

At the première the three principal roles were performed by Marie-Jeanne, Gisella Caccialanza, and William Dollar. In the Ballet Russe de Monte Carlo's revival, Mary Ellen Moylan (considered one of the greatest interpreters of the leading part), Maria Tallchief, and Nicholas Magallanes headed the cast.

Ballet School

(École de Ballet)

> *Choreography, Asaf Messerer; music, Alexander Glazounov, Anatol Lyadov, Dmitri Shostakovitch, arranged by A. Tseitlin. First performed by the Bolshoi Ballet, September 17, 1962, at the Metropolitan Opera House, New York.*

This is a theatricalization, perhaps even a dramatization, of a ballet class. The exercises are all there in abundance, but the drudgery is removed and the highlights as well as the routines of many classes are distilled into this one lesson which builds from *pliés* at *barre* to dazzling combinations of leaps and turns. This being a Bolshoi-style affair, there are even some spectacular lifts and split-timing catches to spark the finale. This work, one of the very best of its kind, is a sort of Russian companion piece to Lander's West European *Études* or the elegant nineteenth-century Danish *Konservatoriet*.

Bartók Concerto

> *Choreography, Ben Stevenson; music, Béla Bartók* (Piano Concerto No. 3). *First performed by the Harkness Ballet,*

Barcelona, Spain, September, 1970. The ballet was first performed by the National Ballet of Washington, Kennedy Center Opera House, Washington, D.C., October 20, 1972, with décor and costumes by Bruce Macadie.

A nonstory ballet, which, however, hints of incidents of love and remembrances, glimpses of nature, and the glow of sunshine. In the National Ballet of Washington performance, Carmen Mathe and Dermot Burke danced the Second Movement *pas de deux*.

Bartók No. 3

Choreography, John Clifford; music, Béla Bartók (Piano Concerto No. 3); *costumes, Ardith Hadow. First performed by the Los Angeles Ballet Theater, Los Angeles, March 27, 1974. Added to the repertory of the New York City Ballet, May 23, 1974.*

A nonnarrative ballet by the New York City Ballet's young dancer-choreographer. It is lively, youthful, and concerned with extending music via motion as Clifford's master, George Balanchine, does in his famous music visualization ballets.

The New York City Ballet's first cast was headed by Sara Leland, Anthony Blum, and Debra Austin.

La Bayadère

(Bayaderka)

Choreography, Marius Petipa; music, Ludwig Minkus. First performed, Russian Imperial Ballet, St. Petersburg, January 23 (Julian or Russian calendar) or February 4 (Gregorian or Western calendar), 1877. The first Soviet version, with choreography by Alexander Gorski and Vasilii Tikhomirov, and décor by Konstantin Korovin, was performed by the Bolshoi Ballet, Moscow, January 31, 1923. The Kirov Ballet version, with choreography by Agrippina Vaganova, and decor by Konstantin Ivanov, Piotr Lambin, Orest Allegri, and Adolf Kvapp, was presented in Leningrad, December 13, 1932.

The Kirov presented the Fourth Act, "Shadows," in London, July 4, 1961, and as "Bayaderka" in New York, September 4, 1961. Rudolf Nureyev mounted the Fourth Act with costumes by Philip Prowse, for the Royal Ballet. It was given its first performance by that company, November 27, 1963. Natalia Makarova staged her production for American Ballet Theatre which gave its first performance of the ballet's Fourth Act on July 3, 1974, at the New York State Theatre, New York.

A young warrior is in love with a Hindu temple dancer and plans to wed her. He vows eternal fidelity, but the Rajah offers the youth his beautiful daughter's hand in marriage and he forgets his vows. At the wedding the bayadère is ordered to dance although she has already tried to kill her rival, but the bride's confidante prevents the murder and hides a poisonous snake in flowers given to the dancing girl. The bayadère dies and her somewhat inconstant lover, now remorseful, dreams that they are reunited in the Kingdom of the Shades. This "dream" act is frequently given as an independent ballet, and even the *pas de deux* from the act itself is often presented as a *divertissement*.

Margot Fonteyn and Nureyev headed the Royal Ballet's first cast.

Le Beau Danube

Choreography, Leonide Massine; music, Johann Strauss; scenery, V. and E. Polunin; costumes, Comte Étienne de Beaumont. First produced by the Ballet Russe de Monte Carlo at Monte Carlo, April 15, 1933. An earlier version was presented in Paris by Comté Étienne de Beaumont, 1924. First American performance by the Ballet Russe, New York, December 22, 1933. The ballet was revived by the City Center Joffrey Ballet, October 4, 1972. The Royal Danish Ballet first performed the ballet under the title Den Skønne Donau, *Copenhagen, March 20, 1948.*

The scene is a Viennese park of the nineteenth century. It is a Sunday. A caretaker is sweeping up and a young artist is busily painting. The crowds, in joyous mood, begin to drift in. There are simple workers, persons of quality, entertainers, pretty girls, and handsome youths in this gay ballet; but the chief figures are a young girl (identified as the Daughter), a Street Dancer, and a Hussar, with the King of the Dandies in a brief but effective part.

The slight plot centers around the Daughter, betrothed to the Hussar, and the Street Dancer, perhaps a former mistress, who claims him for her own. As the Street Dancer flounces in and recognizes the Hussar as a man from her past, the parents of the Daughter are shocked; the Daughter, also shocked, faints and the obstreperous Street Dancer, not to be outdone in matters of femininity, collapses into a spectacular swoon.

Briefly the Hussar and the Street Dancer are reunited and recapture their romance in the intoxicating measures of the "Blue Danube Waltz." But the Daughter returns, forgives, and firmly claims the Hussar, the parents give in to the inevitable, the Street Dancer good-humoredly accepts the situation, and all ends happily.

High points of this durable and popular ballet are, of course, the "Blue Danube" (often presented separate from the ballet on a *divertissement* program), the dance of the Hussar and the Daughter, the dashing number performed by the King of the Dandies, the Street Dancer's initial solo and her ensuing comic dance involving a strong man. There are bright sequences also for the ballet's lesser characters, and lilting, happy dances for the ensemble.

At the first Ballet Russe presentation Alexandra Danilova was the Street Dancer; Massine, the Hussar; Tatiana Riabouchinska, the Daughter; and David Lichine, the King of the Dandies. Frederic Franklin has also danced the Hussar. Lydia Lopoukhova was the Street Dancer at de Beaumont's Soirées de Paris in 1924.

Beauty and the Beast

Choreography, John Cranko; music, Maurice Ravel (excerpts from Mother Goose Suite); *scenery and costumes, Margaret*

Kaye. First produced by the Sadler's Wells Theatre Ballet, London, December 20, 1949. First American performance, Denver, November 14, 1951.

This elaborate, extended *pas de deux* relates in two scenes the meeting of Beauty and the Beast, her terror, his gentle courtship, her flight and remorse, her return, the breaking of the spell, and the changing of the Beast into a handsome youth.

Both scenes are laid in the forest and the mood is one of eeriness touched with unseen magical forces. The focus of interest, however, is upon the two figures as they unfold and resolve the familiar fairy tale through dramatic dance.

Patricia Miller and David Poole created the roles of Beauty and the Beast in this Cranko work.

The Bedbug

Choreography, Leonid Yakobson; music, F. Otkazov and G. Firtich; book, Leonid Yakobson (after Vladimir Mayakovsky's play); designs, Alexander Goncharov, F. Zbarsky, T. Selvinskaya, and Boris Messerer. First performed by the Kirov Ballet, Leningrad, June 24, 1962.

La Belle au Bois Dormant

See *The Sleeping Beauty*

The Bells

Choreography and scenario, Ruth Page; music, Darius Milhaud; scenery and costumes, Isamu Noguchi. First produced, Chicago, April 26, 1946 (Chicago University Composers' Series); presented by the Ballet Russe de Monte Carlo, August 30, 1946, Jacob's Pillow Dance Festival, and in New York, September 6, 1946.

Bhakti

Choreography, Maurice Béjart; Indian folk music; costumes, Germinal Casado. First performed by the Ballet of the Twentieth Century, 1968.

A long, leisurely, contemplative ballet that interrelates Hindu themes and ceremonial gestures, partly of yoga cast, with Western actions and even Western characters.

Les Biches

Choreography, Bronislava Nijinska; music, Francis Poulenc; scenery and costumes, Marie Laurencin. First produced by the Diaghilev Ballets Russes, Monte Carlo, January 6, 1924. Revived by the Marquis de Cuevas' Grand Ballet, November 17, 1947, and first presented in America by that company, New York, November 13, 1950. The ballet was staged for the Royal Ballet and first performed in London by that company, December 2, 1964.

The word *biche* means "doe." In popular usage, it may mean "girl," and some ballet associates prefer to translate it as "gazelle." The ballet has also been given under the title *The House Party.*

This ballet, in eight sequences, opens on a fashionable drawing room. Girls dressed in pink enter and begin a dance which is, peculiarly, part-innocent, part-wanton but altogether gaily thoughtless. They are followed by three young men, clad in bathing suits, who display muscles, expanded rib cages, and athleticism in their actions, first for their own pleasure and then for the delight of the girls, who return to watch them.

The boys show little interest in the flighty ones but their curiosity is aroused by a girl wearing a blue tunic, white tights, and white gloves, who moves swiftly and in self-absorbed manner across the stage. When she returns, she dances briefly and exits with one of the young men.

The Hostess, an older woman, now appears. She is wearing yellow, carries a long cigarette holder and moves about nervously, dancing to capture attention, eager to recapture youth. She joins two of the boys in a lively dance and ultimately selects one as her escort. The girl in blue and her cavalier reenter for a *pas de deux*, two girls follow with a secretive duet designed to disclose the affection they bear toward each other, and the ballet ends with all participants on stage for a brisk finale.

None of the characters in *Les Biches*, with the possible exception of the aging pleasure-seeking hostess, is given detailed definition. Rather do the figures, in their various activities, reflect an atmosphere of decadence, thoughtlessness, self-gratification, and, in the case of the girl in blue, cool waiting. If innocence and wantonness are strangely paired, so also is the clandestine and the overt, for at times, the party members seem to care not at all what they are up to or who sees it, and at other moments some of the girls spy over the back of a sofa at the doings of others.

Les Biches is chic, sophisticated, and certainly an ironic commentary on the emptiness of living among certain social sets of the 1920s. That its choreographer views it as a romantic ballet, the twentieth-century equivalent of the great nineteenth-century *La Sylphide*, is clue enough to her satiric aims.

Among the many celebrated members of the initial cast were Vera Nemtchinova, Anatole Vilzak, Alexandra Danilova, Mme. Nijinska, Felia Doubrovska, Ninette de Valois, and Lubov Tchernicheva. Alicia Markova and Anton Dolin have also danced the principal parts.

The Big City

Choreography, Kurt Jooss; music, Tansman (Sonatina Transatlantique); *costumes, Hein Heckroth. First produced, Ballets Jooss, Cologne, November 21, 1932. Added to the repertory of the City Center Joffrey Ballet, New York, February 28, 1975.*

Post-World War I city scenes with a theme of romance and temptation linking a series of shifting vignettes. The Young Workman loses his girl to the rich libertine who can offer her finery and fun, the rich are juxtaposed against the poor, prostitutes contrasted

with protective mothers. The loneliness, the ephemera, the "passing parade" of the metropolis in which, in the end, anonymity
prevails are captured in the historic Jooss style which interrelates
elementary classical ballet with modern dance and dramatic
gesture.

Mascha Lidolt, Sigurd Leeder, Ernst Uthoff headed the first
cast. Hans Zullig and Noelle de Mosa were especially famous interpreters of the roles of the Young Workman and the Girl.

Billy the Kid

*Choreography, Eugene Loring; music, Aaron Copland; book,
Lincoln Kirstein; scenery and costumes, Jared French. First
produced by the Ballet Caravan, Chicago, October 16, 1938.
Presented by Ballet Theatre (now the American Ballet Theatre), New York, February 13, 1941. Billy the Kid has been
revived several times by the American Ballet Theatre, most
recently, July 17, 1973.*

Billy the Kid has long remained one of the most distinguished
examples of ballets based upon American folk themes. Its movement technique, though stemming from the classical ballet, is augmented by actions and gestures idiomatic to America or evocative
of the American spirit. There are, for example, pirouettes straight
out of the traditional ballet technique but as performed by Billy,
they become an expression of bravado. Western heroes of the
movies often spin their revolvers on a finger before shooting. Billy,
characterized through dancing, spins his body (in a pirouette)
before shooting.

There are pirouettes also in the great processionals which
open and close the ballet, but they do not stand out as balletic
virtuosity; rather are they part of a streaming pattern which suggests the drive Westward, the spaciousness of a new land, the pull
of promise. Some fall back, some simply turn and look back; but
the majority of the figures in the processionals push forward and
the viewer retains in his mind the picture of booted men, their
arms thrust forward, legs raised in preparation of a mighty step.

There are still other actions which give *Billy the Kid* American colorings. The cowboys, with hands on buttocks but near their guns, strut about as they look over the girls, or they ride their imaginary horses in easy canters or furious gallops. The pioneer women step gently but firmly, the Mexican girls swing into their happy rhythms, and the saloon entertainers toss their hips provocatively. Stealth is present as the search for Billy gets under way, the gestures of a card game are silhouetted by campfire light, a roaring gun battle pictures the easy death of the Old West, and in a dream the figure of beauty, moving with classical grace, visits the tormented, hunted hero.

The ballet, although built around the figure and the exploits of Billy the Kid, is not so much a biography of a notorious but peculiarly appealing desperado as it is a perception of the pioneer West in which a figure such as Billy played a vivid role.

Following the opening processional—the Prologue—which carries an unbroken line of people across the front of the stage, the scene shifts to a busy town abustle with the separate but related actions of cowboys, pioneer women, Mexicans, the saloon girls, and others. Billy, as a little boy, enters with his citified mother. A fight breaks out and the mother, standing in the line of the bullet fire, is killed. Billy, hesitating for a moment in unbelieving horror, grabs a knife and stabs the Mexican who fired the shot. The heroic figure who had led the processional steps forth to aid the frightened boy but Billy, his first crime committed, flees.

The dead man returns again and again throughout the ballet in many guises as the figure of Alias, symbol of all the men Billy has killed and also symbol of Billy's ultimate doom. The leader of the pioneers, the would-be friend, is Pat Garrett, who as sheriff must ultimately bring Billy to punishment.

The following scene shows the adult Billy, an arrogant man now thoroughly tempered by viciousness. In a long and elaborate solo, Billy defines himself as he stamps and struts with cold bravado, stalks an enemy, spins and shoots, races in flashing turns across the stage, brandishes his weapons, kicks at his victim, and in a final stance, like a cockerel, laughs at the fallen one.

In the ensuing scenes, Billy kills the leader (it is Alias) of a a trio bent on capturing him, cheats in a card game with Pat Garrett, and takes part in a fight with a large posse, during which he kills Alias and is captured by Garrett. He languishes briefly in jail until he kills his jailer (Alias), escapes to the desert, eludes capture for a spell, and in a romantic interlude dreams of his Mexican sweetheart. As the dream fades, he thinks he hears a noise and cries out "¿Quién es?" There is no answer, no further sound. He laughs nervously, lights a cigarette, and is shot to death by Garrett, who has been led to the spot by Billy's Indian guide (Alias). There is a dance of mourning performed around the body of Billy by heavily draped women and the scene shifts to the processional (Epilogue), for though Billy is not forgotten, he is dead, and the trail Westward has never once been interrupted by the tragic actions of a single man.

In the first performances, the choreographer danced the role of Billy; Lew Christensen, Pat Garrett; Todd Bolender, Alias; and Marie-Jeanne, the dual role of Mother-Sweetheart. Mr. Loring also danced the title role in his own short-lived company, Dance Players, and with Ballet Theatre. Others who have danced Billy with Ballet Theatre are Michael Kidd, John Kriza (one of Kriza's finest characterizations), Eliot Feld, Daniel Levins, and Dennis Wayne.

Billy Sunday

Choreography, Ruth Page; music, Remi Gassmann; scenery, Herbert Andrews; costumes, Paul du Pont. First produced by Miss Page's own company, Chicago, December 13, 1946. Presented by the Ballet Russe de Monte Carlo, New York, March 2, 1948. Chicago production a workshop enterprise without scenery, costumes, or finished staging.

Birthday Offering

Choreography, Frederick Ashton; music, Alexander Glazounov; costumes, André Levasseur. First produced by the Sadler's Wells Ballet (now the Royal Ballet), London, May 5,

1956. First presented in America by the same company, New York, September 11, 1957.

Birthday Offering, described by the choreographer as a *"pièce d'occasion,"* was created in honor of the twenty-fifth anniversary of the Sadler's Wells Ballet, which, as the Vic-Wells Ballet, had given its first full evening of ballet May 5, 1931.

This classical work,without story, was designed to exploit and to celebrate the individual powers of seven ballerinas and their seven partners.

The first cast was composed of Margot Fonteyn, Beryl Grey, Violetta Elvin, Nadia Nerina, Rowena Jackson, Svetlana Berisova, Elaine Fifield; and Michael Somes, Alexander Grant, Brian Shaw, Philip Chatfield, David Blair, Desmond Doyle, and Bryan Ashbridge.

The Bitter Weird

Choreography, Agnes de Mille; music, Frederick Loewe, Trude Rittman. First performed by the Royal Winnipeg Ballet.

The Bitter Weird is a ballet based upon the dances de Mille created for the Broadway musical *Brigadoon.* A highlight: the fight to the death of the rivals for the hand of the heroine.

Black Angel

Choreography, John Butler; music, George Crum (Black Angel); décor, Rouben Ter-Arutunian. First performed by the Pennsylvania Ballet, Philadelphia, March 29, 1973.

A modern-primitive work described as a "satanic mass, a religion without belief, possession by the ritual itself."

Black Swan

(See also *Swan Lake*)

Black Swan is the popular name given to the *pas de deux* for Odile and the Prince in Act III of *Swan Lake*. In extracted form, in which the characters are not specifically identified, it is frequently presented as a highly virtuosic example of bravura dancing on a program with other, unrelated ballets. Just as an area from an opera may be included in a song recital, so certain *pas de deux* may be taken from a ballet and given as a separate item on a ballet bill. The *Black Swan* is the *pas de deux* which contains the famous sequence of thirty-two *fouettés* for the ballerina.

Blood Wedding

Choreography, Alfred Rodrigues; music, Denis Aplvor Ivor; scenery and costumes, Isabel Lambert. First produced, Sadler's Wells Theatre Ballet, London, June 5, 1953. Produced in America in a workshop presentation by the American Ballet Theatre, New York, May 6, 1957 (staged by the choreographer). The ballet was added to the repertory of the Royal Danish Ballet and first performed by that company, January 31, 1960.

Bluebeard

Choreography and book, Michel Fokine; music, Jacques Offenbach; scenery and costumes, Marcel Vertès. First produced by Ballet Theatre (now the American Ballet Theatre), Mexico City, October 27, 1941; New York première by same company, November 12, 1941.

Bluebeard, one of Fokine's last ballets, is a comic work in two prologues, four scenes, and three interludes. It is based on a double plot and each plot has its own exaggerated complications which by the end of the ballet manage to get themselves interwoven.

One plot deals with King Bobiche, ruler of a mythical kingdom, and his fickle wife, Queen Clementine. At the start of the ballet, the King is trying to rid himself of a baby daughter, simply because she is not a boy and proper heir. He places a necklace around the baby's throat and with the aid of Count Oscar, a bumbling but shrewd eunuch-type character, places the child in a basket and sets her afloat on the river. Years pass and the doddering old King catches his wife with a series of lovers. No sooner is one condemned and his neck in the noose than the queen adds another to her collection of amours. Five lovers are sent to the gallows but Count Oscar, because he is kind-hearted and susceptible to bribes, releases them en route to their doom. Now the King, remorseful and lonely, must find his daughter and sends Count Oscar in search of her.

The Count finally discovers her living among shepherds and wildly in love with a shepherd youth, who is really Prince Sapphire in disguise. The Count reveals her identity to the princess but she is afraid that her rustic will love her no longer and the shepherd, in turn, fears that she will reject him if she discovers he is a prince.

Meanwhile, Bluebeard has made his appearance in the second prologue, during which he polishes off five wives in a matter of seconds. Bluebeard returns again during the scene with the shepherds and here, aided by his alchemist, Popoloni, looks about for another wife. Some of the girls are frightened of him, the bolder ones do not interest him; but one, Boulotte, enters, claps him on the back and enchants him with her hearty romancing.

On the way to their wedding Bluebeard and Boulotte pass the discovered Princess on her way back to court. Bluebeard falls in love at sight and makes plans to do away with Boulotte. Back in his castle, Bluebeard turns Boulotte over to the mercies of Popoloni in a room which already contains five graves, all sealed, and a sixth, unused grave. Boulotte is forced to drink a goblet of liquid and falls over dead. Bluebeard mourns briefly and then prances off on his latest quest. But Popoloni tickles the nose of the fallen Boulotte and she returns to life. So also do the five preceding wives.

In the final scene, at court, the Princess and her parents are reunited. The girl is furious when told she must marry Prince Sapphire, but when he comes in, she recognizes her own true love and all seems well. But Bluebeard enters and with threats and flashing swords demands the Princess for himself. A duel is fought between Bluebeard and Prince Sapphire and the latter is wounded, presumably unto death.

Bluebeard claims the weeping Princess but five masked women enter, led by Popoloni, and shortly reveal themselves to the terrified Bluebeard as his ex-wives. In the denouement, the five wives are married to the Queen's five lovers, the Princess and her Prince are reunited, and Bluebeard discovers that Boulotte is really the girl of his choice.

Difficult as it may seem, it is possible to follow the plots of this ballet as it unfolds and it is necessary to do so if one is to get the point of the endless stream of predicaments which beset the chief characters. Pantomime, character dancing, and straight ballet are all employed in the telling of this comedy and the movements devised for each of the figures serve to characterize his qualities and temperament, from the bounding, unpredictable antics of Bluebeard and the kittenish motions of the Queen to the noble actions of Prince Sapphire and the lusty phrases of Boulotte.

The first all-star cast included such luminaries of that period (and some who were destined to become famous later) as Anton Dolin (Bluebeard), Alicia Markova (the Princess), Irina Baronova (Boulotte), Antony Tudor, Ian Gibson, Lucia Chase, Nora Kaye, Rosella Hightower, Hugh Laing, Jerome Robbins, Donald Saddler, Annabelle Lyon, Maria Karnilova, and Dimitri Romanoff.

Bluebird Pas de Deux

(See also *The Sleeping Beauty*)

This *pas de deux,* popularly known as the *Bluebird* (or *Bluebirds*), is contained in the last act of *The Sleeping Beauty*. It is also a part of *Aurora's Wedding* (or *Princess Aurora*), the name given to the closing act of *The Sleeping Beauty* when it is presented as an independent one-act *divertissement.* In turn, the *Blue-*

bird Pas de Deux is frequently given as a separate item on a program of other ballets.

Bogatyri

Choreography and book, Leonide Massine; music, Alexander Borodin; scenery and costumes, Nathalie Gontcharova. First produced by the Ballet Russe de Monte Carlo, New York, October 20, 1938.

A Russian Folk Ballet.

Bolero

This popular musical work by Maurice Ravel has been given many different stagings and wholly different choreographies. It has been conceived as a solo work, a group work, and a mass spectacle. Some choreographers have held it close to the ethnic patterns of Spanish dance while others have used it in a more balletic manner.

Among the innumerable dance versions of Ravel's *Bolero* are those created for the following: Ida Rubinstein, Ballet Theatre (choreography by Argentinita), the Markova-Dolin Ballet, the Philadelphia Ballet, the Royal Danish Ballet, the Marquis de Cuevas' Grand Ballet, Radio City Music Hall. In the Maurice Béjart treatment of the work the dancers are one girl and sixteen men.

Bolt

Choreography, Fedor Lopukhov; music, Dmitri Shostakovitch; book, V. Smirnov; designs, Tatiana Bruni and G. Gorshykov. First performed by the Kirov Ballet at the Leningrad State Academic Theatre of Opera and Ballet, April 8, 1931.

Le Bourgeois Gentilhomme

Choreography, George Balanchine; music, Richard Strauss; scenery and costumes, Eugene Berman; based upon the play of the same name by Molière. Produced by the Ballet Russe de Monte Carlo, New York, September 23, 1944. An earlier production, with scenery and costumes by Alexandre Benois, was presented by the René Blum Ballets Russes.

Bourrée Fantasque

Choreography, George Balanchine; music, Emmanuel Chabrier; costumes, Karinska. First produced by the New York City Ballet, New York, December 1, 1949. The Royal Danish Ballet first performed the ballet, May 5, 1963.

This once popular ballet has no story but each of its three movements has its own special spirit, pace, colors, and humors, qualities suggested by the pieces of Chabrier which compose the ballet's score.

The first movement, called "Bourrée Fantasque," is broadly comic yet highly classical. Even the movements which depart from pure ballet line or behavior are just that, departures, rather than actions unrelated to ballet; and much of the humor stems from the spirit of let's-break-the-rules-and-have-fun.

The second movement, "Prelude," is totally unlike the first. It is a cool, romantic reverie.

"Fête Polonaise" is the third and final movement. It is a joyous celebration dedicated to speed, lightness, and unbounded energy.

At the first performance, the cast (in order of appearance) was headed by Tanaquil LeClercq and Jerome Robbins, Maria Tallchief and Nicholas Magallanes, Janet Reed and Herbert Bliss.

La Boutique Fantasque

Choreography, Leonide Massine; music, Gioacchino Rossini, arranged and orchestrated by Ottorino Respighi; scenery and costumes, André Derain. First produced by the Diaghilev Ballets Russes, London, June 5, 1919. First presented in America by the Ballet Russe de Monte Carlo, New York, March 20, 1935.

Dancing dolls and the notion that toys may have a secret life of their own have long fascinated choreographers and often enchanted their audiences. Two of the most famous and enduring ballets on the doll theme are *Coppélia* (created in the last century) and the twentieth-century *La Boutique Fantasque*.

The scene is a French toyshop of one hundred years ago. As the ballet starts, the Shopkeeper and his Assistant unlock the doors and prepare to receive customers. The first is an unwanted visitor, a thief who is quickly discovered and runs out of the shop just as two prim ladies arrive. They are followed by an American and his family and later by a Russian family.

The Shopkeeper brings out his dolls to perform for his prospective customers. The first are Italian dolls who dance a lively tarantella. Next on display are four dolls dressed like cards—the queen of clubs, the queen of hearts, the king of spades, the king of diamonds—who move through the measures of a mazurka. With the arrival of the Russian family, dancing Cossack dolls are introduced. These are replaced by poodles, a male and a female, who behave so realistically that the Americans are quite shocked.

The prize items in the shop are saved for last. They are the two Cancan Dancers, a man and a woman, who perform with such spirit, with such communicable abandon that the customers need look no further. The Russians decide to buy the high-kicking, skirt-swooshing girl dancer and the Americans, the agile, acrobatic man. In the morning, they will return to claim their dolls.

The Shopkeeper and his Assistant leave, night comes, and all the dolls spring to life. They dance happily, glad of being alone, but there is a problem to be met. The Cancan Dancers, long lovers, are to be separated and they dance what would seem to be their final duet.

In the morning, the Russians and Americans come to pick up their purchases; but the Cancan Dancers have disappeared and the enraged and disappointed customers launch an attack on the Shop-keeper and his helper. The toys band together in a colorful little army and institute a counterattack which propels the Russians and the Americans into the street. As the irate parents and their children look through the shop window, they see the Shopkeeper shake hands with the Cancan Dancers, now returned and still united, and all the toys join in a joyous dance of celebration.

In the 1919 cast, Massine and Lydia Lopoknova were the Cancan Dancers and the great Enrico Cecchetti, founder of a major method of ballet instruction, was the Shopkeeper. At the New York première, Massine and Alexandra Danilova were the Cancan Dolls, roles they played many times in subsequent seasons.

Brahms Quintet

Choreography, Dennis Nahat; music, Johannes Brahms; costumes, Willa Kim. First performed by the American Ballet Theatre, December 10, 1969.

Brahms-Schönberg Quartet

Choreography, George Balanchine; music, Johannes Brahms (Quartet No. 1 in G minor, Op. 25; orchestrated by Arnold Schönberg); décor, Peter Harvey; costumes, Karinska. First performed by the New York City Ballet, New York, April 21, 1966.

Brahms-Schönberg Quartet is a super-Balanchine music visualization ballet in four movements (Allegro, Intermezzo, Andante, Rondo alla Zingarese) that interrelates classical ballet action with excursions into spirited *demi-caractère*, sweeping lyricism and bright bravura, concluding in a rousing Hungarian gypsy finale.

Melissa Hayden, André Prokovsky, Patricia McBride, Kent Stowell, Allegra Kent, Edward Villella, Suzanne Farrell, and Jacques d'Amboise headed the first cast.

Brahms Variations

Choreography, Michael Uthoff; music, Johannes Brahms (Variations on a Theme by Joseph Haydn); *costumes, Carl Michell; décor, James Steere. First performed by the Hartford Ballet Company, Hartford, Connecticut, February 23, 1974.*

A modest classical ballet astutely planned to present a junior company in passages that highlight the dancers' accomplishments and skirt their technical limitations.

Brandenburg Nos. 2 and 4

Choreography, John Cranko; music, Johann Sebastian Bach; décor and costumes, Dorothea Zippel. First performed by the Royal Ballet, London, February 10, 1966. First performed in America by the same company, New York, May 17, 1967.

Cranko's *Brandenburg Nos. 2 and 4* is a lively exercise in virtuosic responses to musical stimuli for eight men and eight women. The team idea is suggested as the groups line up rather like athletes ready for play . . . and play they do.

The Bronze Horseman

Choreography Rostislav Zakharov; music, Reinhold Glière; book, Pyotr Abolimov after Alexander Pushkin's poem; designs, Mikhail Bobyshov. First performed by the Kirov Ballet, Leningrad, March 14, 1949. First presented by the Bolshoi Ballet, Moscow, June 27, 1949.

This tells of a government official who loses his beloved during the flood of St. Petersburg and who blames Peter the Great for his torments. The "bronze horseman" is the statue of the Czar whom the deranged Vevgeny believes is pursuing him.

Natalia Dudinskaya and Konstantin Sergeyev created the principal roles. Galina Ulanova has also danced the part of Parasha, the heroine.

Brouillards

Choreography, John Cranko; music, Claude Debussy. First performed by the Stuttgart Ballet, March 8, 1970.

A forty-five minute poetic ballet that makes the viewer think of mist or snow, of sails on the sea or feathery plants bending in a breeze.

Bugaku

Choreography, George Balanchine; music, Toshiro Mayuzumi; décor and lighting, David Hays; costumes, Karinska. First performed by the New York City Ballet, New York, March 30, 1963.

Bugaku, an adroit, poetic, and visually beautiful combining of certain Western ballet steps and gestures with the deliberate ceremonial air of Eastern dance. A highlight: the nuptial dance, which achieves a scent of eroticism while never departing from the contours of highly refined ritual.

Allegra Kent and Edward Villella were the first principals.

The Cage

Choreography, Jerome Robbins; music, Igor Stravinsky (Concerto Grosso in D for Strings); décor and lighting, Jean Rosenthal; costumes, Ruth Sobotka. First produced by the New York City Ballet, New York, June 14, 1951.

This terrifying and exciting ballet is concerned with a tribe of females who look upon the male as rightful prey. The costumes and certain aspects of the choreography suggest the females are insects while other actions suggest humans. The basic idea of the theme, however, is that certain insects, certain beings (such as the Amazons) devoured or destroyed the male, using him only briefly for the process of procreation. Some have even read into *The Cage* (and perhaps it is there) a psychological allegory to the effect that some women in modern society are destroyers of men.

The savage rite begins as the curtains rise upon a dark stage. A giant web sweeps high to form an eerie canopy, then the lights come on and a band of creatures appears, headed by their Queen. A shrouded figure is drawn from between the Queen's legs, the pupal coverings are removed (except for the face) and the inert Novice is introduced. The feral females dance their celebration of birth and, pulling the Novice to the center of the arena before the Queen, rip the white mask from her face. There is no expression. The huge, black-rimmed eyes blink at the light; the distorted body, crowned with moistly plastered, jagged black hair, stands ready to explore a new life. The Queen touches her, the tribe departs and the Novice begins to move.

From a squatting position, the Novice probes the air with knifelike fingers, stretches her limbs, tests newly discovered muscles. Her angular walk, her weapon-arms are predatory, awaiting the arrival of a victim. The first Intruder enters and reaches for her, but she tumbles him to the ground in a viselike embrace, rolls over him, rises and stabs at his chest with a sharply pointed toe. Then she reached down to the exhausted man, lifts his neck through her legs and with a quick twist of the body strangles him between her thighs.

With a contemptuous kick at the body of the male, she starts a march of victory, her head thrown back and her mouth open in the exultant cry which announces the kill. From the wings, the watching females stride forth and with like steps and cries join the celebration. The Novice has been successfully initiated into her deadly duties.

The happily gruesome party comes to an abrupt end as a warning is sounded, announcing another Intruder. The tribe disappears, leaving the Novice to face a stalwart, handsome male. He grabs her, she resists briefly but a new feeling enters her body and she succumbs to the call of sex. Her movements shed something of their angularity, a glow suffuses her as she joins the male in a love duet. Some of the actions are almost classical, as if a boy and a girl were investigating in movement the beauty and potential sensuality of the body, erect, long of line, elegant. But other gestures— the interweaving and tickling of fingers in the manner of insect antennae—suggest the creatures. In an ironic culmination the male places the Novice's head between his thighs but instead of strangling her he turns about tenderly, as her feet strike the floor in trembling ecstasy and her arms reach up to complete the union.

The tribe returns and for a moment the Novice seeks to protect her lover. But as the Queen issues her orders and the females attack, the Novice's murderous instincts return. The Intruder, after being mutilated by the females and stabbed by the claws of the Novice, is borne aloft in wild triumph and ultimately strangled between the Novice's legs. A wild, whirling dance of evil joy brings the ceremony to a close as the Queen and the triumphant Novice stand twisted and commanding in the center of their vile arena.

The Cage, obviously, is not a pleasant ballet but it is an exciting one, almost hypnotic in its projection of a melodramatic fantasy. The movements, steps and gestures, part balletic and part invented, are fused into a savage vocabulary of action for the telling of a vicious tale and for the characterization of demonic creatures.

The first cast was headed by Nora Kaye (the Novice), Yvonne Mounsey (the Queen), Michael Maule (the First Intruder), and Nicholas Magallanes (the Second Intruder). Others who have danced the Novice are Melissa Hayden, Tanaquil LeClercq, Allegra Kent, Patricia McBride, and Gelsey Kirkland.

Cakewalk

Choreography, Ruthanna Boris; music, Louis Gottschalk (adapted and orchestrated by Hershy Kay); scenery and costumes, John Drew. First produced by the New York City Ballet, New York, June 12, 1951. The ballet was taken into the repertory of the Joffrey Ballet (now the City Center Joffrey Ballet) and first performed by that company, September 6, 1966.

Cakewalk, a spritely example of Americana in the ballet field, is based upon the form and spirit of the minstrel show. It does not attempt to duplicate the minstrel show formula in every detail but rather it exploits the dance equivalents of minstrel entertainment.

The participants, including the two standard end men (they are girls for the ballet), open with a strutting march before the front curtain which, when it rises, discloses the seating arrangement for the show. The performers make their entrances, take their seats and the dancing begins.

The Interlocutor introduces a sweet young thing who, supported by syrupy music, humorously depicts the plight of the wallflower. Next follow the Interlocutor in a number called "Sleight of Feet," the End Men in a fast and complicated number, and an exuberant girl in a flashing dance entitled "Freebee" which eventually draws all the minstrel band into its infectious and exhausting rhythms.

In Part II, the Interlocutor has become the magician. He and his assistants, with a wave of their magical capes, reveal the dancing figures of Venus and the three Graces, next a Wild Pony and finally, Hortense, Queen of the Swamp Lilies, who descends from her garlanded swing to dance a languid, sentimental, dreamy *pas de deux* with a poet.

Part III, the finale, builds to an extended, increasingly dynamic and effervescent cakewalk.

The choreography combines a great many classical ballet steps with elements of the folk dance and popular dance of the minstrel era, but even the ballet movements, except for the deadpan satirical dances, have been adapted by the choreographer to suit the spirit and the action characteristic of minstrel activities.

The initial cast was headed by Janet Reed (the Wallflower and Hortense), Patricia Wilde (Freebee and the Wild Pony), Yvonne Mounsey (Venus), Herbert Bliss (the Poet), Frank Hobi (Interlocutor and Magician), and Tanaquil LeClercq and Beatrice Tompkins (End Men).

Camille

Choreography, John Taras; music, Franz Schubert (arranged by Vittorio Rieti); scenery and costumes, Cecil Beaton; based

*on the novel by Alexandre Dumas, fils. First produced by the
Original Ballet Russe, New York, October 1, 1946. In this
short-lived ballet version of the famous story, Alicia Markova
and Anton Dolin played the leads.*

Cantata

*Choreography, Michael Uthoff; music, Alberto Ginastera
(Cantata para América Mágica); décor, Anni Albers; cos-
tumes, Carl Michell. First performed by the Hartford Ballet
Company, Hartford, Connecticut, February 23, 1974.*

More of a dance ceremony than a ballet, this work combines
modern dance with primitive stress and distortion to suggest
Mayan, or some unidentified Amerindian, ritual.

Canto Indio

*Choreography, Brian Macdonald; music, Carlos Chavez; cos-
tumes, Capuletti. First performed in New York by the Harkness Ballet, November 2, 1967. The ballet has also been performed by the Royal Winnipeg Ballet.*

A spirited *pas de deux*, fast-paced and filled with bits of humor,
which captures something of the unaffected romantic innocence
of Mexican Indian villagers.

Elisabeth Carroll and Helgi Tomasson were its first dancers.

Capital of the World

*Choreography, Eugene Loring; music, George Antheil; scen-
ery and costumes, Esteban Frances; based on the story by
Ernest Hemingway. The ballet was first created for television
and had its world première on TV, December 6, 1953, with
Ballet Theatre (now the American Ballet Theatre) dancers. Its
first stage presentation took place in New York, December 27,
1953, when it was added to the Ballet Theatre repertory.*

Capriccio Espagnol

Choreography, Leonide Massine; music, Rimsky-Korsakoff; scenery and costumes, Mariano Andreù; choreographic collaboration, Argentinita. First produced by the Ballet Russe de Monte Carlo at Monte Carlo, May 4, 1939, same company.

This is a plotless ballet for company and soloists, using for the most part Spanish dance steps, gestures, and postures. Peasant dances, gypsy dances, and dance of a more classical nature in Spanish style constitute the ballet. Little dramatic incidents, village groupings, shifts in mood, lulls, and crescendos of action help to transform *Capriccio Espagnol* from a simple series of dances into a continuous ballet.

Argentinita, Massine, and Alexandra Danilova were in the Monte Carlo production.

Capriccioso

Choreography, Anton Dolin; music, Domenico Cimarosa; scenery and costumes, Nicolas de Molas. First produced by Ballet Theatre (now the American Ballet Theatre), Chicago, November 3, 1940.

Caprichos

Choreography, Herbert Ross; music, Béla Bartók; costumes, Helene Pons. The ballet is based upon the Spanish artist Goya's commentaries on his own series of etchings by the same name; and the Bartók music, played as originally written (not expanded for orchestral use) is his Contrasts for Piano, Clarinet and Violin. *First produced by the Choreographers' Workshop, New York, January 29, 1950. First presented by Ballet Theatre (now the American Ballet Theatre), New York, April 26, 1950.*

In four episodes, which are mainly free dance rather than ballet, Ross gives choreographic extension to the ironic Goya comments and dance form to the harsh and bitter characteristics of the related etchings.

The first scene derives from the note "These good girls have seats enough and nothing to do with them better than carry them on their heads." The two girls, it is immediately apparent, are not very good. Their hair is loose, they wear extremely abbreviated tunics which they keep pulling up over their heads to reveal the full contours of their bodies, they are barefoot, they wear long black gloves and, in sardonic contrast to their behavior, they display large black crucifixes around their necks. Each carries a small stool and their actions consist of playing with the stools, placing them on their heads, lying on them, sliding across the stage with them, and racing, rolling, stretching, sprawling, gesticulating with lascivious aimlessness.

The second episode, "No one ever escapes who wants to be caught," introduces a woman followed by two men. She dances (on *pointe*) a Spanish-style sequence and pretends to reject the amorous advances of the men. As the dance increases in excitement, the men perform with her, rip her shawl apart in the passion of the chase, embrace her, whirl her about, and finally carry her to the wings and lay her down where she cannot be seen but they can, bending over her. Following the swift ravishment, the men flee and the woman spins rapidly across the stage with mute screams and disappears. During the episode, the two girls with the stools watch the proceedings with evil interest.

The third scene, "If he were more gallant and less of a bore, she would come to life again," is a macabre duet for a man and an inert female body. The man at first stands near the wings with arms outstretched and into them, from high in space, falls the body of a woman with long hair. He dances with the limp figure, endeavoring to instill life into it with his own passion. He lifts her, twists her into a myriad of positions, props her up, moves violently with her, but she remains lifeless.

The final episode deals with a martyr. "They are determined to kill this saintly woman. After judgment has been pronounced against her, she is dragged through the streets in triumph, but if they do it to shame her, they are wasting their time. No one can make her ashamed who has nothing to be ashamed of." In an eerie green light, a woman is carried in on a board accompanied by four hooded men carrying huge broomlike branches. The board is set upright, the woman is bound to it and the fire is lighted. As she moves her feet restlessly, draws up her legs in agony, the four men toss their brooms into the pool of red light at her feet and the red intensifies, enveloping her body. She grasps at her head-dress and pulls a white covering over her face, shudders, and dies. Figures standing behind the board move into a pattern of the Cross while the two foul girls with the stools, who have presided over all of the disasters, look on casually, partly amused, partly bored.

As the curtain falls, a voice is heard: *"El sueño de la razón produce monstruos"* ("The sleep of reason produces monsters").

The first cast for the Ballet Theatre included Charlyne Baker and Jenny Workman (the Two Girls), Nana Gollner (the Woman Who Was Caught), John Kriza and Ruth Ann Koesun (the Man and the Dead Girl), and Mary Burr (the Martyr).

Capricorn Concerto

Choreography, Todd Bolender; music, Samuel Barber; scenery and costumes, Esteban Frances. First produced by the Ballet Society (later, the New York City Ballet), New York, March 22, 1948. A later treatment, with wholly new choreography, of Bolender's Zodiac.

Capriol Suite

Choreography, Frederick Ashton; music, Peter Warlock; scenery and costumes, William Chappell. First produced by Ballet Rambert, London, February 25, 1930. First American presentation by the Sadler's Wells Theatre Ballet, San Francisco, December 5, 1951.

Both the music and the choreography were inspired by Thoinot Arbeau's sixteenth-century book *Orchésographie,* in which a young man named Capriol receives instruction in dancing and dance deportment from Arbeau. *Capriol Suite,* Ashton's first ballet, is based upon the *basse danse,* the *pavane,* the *branle,* and other sixteenth-century dances familiar to Arbeau.

Ashton, Andrée Howard, Diana Gould, Harold Turner and William Chappell headed the first cast.

Carmen

Choreography, Roland Petit; music, Georges Bizet; scenery and costumes, Antoni Clavé; based on the opera. First produced by Roland Petit's Ballets de Paris, London, February 21, 1949. First presented in America by the same company, New York, October 6, 1949. Ruth Page has staged several versions of Carmen, *the most recent of which was staged for her Ruth Page's International Ballet, with orchestrations by Isaac van Grove and decor and costumes by Bernard Daydé. This version is in the repertory of the Pittsburgh Ballet Theatre. John Cranko's choreography to a collage of Bizet's music by Wolfgang Fortner and Wilfried Steinbrenner, decor and costumes by Jacques Dupont, was first performed by the Stuttgart Ballet, Stuttgart, February 28, 1971. Alberto Alonso staged a version of* Carmen *for the Bolshoi Ballet, with decor by Boris Messerer and costumes by Salvador Fernandez. It was first performed in Moscow, April 20, 1967. This production was first performed in Western Europe, in London, July 23, 1969. Alonso also staged the work for the Ballet Nacional de Cuba in 1972.*

The Petit version is in five scenes and represents a striking admixture of classical ballet, Spanish-style movement, mime, and freshly invented dramatic dance action.

The opening episode is a street scene. It is Seville and people are idly strolling, standing, chatting, waiting for something of interest to happen. There is occasional, incidental dance but the atmosphere does not become charged until we hear the sounds of a fight coming from the second floor of a building. Down the stairs races a girl with Carmen in hot pursuit. They continue their biting, scratching, hair-pulling row as the assembled crowd happily eggs them on. Into the scene of battle comes Don José. He rescues the loser and is about to arrest Carmen when he suddenly becomes transfixed with her vivid, daring beauty, her voluptuousness, her sullen yet provocative air. Capitulating completely, he asks to meet her later.

The second scene, a tavern, reveals first a group of pleasure-seekers, some blowsy and bored, others young and vital. Don José enters and to the music of the famous *Habañera* dances a fast, bright, stamping, anticipatory dance of happiness. The customers cheer him on with singing and hand-claps and Carmen suddenly appears on top of the bar. She is lifted down and starts a solo dance which is as vicious as it is alluring. Her abbreviated costume reveals most of her body, a fan becomes an instrument of seduction and the gold dust with which her short, black hair and shoulders are sprinkled, spurts in all directions as she engages in a series of violent spins. When, finally, she offers herself to Don José, he picks her up and carries her to the bedroom above while the crowd celebrates his capture by her. At the end of the scene, the lovers return to join the wild festivities and then retire again.

The third scene is in Carmen's bedroom. It is morning and Don José opens the curtains to reveal Carmen lying on a bed. While he is washing his hands, drying them on the curtains and standing deep in reverie, Carmen begins to move. She caresses her body with appreciative hands, inviting her lover to take stock of her charms as she investigates the smooth texture and curves of her legs, arms, face, breasts. At first Don José seems disinterested, tired, and Carmen is annoyed, but as she attempts to turn away from him, his passion is swiftly renewed. The two engage in an intensely amorous duet in which Don José lifts Carmen high and slides her body down against his own, sinks to the floor, where he balances her in a glorious feminine arc upon his knees, and then slowly draws her gently shuddering body to his in total contact. As the exhausted lovers lie there, three of Carmen's friends arrive and urge them to come outside.

Scene four takes place at night in a lonely Seville street.

Carmen, Don José, and some companions enter. Plans for robbery are made and Don José, completely under the spell of Carmen, accepts the dagger she hands him and agrees to follow her orders. Waiting, he moves to the ominous music of a drum until a man enters. Don José stabs him and takes his money; Carmen and her companions come back, snatch the loot and run off, with Don José trailing them.

The fifth and final scene takes place outside the bullring. A group of girls await the arrival of their hero, the toreador, and when he comes in, his eyes single out Carmen, whose cool yet intriguing glance arouses him far more than the adoration of the rest. Don José, who enters at this point, sees the glance and recognizes the same hypnotic power that Carmen had exercised on him. As the crowd goes in to the arena Don José, in a furious fit of jealousy, rushes up to Carmen as if he would strangle her. She tears herself away and the two commence a duel in dance in which one must die. The challenge, the feints, the attacks end as Don José stabs Carmen. She dies in his arms, her legs trembling with the last flood of life.

Petit and Renée Jeanmaire danced the leading roles both abroad and in the United States. Maya Plisetskaya was the first to dance the Alberto Alonso version. Alicia Alonso later danced it in Cuba.

Carmina Burana

Choreography, John Butler; music, Carl Orff; costumes, Ruth Morley; décor, Paul Sylbert. First performed at the New York City Opera November 19, 1959, by Carmen DeLavallade, Glen Tetley, Veronika Mlaker, and Scott Douglas.

This major modern work may be described as an erotic ballet-cantata, for the motivation of the action derives as much from the Latin words as from the Orff score. Both provide images to guide the choreographer. There are several successful stagings of this popular choral work, but the best known is that created by John Butler. It is highly sensual in essence and large in scale, reserving most of the romanticized sexualities for *pas de deux* and making movement statements of sweeping grandeur through a large ensemble. It is cast wholly in modern dance terms but has successfully served in the repertories of opera, ballet troupes, and modern dance companies.

Carnaval

Choreography and book, Michel Fokine; music, Robert Schumann (orchestration of Carnaval, suite for piano); scenery and costumes, Léon Bakst. First performed at a benefit in St. Petersburg by members of the Russian Imperial Ballet in 1910. First performed by the Diaghilev Ballets Russes in Paris, June 4, 1910; American première, by the same company, New York, January 19, 1916. Later revived in America by the Ballet Russe de Monte Carlo and Ballet Theatre (now the American Ballet Theatre), the former March 16, 1934, the latter in 1940. Eliot Feld's American Ballet Company performed Carnaval for the first time at the Brooklyn Academy of Music, October 24, 1969. The ballet has also been in the repertoires of the National Ballet of Canada and the Australian Ballet.

This one-act ballet, highly popular for about three decades, is set in the anteroom to a main ballroom. Here the characters, many of them drawn from the *commedia dell'arte*, gather to flirt, dance in small groups, frolic, and chatter, safe from the demanding formalities of the ball itself.

In addition to the young ladies of the ensemble and their cavaliers, we meet the ever energetic and playful Harlequin, the fickle and charming Columbine, the sad-faced Pierrot, the irritating Pantalon, and other couples engaged in or pursuing amorous dalliance. Little incident follows little incident, dance follows dance as the ballet proceeds on its lightly humorous course.

At the first performance in Russia, the cast included Tamara Karsavina, Vera Fokina, Ludmilla Shollar, Bronislava Nijinska, and Enrico Cecchetti. At the Paris première, the cast was almost the same but one of the exceptions was the appearance of Vaslav

Nijinsky as Harlequin. Adolph Bolm was seen as Pierrot both in Europe and America (he performed the role in the American Ballet Theatre production).

Casse Noisette

See *The Nutcracker*

Catulli Carmina

(The Love Songs of Catullus)

> *Choreography, John Butler; music, Carl Orff; costumes, Jac Venza. First performed at the Caramoor Festival, New York, June 26, 1964, danced by Carmen de Lavallade, Mary Hinkson, Robert Powell, and Buzz Miller. The ballet has since been taken into the repertory of Les Grands Ballets Canadiens.*

Ceremonials

> *Choreography, Norman Walker; music, Alberto Ginastera. First performed by the Harkness Ballet, Providence, Rhode Island, October 12, 1972.*

A nonethnic choreographic synthesis of those historic, and prehistoric, rituals which had to do with courtship, fertility, body strength, racial memory, magicmaking. A ballet both sensual and sensuous.

Ceremony

> *Choreography, John Butler; music, Krzysztof Penderecki; decor, Rouben Ter-Arutunian. First performed by the Pennsylvania Ballet, New York, January 29, 1968.*

Chabriesque

Choreography, Gerald Arpino; music, Emmanuel Chabrier (Trois Valses Romantiques, Souvenirs de Munich, *and* Cortège Burlesque); *costumes, A. Christina Giannini. First performed by the City Center Joffrey Ballet, Chicago, February, 1972. First performance in New York by the same company, March 10, 1972.*

A light and spirited ballet evoking young romance through swift embraces, darting departures, joyous arrivals, exuberant lifts, all relating male and female bodies in innocent but warm proximities.

La Chatte

Choreography, George Balanchine; music, Henri Sauget; book by Boris Kochno based on one of Aesop's fables; scenery and costumes, Gabo and Pevsner. First produced by Diaghilev's Ballets Russes, Monte Carlo, April 30, 1927.

Checkmate

Choreography, Ninette de Valois; music, Arthur Bliss; scenery and costumes, E. McKnight Kauffer. First produced by the Vic-Wells Ballet (later the Sadler's Wells Ballet and now the Royal Ballet), Paris, June 15, 1937; first London performance, October 5, 1937; first American performance (same company), November 2, 1949.

This allegorical ballet opens with a Prologue in which two armored chess players, Love and Death, sit facing each other across a chessboard. In a few moves Love has lost, an omen of the course of the ballet. The players now disappear and a curtain rises to reveal the stage as a chessboard. The dancers who enter are dressed like red and black chessmen.

The reds are to be attacked by the blacks and the outcome

is almost apparent at the start (in addition to the omen of the Prologue), for the invading blacks, led by their queen, advance inexorably, demolishing the besieged. Only a red knight fights valiantly for his queen and feeble king but he too is defeated, for he cannot bring himself to kill the black queen when the opportunity presents itself. At the close, the red king is left alone to face torture and death at the hands of the black queen.

The role of the Black Queen was created by June Brae, and Beryl Grey was the first to dance it for American audiences.

Chopin Concerto

Choreography, Bronislava Nijinska; music, Frédéric Chopin; costumes, Alexander Ignatiev. First produced by the Ballet Russe de Monte Carlo, New York, October 12, 1942. (An earlier version was presented in Paris in 1937.)

Chopin Concerto is a storyless ballet, now rarely given, which featured at its première Alexandra Danilova, Nathalie Krassovska, Igor Youskevitch, and Frederic Franklin.

Chopiniana

(See also *Les Sylphides*)

Choreography, Michel Fokine; music, Frédéric Chopin, orchestrated by Glazounov. First produced in St. Petersburg, March 8, 1908, by members of the Russian Imperial Ballet, with Anna Pavlova and Anatole Oboukhoff. (An earlier version, using the figure of Chopin, was presented in 1906; Russian, English, and American authorities and Fokine himself are not in agreement on the date of the first performance of the second version, although the year is most probably 1908 and the month February or March.) Later revised and renamed Les Sylphides, *and with scenery and costumes by Alexandre Benois, it was presented by Diaghilev's Ballets Russes in Paris, June 2, 1909. Pavlova and Vaslav Nijinsky danced in the Paris première.*

This abstract, romantic ballet, composed of a series of dances for soloists and ensemble, was designed to evoke the flavor of the Romantic Age of ballet as it was introduced nearly a century earlier in the Taglioni *La Sylphide*.

Chopiniana or *Les Sylphides* is a standard production in almost every ballet repertory. One of the several companies which presents it under its original title, *Chopiniana*, is the Royal Danish Ballet, whose production was staged by Fokine himself in 1925 in Copenhagen. The Danish staging was first seen in America in 1956. The Bolshoi Ballet's production (starring Galina Ulanova) was first presented in America (New York), April 23, 1959. For details on the choreography, see *Les Sylphides*.

Choral Variations on Bach's "Vom Himmel hoch"

Choreography, George Balanchine; music, Igor Stravinsky; decor, Rouben Ter-Arutunian. First performed by the New York City Ballet, Stravinsky Festival, June 25, 1972.

Choreartium

Choreography, Leonide Massine; music, Johannes Brahms (Symphony No. 4); scenery and costumes, Constantine Terechkovich and Eugene Lourie. First produced by the Ballet Russe de Monte Carlo, London, October 24, 1933. First American presentation, New York, October 16, 1935.

This is the second of Massine's symphonic ballets (the first, *Les Présages* to Tchaikovsky's Fifth Symphony). It has no plot, although mood, situation, and relationships are suggested. Basically, it falls into that category of choreography which the nonballet Denishawn Dancers used to term "music visualization," a concept of reflecting or extending into dance form the rhythms, phrases, intensities, colors, and moods of the selected music.

Of special interest in *Choreartium* was the second movement. Here Massine departed from ballet technique to employ, in somewhat adapted form, the style of modern dance (probably the Cen-

tral European type of modern dance rather than the American).
The key design was carried by a line of women dancing a lamentation led by a figure whose body movements—freely used torso,
angular lines—were closely allied to modern dance.

The first cast included Irina Baronova, Alexandra Danilova,
Tatiana Riabouchinska, Vera Zorina, Roman Jasinsky, David Lichine, Paul Petroff, Yurek Shabelevski, and, as the principal dancer
of the second movement, Nina Verchinina.

Choreographic Miniatures

*Choreography, Leonid Yakobson; music, Edvard Grieg,
Claude Debussy, Peter Ilyich Tchaikovsky, Johann Strauss,
Maurice Ravel, Serge Prokofiev, Serge Rachmaninoff, Alex-
ander Scriabin, Igor Stravinsky, and others; designs, Simon
Virsaladze, Valery Dorrer, and Tatiana Bruni. First performed
by the Kirov Ballet, Leningrad, January 6, 1959.*

Cinderella

*Choreography, Frederick Ashton; music, Serge Prokofiev;
scenery and costumes, Jean-Denis Malclès. First produced by
the Sadler's Wells Ballet (now the Royal Ballet), London, December 23, 1948. First American presentation by the same
company, New York, October 18, 1949. Other stagings of
Cinderella include the following: Soviet ballet, choreography,
R. Zakharov, music of Prokofiev, Moscow, January, 1945 (the
Bolshoi Theatre); the Russian Imperial Ballet, choreography
by Ivanov, Cecchetti, St. Petersburg, December 5, 1893 (a
still earlier Russian Cinderella was staged in Moscow, January
6, 1825); Original Ballet Russe, choreography by Michel Fokine, music by Frédéric d'Erlanger, scenery and costumes by
Nathalie Gontcharova, first presented in London, July 19,
1938, and in New York November 16, 1940. (As Cendrillon,
produced May 8, 1815, St. Petersburg; produced May 13,
1823, Paris Opera with choreography by Didelot; in these and*

subsequent productions, various choreographers, composers, designers were employed; Russian title for Cinderella *is* Zolushka.) *The ballet, with choreography by Celia Franca and décor by Jürgen Rose, was first presented by the National Ballet of Canada in 1969. A new production by the National Ballet of Washington, created by Ben Stevenson, was premièred in April, 1970. The Ballet West production, choreographed by Willam Christensen, with décor and costumes by Kenneth MacClelland, was presented in 1969. A new Royal Ballet production, with Ashton's choreography, décor by Henry Bardon, and costumes by David Walker was presented December 23, 1965, and presented by the same company for the first time in the United States, April 18, 1967.*

The Ashton ballet, choreographed in classical style, is in three acts. The Sadler's Wells Ballet had mounted program-length traditional ballets before, but *Cinderella,* with original choreography by Ashton, represented the first English creative effort in the full-length ballet medium.

The ballet follows the familiar lines of the fairy tale itself, but Ashton, in addition to choreographing the actions of the story's principal figures, has introduced dances and *divertissements* which color, enhance, augment the theme.

In Act I, we are introduced to the drab Cinderella, dreaming of better days, obeying the orders of her ugly stepsisters, dancing gracefully with a broom. During the course of this act, the ugly ones fight over a scarf, scorn a begging hag (to whom Cinderella gives a piece of bread), prepare themselves in finery for the ball and, under the direction of a dancing teacher, engage in a hilarious sequence of attempts to master dance steps and party etiquette. With the departure of the stepsisters, the hag returns and reveals herself to Cinderella as a good fairy, the fairy godmother. The room seems to dissolve, and four fairies, representing spring, summer, autumn, and winter, dance their measures and prepare Cinderella for the ball. The neglected girl is now dressed in beautiful clothes, the pumpkin has been transformed into a coach and the joyous departure for the ball begins.

In Act II the ball at the palace is being held. There is a series of court dances, one of them involving the two ugly stepsisters and their terpsichorean inadequacies. But the romantic highpoint comes with the *pas de deux* for the handsome prince and the now glittering Cinderella. The act, quite naturally, concludes with a vivacious ensemble dance, led by the two young lovers, interrupted by the striking of midnight and Cinderella's swift departure.

The concluding act, in two scenes, opens with Cinderella sitting by the fireplace in her home. Only a single slipper convinces her that her experience was not a dream. In keeping with the familiar story, the prince enters, seeking the owner of the slipper dropped by Cinderella at the ball. It fails to fit the ugly sisters and when it slips easily onto the foot of Cinderella, the prince declares that she shall be his wife. The girl forgives her stepsisters for their cruelty, and the fairy godmother appears to transform the scene into a magical garden where dancing fairies and the prince's companions await the arrival of the couple. After dancing with their guests, the young lovers board their magical boat and sail away to happiness.

The role of Cinderella was choreographed by Ashton for Margot Fonteyn but because of illness the ballerina did not appear in the first performances, although subsequently she assumed the role. Moira Shearer was the first to dance the part, with Violetta Elvin as her immediate successor. Michael Somes was the first Prince and the roles of the ugly Stepsisters were created by Ashton and Robert Helpmann. Pamela May was the Fairy Godmother.

In the 1893 Ivanov ballet, Pierina Legnani created the title role; in the Bolshoi version of 1945, Galina Ulanova was the Cinderella; the Fokine production of 1938 starred Tatiana Riabouchinska. In 1906, Adeline Genée, the great Danish ballerina, appeared in her own production of *Cinderella* in London.

Cirque de Deux

Choreography, Ruthanna Boris; music, Charles Gounod (Walpurgis Night); *scenery and costumes, Robert Davison. First* produced by the Ballet Russe de Monte Carlo, New York, September 10, 1947. (A pre-Broadway performance took place the preceding month in Hollywood, August 1, 1947).

Clarinade

Choreography, George Balanchine; music, Morton Gould (Derivations for Clarinet and Jazz Band). First performed by the New York City Ballet, New York, April 29, 1964.

Clockwise

Choreography, Bruce Marks; music, Jean Françaix (L'Horloge de Flor); costumes, Stanley Simmons; lighting, Jules Fisher. First performed by Eliot Feld's American Ballet Company, October 23, 1970, at the Brooklyn Academy of Music, New York.

A first choreographic effort by an internationally famous dancer schooled in both classical ballet and modern dance.

The Clowns

Choreography, Gerald Arpino; music, Hershy Kay; costumes, Edith Luytens Bel Geddes. First performed by the City Center Joffrey Ballet, New York, February 28, 1968.

Clowns, in which props and lighting effects are an essential aspect of production, is a view of the clown as the perennial victim of insult, derision, even physical harm. He is also a sort of Everyman and in this ballet he seems to be swept up in a maelstrom of atomic war's aftermath, evil, and terror. Comedy and buffoonery are juxtaposed with the terror of loss.

Robert Blankshine created the role of the chief clown.

Le Combat

See *The Duel*

Commedia Balletica

Choreography, Todd Bolender; music, Igor Stravinsky (Pulcinella); scenery and costumes, Robert Davison. First produced by the Ballet Russe de Monte Carlo, New York, September 17, 1945. A pre-Broadway première was presented a few weeks earlier at the Jacob's Pillow Dance Festival, Lee, Massachusetts. The ballet was called Musical Chairs *at Lee and when it was produced by Jerome Robbins' Ballets: U.S.A.*

Con Amore

Choreography, Lew Christensen; music, Gioacchino Rossini; libretto, James Graham-Lujan; scenery and costumes, James Bodrero. First produced by the San Francisco Ballet in its home city March 10, 1953. Added to the repertory of the New York City Ballet, New York, June 9, 1953. The scenery and costumes for the New York City Ballet production were designed by Esteban Frances. The work was added to the repertory of Ballet West, with sets and costumes by Ariel Ballif, in 1962. The National Ballet of Washington first performed the work, with scenery and lighting by James Waring and costumes by Joseph Lewis, in Washington, D.C., October 10, 1963.

This ballet of militant and frivolous love is couched in the theatrical and pictorial styles of the nineteenth century. The first episode treats with a corps of pretty Amazons, headed by a handsome female captain and her two lieutenants, whose camp is invaded by a heroic-looking bandit. The ladies capture him but his charm is such that they fall in love with him. He, however, spurns their advances and even dares to say "No!" to the captain herself. In entreaty, they break their guns across their knees and the captain relinquishes her pistols but he will not be swayed. At the close of the scene, he kneels, chest brazenly bared, willing to be shot rather than submit to a love he does not want.

The second scene carries us to the home of a lovely and restless lady who hurries her husband on his way in a clear demonstration that someone else is expected momentarily. As soon as her husband departs, she admits a gentleman, who pursues her amorously. She eludes him for a bit but when he produces a shining bauble, she submits happily to his advances. There is a knock on the door and the lover conceals himself as a sailor enters and commences his ardent wooing; but a third knock sends him scurrying and a young scholar enters, reading a book and, obviously, far more interested in his studies than in romance. The fickleness of woman asserts itself and the lady makes an effort to woo him. The two who are hidden emerge and all engage in frantic attempts to seduce the lady. While they are holding her in an embrace, the husband returns and stands aghast as the lights go out.

The third and final scene is designed to resolve these mixed-up love affairs. Cupid or Love, embodied as a girl, enters to see what she can do. The scenes shift to the concluding tableaux of each of the preceding dramas; the Amazons, bandit, wife, husband, lovers grab little trees, which have been handily made available to them, and hide behind them, peer from behind them, and race about in what appears to be a hopeless melee. But Love's arrows do the trick and, placed in the right hearts, they bring together in passionate affection the Captain and her bandit, the wife and her husband, the first two lovers and the Amazon lieutenants. Feeling sorry for the lonely scholar, Love lets fly with a final shaft, he looks up and sees Love herself, drops his books, and chases after her.

Sally Bailey, Nancy Johnson, and Leon Danielian created the leading roles (Captain, Wife, Bandit) with the San Francisco Ballet.

The Concert

Choreography, Jerome Robbins; music, Frédéric Chopin (various selections); costumes, Irene Sharaff. First produced by the New York City Ballet, New York, March 6, 1956. Extensively revised and restaged (with décor by Saul Steinberg) by Robbins for his Ballets: U.S.A., Spoleto, Italy, June 8, 1958; New York, September 4, 1958. The work was revived by the New York City Ballet on December 2, 1971.

The choreographer describes his ballet as "a charade" and the motivating idea is that while listening to music, all sorts of images can freely cross the mind.

A piano is on stage and a pianist is performing. A motley group enters—the devoted music student, the eager woman, the bored husband, others—and sit on chairs to listen to the music. Then the images appear. A girl arises and flings herself into a whirlwind of action so violent that her hair lashes her face, and so dynamic that she ends in a complete collapse. A man attempts to polish off the "Minute Waltz" in record time. Groups of enraged butterflies emerge as the "Butterfly Etude" is played. Other reveries—the dreamers are aided in filling out their secret thoughts by a handy *corps de ballet*—include a woman bent on killing her husband by firearms, poison, and other methods; a ballet episode in which the dancers have conflicting ideas on tempo and design and utterly destroy the choreography; and a wistful, dreamy solo of great beauty and nostalgia. There are still other images, some pretty, some sad, some hilarious and some ineffectual.

Tanaquil LeClercq and Robert Barnett were among the principal dancers in the New York City Ballet production. In the revised, New York production, Maria Karnilova scored in one of the principal roles.

Concerto

Choreography, David McLain; music, Francis Poulenc. First performed by the Cincinnati Ballet, Cincinnati, April 7, 1969.

The ballet finds its choreographic form and its production plan in the architecture of the Corbett Auditorium of the College-Conservatory of Music, University of Cincinnati, where it was first presented. It is a classical work, reflecting the architecture of its housing. When performed on tour, the ballet's architectural designs are simulated not only by the costuming but by lighting effects. Edward Schulte was the auditorium's architect.

Concerto

Choreography, Kenneth MacMillan; music, Dmitri Shostakovitch; décor, Jürgen Rose. First performed by the American Ballet Theatre, New York, March 18, 1967. The ballet was first presented by the Royal Ballet, London, May 26, 1967. (Initially presented by the Berlin Opera Ballet, November 30, 1966.)

A ballet of moods—buoyant, sad, graciously pleasant—inspired by the characteristics and qualities of the music.

The American Ballet Theatre staging had Eleanor D'Antuono, Cynthia Gregory, Toni Lander, Bruce Marks, and Scott Douglas as the principals.

Concerto Barocco

Choreography, George Balanchine; music, Johann Sebastian Bach (Concerto in D Minor for Two Violins); scenery and costumes, Eugene Berman. First produced by the American Ballet, New York, May 29, 1941. Presented by the Ballet Russe de Monte Carlo, New York, September 9, 1945, without the Berman scenery and costumes. Added to the repertory of the Marquis de Cuevas' Grand Ballet, 1948, in Europe. Revived by the New York City Ballet, New York, October 11, 1948, with original Berman setting and costumes. Restaged by the New York City Ballet, New York, September 13, 1951, without the Berman scenery and costumes and using instead (as did the Ballet Russe) black practice costumes and an un-

adorned cyclorama as a background. The ballet is also in the repertory of the San Francisco Ballet. The ballet was added to the repertoire of Ballet West in 1964. It is also in the repertory of the National Ballet of Washington (1967), the Boston Ballet (1964), the Pennsylvania Ballet, and the Dance Theater of Harlem.

An abstract ballet in three movements designed to mirror the rhythms, sequences, intensities, emotional hues, and forms of the Bach score. Three soloists—two women and a man—and an ensemble of eight girls represent the physical extensions of the music.

In the first movement, the patterns reflect the interrelations of the two violins with each other (danced by the two ballerinas), and with the other instruments of the orchestra (embodied as a unit by the corps). The qualities of the two solo instruments are sensitively reproduced in the two dancing bodies—one, light, high, and bright; the other, of darker tone, more solid of movement, closer to the ground, glowing rather than shining.

The second movement centers mainly about the ballerina of the first violin and her cavalier. It is an adagio with soaring but effortless lifts in which the ballerina's body mounts into arcs along with the sweeping melodies of the first violin. There are delicate leanings out into space, soft resistances to gravity and even long sliding steps culminating in sharply defined arabesques as the patterns of the music move through surges and rests, calm introductions of a theme, and brilliant climaxes.

The final allegro movement brings on the ten girls, including the two soloists, in swift, bright, and crisp actions, many of them syncopated, fused into a series of masterful designs.

Indeed, the wealth of design in *Concerto Barocco*, its freshness and yet its undeviating classicism, is equal in its musicality to the great Bach score. Although it has no story and is usually done in practice clothes, it remains one of Balanchine's most popular ballets, appealing to the ballet novice and to the casual theatergoer as well as to the balletomane.

The on-again, off-again status of the Berman décor and costumes is indicative of the ballet's inherent purity. Many have felt that the costumes and scenery, though beautiful and appropriate, obscure the details of body movements, and so beautiful are these movements that many have preferred to see them as unencumbered as modesty will permit. Hence, the use of simple black practice costumes has proved advantageous and desirable.

Marie-Jeanne, Mary Jane Shea, and William Dollar headed the cast for the American Ballet. Marie-Jeanne, Patricia Wilde, and Nicholas Magallanes danced in the Ballet Russe revival. Marjorie Tallchief, Ethery Pagava, and George Skibine created the parts for the Marquis de Cuevas' Grand Ballet. The New York City Ballet's 1948 staging had Marie-Jeanne as the first ballerina; and the 1951 revival by the same company, Maria Tallchief, Diana Adams, and Magallanes in the leading parts.

Concerto Grosso

Choreography, Michael Uthoff; music, Antonio Vivaldi (Concerto Grosso No. 8 in A Minor); *costumes, David James. First performed, Mexico City, March, 1972, Ballet Clásico de Mexico. Added to the repertory of the Hartford Ballet, November 11, 1972.*

La Concurrence

Choreography, George Balanchine; music, Georges Auric; scenery, costumes, and libretto, André Derain. First produced by the Ballet Russe de Monte Carlo, Monte Carlo, April 12, 1932.

Confetti

Choreography, Gerald Arpino; music, Gioacchino Rossini (Overture to Semiramide). *First performed by the City Center Joffrey Ballet, New York, March 3, 1970.*

Dancing as light as its title suggests. Swift images of gaiety. Little trillings of the feet similar to coloratura trills in arias suggesting birdcalls.

The Consort

Choreography, Eliot Feld; music, John Dowland, Neusiedler, and Thomas Morley (orchestrated by Christopher Keene); costumes, Stanley Simmons. First performed by Eliot Feld's American Ballet Company, Brooklyn Academy of Music, October 24, 1970. First performed by the Royal Swedish Ballet under the title Herrskapslekar, *Stockholm, October 24, 1973.*

Dances that evoke both the elegance and the bawdiness of the Elizabethan age. Court dances developing into more advanced ballet actions and into activities which come close to bending a *branle* into a brawl.

Constantia

Choreography, William Dollar; music, Frédéric Chopin (Piano Concerto in F Minor); scenery, Horace Armistead; costumes, Grace Houston. First produced by the Ballet International, New York, October 31, 1944. Added to the repertory of the Original Ballet Russe, New York, October 16, 1946. Staged by the Marquis de Cuevas' Grand Ballet, 1947–1948. Remounted by Ballet Theatre (now the American Ballet Theatre), New York, April 9, 1951, with scenery and costumes by Robert Davison.

Coppélia

Choreography, Arthur Saint-Léon; music, Léo Delibes; book, Charles Nuitter and Saint-Léon. First presented at the Paris Opera, May 25, 1870. First American performance by the National (formerly, American) Opera Company, New York, March 11, 1887 (possibly seen earlier on tour), in a production staged by Mamert Bibeyran. First presented in St. Petersburg in 1884 by the Russian Imperial Ballet with Saint-Léon choreography as reconstructed by Marius Petipa. Produced by the Royal Danish Ballet, Copenhagen, December 27, 1896,

*in a version adapted from the Saint-Léon original by Hans
Beck (later revised by Harald Lander). The Russian version of
Coppélia was first performed in America by Anna Pavlova
and Mikhail Mordkin, with the Metropolitan Opera Ballet, in
New York (at the Met), February 28, 1910. The ballet was
first danced in London in 1906 in a production starring Adeline Genée. While the contemporary French and Danish stagings of Coppélia are direct descendants of the Saint-Léon
original, the English and American mountings derive from the
Imperial Russian version. The Vic-Wells Ballet presented it
in London, March 21, 1933; as the Sadler's Wells Ballet, restaged it October 25, 1946; and the junior company, the
Sadler's Wells Theatre Ballet, presented a new production in
London, September 4, 1951, and performed it in New York,
March 27, 1952. The Ballet Russe de Monte Carlo production,
staged by Serguev after Petipa, Iavnov, and Cecchetti, was
presented in London in September 1938 and given its first
New York performance, October 17, 1938. A shortened Coppélia, arranged by Simon Semenov was produced by Ballet
Theatre (the American Ballet Theatre), New York, October
22, 1942. A production of Coppélia, staged by Ivan Clustine,
was in the repertory of Anna Pavlova and her touring company. There have been and are many other mountings of this
perennial ballet favorite. Among them are the John Cranko
production, first presented by the Stuttgart Ballet, Stuttgart,
June 10, 1962, and the National Ballet of Washington production, staged by Frederic Franklin, décor by James Waring,
costumes by Joseph Lewis, Washington, D.C., December 27,
1963. George Balanchine and Alexandra Danilova mounted a
production for the New York City Ballet, Saratoga Springs,
July 17, 1974.*

Act I. The scene is a village square. On one side of the stage is
the house where Swanilda, the heroine, lives and on the other
is the mysterious workshop of Dr. Coppélius, a toymaker suspected
of possessing magical gifts. In the upstairs window of the toymaker's house sits Coppélia, a doll, with a book in her hands. Swanilda

enters and engages in a dance which characterizes her youthful exuberance, her gaiety of spirit and suggests that she must be a girl in love. She sees the doll and bows to it, not knowing it is a doll, but her friendly bows, gestures, and greetings make no impression and she stamps her foot in irritation.

Hearing the arrival of Franz, her sweetheart, she darts away, suspicious of his interest in the remote Coppélia. Her thoughts are justified, for the young man flirts with the doll until the old Doctor, (who had left the house at the start of the ballet and hobbled about the square before returning inside), makes the doll move and then closes the curtains before Franz can get more than a brief look at her actions. Thwarted, he turns to Swanilda's home. The girl appears from her hiding place, where she has been able to observe her swain's interest in the mysterious girl, and pretends to chase a butterfly. Franz joins her, pins the butterfly to his jacket; Swanilda cries out as if her own heart had been pricked. Franz's protestations of devotion fail to convince her.

The two lovers are interrupted by the villagers, who run onto the stage to perform the *Mazurka*, one of the highlights of the ballet. At the conclusion of the *Mazurka*, the Burgomaster arrives to announce a special festival to be held in honor of a new bell given by the local lord for the town clock. Dowries will also be presented to girls wed on the festival day. Swanilda, not quite sure of Franz, dances with an ear of wheat, listening for the goodluck sound which will say that Franz is true to her. Although she shakes the ear, she hears nothing, her friends fail to hear a sound; and although Franz says he hears it, she refuses to believe him. The marriage appears to be canceled as the lovers part.

A *Czardas*—another highlight of the ballet—follows, and at its close dusk begins to settle and the celebrants depart. The old Doctor emerges from his house, carefully locks the door and places the key in his pocket. But some of the town bullies push him around and the key falls to the ground. A bit later, Swanilda and her girl friends appear, find the key and under Swanilda's urging sneak into the house of the toymaker. Franz, meanwhile, is determined to satisfy his curiosity about Coppélia. With a ladder he attempts to scale the wall to her window but the return of Dr.

Coppélius interrupts his plan. The bent, hobbling old man cannot find his key and noting that his door is open, he rushes in. Franz, still determined, comes back with his ladder and starts to climb as the curtain falls.

Act II. The large workroom in Coppélius' house. Life-sized dolls in various poses are scattered about the room. Swanilda and her friends enter and in the dimness are frightened by these figures. A Chinaman, a drummer, Harlequin, an astrologer, and other dolls (they vary in different productions) suffer the inspection of the girls but Swanilda is mainly interested in the girl seen in the window. She pulls back the drapes in an alcove and discovers her sitting there. Neither greetings nor a tug at the dress bring response and Swanilda discovers that Franz's long-distance love is nothing but a doll. And so are the other figures, for one of the girls brushes up against the Chinaman and he starts his mechanical dance.

The girls wind up all the dolls and are enjoying them when the old Doctor races in, infuriated by this invasion. The girls flee but Swanilda darts behind the alcove curtains. Then, Coppélius hears a sound and Franz crawls in the window. At first the old man is furious but then he decides here is an opportunity to test his magic. He gives Franz a drugged drink and when Franz is unconscious, rolls out Coppélia, who, the audience can see, is really Swanilda dressed in the doll's clothes.

With the aid of a big book of magical directions, Coppélius attempts to bring his favorite doll to life. He sweeps his hands over Franz's body, as if drawing life forces from it and its various parts—shoulders, eyes, limbs, heart—and then dashes the unseen essences at the doll. Her eyes bat, her shoulders shrug, the arms move stiffly, she steps, she dances. When the magician is not watching, Swanilda attempts to awaken Franz, but in vain. For the rest, she dances as ordered, sometimes slapping Coppélius with her stiff arms (as if it were unintentional), again engaging in a bright Italian dance or a fast and amusing Scottish dance. Finally she stirs Franz, races about the room, raising havoc with the magic book and the dolls, then departs, recognized by Franz as his own true love, Swanilda. Dr. Coppélius, his dreams shattered, pulls back the curtains of the alcove and finds the limp, undressed body of his doll, a doll who never came to life except in the heartless impersonation by Swanilda.

Act III. The village square. The festival has begun and Swanilda and Franz are happily reunited. Coppélius interrupts the joyous scene with demands of payment for the damage he has sustained. Swanilda offers him her dowry but the lord tells her to keep it and gives the distressed and greedy Doctor a bag of gold. Now the festivities truly begin, with happy dances, most of them depicting the hours of the day as recorded by the new bell in the village clock. There are solos for Dawn and for Prayer, ensemble dances and, of course, a brilliant *pas de deux* for Swanilda and Franz. With the plot resolved, the time has come to dance and Act III is mainly a *divertissement*.

Coppélia is to comic ballet what *Giselle* is to tragic ballet in the nineteenth-century roster of masterworks. Its first ballerina was Giuseppina Bozzacchi. Among the later ballerinas who appeared as Swanilda were Pavlova, Lydia Lopokova and Catherine Geltzer. Beginning with the Ballet Russe's 1938 production, Alexandra Danilova was hailed as the most perfect Swanilda of her generation and for many balletgoers in America and Western Europe, Swanilda and Danilova were synonymous for two decades. Among other ballerinas associated with this role have been Inge Sand, Nadia Nerina, Natalia Makarova, Carla Fracci. The role of Franz has been done by Frederic Franklin, Fredbjørn Bjornsson, Niels Kehlet, Ivan Nagy.

Le Coq d'Or

Choreography, Michel Fokine; music, Nicholas Rimsky-Korsakov; based on the Rimsky-Korsakov opera, with libretto by Byelsky, suggested by a poem of Pushkin; scenery and costumes, Nathalie Gontcharova. First produced by the Ballet Russe de Monte Carlo, New York, October 23, 1937. Earlier productions included one as an opera-pantomime presented by Diaghilev in Paris, May 21, 1914. On March 6, 1918, an opera-pantomime staging by Adolph Bolm was given at the Metropolitan Opera House.

The Fokine ballet, in three acts, a prologue, and an epilogue, tells of an Astrologer who falls in love with the Queen of Shemakhan, daughter of the air. In order to win her for himself, he works out an elaborate ruse whereby he gives to the stupid King Dodon a magical Golden Cockerel which will give warning of the approach of enemies, in return for a gift yet to be named. The Cockerel gives two warnings: at the first one the King sends out his two rival sons to do battle; and at the second he heaves his immense, lazy weight onto a horse to protect the kingdom himself. He finds no enemies, but the sons have killed each other, the armies are disrupted, and he is frightened by the sudden emergence of a great tent. The tent, however, contains no recognizable enemy, only the beautiful Queen of Shemakhan and her attendants.

King Dodon, after making a fool of himself over the Queen, returns with her to his city and presents her as his queen. The Astrologer comes to claim his gift, the Queen of Shemakhan, and is killed by the King for his impertinence. The flashing Golden Cockerel pecks the King to death as the Queen of Shemakhan laughs and disappears.

Irina Baronova as the Queen of Shemakhan and Tatiana Riabouchinska in the title role, headed the initial cast in the Fokine work.

Le Corsaire

Choreography, Jules Perrot (revised in subsequent productions by other choreographers); music, Adolphe Adam. First produced Paris Opera, January 23, 1856. Later added to the repertory of the Russian Imperial Ballet, St. Petersburg, January 24, 1858. Succeeded by a new version January 25, 1899.

This three-act ballet, based on a poem by Byron, has a fairly complicated plot involving a pirate (the corsair) and a beautiful girl, who is sold to a rich pasha by her guardian and who is, after many adventures, united with the man she fell in love with on sight, the pirate. The ballet is performed in the Soviet Union but audiences in Western Europe and America know it primarily through its famous excerpted *pas de deux*.

Margot Fonteyn and Rudolf Nureyev were the first to dance the *pas de deux* with the Royal Ballet.

Cortège Burlesque

Choreography, Eliot Feld; music, Emmanuel Chabrier (Cortège Burlesque, Souvenirs de Munich); orchestrated by Hershy Kay; scenery, Robert Munford; costumes, Stanley Simmons. First presented by the American Ballet Company, Festival of Two Worlds, Spoleto, Italy, June 27, 1969.

Cortège Burlesque is a circus satire in *pas de deux* form.

The dancers at the first performance were Eliot Feld and Christine Sarry.

Cortège Hongrois

Choreography, George Balanchine; music, Alexander Glazounov (last act of Raymonda*); décor and costumes, Rouben Ter-Arutunian. First performed by the New York City Ballet, New York, May 7, 1973.*

A *piece d'occasion*. A potpourri of passages from Petipa's *Raymonda*, Balanchine's later staging of *Ramonda*, his *Pas de Dix*, *Grand Pas–Glazounov*, and additional sequences, honoring the ballerina Melissa Hayden on the occasion of her retirement from the New York City Ballet.

Cortège Parisien

Choreography, Eliot Feld; music, Emmanuel Chabrier ("Fête polonaise"); costumes, Frank Thompson; lighting, Jules Fisher. First performed by Eliot Feld's American Ballet Com-

pany, *Brooklyn Academy of Music, New York, October 21, 1970.*

Ballet froth and bubbles, a sort of sip of *Gaîté Parisienne.*

Cotillon

Choreography, George Balanchine; music, Emmanuel Chabrier (various selections); book, Boris Kochno; scenery and costumes, Christian Bérard. First produced by the Ballet Russe de Monte Carlo, Monte Carlo, April 12, 1932. Later presented in America by the Original Ballet Russe.

Courante

Choreography, Ben Stevenson; music, Johann Sebastian Bach (Cello Suite in G, transcribed for lute); *décor, Robert Troll; costumes, Catherine Gentilucci and Patricia Sorrell; lighting, Jennifer Tipton. First performed by the National Ballet of Washington, Kennedy Center Opera House, Washington, D.C., June 1, 1973.*

A modern ballet that artlessly bridges the gap between youth of the Elizabethan Age and of today through romantic, gay, and antic dances suitable to any era.

Carmen Mathe headed the first cast. Howard Bass was the lutenist.

Creation of the World

Choreography, Natalia Kasatkina and Vladimir Vasiliov; music, Andrei Petrov; based on drawings by Jean Effel. First performed by the Kirov Ballet, Leningrad, March 23, 1971.

La Croqueuse de Diamants

(The Diamond Cruncher)
Choreography and songs, Roland Petit; music, Jean-Michel Damase; lyrics, Raymond Queneau; book, Roland Petit and

*Alfred Adam; scenery and costumes, George Wakhevitch.
First produced by Roland Petit's Ballets de Paris, Paris, September 25, 1950. First American performance (same company), New York, October 31, 1950.*

This ballet-revue in four scenes presents the strange character
of a woman whose avid interest in diamonds is not to fill her decorative needs but to satisfy her appetite. She eats them. Through
lusty song, dance, and pantomime, the choreographer takes us to
a part of Paris occupied by thugs, thieves, and other interesting,
disreputable characters, as well as by ordinary merchants, and tells
his tale of the Diamond Cruncher. Her hand reaches through a wall
to pick a pocket or to receive the glittering loot from her band of
robbers. There is sex and romance and rough humor in the Diamond Cruncher's life, but the high points come when this desirable
gamine holds the gems up to her gleaming teeth and sings in sexy
style about her peculiar appetite.

Renée Jeanmaire created the title part both in Europe and
America, and Petit himself played the male lead.

Cupido

(Cupid Out of his Humor)

*Choreography, Mary Skeaping; music, Henry Purcell. First
performed at the Court Theatre at Drottningholm (a royal
summer residence on the island of Lovön, built in the seventeenth century) by the Royal Swedish Ballet, June 14, 1956.*

Mary Skeaping's twentieth-century rendering of an old Swedish libretto of a ballet danced for Queen Christina in 1649, performed in the appropriate milieu of the old court theatre.

The first cast was headed by Bjørn Holmgren and Elsa-Marianne Von Rosen.

Cyrano de Bergerac

*Choreography, Roland Petit; music, Marius Constant; décor,
Basarte; costumes, Yves Saint Laurent; libretto, Roland Petit*

(after the play by Edmond Rostand). First performed by the Royal Danish Ballet, Copenhagen, February 18, 1961.

Dances at a Gathering

Choreography, Jerome Robbins; music, Frédéric Chopin; costumes, Joe Eula. First presented by the New York City Ballet, May 23, 1969. The Royal Ballet gave its first performance of the ballet, October 19, 1970, and gave its American première May 16, 1972.

Dances at a Gathering is Jerome Robbins's inspired choreographic responses to études, mazurkas, waltzes, a scherzo, and a nocturne by Chopin. Rooted in classical ballet technique, it transcends ballet as such to become a total dance expression. One solo for ballerina does not use *pointe* steps at all, yet she wears toe shoes; occasionally the booted males echo in sturdy step and strong arm gestures the composer's Polish heritage; and there are steps and gestures evocative of male bravado, girlish coquetry, playfulness, reverie, celebration. It seems to spring from the pure, clean, uncalculating, ecstatic impulse to dance. It captures you, the onlooker, in an unseen embrace and makes you an unquestioning, elated participant in your own *Dances at a Gathering*.

The cast for the first performance was Edward Villella, Allegra Kent, Kay Mazzo, Sara Leland, Patricia McBride, Violette Verdy, Anthony Blum, John Clifford, John Prinz, and Robert Maiorano.

Dance Symphony

Choreography and book, Fedor Lopukhov; music, Ludwig van Beethoven (Symphony No. 4); costumes, Pyotr Goncharov. First performed by the Kirov Ballet, Leningrad, March 7, 1923.

Danse Brillante

Choreography, Frederic Franklin; music, Mikhail Glinka; costumes, Regina Quintana. First performed by the National Bal-

let of Washington, Lisner Auditorium, Washington, D.C.,
April 22, 1966.

Roni Mahler, Ivan Nagy, and Anita Dyche danced the first performance.

Danses Concertantes

*Choreography, George Balanchine; music, Igor Stravinsky;
scenery and costumes, Eugene Berman. First produced by the
Ballet Russe de Monte Carlo, New York, September 10, 1944.
Another version of the ballet, with totally different choreography by Kenneth MacMillan and scenery and costumes by
Nicholas Georgiadis, was presented by the Sadler's Wells
Theatre Ballet, London, January 18, 1955. The MacMillan
version was presented by the American Ballet Theatre for the
first time, New York, October 10, 1967. The Balanchine version was revived by the New York City Ballet for its Stravinsky Festival and performed on June 20, 1972; it has remained
in the repertory. The Royal Danish Ballet presented the Mac-
Millan version for the first time, December 16, 1961.*

The Balanchine *Danses Concertantes* is without a story. It is
a ballet of bright movement, wit, and invention in which the choreographic designs capture the flow, the rhythmic surprises, and the
formal sequence of the music. The dancers, in costumes that are
both chic and glittering, appear first in a march for full company;
then follows an episode for the ballerina and ensemble, four variations for subgroups of the corps, a *pas de deux* for the ballerina and
the premier danseur, and finally a concluding march for the entire
company.

The music, because it is dance music and was conceived with
dance presentation in mind, dictates the form, rhythmic design,
and quality of dance, yet choreographic differences are possible.
Balanchine and MacMillan have used different patterns of action
and even different steps, although both, of course, selected movements in keeping with the style and texture of the music. Another
point of difference in the two versions was that the mature Balan-

chine colored his ballet with sophistication while the then youthful MacMillan flavored his with the almost rompish (though still elegant) exuberance of youth.

Alexandra Danilova and Leon Danielian were the stars in the first Ballet Russe presentation.

Dante Sonata

Choreography, Frederick Ashton; music, Franz Liszt; scenery and costumes, Sophie Federovitch; based on Dante's Divine Comedy, *as considered by Victor Hugo in his poem "After a Reading of Dante." First produced by the Sadler's Wells Ballet (now the Royal Ballet), London, January 23, 1940. First American performance by the same company, New York, September 23, 1950.*

This is a dramatic ballet, in one act, which combines a free-style (toe slippers are not used) ballet technique with some plastic action. There are two opposing groups, the Children of Light and the Children of Darkness, and the ballet is based upon the conflict between good and evil. The Children of Light, dressed in white, move with serenity, gracefulness, and a flowing, spiritual quality, while their dark-clad opponents writhe, move harshly. In battle evil triumphs; but at the close of the work both leaders are killed by crucifixion.

By American standards Ashton's free dance usages seem elementary, neither as complex nor as physically powerful as those American contemporary ballets which employ modern dance principles, but his mastery of overall design and his effective tableaux have been appreciatively received here.

Margot Fonteyn and Robert Helpmann were the chief figures in the first performance in London, and Fonteyn and Michael Somes were the principals in New York.

Danza a Quattro

Choreography, Michael Uthoff; music, Gaetano Donizetti (La Favorità); costumes, José Coronado. First performed by the

Hartford Ballet, Jacob's Pillow Dance Festival, Lee, Massa-
chusetts, July 10, 1973.

Daphnis and Chloë

Choreography and book, Michel Fokine; music, Maurice Ra-
vel; scenery and costumes, Léon Bakst. First produced by
Diaghilev's Ballets Russes, Paris, June 8, 1912. In 1936 the
Philadelphia Ballet produced Daphnis and Chloë *with new*
choreography by Catherine Littlefield. On April 5, 1951, in
London, the Sadler's Wells Ballet (now the Royal Ballet) pre-
sented Daphnis and Chloë *with wholly new choreography by*
Frederick Ashton and scenery and costumes by John Chax-
ton. The Ashton ballet had its American première by the
same company, New York, September 25, 1953. John Cranko's
version of Daphnis and Chloë, *with costumes by Nicholas*
Georgiadis, was first performed by the Stuttgart Ballet, July
15, 1962.

The Ashton ballet, set to the full Ravel score for chorus and
orchestra and presented in three scenes, is cast in modern, rather
than classical, Greece. The modern approach gives the love story
of Daphnis and Chloë immediacy, but the choreographer has not
neglected the ancient connotations of the tale, for the folk measures he has devised for the villagers seem ageless and the spirit of
the god Pan seems still to exert an influence upon the doings of
men.

As the ballet begins, beautiful and dedicated processionals,
ancient circle dances, and lusty acts of celebration provide an
ecstatic and pertinent setting for the two young lovers. They are a
part of this scene but they are special, for their love is rare, un-
touchable. Not even Dorkon's rough and manly wooing can capture Chloë's interest nor can the hot and alluring actions of Lyka-
nion tempt Daphnis. In their glowing solo moments and in their
radiant passages together, the unswerving course of their love is
clearly etched.

Chloë's abduction by a bandit, a wrenching tragedy to both

Above: Lucile Grahn in *La Sylphide* (1836)

Left: Le Ballet Comique de la Reine (1581)

Below: Lafontaine (left), the first professional ballerina, shown with a partner in Louis XIV bronze figures of the Paris Opera performance of *Le Triomphe de l'amore* (1681)

Right: Michaël Denard with the Paris Opera Ballet nearly 300 years later

Collection of Louis Peres

Above: Pas de Quatre (1845). Carlotta Grisi, Marie Taglioni, Lucile Grahn, Fanny Cerrito

Left: Fanny Elssler (1840)

Galina Ulanova coaches the young Ekaterina Maximova (1960s)

Above: Alexandra Danilova as Odette in The Ballet Russe de Monte Carlo's *Swan Lake*

Above right: American Indian Ballerinas: Moussia Larkin (Shawnee), Marjorie Tallchief (Osage), Rosella Hightower (Choctaw), Yvonne Chouteau (Cherokee)

Above: Mikhail Baryshnikov with American Ballet Theatre in *Le Corsaire*

Left: Anneli Alhanko and Per Arthur Segerström in the Royal Swedish Ballet's *Adam och Eva*

Natalia Makarova and Ivan Nagy in American Ballet Theatre's *Apollo*

Knut Evensen

Above: Rudolf Nureyev with Anne Merele Sundberg, Leonie Leahy, and Inger Johanne Rütter in The Norwegian National Ballet's *Apollo*

Right: Michaël Denard in Amercian Ballet Theatre's *Apollo*

Left: Carmen Mathe and Dermot Burke in The National Ballet's *Bartok Concerto*

Right: Maximiliano Zomosa in City Center Joffrey Ballet's *Astarte*

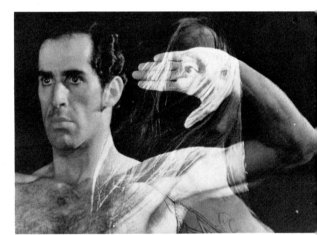

Jack Mitchell

Below: The Leningrad Kirov Ballet's *Bayaderka*

Left: Miriam Golden, Irina Baronova, Margaret Banks, and Anton Dolin in The Ballet Theatre's *Bluebeard. Right:* Tanaquil LeClercq and Jerome Robbins in New York City Ballet's production of George Balanchine's *Bourrée Fantasque*

Left: Alexandra Danilova and Leonide Massine in The Ballet Russe de Monte Carlo's *Capriccio Espagnol. Right:* Erik Bruhn and Kirsten Simone in the Royal Danish Ballet's *Carmen*

MIRA

Above: Fiona Fuerstner in the Pennsylvania Ballet's production of John Butler's *Carmina Burana*

Left: Sir Frederick Ashton in The Royal Ballet's *Cinderella*

Below: The New York City Ballet's production of Jerome Robbins' *The Concert*

Martha Swope

Husband and wife Fokine and Fokina in their own production of *Daphnis and Chloe*

Marian Sarstadt and Gerard Lemaître in the Netherlands Dance Theater's *Le Diable à Quatre*

Anthony Crickway

Left: George Balanchine rehearses New York City Ballet's production of his *Don Quixote. Right:* Ekaterina Maximova and Vladimir Vasiliev in The Bolshoi Ballet's *Don Quixote*

Rudolf Nureyev and Lucette Aldous in the Australian Ballet's production of Nureyev's *Don Quixote*

Left: Antoinette Sibley and Anthony Dowell in The Royal Ballet's *The Dream*

Below: The Royal Swedish Ballet's *Echoing of Trumpets*

Enar Merkel Rydberg

MIRA

Derek Rencher and Svetlana Beriosova in The Royal Ballet's *Enigma Variations*

MIRA

Martha Swope

Left: Marcia Haydée, Egon Madsen, and Susanne Hanke in The Stuttgart Ballet's *Eugene Onegin. Right:* Lucia Chase, Gayle Young, and Sallie Wilson in American Ballet Theatre's *Fall River Legend*

Jerome Robbins, John Kriza, Harold Lang, Janet Reed, and Muriel Bentley in The Ballet Theatre's *Fancy Free*

Walter Terry Collection

Tommy Frishoi and Vivi Flindt in The Royal Danish Ballet's *Far from Denmark*

Right: Engraving by Choffart for P. A. Baudouin's *Une Jeune Fille Querellée par sa Mère*, the inspiration for *La Fille Mal Gardée*

Below: Opening scene of The Royal Ballet's *La Fille Mal Gardée*

Right: Nadia Nerina and David Blair in The Royal Ballet's *La Fille Mal Gardée*

Below and center: Maria Lang and Nils Äke Hägghom in The Royal Swedish Ballet's *Firebird*

Bottom: Annette av Paul and Jens Graff in The Royal Swedish Ballet's *The Fishermen's Dance*

Houston Rogers

Enar Merkel Rydberg

Enar Merkel Rydberg

Above left: Gelsey Kirkland and Helgi Tomasson in New York City Ballet's *Four Bagatelles. Right:* Nana Gollner in the mad scene of The Ballet Theatre's *Giselle*

Left: Natalia Makarova and Ivan Nagy in American Ballet Theatre's *Giselle*

Melissa Hayden in New York City Ballet's *Glinkiana*

Left: Miriam Golden and Eugene Loring in The Ballet Theatre's *The Great American Goof.* *Right:* Maris Liepa in The Bolshoi Ballet's *Hamlet*

Tanaquil LeClercq, Nicholas Magallanes, and Melissa Hayden in New York City Ballet's *Illuminations*

The Ballet Theatre's *Interplay*. Melissa Hayden, John Kriza, *center*

Violette Verdy and Conrad Ludlow in "Emeralds" from New York City Ballet's *Jewels*

Below left: Kerstin Lidström, Jens Graff, and Maria Lang in The Royal Swedish Ballet's *Konservatoriet. Right:* Kirsten Simone and Flemming Flindt in The Royal Danish Ballet's *Le Loup*

the lovers, demands that the almost forgotten powers of Pan be reborn in order that this romance may be preserved. Chloë is rescued and returned to the arms of her lover.

The Ashton ballet, which is different choreographically from the Fokine version and varies slightly from the older version in certain details of the narrative, carries its action into three settings: outside a cave sacred to Pan and his nymphs, the bandits' headquarters, the seashore.

Margot Fonteyn and Michael Somes created the title roles.

In the Fokine production of 1912 Tamara Karsavina and Vaslav Nijinsky were the young lovers; and in a later London presentation, Fokine himself and his wife, Vera Fokina, were the principals.

Dark Elegies

Choreography, Antony Tudor; music, Gustav Mahler (Kindertodtenlieder); scenery and costumes, Nadia Benois. First produced by the Ballet Rambert, London, February 19, 1937, and later presented by the Vic-Wells Ballet. First American production by Ballet Theatre (now the American Ballet Theatre), New York, January 24, 1940, with scenery and costumes by Raymond Sovey based on the Benois originals. Also in the repertory of the National Ballet of Canada, the Royal Swedish Ballet, the Norwegian National Ballet, and Ballet Rambert.

This dance of lamentation, set to the Mahler song cycle, makes little use of the brilliant steps of the traditional ballet. *Pointes* are used but the risings onto them are reflections of emotional states rather than manifestations of technical facility.

The lamentation is mainly communal, a sharing of sorrow, and although separate figures establish their individual feelings of anguish and loss, the presence of the community, the return to it, are continuing patterns. The drab, peasant-like constumes and the frequent use of the old circle form of dance invest *Dark Elegies* with the characteristics of a folk ritual.

It is an unsmiling ballet and its elements of tragedy are ex-pressed entirely through dance action and not by pantomimic means. The movements are tempered by the wide dynamic range of modern dance and the characteristics of the steps, gestures, and body motions are close to those of modern dance although the underlying technique is that of ballet.

These dances of sadness, desperation, resignation, mourning, and quiet hope require highly expert dancers to evoke their intrinsic powers. Nora Kaye and Hugh Laing have been among the most successful interpreters of the leading roles.

Day on Earth

Choreography, Doris Humphrey; music, Aaron Copland (Piano Sonata); costumes, Pauline Lawrence. First danced at the Beaver Country Day School, Brookline, Massachusetts, May 10, 1947. Restaged for the Hartford Ballet Company by Muriel Topaz and Christine Clark, March 3, 1973.

A modern dance work that has become a part of ballet repertory. It is a dance for four figures: man, wife, girl, child. During its course, it suggests the carefree days of childhood, adolescent gaiety and flirtation, young romance, mature love, parental concern, and finally, the continuity of life as the child presides over a new generation.

José Limón, Letitia Ide, Miriam Pandor, and Melisa Nicolaides constituted the first cast.

Death and the Maiden

Choreography, Andrée Howard; music, Franz Schubert; costumes, Andrée Howard. First produced by the Ballet Rambert, London, February 23, 1937. Restaged by Ballet Theatre (now the American Ballet Theatre), New York, January 18, 1940.

Les Demoiselles de la Nuit

(The Ladies of Midnight)

Choreography, Roland Petit; music, Jean Françaix; book, Jean Anouilh; scenery and costumes, Léonor Fini. First produced by Roland Petit's Ballets de Paris, Paris, May 21, 1948. First presented in America by Ballet Theatre (now the American Ballet Theatre), April 13, 1951.

Designs with Strings

Choreography, John Taras; music, Peter Ilyich Tchaikovsky (second movement of Trio in A Minor); costumes (for the American presentation), Irene Sharaff. First produced by the Metropolitan Ballet, Edinburgh, Scotland, February 6, 1948. American première by Ballet Theatre (now the American Ballet Theatre), New York, April 25, 1950.

Two boys and four girls constitute the cast of this ballet of mood. It opens with a silhouette pattern from which the dancers emerge to perform sequences together and in smaller groups, including a *pas de deux*. The atmosphere is romantic throughout, sometimes sadly sentimental, at other times carefree. If there is no plot, there is an indication of incident as the principal boy and girl are pulled apart from each other at the close of the ballet; as two girls, earlier in the work, seem to share a secret together; as a boy and two girls engage in gracious reverie. The ballet culminates with a return to a silhouette pattern.

In the American première Erik Bruhn, Michael Lland (then known as Holland Stoudenmire), Diana Adams, Norma Vance, Lillian Lanese, and Dorothy Scott constituted the cast.

Devil's Holiday

Choreography, Frederick Ashton; book and music, Vincenzo Tommasini; (on themes of Niccolò Paganini); scenery and cos-

tumes, Eugene Berman. First produced by the Ballet Russe de Monte Carlo, New York, October 26, 1939.

This ballet, in a prologue and three scenes, relates the story of the Devil, in disguise, who seeks to amuse himself on a holiday with mortals and their affairs. He aids a poverty-stricken nobleman with his pressing debts and enables a Beggar to win the affection of the nobleman's daughter. Then, through his malevolent presence, he separates the daughter from her fiancé, tempts the adoring Beggar with dreams of a gypsy girl, and generally plays havoc with the lives of men. At the close the Devil is unmasked, and as he disappears the temporarily frightened revelers return to the capers of a Venetian carnival.

Principal roles in this ballet, not for many years an active part of ballet repertory, were danced by Alexandra Danilova (Daughter), Frederic Franklin (Beggar), George Zoritch (Fiancé), and Marc Platoff (Devil). This was the first Ashton ballet to be seen in America.

Diable à Quatre (Pas de deux)

Choreography, Benjamin Harkarvy; music, Adolphe Adam. First performed by the Harkness Ballet, November 7, 1969.

Elisabeth Carroll and Helgi Tomasson were its first dancers.

Dichterliebe

Choreography, Bruce Marks; music, Robert Schumann; libretto, Heinrich Heine; decor, Søren Frandsen; costumes, Yves Harper; lighting, Jørgen Mydtskov. First performed by the Royal Danish Ballet, November 4, 1972.

Dim Lustre

Choreography, Antony Tudor; music, Richard Strauss (Burlesca); scenery and costumes, Motley. First produced by Bal-

let Theatre (now the American Ballet Theatre), New York,
October 20, 1943. The New York City Ballet first performed
the ballet, May 6, 1964.

This is a ballet built upon images evoked from memory. At a
formal party, a man and woman, presumably attracted to each
other, are dancing together but little gestures, incidents, a scented
handkerchief, a necktie recall past experiences. As the boy kisses
the girl on the shoulder, her mind darts back to her first love and
for a moment she recaptures in dance images this episode of innocent romance. A touch on the shoulder causes the man to recall a
summer day spent with three attractive and coquettish girls. The
evocations continue with visions of earlier loves, first young and
pure, and later more passionate and experienced. At the close the
partners separate, somewhat sadly but with resignation, knowing
they cannot escape from the past.

Between the dream episodes, the choreographer, turning to
sophisticated fantasy, brings in doubles of the two leading figures.
The girl dances with her own image; the man with his. In the
mirror of themselves, they find the pathway back to the past.

In the first presentation, Nora Kaye and Hugh Laing were the
partners, with Muriel Bentley and Michael Kidd as their reflections. John Kriza, Rosella Hightower, Janet Reed, Albia Kavan,
Virginia Wilcox, and Tudor danced the images from the past.

A Distant Planet

Choreography, Konstantin Sergeyev; music, B. S. Maizel; li-
bretto, Konstantin Sergeyev and B. S. Maizel; designs, Valery
Dorrer. First presented by the Kirov Ballet, Kirov Theatre,
Leningrad, April 12, 1963.

Divertimento

Choreography, George Balanchine; music, Alexei Haieff; prac-
tice costumes. First produced by the Ballet Society, New York,

January 13, 1947. Later added to the repertory of the New York City Ballet in original and then revised versions.

Mary Ellen Moylan and Francisco Moncion danced the leading roles in the Ballet Society première.

Divertimento No. 15

(formerly called *Caracole*)

Choreography, George Balanchine; music, Wolfgang Amadeus Mozart; costumes, Christian Bérard. First produced by the New York City Ballet under the title Caracole, *New York, February 19, 1952. Using the musical title* Divertimento No. 15, *the ballet, with entirely new choreography by Balanchine, was presented as a new work by the New York City Ballet in New York, December 19, 1956. The reason for the new version had nothing to do with the merits of* Caracole, *which had been a success; while* Caracole *was resting from repertory duty for a few seasons, the choreographer forgot his original choreography (and the dancers did also) and was compelled to create a wholly new ballet to the same music. The production was also new, with costumes by Karinska and a setting, borrowed from* Symphonie Concertante, *by James Stewart Morcom.*

Divertimento No. 15 is an abstract work that takes its form and colors from the musical score, which is in five movements: Allegro, Andante Grazioso, Theme and Variations; Minuet; Andante; Allegro Molto, Andante.

The ballet requires a *corps de ballet,* skilled male soloists, and five female dancers of ballerina stature. It is a classical ballet in which the highly inventive designs, individual movements, bursts of virtuosity, and flowing lyricisms parallel like elements in the score. The peaks of brilliance are reached primarily in the variations for the ballerinas and for one of the male soloists.

For *Caracole,* the cast was headed by Maria Tallchief, Tanaquil LeClercq, Melissa Hayden, Diana Adams, Patricia Wilde, André Eglevsky, Nicholas Magallanes, Jerome Robbins. The first cast for *Divertimento No. 15* included Hayden, Adams, Wilde, Yvonne Mounsey, Barbara Milberg, Magallanes, Roy Tobias, Jonathan Watts.

Donald of the Burthens

Choreography and book, Leonide Massine; music, Ian Whyte; scenery and costumes, Robert Colquhoun and Robert Mac-Bryde. First produced by the Sadler's Wells Ballet (now the Royal Ballet), London, December 12, 1951.

This is a dramatic ballet in two scenes based upon a Scottish story, closely allied to the Faust theme, of a mortal's bargain with Death.

Using Scottish dances as a choreographic base, *Donald of the Burthens* relates how a woodcutter, weary of his heavy labors, makes a pact with Death (the figure of a woman), whereby he promises never to pray, in return for a career as a great doctor. Donald achieves his goal and saves a king from dying by tricking Death, but is ultimately claimed by her when he turns to prayer.

Alexander Grant created the title part and Beryl Grey danced the role of Death.

Donizetti Variations

Choreography, George Balanchine; music, Gaetano Donizetti (from Don Sebastian); costumes, Karinska; lighting, David Hays. First performed by the New York City Ballet, November 16, 1960, at City Center, New York. Melissa Hayden and Jonathan Watts headed the first cast.

One of the most popular of Balanchine's "music visualization" creations. Its overall air is one of lightness and joy, its total impression is of fleetness of foot and its muscle memories for the viewer are of explosive feats of virtuosity. As a dividend, there is one short passage, quite unexpected, of near slapstick humor in which the choreographer seems to be kidding himself while at the same time retaining his celebrated concern for the dictates of music.

Don Juan

Choreography, Michel Fokine; music, Christoph Willibald Gluck; scenery and costumes, Mariano Andreù; based on Gluck's ballet (derived from the Molière play) first presented in Vienna, 1761, with choreography by Angiolini. The Fokine ballet was given by the Ballet Russe de Monte Carlo, London, June 25, 1936, and in New York, October 22, 1938. Another version, with choreography by John Neumeier, additional music by Tomás Luis de Victoria (Requiem), and decor by Filippo Sanjust, was first performed in Frankfurt, Germany, November 25, 1972. This version was later staged for the National Ballet of Canada, featuring Rudolf Nureyev in the title role, and had its first American performance, New York, April 26, 1974.

This is the familiar story of Don Juan, his courtship of Donna Elvira, his slaying of Elvira's father in a duel, the return of the father's ghost as Don Juan entertains his mistresses, the anguish of the forsaken Elvira, and the death of Don Juan, victim of the father's mobilized statue and ghoulish attacks by his dead mistresses.

Anatole Vilzak created the title role in London, and Michael Panaieff in New York. Jeannette Lauret was the Donna Elvira in both presentations.

Frederick Ashton's *Don Juan*, first produced by the Sadler's Wells Ballet (the Royal Ballet), London, November 25, 1948, and presented in New York, September 24, 1953, to the music of Richard Strauss, with scenery and costumes by Edward Burra, is more of a "choreographic impression" of the theme than a dramatic telling of the story. The ballet opens in silence, lovely women making a dance frame around the Don, and continues its series of love-search images to the accompaniment of the Strauss tone-poem.

Robert Helpmann created the title role in the Ashton ballet.

The Neumeier version is a lavish production with a vast set which permits for a play within a play. At a party, the Don's servant arranges for players to enact scenes from his master's amorous life and the playlets indicate that all of the Don's loves are trivial and that he is not the lover that legend would have it. The servant plays the Don but Neumeier, mingling reality with fantasy and exact times with dreamed time, occasionally makes the two interchangeable so that the real Don actually participates in the drama of his staged biography. A woman in white who moves mysteriously in and out of the proceedings is the only woman who attracts the Don deeply. At the close of the ballet, we learn that the lady in white is Death.

Don Quixote

(or *Don Quichotte*)

Choreography, Marius Petipa; music, Leon Minkus; libretto by Petipa based on the novel by Miguel de Cervantes. First produced by the Russian Imperial Ballet, December 14, 1869, in four acts and eight scenes. A later staging of the Petipa ballet in five acts and eleven scenes was presented in St. Petersburg, November 9 (Julian or Russian calendar) or November 21 (Gregorian or Western calendar), 1871, and a revised version by Gorsky was given in Moscow, January 20 (Julian) or February 2 (Gregorian), 1902. Don Quixote remains in the repertories of the Soviet State Ballet. Don Quichotte Chez la Duchesse, a three-act comic ballet, was produced in Paris, February 12, 1743. A version of the Petipa-Minkus ballet staged by Laurent Novikoff in a prologue and two acts was in the repertory of Anna Pavlova's company. A contemporary Don Quixote, with choreography by Ninette de Valois, music by Robert Gerhard, and scenery and costumes by Edward Burra, was produced by the Sadler's Wells Ballet (now the Royal Ballet), London, February 20, 1950, and September 29, 1950, in New York. Other historical productions of Don Quixote include one by Jean Georges No-

verre in the mid-eighteenth century and one by Paul Taglioni in the 1830s. A totally new version with choreography by George Balanchine, music by Nicholas Nabokov, décor, costumes, and lighting by Esteban Frances, was first performed by the New York City Ballet, New York, May 28, 1965.

In this telling of the famous Cervantes tale, the figures of the would-be knight, Don Quixote, and his faithful Sancho Panza are almost, but not quite, incidental in a story centered upon the lusty and high-spirited love of Kitri, an innkeeper's daughter, and Basil, a barber. The funny and poignant quests of Don Quixote are interwoven with the adventures of the young lovers in a ballet noted for its drama, its roaring comedy, its colorful folk sequences, and the virtuoso passages for its principals. The Balanchine production omits Kitri and Basil, focusing upon the Don and his fantasies, symbolized by Dulcinea.

It has been danced by Sobeshamskaya (the first Kitri), Pavlova, Karsavina, and, with the Bolshoi Ballet, Plisestskaya, Maximova, and others. A full-length movie featuring the Australian Ballet—with Sir Robert Helpman in the title role, Rudolf Nureyev as Basil, and Lucette Aldous as Kitri—was produced in a version conceived by Nureyev.

Balanchine's production, in three acts, is one of the New York City Ballet's most spectacular productions, including live animals, prop dragons and giants, enormous magical books, windmills of course, and rich costumes. The choreographer danced the title role at the première and Suzanne Farrell was the recurring figure of Servitude, Fidelity, Romance, and Youth.

Double Exposure

Choreography, Joe Layton; music, Alexander Scriabin (piano pieces) and Henri Pousseur (electronic music). First produced by the City Center Joffrey Ballet, Chicago, February 4, 1972, and in New York, March 3, 1972. A ballet treatment of Oscar Wilde's The Picture of Dorian Gray.

The Dream

Choreography, Frederick Ashton; music, Felix Mendelssohn; scenery and costumes, Henry Bardon. First performed by the Royal Ballet, April 2, 1964. First performed in America by the same company, April 30, 1965. First performed by the City Center Joffrey Ballet, October 10, 1973. The Dream is also in the repertory of the Australian Ballet.

The Dream is a one-act ballet treatment of Shakespeare's *A Mid-Summer Night's Dream.* It omits the characters of Hippolyta and Theseus and minimizes the subplot of Bottom and his fellow rustics, but it encompasses the two main threads of the story: the argument between Titania and Oberon over which is to have the Changeling Indian Boy, and the mixed-up loves of Helena, Hermia, Demetrius, and Lysander. Sir Frederic treats the whole in romantic ballet style, incorporating the acting with the dancing and avoiding traditional mime completely. The complicated story is presented with succinctness and clarity, and the choreography is highlighted by light and airy dances for the ensemble of fairies, a lyrical *pas de deux* for Titania and Oberon, comedy chases and clashes involving the four confused lovers, a character dance *sur les pointes* for Bottom with his ass's head, and fast, high-flying, virtuosic antics for Puck.

Antoinette Sibley, Anthony Dowell, and Alexander Grant headed the first cast.

Dream Pictures

Choreography, Emilie Walbom; music, Hans Christian Lumbye; scenery and costumes reproduce Copenhagen's Tivoli Gardens in the Biedermeier period. First produced by the Royal Danish Ballet, Copenhagen, April 15, 1915. First full-scale American presentation by the same company, New York, September 19, 1956. In the summer of 1955, an abridged version was given at the Jacob's Pillow Dance Festival at Lee, Massachusets, and at New York's Lewisohn Stadium.

The Duel

(also *Le Combat* and *The Combat*)

Choreography, William Dollar; music, Rafaello de Banfield. First presented in America as Le Combat *by Roland Petit's Ballets de Paris, New York, October 6, 1949. First presented in a revised and enlarged version as* The Duel *by the New York City Ballet, New York, February 24, 1950. As* The Combat, *with scenery and costumes by Georges Wakhevitch, it was added to the repertory of Ballet Theatre (now the American Ballet Theatre), London, July 23, 1953. The Petit production, which had its world première in London, February 24, 1949, was an elaborate pas de deux. The New York City Ballet production, with costumes by Robert Stevenson, was rechoreographed to include three supporting male dancers in addition to the two principals. The ballet was first danced by the National Ballet of Washington at Lisner Auditorium, Washington, D.C., February 26, 1966. It is also in the repertory of the Boston Ballet.*

This is the story of Tancred, the Christian warrior, and Clorinda, a pagan girl, who meet during the era of the Crusades, fall in love and, as unwitting opponents, battle to the death. The incident was derived from Tasso's *Jerusalem Delivered.*

Colette Marchand and Milorad Miskovitch danced the lovers in the Roland Petit production. Melissa Hayden and Dollar created the principal roles in the New York City Ballet version, with Francisco Moncion replacing Dollar in later presentations. At the London première of the Ballet Theatre staging, Hayden and John Kriza were the stars. In the National Ballet of Washington production Roni Mahler danced Clorinda and Ivan Nagy was Tancred in the first performance.

Dumbarton Oaks

Choreography, Jerome Robbins; music, Igor Stravinsky; costumes, Patricia Zipprodt. First performed by the New York City Ballet, New York, Stravinsky Festival, June 23, 1972.

A joyous, jazzy ballet that includes high kicks as well as high jinx and a tennis game that ends in a "love" score. It is of the genre of Vaslav Nijinsky's *Jeux* and Bronislava Nijinska's *Les Biches* without in any way being imitative.

Anthony Blum and Allegra Kent headed the first cast.

Duo Concertant

Choreography, George Balanchine; music, Igor Stravinsky; lighting, Ronald Bates. First performed by the New York City Ballet, Stravinsky Festival, June 22, 1972.

An extended *pas de deux* in which the dancers respond to the music in movement, or at times simply listen to it with quiet intensity and alertness. This duet, conceived in what might be called modern classical terms, is both active and contemplative in its musical mingling.

At the première, the dancers were Kay Mazzo and Peter Martins.

Dybbuk

Choreography, Jerome Robbins; music, Leonard Bernstein; scenery, Rouben Ter-Arutunian; costumes, Patricia Zipprodt; lighting, Jennifer Tipton. First produced by the New York City Ballet, New York, May 16, 1974 (following a gala benefit preview, May 15).

The Robbins ballet is not a literal translation into ballet terms of the Ansky story, but, rather, a series of variations on the theme. Indeed, the work itself is not balletic in the classical sense. It uses freely invented dance movement, much of it, especially in the group passages, evocative of primitive forces like those Robbins used in his version of *Les Noces*. It is Jewish in inspiration but universal in mold, just as *Noces* was Russian-rooted but treated as a ritual common to humankind. Choreographic highlights of *Dybbuk* include the opening dance for men, a virile ceremonial-flavored section that suggests the strength of warriors, and the gentle but passionate duet for the boy and girl in the core of possession.

The first cast was headed by Patricia McBride and Helgi Tomasson. The composer conducted at the gala preview and the official première.

The Dying Swan

(or *Le Cygne*)

Choreography, Michel Fokine; music, Camille Saint-Saëns. First produced in 1905 in St. Petersburg at a concert and danced by Anna Pavlova.

This is a solo, quiet and delicate, which seeks to capture the fluttering movements, the grace of a swan as it moves to a trembling death.

The Dying Swan was always associated with Pavlova and came almost to be her trademark. She danced it continuously throughout her long career, for it was an enduring favorite with her worldwide audiences. Many others have danced *The Dying Swan*—most of them in memory of or in tribute to Pavlova—among them, Alicia Markova, Tamara Toumanova, Galina Ulanova, Nathalie Krassovska, Maya Plisetskaya, Natalia Makarova. Many lesser figures and even students have attempted it but it remains forever identified with the now legendary magic of Pavlova.

Early Songs

Choreography, Eliot Feld; music, Richard Strauss; costumes, Stanley Simmons. First performed by the American Ballet Company, Brooklyn Academy of Music, New York, April 3, 1970.

A ballet of solo, duo, and ensemble dances in which the choreographer attempts not to interpret the songs but, rather, to respond to their moods and cadences. Thus, the dances have their own distinct identities, an existence that is in harmony with the *Lieder*. A musical lilt may fall upon the ear harmoniously with the sight of a gentle ballet lift, or a musical flutter may be kinetically echoed in lightly executed leg beats. In other sequences there are no music-dance counterparts but simply concord of mood and style.

Eaters of Darkness

Choreography, Walter Gore; music, Benjamin Britten. Presented by the Norwegian National Ballet, 1968. The National Ballet of Washington first presented the ballet in Washington, D.C., November 30, 1973. (An earlier staging, January 29, 1958, was mounted by the Frankfurt State Opera Ballet.)

A young, normal wife is wrongfully placed in an insane asylum. Succumbing to the pressure of her surroundings, she actually goes insane.

Paula Hinton was the Bride in the Frankfurt production.

Ebony Concerto

Choreography, John Taras; music, Igor Stravinsky; décor, David Hays. First performed by the New York City Ballet, New York, December 7, 1960. Another version, with choreography by John Cranko and costumes by Silvia Strahammer, was premièred in Stuttgart, Germany, by the Stuttgart Ballet, December 29, 1970. The first American performance of the Cranko version was April 30, 1971, at the Metropolitan Opera, New York.

The Stuttgart treatment is built upon three clowns who are as lovable as they are funny.

Echoing of Trumpets

Choreography, Antony Tudor; music, Bohuslav Martinu; decor, Birgen Bergling. First performed by the Royal Swedish Ballet, Stockholm, September 28, 1963. First performed by the American Ballet Theatre, New York, November 11, 1967.

Echoing of Trumpets is an antiwar ballet in which hate, barbarism, and death of the soldiers on the battlefields spill over into the life of a village and its villagers.

The Ecstasy of Rita Joe

Choreography, Norbert Vesak; music, Ann Mortifée; costumes and lighting, Vesak; orchestration, Carlos Rausch; film direction, S. Williams; lyrics and dialogue, George Ryga. Commissioned by the Manitoba Indian Brotherhood to mark the centenary of the signing in Manitoba of Indian Treaties Numbers 1 and 2, and first presented by the Royal Winnipeg Ballet, July 27, 1971, in Ottawa.

This one-act multimedia Canadian ballet, based on the play by George Ryga, has a Canadian theme that tells the tragedy of the Indian girl, Rita Joe, who leaves the reservation for life in the city. The ballet follows her downward path in the city to prostitution and death as it symbolizes the profound problems the Indian faces when leaving the ways of his people for the environment of a white society.

Ana Maria Gorriz created the title role, Jaimie Paul was played by Salvatore Aiello. The singer was Ann Mortifée; the Voice of the Magistrate, Peter Howarth; and the Voice of the Father, Chief Dan George.

Eden—Pas de Deux

See *Adam och Eva*

Les Elfes

(The Elves)

Choreography, Michel Fokine; music, Felix Mendelssohn (Overture to A Midsummer Night's Dream, Andante and Allegro from Concerto in E Minor for Violin). First produced by the Fokine Ballet, New York, February 26, 1924. Restaged, with costumes by Christian Bérard, by the Ballet Russe de Monte Carlo at Monte Carlo, April 24, 1937. Revived by the same company in America, March 22, 1939. Later revived by the same company, New York, April 20, 1950.

Embrace Tiger

Choreography, Glen Tetley; music, Morton Subotnick (Silver Apples of the Moon); décor, Nadine Baylis. First performed by Ballet Rambert, London, November 21, 1968. Glen Tetley and Company first presented the ballet, New York, May 13, 1969.

Enigma Variations

Choreography, Frederick Ashton; music, Edward Elgar; décor and costumes, Julia Trevelyan Oman. First performed by the Royal Ballet, October 25, 1968.

A major creation by Ashton and a major production by the Royal Ballet of a biography in dance with the composer, Sir Edward Elgar, as the subject. Scenes and episodes, projected through mime and dance action, recreate not only a life's characters and events, some sad and others gay, but also the Edwardian Age. Derek Rencher created the role of Elgar.

Episodes

*Choreography, Martha Graham and George Balanchine;
music, Anton Webern* (Passacaglia, Op. 1; Six Pieces, Op. 6;
Symphony, Op. 21; Five Pieces, Op. 10; Concerto, Op. 24;
Variations, Op. 30; Ricercata in Six Voices from Bach's "Musical Offering"); *costumes, Karinska; scenery, David Hays. First
produced by the New York City Ballet, New York, May 14,
1959.*

Episodes, set to the orchestral works of the avant-garde twentieth-
century composer Anton Webern, was not only the first collaboration between George Balanchine, artistic director and chief choreographer of the New York City Ballet, and Martha Graham,
America's most famous modern dancer, but also the first work
Graham choreographed for a company other than her own. The
Graham section was choreographed in her own modern dance
style.

The dance itself portrays the terror that the doomed Mary,
Queen of Scots, experienced as she approached death; her restored
poise as she looked at the discarded robe of royalty, which she
must honor with courage; her memories of Bothwell, who loved
her but wanted her crown; a fantastic long-distance tennis game
between herself and Queen Elizabeth, whom she never met but
who ordered her death; her visions of other men in her life; the
placing of her head on the block.

The Balanchine section, which soon constituted the total ballet (the Graham episode was soon dropped), is without narrative.
Incident is suggested, but the work is cast in abstract terms in
which movement and movement designs are all important. Except
for the closing episode (*Ricercata*), couched in classical, noble
style, the Balanchine choreography introduces lifts (a girl is held
upside down with legs extended), gestures, and movements (such
as leg extensions with foot flexed instead of pointed) never, or
rarely, used in classical ballet.

In the *pas de deux* (*Five Pieces, Opus 10*) there is an indication of incident as the girl and boy seem to reach for each other,
perhaps romantically, in movements that miss connections. Be-

tween movements, in the silences in the music (and Webern uses silence as well as sound in his scores), the dancers stand still as if considering more successful strategic approaches to each other. Another section, a solo, in pure modern dance form and performed by a modern dancer, was later eliminated.

At the first performance, Graham danced Mary; Bertram Ross (of the Graham company), Bothwell; Sallie Wilson (of the New York City Ballet), Queen Elizabeth; and members of both companies danced the remaining roles. Principals in the Balanchine episodes were Violette Verdy, Jonathan Watts, Diana Adams, Jacques d'Amboise, Allegra Kent, Nicholas Magallanes, Melissa Hayden, Francisco Moncion (all of the New York City Ballet), and Paul Taylor, modern dancer (guest artist).

Errante

(The Wanderer)

> *Choreography, George Balanchine; music, Franz Schubert; scenery and costumes, Paul Tchelitcheff. First produced by Balanchine's Les Ballets 1933, Paris, 1933. First American performance by the American Ballet, New York, March 1, 1935. Staged by Ballet Theatre (now the American Ballet Theatre), May 21, 1943.*

The theme and the mood of this ballet are indicated by the title. Tilly Losch was the first to dance the leading role. Tamara Geva headed the cast at the American première and Vera Zorina danced it with Ballet Theatre.

La Esmeralda

> *Choreography and book, Jules Perrot; music, Cesare Pugni; scenery, William Grieve; costumes, Mme. Copère. First produced in London, March 9, 1844. First presented in America by the Monplaisir Ballet Company, New York, September 18, 1848. Russian première, St. Petersburg, December 21 (Julian*

or Russian calendar), 1848, or January 2 (Gregorian or West-ern calendar), 1849. Restaged in 1954 by the London Festival Ballet, London, with choreography by Nicholas Beriosoff and presented in America as a divertissement (Act II) on a tour, with the New York première taking place in Brooklyn, Febru-ary 18, 1955. Esmeralda remains in the repertory of the Soviet State Ballet.

A three-act ballet based upon Victor Hugo's *Notre-Dame de Paris*. The story of the Hunchback's love is too well known to need re-telling here.

At the première the title role was played by Carlotta Grisi, with Perrot as the poet whose life she saves and whom she mar-ries. The complete ballet remains in repertory in the Soviet Union. An excerpted *pas de deux* is popular in *divertissement* programs in Western Europe and America.

L'Estro Armonico

Choreography, John Cranko; music, Antonio Vivaldi. First performed by the Stuttgart Ballet, April 27, 1963.

Et Cetera

Choreography, Louis Johnson; electronic music, Paul Mar-tin Palombo; scenic and lighting design, Jay Depenbrock; with projections of crystal photomicrographs (chemical crystals photographed through a microscope and enlarged for stage by fourteen projectors), Alice Weston, artist, and R. Marshall Wilson, chemist. First performed by the Cincin-nati Ballet Company, Cincinnati, November 28, 1973.

A multimedia jazz ballet in which fantasy seems more real than reality. Figures in white tights move in heavenly spheres and are juxtaposed with earthly creatures. Hardhat laborers, so captured by the machine that is television, refuse to notice a live girl, and in order to get their attention, she moves behind a TV screen and only then, as a two-dimensional image, is she able to attract their notice.

The Eternal Idol

Choreography, Michael Smuin; music, Frédéric Chopin; costumes, Marcos Paredes. First performed by the American Ballet Theatre, New York, December 4, 1969.

The Eternal Idol is a duet inspired by the art of the sculptor Auguste Rodin. It is not a ballet of "living statues," although Rodin's Eternal Idol pose introduces the work; rather, it is an essay in concepts of form, from mass to shape to movement to flight. It is a frank presentation of the most beautiful human bodies in which Rodin himself found "unknown depths and the very substance of life."

Cynthia Gregory and Ivan Nagy were the dancers on which Smuin built his ballet.

The Eternal Struggle

Choreography, Igor Schwezoff; music, Robert Schumann (Symphonic Études); scenery and costumes, Kathleen and Florence Martin, New York showing by the Original Ballet Russe, New York, November 25, 1940.

This work, representing one of the comparatively early attempts to fuse ballet with free-style movements related to modern dance, deals with the struggle of an idealist to free himself from "the wretchedness and helplessness of mankind."

The protagonist was danced by George Skibine, and others featured at the New York première were Tamara Toumanova (as Illusion), Sono Osato (Beauty), and Marina Svetlova (Truth).

The Eternal Struggle was first staged for the Original Ballet Russe by Schwezoff during a tour of Australia and was first performed in Sydney, July 29, 1940.

Études

Choreography, Harald Lander; music, Knudage Riisager. The first performance was by the Royal Danish Ballet, Copenhagen, January 15, 1948. A new version, with décor by Erik Nordgreen and costumes by Bernard Daydé, was first performed, March 4, 1962. First performed by American Ballet Theatre, October 5, 1961, with costumes by Rolf Gerard. The Paris Opera first presented the ballet, Paris, November 19, 1952. The London Festival Ballet first performed it August 8, 1965.

A staged ballet class, beginning with a single figure demonstrating the basic ballet positions and ranging from there through exercises at the ballet *barre*, through precise *adagio* in "center" floor work without *barre* support, to dazzling displays of turns, leaps, beats, and combinations. Included is a scene evocative of the Romantic Age of Ballet in the style of the nineteenth-century Danish choreographer, August Bournonville. The ballet is for a large company with every member a virtuoso performer and the three principals—two *danseurs* and the ballerina—supervirtuosi. *Études* can be viewed as a twentieth-century extension of Bournonville's *Konservatoriet* (1849), indicating the solid foundations and increasing technical skills of classical ballet over a century. (The Bolshoi Ballet's *Ballet School* is a work of this genre. There are others, some in the folk-dance field—Moiseyev, for one.)

Margot Lander, Hans Brenaa, and Svend Erik Jensen starred at the Danish première.

Toni Lander, Royes Fernandez, and Bruce Marks headed the American Ballet Theatre cast.

Eugene Onegin

Choreography, John Cranko; music, Peter Ilyich Tchaikovsky (arranged and orchestrated by Kurt-Heinz Stolze); scenery and costumes, Jürgen Rose. First performance by the Stuttgart

Ballet, April 13, 1965. A new production of the ballet was presented by the Stuttgart Ballet, October 27, 1967.

A major full-length ballet-drama based upon Alexander Pushkin's story, but with a musical score composed not of themes from the opera but from other Tchaikovsky material. Cranko, famed for his command of dramatic ballet, includes among his scenes striking ensemble dances for breezy out-of-doors celebrations and glittering ballroom events to the spareness of a duel scene and the ultimate loneliness of the heroine standing alone in helpless anguish on a great stage. The characterizations for Tatiana, the heroine, the two men in her life, her family, and her friends are skillfully defined in full-scale dance and in incidental gesture. A highlight of the ballet is the letter scene, which for ballet becomes a vision scene, in which Tatiana dreams that her lover comes to her in her room and that they celebrate their enduring love.

Marcia Haydée created the role of Tatiana.

Evening Dialogues

Choreography, Jonathan Watts; music, Robert Schuman; costumes, Joe Eula. First performed by the City Center Joffrey Ballet, Chicago, Illinois, August 22, 1974.

A light, abstract ballet belonging in that genre which is epitomized by Robbins' "Dances at a Gathering."

Heading the cast were Burton Taylor and Denise Jackson, Gregory Huffman and Francesca Corkle, and James Dunne and Beatrice Roderigues.

The Exiles

Choreography, José Limón; music, Arnold Schönberg (Chamber Symphony No. 2, op. 38); décor, Anita Weschler; costumes, Pauline Lawrence. First performed by José Limón and

Company, Connecticut College American Dance Festival, August 11, 1950. Also presented by the Royal Swedish Ballet.

This modern dance work, which has moved into ballet repertory, depicts Adam and Eve after the expulsion from Eden. The two-character dance was first performed by the choreographer and Letitia Ide.

Façade

Choreography, Frederick Ashton; music, William Walton; scenery and costumes, John Armstrong; based upon poems by Edith Sitwell. First performed by the Camargo Society, London, April 26, 1931. Presented by the Ballet Rambert, London, May 4, 1931. Added to the repertory of the Sadler's Wells Ballet (now the Royal Ballet), London, October 8, 1935. First presented by the Sadler's Wells Ballet in America, New York, October 12, 1949. The City Center Joffrey Ballet added Façade to its repertory, New York, February 17, 1969. The work is also in the repertory of Ballet Rambert.

Façade, a series of short dances, takes place in front of a Victorian house. All of the numbers (there are nine) are either light or comic. Among them are a "Scottish Rhapsody"; a "Yodeling" bit for a milkmaid and three mountain lads; a solo "Polka"; a "Popular Song" done in the vaudeville hoofing manner by two young men; and a hilarious "Tango"—with many elaborate backbends, swoops, stalkings, and amorous gestures—performed by a gigolo and a debutante.

Lydia Lopokhova, Ashton, and Alicia Markova were starred in the Camargo Society production. At the New York première Moira Shearer and Ashton danced the "Tango."

Facsimile

Choreography, Jerome Robbins; music, Leonard Bernstein; scenery, Oliver Smith; costumes, Irene Sharaff. First pro-

duced by *Ballet Theatre (now the American Ballet Theatre),
New York, October 24, 1946.*

Fadetta

*Choreography, Leonid Lavrovsky; music, Léo Delibes (Syl-
via), Jules Massenet, François Auber, and Riccardo Drigo,
arranged by Yevgeny Dubovsky; book, Leonid Lavrovsky and
V. Soloviov, based on George Sand's* Little Fadette; *designs,
N. Nikiforov. First presented by the graduating class of the
Leningrad Choreographic School on the stage of the Leningrad State Academic Theater of Opera and Ballet (Kirov),
March 21, 1934. Another version, with choreography by Lavrovsky, was performed at the Maly Theater, Leningrad, June
9, 1936, with designs by B. Erbshtein. A Bolshoi production,
with choreography by Lavrovsky and designs by T. Starzhenetskaya, was performed June 20, 1952.*

The Fairy's Kiss

See *Le Baiser de la Fée*

Fall River Legend

*Choreography, Agnes de Mille; music, Morton Gould; scen-
ery, Oliver Smith; costumes, Miles White. First produced by
Ballet Theatre (now the American Ballet Theatre), New York,
April 22, 1948. The ballet was added to the repertory of the
Boston Ballet, April 4, 1974.*

The ballet is based upon the true story of Lizzie Borden, an unmarried woman of Fall River, Massachusetts, who was accused of
killing her father and stepmother with an ax in the year 1892. She
was acquitted of the crime and lived out her life in her home
town, but in the ballet the figure of the Accused is condemned to

death on the gallows. There are a Prologue and eight scenes to
the ballet.

In the Prologue the Accused is seen standing with her Pastor
near the gallows as the foreman of the jury states the findings. As
he refers to the Accused's past the scene changes, the gallows is
swung back to form part of a Victorian home. It is a frame with
a door and we can see inside. Nearby stands a block for chopping
wood.

Scene One. The Accused stands, looking back over her life.
She sees a child (herself) dancing happily with her father and her
own mother, both beloved. There are passers-by and among them
a severe woman dressed in black, whom the child obviously dis-
likes, but she seems to be a close friend of the family. The mother
has an attack, a fainting spell, and the child is frightened, but she
recovers temporarily and there are again moments of joy. But
death finally comes and the mourning husband turns to the domi-
neering woman in black for assistance and consolation. Soon she
is to become the stepmother. Watching this scene is the adult
Accused, torturing herself in restrospective vision, for she knows
what is to become of the child, of the household itself.

Scene Two. The child has grown now to spinsterhood and
sits with her father and stepmother in their sitting room. They
rock in their chairs, but while the parents read, the girl nervously
snaps her fingers and finally runs upstairs. The stepmother whispers to her husband and we may be sure she is suggesting that the
girl is not quite all there. The heroine returns again to rocking but
the empty, loveless atmosphere of the house, the cruel attitude of
her stepmother, and now the seeming coldness of her father drive
her outside. Here she meets the young Pastor and finds with him
friendship, warmth, understanding, and perhaps the beginning of
romance. They dance joyfully together but the girl is recalled to
the house by her disapproving parents. She sits as long as she can
and then goes for an ax. The stepmother cringes in terror but the
girl merely goes out the door and chops some wood. When she
returns with the wood, she suddenly realizes the cause for her
stepmother's fear and shakes with near-hysterical laughter. An
idea, not fully shaped, has been born.

Scene Three. The girl, sitting on her doorstep, muses on the happiness of normal young folk. She sees friends and lovers dancing and trysting and envies them their joys. In defiance of her lot, she heads toward the chopping block and reaches for the ax, but the savagery of her thoughts frightens her and she pulls her hand away. The Pastor enters with flowers for her and an invitation to attend a picnic at the church. They dance together but are interrupted by the parents, who disapprove of this new friendship. Near the breaking point, the girl throws herself on the ground in a fit of rage, claws at her stepmother, who has whispered to the Pastor that the girl is out of her mind. The parents beckon her to come with them, she looks at them for a moment, and then calmly ignores their orders and leaves with the Pastor.

Scene Four. At a prayer meeting the girl, soon to be the Accused, is accepted into the hearts of the members of the congregation. Full of gratitude for the unaccustomed kindnesses, her hopes rise and, as the congregation departs, she joins the Pastor, and in appealing, childlike gestures indicates her need for him. He returns her affections and, with the return of the congregation, she takes part as a free spirit in a dance of gladness. The stepmother's arrival not only destroys her happiness but also her mind, for as the evil woman whispers to the Pastor, the girl seems to take leave of her senses. At the close of the scene, she leaves with her stepmother.

Scene Five. The Accused is sitting on the steps of her home, her parents inside. In a moment, she makes up her mind, walks over to the block, withdraws the ax, and enters the house, driven to the act of murder by desperation. The two sitting there jump up in fright but the Accused merely looks at them and there is a blackout.

Scene Six. This is a dream. The house has disappeared and a backdrop showing a bloodied room has been lowered. The Accused finds the image of her own mother to seek consolation and approval for her deed. Her dress has been removed and her underdress is splotched with blood. The mother-figure embraces the Accused, dances with her, and then, seeing the smears of blood, slaps her as she might a mischievous child. The Accused, crushed by this reprimand, comes close and the mother rocks her gently, then leaves.

Scene Seven. Townspeople mill about outside the house, knowing that something dreadful has occurred. The Accused appears from another room, makes a futile attempt to straighten the scene of the crime and then, miming a wild cry, rushes out the door. Two men enter the house and reemerge shortly carrying the ax and the white shawl which had belonged to the girl's mother and had been worn later (and this was an act of desecration in the eyes of the girl) by the stepmother. She kisses the shawl tenderly and, with the arrival of the Pastor, throws herself into his protective arms.

Scene Eight. This is a return to the Prologue. The Accused has heard the verdict and is calm as memories pass swiftly before her. The Pastor gives her his final comfort and she turns to the gallows. As the ballet ends she moves in a shudder and her head falls limply in death.

At the first performance Alicia Alonso danced the role of the Accused; John Kriza, the Pastor; Muriel Bentley, the Stepmother; Peter Gladke, the Father; Diana Adams, the Mother. The leading part had been created especially for Nora Kaye; but illness kept the ballerina from dancing the première. Dania Krupska as well as Alonso danced the Accused, but when Miss Kaye assumed the stellar role, it was considered to be another splendid addition to her gallery of dramatic dance characterizations. At a later date Lucia Chase replaced Bentley as the Stepmother. Sallie Wilson has also danced Lizzie.

Fancy Free

Choreography, Jerome Robbins; music, Leonard Bernstein; scenery and costumes, Oliver Smith. First produced by Ballet Theatre (now the American Ballet Theatre), New York, April 18, 1944.

The ballet takes place on a minor street in New York and in a small neighborhood bar. Three sailors, dressed in their whites, are on shore leave and looking for a good time. As they enter, they case the scene, straightening their hats and uniforms and horse about among themselves, performing antics which show their high spirits and comradeship. They are in search of fun but not quite sure where to find it. One of them notices the bar and walks in, quickly followed by his two chums. They swagger up to the bar in a jaunty sailor gait, down their drinks, and two of them trick the third into paying for all.

Outside again, they settle into restless boredom until suddenly a flashy girl with a bright-red handbag swishes by. The boys are galvanized to action. Each tries to attract her attention and her seeming aloofness only spurs them on. They grab her handbag, play catch with it, imitate her walk, and tease her, but when she shows signs of friendliness, they start to scrap among themselves to see which one is to have her for a date. One of the sailors is kocked down and the other two chase off after the girl.

The lone sailor starts back for the bar when he meets a young and beautiful girl. He invites her for a drink and she accepts. Once in the bar, he feels his way cautiously. Rather than launch into amorous action (and we can see he is tempted), he tells her about his war experiences. He indicates that single-handed he shot down scores of enemy planes, but with a concluding shrug, suggests that it really wasn't much. As the two are drawn closely to each other, they commence to dance a lovely, romantic, and gentle *pas de deux* to blues music. At its close he kisses her gently and she shyly wipes the lipstick from his face.

A roar and a clatter announce the arrival of the other two sailors and their girl. There is no escape now for the two new lovers and the rivalry intensifies as some decision must be made about the distribution of two girls among three boys. The girls, apparently old friends, gab happily together. The boys lead them to a table and a riot nearly breaks out over the seating arrangements. They try dancing but the cutting-in gets things hopelessly snarled and it is finally decided that a dance contest involving the three sailors is the only way to reach a decision. The girls are to be the judges.

The first solo is a showoff affair using almost every trick in the dance book. It starts with a double air turn, landing in a split, and goes on from there into all manner of virtuosic actions, including high leaps, a cancan leg extension with the dancer holding onto his foot as he stretches the leg ear-high, and a vaulting jump to the top of the bar.

The second solo (usually danced by the sailor who has performed the earlier blues duet) is quite different. It is both sinuous and insinuating. The turns are slow and sustained rather than fast, and there is a gentle provocativeness about most of the movements, although there is a brief razzle-dazzle hoofing sequence by way of contrast. The dance ends as the sailor does a turn and winds up gracefully on the floor with his legs in the air, his back arched, and an expression on his face which pleads mutely for acceptance by the girl of his choice.

The third and final solo in the contest (originally danced by the boy of the blues duet) is a Latin American affair with complicated rhythms, loose hips, and an aura of pleasantly satiric sophistication about it.

The girls can't decide, the boys know that one of them has to be eliminated if the evening is to be any fun at all, so they engage in a wild fight. Bodies hurl about, fists fly, and when the battle subsides, they discover they have all lost. The girls have left. The boys nurse their wounds, and after a restorative drink stroll outside again. They repeat the leitmotif movement which had introduced them, divide a stick of gum as they have done earlier, and settle back to wait. A beautiful girl walks by. They lean forward but they are not going to get into trouble again; yet each is wary of the others. Suddenly, one of the boys bolts after the girl, the others race after him, and the whole process starts again as the curtain falls.

This was Jerome Robbins' first ballet and it was an instant hit. Wartime audiences loved the American sailors and their antics; but the ballet has remained popular because the theme was projected in movement terms which were fresh, witty, and energetically American, a perfect fusion of classical ballet with popular dance idioms, comic gesture, and dramatic incident. (From *Fancy Free* evolved a hit musical, *On the Town,* which continued the successful collaboration of Robbins, Bernstein, and Smith.)

The first cast, which has been reunited on several occasions since the première, included Robbins, Harold Lang, and John Kriza as the Three Sailors, Muriel Bentley as the Girl with the Handbag, Janet Reed as the Second Girl, and Shirley Eckl as the last Temptress. Rex Cooper was the Bartender.

Fanfare

Choreography, Jerome Robbins; music, Benjamin Britten (The Young Person's Guide to the Orchestra); scenery and costumes, Irene Sharaff. First produced by the New York City Ballet, New York, June 2, 1953. Added to the repertory of the Royal Danish Ballet, Copenhagen, April 29, 1956.

The form of the ballet reflects exactly the form of the music itself, which is composed on a majestic theme by Henry Purcell: first comes a statement of the theme, then a set of variations, which introduces the four sections of the orchestra and the instruments, one by one; a fugue, which brings the instruments back together again, one by one; and a restatement of the Purcell theme. The dancers' costumes are blue for the woodwinds, pink for the strings (the harp alone is white), yellow for the brass, and black for the percussion. Instrumental designs on the fronts of the costumes designate the various musical instruments and define a specific dancer as a flute, harp, violin, etc. All the dancers wear crowns, and above them on stage hang heraldic pennants glorifying ancient musical instruments.

The entire company dances the great Purcell air with courtly dignity and aristocratic *élan*. Then it departs as the variations for the separate instruments, or groups of instruments, commence. A piccolo and two flutes, danced by three girls, are followed by a duet for two clarinets, a boy and a girl. A solo for oboe, danced by a girl, and a lightly comic variation for two boys, as bassoons, close the woodwind section.

In the string section, the first and second violins are represented by two groups of girls; the violas by a boy and a girl; the cellos by two girls; the double bass by a boy who staggers and flounders about as the complexities of the music for this instrument increase; and the harp by the ballerina, whose light and airy actions and concluding cartwheel and descent to the floor mirror the swiftly cascading notes of the instrument.

Horns, trumpets, tubas, and trombones, danced by men (except for the horns), come next, and here there is an increasing accent on humor, as two of the figures slap each other and hammily edge for top position or, in the case of the tubas, as a drill sergeant (miming shouted commands) leads them through their paces, modestly taking full credit.

Three boys are the percussion figures—drums, gongs, cymbals, etc. They cavort about the stage and intersperse each sequence with a stately and ridiculous rope-skipping routine. The leader of the three indulges in all sorts of antics, among them a takeoff on a presumably tempestuous Spanish dancer armed with castanets.

The Narrator, who has explained the purpose of the ballet and the divisions of the orchestra, and who has introduced the various instruments, now states, "We have taken the orchestra to pieces. It remains to put it back together again. We shall do this in the form of a fugue." The fugue, reintroducing the instruments in the order of their earlier appearances, finally leads to the reunification of the four musical families of the orchestra and merges into the opening theme as the dancers, united in action, move with grandeur to the noble music of Purcell.

The ballet was first presented on the day of the Coronation of Queen Elizabeth II and represented an American greeting in ballet form to the new British monarch. Yvonne Mounsey as the Harp and Todd Bolender as the chief percussion figure headed the cast.

Fanfarita

> *Choreography, Gerald Arpino; music, Ruperto Chapi y Lorente, Zarzuela music adapted by Rayburn Wright. First performed by the City Center Joffrey Ballet, New York, October 9, 1968.*

Fanfarita, a little fanfare, Spanish-style, mixing ballet virtuosities with castanets and flamenco stances in this *pas de trois*.

Luis Fuente, Susan Magno, Erika Goodman headed the first cast.

Fantasies

Choreography, John Clifford; music, Ralph Vaughan Williams; costumes, Robert O'Hearn. First performed by the New York City Ballet, January 23, 1969.

First cast was Kay Mazzo, Anthony Blum, Sara Leland, and Conrad Ludlow.

The Fantastic Toyshop

See *La Boutique Fantasque*

Far from Denmark

(Fjernt Fra Danmark)

Choreography, August Bournonville; music, Hans Christian Lumbye, Louis Gottschalk, Edouard Du Puy, Andreas Lincke, and Joseph Glaeser; revised décor and costumes, after the originals by Christian Ferdinand Christensen, Troels Lund, and Edward Lehmann. First produced by the Royal Danish Ballet, Copenhagen, April 20, 1860.

In two acts and subtitled "A Costume Ball Aboard Ship" (Et Costumebal Onbord), this is a story-ballet about a Danish frigate stopping in an Argentine harbor, and a three-way romantic complication involving a Danish naval officer, the daughter of a consul, and her suitor. The first act, set in the consul's home on a veranda open to the sea with the Danish ship (which shoots ceremonial cannon!) in sight, is mainly pantomimic except for an African servants' dance. Act II is the costume ball in which the sailors dress up as members of various nationalities and perform dances suggesting the regions of origin. A courtly dance of Spanish flavor is also included. In contemporary times the role of the flirtatious heroine has been danced by Kirsten Ralov, Vivi Flindt, and others. The most spectacular dances, however, are performed by the disguised sailors as Eskimos, Chinese, American Indians, and so on, with star dancers almost always cast in these brief but all-important parts.

Feast of Ashes

> *Choreography, Alvin Ailey; music, Carlos Surinach; costumes, Jac Venza. The ballet was added to the repertory of the Robert Joffrey Ballet, Lisbon, Portugal, November 30, 1962. First performed by the Harkness Ballet, Cannes, France, February 19, 1965.*

Feast of Ashes is couched in modern dance terms, especially with respect to dramatic gestures and movement to present the theme of Federico García Lorca's *The House of Bernarda Alba*. However, contemporary ballet dancers have no trouble producing actions which interweave ballet technique with modern dance and pure acting. For the Harkness Ballet the role of the Matriarch was danced by Bonnie Mathis. With the Joffrey, Diana Cartier was featured.

Field Figures

> *Choreography, Glen Tetley; music, Karlheinz Stockhausen; scenery and costumes, Nadine Baylis. First performed by the Royal Ballet, Nottingham, England, November 9, 1970. First American performance by the same company, May 22, 1972.*

La Fille Mal Gardée

(The Unchaperoned Daughter; also presented in Russia as *Useless Precautions* and in America, in the past, as *The Wayward Daughter* and *Naughty Lisette)*

> *Choreography and libretto, Jean Dauberval; music, Peter Ludwig Hertel. First produced in Bordeaux, France, in 1786*

(often called the oldest ballet extant). First performed in America early in the nineteenth century. Revived in New York by the Mordkin Ballet, 1937 (first New York performance, November 12, 1938) and restaged January 19, 1940, in New York by Ballet Theatre (the American Ballet Theatre) with choreographic revisions by Bronislava Nijinska and scenery and costumes by Serge Soudeikine. Two other versions seen in Europe and America are those by Frederick Ashton and Fernand Nault. Ashton's was premièred by the Royal Ballet, December 8, 1960, and by the Royal Danish Ballet, Copenhagen, January 16, 1964. It is also in the repertory of the Australian Ballet. The Nault choreography has been in the repertories of the Joffrey Ballet, Les Grands Ballets Canadiens, and the Boston Ballet. Alicia Alonso staged a version after the Nijinska, for the Ballet Alicia Alonso in Havana, May 21, 1952, and for the Ballet Nacional de Cuba in 1959. The score used by Ashton is by Ferdinand Hérold, adapted and orchestrated by John Lanchberry.

Little of Dauberval's original choreography, presumably, has survived the years, the extensions in ballet technique, and travels from land to land. The Nijinska version is in three scenes and tells the story of Lisette, a vivacious peasant girl; Colin, her sweetheart; Madame Simone, her ambitious mother; Alain, a nitwit selected by Madame to marry her daughter because of his father's wealth; and Alain's father, Thomas, a successful wine producer.

Scene One. Outside Madame Simone's cottage, Lisette waters her plants. Colin enters, puts down his rake, and joins Lisette shortly in a lively and affectionate dance. The mother interrupts this happy scene and chases Colin away. Colin sneaks back from time to time to dance with Lisette and some of her village friends and to enjoy a few fleet moments of sparking with his beloved. As the scene nears its end, Thomas and his butterfly-chasing son arrive and arrangements are made for the marriage of the two young folks. The parents are pleased but Lisette and Alain look at each other in mutual horror and wild despair as the curtain falls.

Scene Two. In this outdoor scene, villagers dance at the close of work, Madame Simone and Thomas, both ugly and aging, appear to be courting each other and Colin sulks as he learns of his sweetheart's engagement to another. Lisette convinces him that she is not to blame and the two demonstrate their lasting love for each other and their momentary happiness in a tender duet and two vivid solos. Gypsies enter the scene to dance and Alain, in high-flying leaps, has also passed this way. But the skies darken, thunder is heard, and everyone scurries to find shelter.

Scene Three. It is Madame Simone's house and the owner and her daughter rush in to escape the storm. The mother sits at her spinning wheel with Lisette at her feet and although the girl tries to sneak off, the alert mother catches her. Colin appears at the transom and Lisette, handing her mother a tambourine, pretends to dance for her. The old lady falls asleep and Lisette attempts to steal her key so that she can get out to Colin; but the mother stirs into wakefulness and Lisette returns desperately to her dancing. Villagers enter with sheaves of wheat and stack them against a table. Madame Simone sees to it that her daughter doesn't leave with them and, seating her at the spinning wheel, makes her own departure.

Lisette sulks for a moment and then dreams of Colin, pretending they are married and have an increasing number of children. Just as she is pantomiming these intimate wishes, the sheaves fly apart and there is Colin. Lisette is furious and embarrassed but soon the lovers make up and exchange scarves. Madame Simone is heard and Lisette tries desperately to hide Colin in the wheat again, but she cannot stack it properly nor can she force his large body into a small chest. Finally, she pushes him into the hayloft and races back to her spinning wheel as her mother enters. Madame Simone notices the scarf belonging to Colin around her daughter's neck, and to punish her, banishes her to the hayloft and locks her in.

Thomas and Alain arrive with the notary, villagers, and friends for the signing of the marriage contract. Madame gives the hayloft key to Alain and sends him to fetch his fiancée. The two lovers emerge with straw in their hair and Madame Simone almost faints from shock. But it is too late now to rectify the situation or to force a marriage, and Madame Simone finally gives her consent to Lisette and Colin becoming man and wife.

La Fille Mal Gardée has had many distinguished interpreters in the role of Lisette during its long history. Fanny Elssler danced it in the last century and Anna Pavlova, Adeline Genée, and Lydia Kyasht performed it in the early part of this century. Later ballerinas in the part have included Irina Baronova, Nana Gollner, Alicia Alonso, and Natalia Makarova.

The Ashton ballet is built upon the same story but the choreography is wholly different except for the essential mime scenes. Ashton highlights include a clog dance for Mother Simone, an opening dance for a rooster and his hens, a maypole dance and a pas de deux in the last scene in which the boy hangs over a transom to partner the girl on the floor below. Nadia Nerina, David Blair, Alexander Grant and Stanley Holden headed the first Ashton cast.

Filling Station

Choreography, Lew Christensen; music, Virgil Thomson; book, Lincoln Kirstein; scenery and costumes, Paul Cadmus. First produced by the Ballet Caravan, Hartford, Connecticut, January 6, 1938. Revived by the New York City Ballet, New York, May 12, 1953.

Filling Station is a comedy ballet indelibly American in tone. The characters are almost comic strip in outline; but this does not mean they are always funny, for modern comics deal with clean-cut heroes and beautiful heroines as frequently as they do with clowns. Thus, the hero of this ballet is Mac, the filling-station attendant, a strong, good-natured, handsome, clean-cut youth.

As the ballet starts, Mac is reading a newspaper. It is night and business is slow. He puts the paper down and begins to dance for his own pleasure in powerful spins and great leaps and in some quieter movements equally common to ballet or to swing-style dancing. He is interrupted by a motorist, a small, knickered, cigar-smoking comic-strip character, who has lost his way. Mac drags out a huge map and gives directions in dance terms with leg extensions, *port de bras* and the like. Behind the map hide two tough truck drivers, friends of Mac. As the tourist leaves, they join their pal in a rough-and-tumble *pas de trois*, featuring somersaults, cartwheels, and a final exit in which one of the drivers jumps on Mac's back, sticks his legs straight out under Mac's arms and with extended legs scoops up the third, in a sitting position, Mac bearing the weight of the two men.

A State Trooper enters, chides the drivers for some infraction, and leaves. The motorist returns, now with his huge overbearing wife and horrid little child, who is obviously desperate to get to the restroom. The wife scolds the husband and waddles off with the child, leaving the relieved man to practice golf swings with Mac.

With the departure of the tourists, a highly inebriated couple stagger in from a dance. The two engage in a reeling adagio, the girl so limp that her beau has to maneuver her about. At the close of the duet Mac and the drivers join in and the girl, no longer glassy-eyed but delighting in the whole affair, pitches herself with abandon at first one and then the other. Quick grabs save her from falling on her face (or into the orchestra pit) and at the close she leaps into the arms of the motorist, who has rejoined the group, just as the wife and child return.

The succeeding dance, "The Big Apple," is interrupted by the arrival of a gangster who lines up everyone in the filling station and robs each of cash and jewelry. Mac manages to turn off the lights and a chase ensues. The dancers cross the stage in turns and leaps, shining flashlights briefly on all parts of the stage and into the audience. A shot rings out, the lights come on, and the drunken girl appears to have been killed. The trooper takes his prisoner and the girl, borne high in the air by the men, is carried off slowly as if in a cortege, but just before she is carried out of sight, she lifts her head, and winks and waves to Mac. The handsome attendant dances for a moment and returns to his reading as the ballet ends.

Lew Christensen danced Mac at the première, with Marie-Jeanne as the Girl. Erick Hawkins, Michael Kidd, Todd Bolender,

Eugene Loring, and Fred Danieli were also in the original cast. For the New York City Ballet revival, Jacques d'Amboise danced Mac, with Janet Reed as the Drunken Girl, Michael Maule as her equally intoxicated Playmate, Edward Bigelow and Robert Barnett as the Truck Drivers, Stanley Zompakos as the Motorist, Shaun O'Brien (in travesty) as the Wife, and Edith Brozak as the Child.

Le Fils Prodigue

See *The Prodigal Son*

Firebird

(L'Oiseau de Feu)

> *Choreography, Michel Fokine; music, Igor Stravinsky; scenery and costumes, Golovine. First produced by Diaghilev's Ballets Russes, Paris, June 25, 1910. First presented in America by the same company, January 17, 1916. Revived in 1926 with scenery and costumes by Nathalie Gontcharova. Presented by the Ballet Russe de Monte Carlo, New York, March 20, 1935, and presented by the Original Ballet Russe, New York, December 6, 1940, both productions using the Gontcharova settings and costumes. Restaged, with choreography by Adolph Bolm and scenery and costumes by Marc Chagall, by Ballet Theatre (now the American Ballet Theatre), New York, October 24, 1945. Produced by the New York City Ballet, with new choreography by George Balanchine and with the Chagall settings and costumes, November 27, 1949. The Fokine original, staged by Serge Grigoriev and Lubov Tchernicheva (members of the Diaghilev company), with scenery and costumes by Gontcharova, was produced by the Sadler's Wells Ballet (now the Royal Ballet), Edinburgh, August 23, 1954, and presented in New York, September 20, 1955. A totally new production, with choreography by Brian Macdonald and costumes and scenery by Rouben Ter-*

Arutunian, was presented by the Harkness Ballet, November 1, 1967. A production with choreography by Maurice Béjart and costumes by Joelle Roustan was first performed, October 31, 1970. George Balanchine, with Jerome Robbins, created a new production with new Chagall decor and costumes, which was first presented by the New York City Ballet, May 28, 1970. The Macdonald version is also in the repertory of the Royal Swedish Ballet.

The New York City Ballet production, with a shorter score (arranged by the composer himself) than the original, is in three scenes.

Scene One. In a dense and mysterious forest, Prince Ivan is hunting. He hears strange and ominous sounds and then sees a golden light, which sweeps the air and suddenly turns into the glittering image of the Firebird. Frightened, he runs to hide as the shining creature leaps onto the scene and moves swiftly, restlessly, and with uninterrupted action through skimming steps, dartings, turns, soaring balances. Ivan returns and, fascinated with this shimmering creature, part magical bird and part beautiful woman, attempts to capture her. As she completes a dizzying sequence of turns, Ivan steps forth and seizes her. Terrified, she alternates between frozen immobility and wild flutterings of escape. She pleads for her freedom and Ivan releases her. In gratitude she dances for him and with him, nestling close in his arms or sliding across the stage in near-splits or, as he holds her extending arm, arcs her back, extends a leg high into space, and whirls about him in a band of flame. Before she leaves, she takes a feather from her breast, indicates that it is a magical feather that will protect him from danger; then she leaps high into the air and disappears from view.

Scene Two. In the gardens of the evil magician Kastchei, Ivan comes upon a group of captive princesses, led by the lovely Tsarevna, dancing Russian folk measures. He watches their simple and joyous dances for a moment and then steps forth from his hiding. The girls are alarmed and particularly so when Ivan beckons to one of them to come forth. He whispers in her ear and tells her that he wishes to meet the Tsarevna. The Tsarevna steps forward and the two bow to each other. Then Ivan and the Tsarevna lead the princesses in a Russian round dance, which includes not only circular actions, but advances and retreats and elaborate inter-weavings of arms and bodies.

Suddenly darkness settles over the scene and with a crash of music, an army of monsters appears. Costumes, masks, and actions are grotesque. Ivan starts to flee but he remembers that the magic feather will protect him. He stands his ground against Kastchei, who has entered, and moves among the monsters waving the feather. The princesses plead for Ivan's life but neither Kastchei nor his evil band can harm the young prince.

There is a flash and the Firebird appears. She hands Ivan an unsheathed sword and, with incredible swiftness, circles the stage in traveling turns which seem to leave a wake of fire. Ivan kills Kastchei and the stage darkens as he stands among the fallen monsters. The Firebird returns, Ivan discovers the Tsarevna, and both bow low in gratitude before her. The two lovers and the princesses depart, leaving the Firebird to complete her mission. Followed by her single light, the Firebird, with brilliant, commanding actions, revives the fallen monsters and, making signs over them, destroys their powers forever. In a final, softly shining lullaby, she brings peace to the forest and flutters out of view.

Scene Three. This is the court of the Prince. Courtiers, attendants, bearers of pennants celebrate the wedding of Ivan and the Tsarevna in this final tableau. A red carpet is unrolled, and the two walk forward as the curtain falls.

In the New York City Ballet production, Maria Tallchief and Francisco Moncion created the principal roles.

At the Paris première of the Fokine original, Tamara Karsavina and Fokine were the leading dancers; and at the New York première, Xenia Maclezova and Leonide Massine were the Lovers, with Enrico Cecchetti as Kastchei. Alexandra Danilova was the Firebird at the first New York presentation by the Ballet Russe de Monte Carlo; and Irina Baronova, at the first New York performance by the Original Ballet Russe. Alicia Markova and Anton Dolin danced in the Bolm version for Ballet Theatre. The Sadler's Wells Ballet restoration of the Fokine original had Margot

Fonteyn (coached by Karsavina herself) in the title role and Michael Somes (Ivan), Svetlana Beriosova (Tsarevna), and Frederick Ashton (Kastchei) heading the cast for the Edinburgh and New York premières. Still other choreographers than those mentioned here have used the Stravinsky score and many other ballerinas have performed in the title part. In the Béjart choreography the role of the Firebird is danced by a male dancer. It has featured Paolo Bortoluzzi and Jorge Donn in the title role.

The Flames of Paris

Choreography, Vasily Vainonen; music, Boris Asafiev (based on French Revolutionary themes); book, Vladimir Dmitriev and Nikolai Volkov; designs, Vladimir Dmitriev. First performed by the Kirov Ballet, Leningrad, November 6, 1932. A new version was performed by the Kirov, November 6, 1936. The Bolshoi Ballet first performed the Third Act of the ballet, November 6, 1932, and the full work, June 6, 1933.

The Flames of Paris is one of the popular contemporary ballets in the repertory of the Soviet State Ballet. Its story deals with the French Revolution and its action is composed of classical ballet, court dances, folk dancing, pantomime, and general dramatic action. In abbreviated form it has been produced in motion pictures. A *pas de deux* from this ballet was presented by the Bolshoi Ballet in New York City, April 23, 1959, with Ekaterina Maximova and Gennadi Lediakh as the dancers. The *pas de deux* was staged and performed by the American Ballet Theatre for the first time, New York, January 13, 1973.

Die Fledermaus

Choreography, Ruth Page; music, Johann Strauss, arranged and orchestrated by Isaac Van Grove; décor and costumes, André Delfau. First performed by Ruth Page's Chicago Opera Ballet, 1958. Now in the repertory of the Pittsburgh Ballet Theatre.

Les Fleurs du Mal

Choreography, Maurice Béjart; décor and costumes, Joelle Roustan and Roger Bernard. Suggested by the collection of Baudelaire's poems of the same name. First produced by Ballet of the Twentieth Century, 1971, and given its first American performance by the same company, New York, November 26, 1971.

Figures, suggesting Aubrey Beardsley illustrations, expose decadent love in many guises: man and woman, man and man, woman and woman.

Et Folkesagn

(A Folk Tale)

Choreography, August Bournonville; music, Niels W. Gade and J.P.E. Hartmann; décor and costumes, Svend Johansen. First performed by the Royal Danish Ballet, Copenhagen, March 20, 1854. A revised version by Hans Brenaa, assisted by Kirsten Ralov, was presented November 2, 1969.

Les Forains

Choreography, Roland Petit; music, Henri Sauget; book, Boris Kochno; scenery and costumes, Christian Bérard. First produced by the Ballets des Champs-Elysées, Paris, March 2, 1945. First presented in America by Roland Petit's Ballets de Paris, New York, October 8, 1950.

The Fountain of Bakhchisarai

Choreography, Rostislav Zakharov; music, Boris Asafiev; book, Nikolai Volkov, with prologue and epilogue based on Alexander Pushkin's poem; designs, Valentina Khodasevich. First performed by the Kirov Ballet, Leningrad, September

28, 1934. The Bolshoi Ballet performed it with the same choreography and sets, June 11, 1936.

This popular Soviet ballet deals with the story of Princess Maria, her capture by a Tatar Khan, her refusal to respond to his romantic advances and her death at the hands of Zarema, favorite of the harem.

The ballet contains a rousing warriors' dance, virtuosic and semi-Oriental movements for Zarema, classical episodes for Maria, and dramatic action. In a shortened version, it has been produced in motion pictures with Galina Ulanova as Maria and Maya Plisetskaya as Zarema.

Four Bagatelles

Choreography, Jerome Robbins; music, Ludwig von Beethoven (Bagatelles, op 33, No.'s 4, 5, 2; op 126, No. 4); costumes, Florence Klotz. First produced, New York City Ballet, New York, January 10, 1974.

A series of *pas de deux* based upon the sheer joy of dancing. There is no storyline, and the characters are not specific figures from a drama or story, but Robbins has asked his dancers simply to be warm, almost radiant, human beings experiencing moods which may be frolicsome, romantic or daredevil.

The dancers of the first cast were Violette Verdy, Jean-Pierre Bonnefous.

The Four Marys

Choreography, Agnes de Mille; music, Trude Rittmann; costumes, Stanley Simmons. First performed by the American Ballet Theatre, New York, March 23, 1965.

The Four Marys, a ballet-drama about the status of the black and white races in the South. The four Marys are servants. Three keep to their places as dutiful servants. The fourth is the mother of a child sired by the white suitor of the mistress of the mansion.

The father flees social censure. The mother is forced to murder her child and is punished for the crime.

Principals at the première were Carmen de Lavallade (heroine), Judith Lerner (the lady of the house), Paul Sutherland (suitor-lover).

Four Moons

Choreography, Rosella Hightower, Roman Jasinsky, George Skibine, and Miguel Terekoff; music, Louis Ballard; decor, Jerome Tiger. First performed at the Oklahoma Indian Ballerina Festival, Tulsa, October 28, and Oklahoma City, November 2, 1967.

A *pièce d'occasion,* an American Indian ballet, presented in Oklahoma City and Tulsa in 1967 in celebration of the sixtieth anniversary of Oklahoma's statehood. The event was called the Oklahoma Indian Ballet Festival and the four native Oklahomans who starred were all internationally famous ballerinas of Indian heritage: Marjorie Tallchief (Osage), Rosella Hightower (Choctaw), Yvonne Chouteau (Cherokee), Moscelyne Larkin (Shawnee). Ballard, the composer, is Cherokee; the designer, Tiger, a Creek Indian. A single example of how ballet technique originating in Paris was used to express an American Indian theme could be found in the "Trail of Tears" episode in which the key steps were tremulous *bourrées* evoking the forced migration, at great loss of life, of the Cherokees from their ancestral lands to new reserves.

The Four Temperaments

Choreography, George Balanchine; music, Paul Hindemith; scenery and costumes, Kurt Seligmann. First produced by Ballet Society (later the New York City Ballet), New York, November 20, 1946. Revived by the New York City Ballet, October 25, 1948, and, in November of 1952, the scenery and costumes were discarded in favor of a plain backdrop and simple practice clothes. The ballet was first presented by the National Ballet of Washington, Washington, D.C., February

*21, 1964, and by the Royal Danish Ballet, Copenhagen, May
4, 1963. The Pennsylvania Ballet added the ballet to its repertory, May 13, 1969. It is also in the repertories of the Norwegian Ballet, the Boston Ballet, the Royal Swedish Ballet,
the National Ballet of Canada, and Het Nationale Ballet.*

The ballet, like the score, is divided into five parts, a theme and
four variations. The variations reflect the temperaments or the
humors promised by the title: "Melancholic," "Sanguinic," "Phlegmatic," "Choleric."

The choreography is basically classical throughout, but Balanchine used traditional actions in new and surprising sequences
and departed from classical action where necessary to give clear
definition to the temperaments and their essential colorings.

The chief figure in the "Melancholic" variation is a man. He
moves alone through movements that indicate loss, uncertainty,
search. Subsequently he is joined by four girls, but at the close of
the variation his melancholy solitude is reestablished.

"Sanguinic" is for a ballerina and her partner, and this variation is open, bright, and free. In "Phlegmatic," the solo male
dancer moves limply through his sequences, using his hands aimlessly, doubling up, resting. A small ensemble stirs him briefly
from his lassitude.

In "Choleric" the ballerina moves with quick, angry, almost
impulsive movements, joined shortly by the entire company for
the finale.

Maria Tallchief, Herbert Bliss, Tanaquil LeClercq, and Todd
Bolender headed the cast for the 1948 revival. The soloists—the
temperament figures and supporting leads—for the première were
Gisella Caccialanza, LeClercq, Mary Ellen Moylan, Elise Reiman,
Beatrice Tompkins, Bolender, Lew Christensen, Fred Danieli, Wil-
liam Dollar, José Martinez, and Francisco Moncion.

À la Françaix

*Choreography, George Balanchine; music, Jean Françaix.
First produced by the New York City Ballet, New York, September 11, 1951.*

Frankie and Johnny

Choreography, Ruth Page and Bentley Stone; music, Jerome Moross; book, Michael Blandford and Moross; scenery and costumes, Paul Dupont. First produced by the Page-Stone Ballet for the dance theater project of the Works Progress Administration, Chicago, June 19, 1938. Restaged, with new scenery by Clive Rickabaugh, for the Ballet Russe de Monte Carlo, New York, February 28, 1945.

The ballet, based upon the famous song-ballad of the same name, relates in movement how Johnny was unfaithful to Frankie when "he done her wrong" and how she shot him. The choreographers have presented their treatment of the tale with sensual boldness and lusty humor. At one time, on the occasion of its first New York performances, *Frankie and Johnny* ran into trouble with the censors, but survived the bout and became an enormously popular ballet.

Ruth Page and Bentley Stone danced the title parts both in Chicago and in New York. At later performances Ruthanna Boris and Frederic Franklin were the ill-fated lovers.

Gaîté Parisienne

Choreography, Leonide Massine; music, Jacques Offenbach; book, scenery, and costumes, Comte Étienne de Beaumont. First produced by the Ballet Russe de Monte Carlo, Monte Carlo, April 5, 1938. First American performance by the same company, New York, October 12, 1938. The ballet was revived under the personal supervision of Massine, for American Ballet Theatre, and was given its first performance by that company at the New York State Theatre, New York, June 17, 1970.

This one-act ballet is set in a fashionable restaurant in the Paris of the last century. As the curtain rises the waiters and the maids are readying the place for the evening's guests, but their labors are casual as they anticipate the spirit of the evening with lively, whirling, head-tossing dances. The Flower Girl, the first of the soloists, enters and in a vivacious dance gives a bouquet to each of the boys and merrily sprays a drink in their direction as she alternates sipping and kicking.

The customers begin to drift in and soon the heroine of the ballet arrives, the beautiful and coquettish Glove Seller, who sets up her little stand and prepares for business. The men, of course, are fascinated with her and s>on set her to spinning about in a vivid introductory dance.

The next arrival is the rolling-eyed, wriggling, excited Peruvian, who comes bounding in with his carpetbags, unwilling to wait another second to taste the joys of Paris. As he finishes his swift and comical dance, he goes first to the Flower Girl and then squirms delightedly as the Glove Seller fits him (or tries to) for gloves. But the Peruvian's romantic hopes are dashed when the handsome Baron enters, spies the Glove Seller, and leads her into a glorious waltz. They are oblivious of everything but each other and they dance as if fate had long since arranged for their meeting.

The Peruvian entertains the girls with wine; a group of soldiers and an officer march in and dance, finishing with a smart salute as a string of girls hangs from their necks. La Lionne and her entourage arrive, and finally jealousy flares up and a fight ensues. La Lionne's escort, the Baron, the officer, the Peruvian, young artists in their berets, indeed everyone becomes involved in the fracas. At the end of the fight the little Peruvian, who has taken refuge under one of the tables, scurries off with it on his back as a waiter flicks him with his napkin.

Now the Glove Seller and the Baron return for their second romantic waltz, mirroring their love in the swoops, dips, lifts, gestures of adoration and glowing proximity of their dance. At its close the cancan dancers take over the stage for a rousing display of high kicks, splits, and spins. But the evening is ending and the guests depart, the various sets of lovers happily paired and the Peruvian left alone with the memories of a gay, if not romantically fruitful, evening.

Gaîté Parisienne, which has remained one of the most popular ballets in the repertory of the Ballet Russe de Monte Carlo, long served as the special vehicle of Alexandra Danilova, whose Glove Seller represented one of her most celebrated roles. After leaving the company, Danilova returned to the part on occasion as guest artist with the Ballet Russe and frequently danced the second waltz on her own programs with her own company or at festival events. Frederic Franklin was almost always associated with her as the Baron.

Principals in the first performance at Monte Carlo included Nina Tarakanova (Glove Seller), Eugenie Delarova (Flower Girl), Jeannette Lauret (La Lionne), Massine (Peruvian), Franklin (Baron) Igor Youskevitch (Officer). At the New York première Danilova danced the Glove Seller. Among others who have danced the leading parts are Leon Danielian as the Peruvian, George Zoritch as the Baron, Mia Slavenska and Maria Tallchief as the Glove Seller.

Gaîté Parisienne, renamed *The Gay Parisian*, was produced as a short color movie with Massine and Franklin in their usual roles and with Milada Mladova as the Glove Seller.

The American Ballet Theatre revival featured Michael Smuin as the Peruvian, Mimi Paul as the Glove Seller, and Bruce Marks as the Baron.

Gala Performance

Choreography, Antony Tudor; music, Serge Prokofiev; scenery and costumes, Hugh Stevenson. First produced by the London Ballet, London, December 5, 1938. First presented in America by Ballet Theatre (now the American Ballet Theatre), with scenery and costumes by Nicholas de Molas, New York, February 11, 1941. The ballet was added to the repertory of the Royal Danish Ballet, December 9, 1970.

This comic ballet deals with the violent rivalry of three ballerinas brought together for the first time to take part in a gala performance. The choreographer has sought not only to make fun of their behavior but to satirize, through exaggeration, the three styles of ballet they represent. The Queen of the Dance is from

Russia; the Goddess of the Dance from Italy; the Daughter of
Terpsichore from France.

Scene One (set to the Piano Concerto No. 3) is a backstage
setting with the backdrop representing the stage side of the theatre curtain. The dancers are warming up for the performance as
the wardrobe mistress and the ballet master come in. But the stir
is really caused by the arrival of the Russian ballerina, who accepts
homage with great hauteur, practices her bows, and causes one
of the girls to burst into tears. The French ballerina, coquettish instead of arrogant, skips in and makes her wishes known. The third
to appear is the Italian ballerina, who stalks in with cold grandeur
and offers her hand to be kissed. Regal as she is, there is a pettish
side to her and the wardrobe mistress receives a slap when she
fails to hold the mirror at the desired angle.

The ballerinas have left and there is a sudden rush as the
performance is about to begin. There is a last trip to the rosin box
to assure no-skid slippers, one girl crosses herself frantically, and
the ensemble scurries into position, their backs to the real audience as they face the curtain about to rise on the imaginary
audience. There is a blackout.

Scene Two (set to the Classical Symphony) reverses the position seen at the end of Scene One. The dancers are facing front
and are backed by an elaborate setting. Eight girls commence to
dance and each, with loving ogles at the audience, attempts to
enchant the viewers with her own hammy charm. Now the Russian ballerina enters, escorted by her cavaliers. Many of her steps
are exceptionally difficult but the accent falls on her method of
execution. She leers at the audience as she jumps, turns, travels,
and ultimately gets around to a series of pirouettes which she
starts in a crouching position and builds to an upright pose before
reversing the procedure. Her curtain calls are ludicrous; she responds to applause with wildly thrown kisses and clutches the scenery as if she could not bear to tear herself away from her adoring
public.

The Italian ballerina enters next with the cold assurance of a
marble monument. She takes her time getting into position, nods
to the orchestra conductor, and commences her dance, based

mainly upon difficult balances interspersed with startlingly abrupt bits of energetic action. Her cavalier is merely a prop to get her into position, and she dismisses him once her position is firmly planted. The cavalier is nothing to her and neither is the audience. She is superior to all. Her curtain calls are accomplished with measured pace and only a frigid nod of the head acknowledges the applause. However, she will brook no sharing of this honor she is subjected to and imperiously dismisses her cavalier so that she may take her bows alone.

Finally, the French ballerina skips on and enchants her audience with high-flying leaps and skittish activities that make it seem that she couldn't possibly stand still and that she is just a cuddly bundle of fluff. Her curtain calls are accomplished at such speed and originate from so many different entrances that her bewildered cavalier cannot keep track of her.

For the finale, the Russian ballerina, covered with jewels and wearing red; the Italian ballerina, with her severe black costume and plume; and the blond French ballerina with her fluffy costume take part in the coda, each attempting to outdo the others. The French and Russian ballerinas do everthing but chew up the scenery in order to attract attention but the Italian ballerina goes on her Olympian way as if no one else of importance were present.

At the close, when flowers are presented, the Italian ballerina manages to snatch the greatest collection and in succeeding curtain calls the battle over the flowers continues as we catch unanticipated glimpses of a floral tug of war.

At the London première the principal parts were danced by Maude Lloyd, Gerd Larsen, Peggy van Praagh, Hugh Laing, and Tudor. The first New York performance had Nora Kaye (Russian Ballerina), Nana Gollner (Italian Ballerina), Karen Conrad (French Ballerina), and Laing and Tudor as the stars.

Gamelan

Choreography, Robert Joffrey; music, Lou Harrison; costumes, Willa Kim. First performance (preview) by the Robert Joffrey Ballet (now the City Center Joffrey Ballet), at the

Fashion Institute of Technology, New York, September 30, 1962. World première by the same company, Kirov Theatre, Leningrad, October, 1963. The first American performance by the Joffrey Company was in Washington, D.C., June 14, 1965.

In colors and in movement tone, a pastel-hued ballet evocative of Japanese images.

Gartenfest

Choreography, Michael Smuin; music, Wolfgang Amadeus Mozart; décor, Jack Owen Brown; costumes, Marcos Paredes. First performed by the American Ballet Theatre, New York, December 18, 1968.

A classical ballet in six movements, ranging from a lyrical *"Traum"* to an exuberant *"Fest."* The choreographer best described the spirit of his ballet with his comment on his reaction to the music of Mozart (composed when he was only thirteen): "It begged to be danced."

Cynthia Gregory, Sallie Wilson, Ivan Nagy, Ted Kivitt headed the first cast.

Gayane

Choreography, Nina Anisimova; music, Aram Khachaturian; book, Konstantin Derzhavin; décor, Natan Altman; costumes, Tatiana Bruni. First performed by the Kirov Ballet, Perm, December 9, 1942. A new production, with choreography by Anisimova and designs by Valery Dorrer, was performed by the Kirov, June 13, 1952.

Gemini

Choreography, Vincente Nebrada; music, Gustav Mahler. First performed by the Harkness Ballet, New Paltz, New York, February 13, 1972.

A tour de force in muscularly powerful and sustained movement, some of it balleticized acrobatics or gymnastics, for two men. As the title suggests, the extremely close relationship of the two, in terms of awareness of each other and in extended tactile design, is a paean to beautiful male bodies in proximity and to the "oneness" mystique usually associated with twins.

Darrell Barnett and Rafael Reyes were the first to dance this ballet.

Gemini

Choreography, Glen Tetley; music, Hans Werner Henze; scenery and costumes, Nadine Baylis; lighting, John B. Read. First performance, Australian Ballet, 1973.

Four dancers, wearing body-encasing costumes of curious luminosity, move against a shimmering background. The movements are a blend of classical ballet and modern dance (essentially derivative of Martha Graham) and are devised to display the disciplines and the virtuosities of the dancers in complex lifts, precarious balances in unusual body positions, leaps, sustained legato patterns and, in fact, a gamut of body gestures which might be considered body testings. The ballet suggests moods but they are fleeting and the accent is on metallic sheen in design and in action.

The first cast for the American Ballet Theatre première January 23, 1975, was composed of Cynthia Gregory, Martine Van Hamel, Jonas Kage, Charles Ward.

Ghost Town

Choreography, Marc Platoff; music and libretto, Richard Rodgers; scenery and costumes, Raoul Pène duBois. First produced by the Ballet Russe de Monte Carlo, New York, November 12, 1939.

The only ballet score ever composed by one of the most famous composers of the American musical theatre.

Giselle

*Choreography, Jean Coralli and Jules Perrot; music, Adolphe
Adam; book, Coralli, Théophile Gautier, and Vernoy de Saint-
George; scenery, Pierre Ciceri; costumes, Paul Lormier. First
presented in Paris, June 28, 1841. London première, March
12, 1842; St. Petersburg première, December 18, 1842; Amer-
ican première, Boston, January 1, 1846. The first performance
by the Royal Danish Ballet was September 24, 1862. Recent
productions in that company's repertory have been by Erik
Bruhn, first performed September 6, 1964, and Anton Dolin,
March 30, 1968. Dolin staged the first Ballet Theatre (now
American Ballet Theatre) production, first performed January
11, 1940. The ballet was first performed by the Sadler's Wells
Ballet (now the Royal Ballet) with choreography by Nicolai
Sergeyev after Petipa, Coralli, and Perrot, on June 12, 1946,
in London. The current Royal Ballet production was produced by Peter Wright, first performed May 15, 1968, with
choreography by Frederick Ashton after the traditional choreography, with décor and costumes by Peter Farmer.
Peter Wright produced the* Giselle *first performed by
the Stuttgart Ballet, March 26, 1966, and the National Ballet
of Canada production, 1970/71. The Bruhn version is also
performed by the Royal Swedish Ballet. Dolin staged the Les
Grands Ballets Canadiens production. The National Ballet of
Washington production, staged by Frederic Franklin, with
décor and costumes by Peter Farmer, was first performed
April 12, 1968. Alicia Alonso staged* Giselle *for the Ballet
Nacional de Cuba in 1959. The current Bolshoi Ballet production has choreography by Leonid Lavrovsky after Petipa, Coralli, and Perrot, and was first presented in 1944.*

For more than a century, *Giselle* has been a success. At its première, it was hailed as one of the greatest of all ballets, topping even
La Sylphide, which had ushered in the Romantic Age of Ballet
several years before; and it remains today the supreme achievement of that era. It has often been called "the Hamlet of the

dance," not merely because of its enduring qualities but rather because it provides the ballerina with a double challenge: those of dancer and actress.

How much of the original choreography remains would be hard to say, for no notational system was used to record its exact movements. During its travels from country to country and company to company, with changing tastes and an array of highly individual ballerinas, each bringing to it her own powers as well as idiosyncrasies, it is probable that many changes have been wrought, some of them perhaps for the better. Still, *Giselle* continues to exert its magic weaving together in expert form love and fantasy, mortal, and mystical melodrama.

Adam's delightful (if somewhat quaint) music does more than provide rhythmic support to the isolated dances. It possesses dramatic unity and, anticipating ballet music of a later day, it boasts both musical continuity and the use of leitmotifs for identifying specific characters, conditions (anger, madness, adoration, fear, mystery), and locales.

The scene of Act I is in a Rhine village. On one side of the stage is the cottage where Giselle lives, on the other a hut. Peasants pass by on their way to celebrate vintage time. The rough Hilarion, a gamekeeper, enters and walks toward the house of Giselle, with whom he is in love. He is startled by someone's approach and hides as he watches Albrecht, a duke disguised as the peasant Loys, enter with Wilfred, his attendant. Albrecht, removing his noble cloak and sword and handing them to Wilfred, stands dressed as the peasant he pretends to be. Dismissing Wilfred, who conceals the cloak and sword in the hut, he turns rapturously to Giselle's home and through pantomime, indicates his love for her.

He raps on the door and then quickly hides as Giselle comes out. She looks around and is about to subside into unhappiness when Albrecht sneaks up and nudges her affectionately. Her little dance on her entrance has shown us her gaiety. Now, with Albrecht, she is shy and demure, and when he vows his love, almost frightened. She picks a flower to test the he-loves-me-he-loves-me-not method and bursts into tears when the answer comes out wrong. Albrecht retrieves the half-used flower and pulls off the remaining petals with a "yes" for each one. Together they dance happily.

Now the jealous Hilarion interrupts the lovers, a fight ensues, and although Hilarion begs Giselle for her love, she dismisses him and he goes off, angry and suspicious. The peasants come onto the scene and Giselle and Albrecht join in their folklike measures until Berthe, Giselle's mother, appears and warns her daughter to cease dancing because of her heart (some ballerinas indicate the existence of a weak heart or frailty earlier in the ballet); if she should die before her wedding day, she will be forced to join the Wilis, restless ghosts of unmarried maidens. Grudgingly, Giselle obeys her mother and returns to her home. Albrecht and the villagers depart.

Hilarion returns to try and persuade Giselle that Albrecht is not for her but the sound of a hunting horn distracts him and he hides in the little hut. Wilfred now enters to seek a place of rest and refreshment for the hunting party of the Prince of Courland and his daughter, Bathilde.

Giselle and her mother welcome the noble party with simple refreshments and Giselle, fascinated with Bathilde's rich robes, presses her cheek against the hem of the skirt. Bathilde is delighted with such admiration and asks Giselle what her duties are. The girl, in mime, relates that she sews and spins but that she likes to dance best of all. Bathilde, with the Prince's permission, gives her a necklace and the party retires to the cottage to rest.

Hilarion now emerges from Albrecht's hut with the noble cloak and sword in hand. He makes a triumphant, vengeful gesture, for he knows now that Albrecht is truly a noble and he can prove it. He hides the evidence as the peasants return. The young folk dance joyously—in some versions there is a charming *pas de six* for a group of the girls—and eventually beg Berthe to let Giselle join them. The mother finally gives in to the pleas and Giselle dances a shining and difficult solo. At the close of the episode, she and Albrecht join their friends in an ensemble dance.

Hilarion now runs forth, rips the lovers from their embrace, and tells of his discovery. The sword is brought forth, the two men fight and, through Wilfred's interference, when he protects his master from the crime of killing Hilarion, the sword is dropped to the ground. Hilarion, determined to prove his point, grabs the hunting horn of the noble party and blasts a call. The Prince and Bathilde come out of the cottage and Bathilde asks Albrecht what he is doing in such peasant garb. He kneels and kisses the hand of his fiancée. Giselle, who has been greatly disturbed by the events but not quite convinced that Hilarion has been speaking the truth, now rushes toward Bathilde. She points to the engagement ring on her finger but so does Bathilde point to her own and Giselle realizes the dreadful truth.

Giselle tears the necklace off and hurls it to the ground. Broken-hearted, bereft of her senses, in a mad dance she seeks to recapture earlier joys and once again picks the flower petals in her imagination. Her foot touches the fallen sword. Quickly she picks it up, drags it in a circle swiftly around the stage and, before Albrecht can stop her, stabs herself.

Dying, Giselle tremulously stumbles through the steps she and Albrecht had danced together. She has forgotten the recent tragedy and in her madness is living again fragments of a happy romance. Coldness touches her, and with a last frightened run she falls into her mother's arms. The Prince and Bathilde have left, but Albrecht and the others have remained, transfixed by the awesome madness. Now he rushes forward to tell Giselle of his deathless love and, with a little gesture, she seems to forgive him just as she dies. Albrecht angrily drags Hilarion forth to show him the enormity of his crime and then kneels beside the body of his beloved as the curtain falls.

Act II takes place in a forest glade. It is night and the musical theme as well as the presence of darkness cast an eerie spell. Homeward-bound huntsmen pause, but the legend of the Wilis is strong and they soon leave, urging along the sorrowing Hilarion, who has sought out the tomb of Giselle.

Now a veiled figure glides swiftly by. It is Myrtha, all-powerful Queen of the Wilis. She returns, unveiled, and commences her glittering solo, cold but perfect, the dance of an imperious queen. She plucks two branches and with them defines the sacred area. Next, she calls forth the Wilis, orders them to remove their veils and to prepare for the ceremony. The ghost-maidens move with unemotional perfection through their patterns while Myrtha culminates her commanding directions with virtuosic measures, which include leaps, flashing leg-beats, and sweeping turns.

Now Myrtha points her wand toward the tomb of Giselle and the ghostly heroine emerges from her grave. The veil is suddenly, mysteriously withdrawn and Giselle, as if in a trance, steps down and bows to her queen. Myrtha touches her with her wand and Giselle begins a rapid spin which grows into an elaborate dance. At its close, she disappears into the forest, the Wilis leave and the scene is desolate.

The mourning Albrecht, followed by the faithful Wilfred, enters in search of Giselle's tomb. Wilfred urges his master to leave this ensorcelled spot but Albrecht dismisses him and walks to the tomb and places flowers upon it. As he thinks of Giselle, she appears, but he does not see her, although he feels her presence. She touches him, leaves, then speeds in front of him; for a moment he has her in his arms before the vision departs. A flash of movement behind him tells him that Giselle has skimmed by once again. Despairing, he kneels, and Giselle returns once more. This time she remains, and the two dance gently and lovingly together. Giselle now picks two lilies and, running, tosses first one and then the other over her head as Albrecht leaps to catch them in midair. The two disappear and Hilarion returns. As he appears, the Wilis rush forth from their place of concealment and cut off all avenues of escape.

With the arrival of Myrtha, the Wilis form a diagonal line and Hilarion rushes to the queen to beg for his life. Her implacable answer is "No," and down the line of Wilis Hilarion is pushed and whirled until the two final members of the band grasp him and propel him into the lake to drown. Myrtha now leads her Wilis off, two by two, in a leaping figure. They return immediately to their posts. A second remorseless trial is to begin, for Albrecht enters and asks for his life. The queen's reply is, of course, negative but Giselle, whose love has spanned death, comes to his aid and tells him to seek sanctuary by the cross which stands over her grave.

Myrtha raises her magical wand to order him to return but the wand breaks in two as it meets the power of the Cross. Angrily she orders Giselle to lead the mortal Albrecht in an endless dance, which will bring exhaustion and death. Giselle must obey. The two dance together in a *pas de deux* with slow and high lifts, giving it a ghostly beauty. Then Giselle dances a difficult solo, followed by Albrecht, who cuts the air with leaps and shimmering leg-beats. Relentlessly the Wilis drive them on. Repeated pleas are to no avail, for the Wilis return again and again to dance and so do Giselle and Albrecht. The hero falters from time to time and finally a series of jumps exhausts his last reserves and he falls.

The dawn is heralded, the hours of magic are fading. Ironically, Giselle holds the fallen Albrecht in her arms as he once held her when she was dying. The Wilis and their queen disappear and Giselle, called by the grave, returns to her tomb. The earth opens up and she sinks from view. Albrecht, who has sought to grasp her in his arms, falls to the ground.

In some versions Giselle is placed upon a grassy bank by Albrecht and slowly sinks into the earth. In others, she mounts the steps of her raised tomb and fades from view behind the cross. And there are still different treatments of the return to the grave just as there are variations in procedure and setting elsewhere in the ballet, depending upon production facilities and the judgment of the choreographer engaged to stage the work.

At the première in Paris Carlotta Grisi danced the title role, Lucien Petipa was Albrecht, and Adèle Dumilâtre was Myrtha. *Giselle* placed Grisi in the very top rank of the great ballerinas of her day, on a par with Marie Taglioni and Fanny Elssler. Indeed, it has been said that Grisi combined in her dancing the ethereal quality which distinguished Taglioni and the fire and warmth of the earthy Elssler. *Giselle*, calling for a warmhearted and exuberant peasant maid in the first act and a creature of fantasy in the second, enabled Grisi to disclose her powers in both areas as well as to give outlet to her dramatic skill. Coralli himself danced the part of Hilarion.

At the London première, Perrot, who quite probably created the variations for his wife, Grisi, danced the part of Albrecht. Elena

Andreyanova was the first to dance *Giselle* in Russia and Mary Ann Lee introduced it to America in Boston.

So successful was *Giselle* that Elssler added it to her repertoire for European tours (Elssler used it for her Russian debut) and Fanny Cerrito and Lucile Grahn, rounding out the quintet of the greatest ballerinas of the Romantic Age, also performed it.

Later ballerinas who distinguished themselves as Giselle included Olga Preobrajenska, Anna Pavlova, Tamara Karsavina, Olga Spessivtzeva, Alicia Markova, Alicia Alonso, Margot Fonteyn, Merle Park, Carla Fracci, Galina Ulanova, Natalia Makarova, Yvette Chauvire.

The Albrechts have included Vaslav Nijinsky, Mikhail Mordkin, Anton Dolin (united with Markova as a celebrated duo in this ballet), Igor Youskevitch, André Eglevsky, Serge Lifar, Frederic Franklin, Erik Bruhn, Rodolf Nureyev, Ivan Nagy, Michael Denard, Anthony Dowell, Edward Villella, Mikhail Baryshnikov.

Glinkiana

Choreography, George Balanchine; music, Mikhail Glinka; décor, costumes and lighting, Esteban Frances. First performed by the New York City Ballet, New York, November 23, 1967. (see *Valse Fantaisie*)

Balanchine's *Glinkiana*, popularly known as "Glink" among dancers, is a plotless ballet consisting of "Polka," "Valse Fantaisie" (see separate listing), "Jota Aragonesa," "Divertimento Brillante." This engaging, lighthearted and popular ballet echoes Imperial Russia's affection in the Petipa era of ballets containing theatricalized folk and/or popular dance materials.

Heading the first cast were Violette Verdy, Paul Mejia, Mimi Paul, John Clifford, Melissa Hayden, Patricia McBride, Edward Villella.

The Gods Amused

Choreography, Eliot Feld; music, Claude Debussy (Danses Sacrées et Profanes); *costumes, Frank Thompson; lighting,*

Jennifer Tipton. First performed by Eliot Feld's American Ballet Company, Brooklyn Academy of Music, New York, April 28, 1971.

A *pas de trois* for male and two female dancers. A slight echo of Balanchine's *Apollo*.

The Gods Go A-Begging

Choreography, George Balanchine; music, George Frederick Handel, arranged by Sir Thomas Beecham; scenery, Léon Bakst; costumes, Juan Gris. First produced by Diaghilev's Ballets Russes, London, July 16, 1928. Later revived by the Ballet Russe de Monte Carlo and presented in New York, October 28, 1937. Another version, with choreography by David Lichine, was mounted for the Original Ballet Russe. In 1936 the Sadler's Wells Ballet (now the Royal Ballet) produced the work with new choreography by Ninette de Valois and scenery and costumes by Hugh Stevenson.

The Goldberg Variations

Choreography, Jerome Robbins; music, Johann Sebastian Bach; costumes, Joe Eula. First presented by the New York City Ballet, May 27, 1971. (A preview "open rehearsal" was held earlier at Saratoga Springs, New York, July 30, 1970.)

This major Robbins creation is a classical ballet in form and in step, but its movement invention carries it far beyond the academic and into the area of total dance. There is no story as such, but the choreographer responds to the music in ways that suggest incident, romance, humor, courtly elegance, and even antics. Indeed, there are sections closely rooted in preclassic dance forms (as is some of the music) and others that incorporate the mid-twentieth century's most advanced examples of dance virtuosity as if the past and the present met in total harmony. Solos, duos, and both small and large ensemble actions provide images of continuing variety during the hour-and-a-half course of a ballet that uses the Bach score uncut. (It has been performed with both harpsichord and piano accompaniments, with the choreographer stating his preference for the latter instrument with respect to his ballet.)

Patricia McBride, Helgi Tomasson, Allegra Kent, Anthony Blum, Karin von Aroldingen, Peter Martins were among the principals at the first cast.

The Golden Age

Choreography, Vasily Vainonen, Leonid Yakobson, and V. Chesnakov; music, Dmitri Shostakovitch; book, A. Ivanovsky; designs, Valentina Khodasevich; regisseur, Emanuel Kaplan. First performed by the Kirov Ballet, Leningrad, October 26, 1930.

Gorda

Choreography, Vakhtang Chabukiani; music, David Toradze; book, Vakhtang Chabukiani and O. Egadze; designs, P. Lapiashvili. First performed by Tbilisi's V. Paliashvili State Academic Theater of Opera and Ballet, December 30, 1949.

Gounod Symphony

Choreography, George Balanchine; music, Charles Gounod (Symphony No. 1); scenery, Horace Armistead; costumes, Karinska. First produced by the New York City Ballet, New York, January 8, 1958.

Graduation Ball

Choreography, David Lichine; music, Johann Strauss; scenery and costumes, Alexandre Benois. First produced by the Original Ballet Russe, Sydney, Australia, February 28, 1940. First American performance, Los Angeles, November 10, 1940. Presented by Ballet Theatre (now the American Ballet Thea-

tre), with scenery and costumes by Mstislav Doboujinsky, New York, October 8, 1944. The Royal Danish Ballet first performed the ballet, March 22, 1952. The National Ballet of Washington added it to its repertory January 26, 1973. It is also performed by the Boston Ballet, Het Nationale Ballet, and Les Grands Ballets Canadiens (as Le Bal des Cadets).

The bright and gay *Graduation Ball* is set in the formal drawing room of a fashionable girls' school. With much liveliness and mischief, the girls prepare for the arrival of the cadets from a nearby military academy for a dance and entertainment. The boys arrive in strict formation and their manners are so stiff and their bows so formal that the girls are almost frightened. One indeed sits down suddenly out of sheer alarm. Finally, however, the ice is broken and the chief cadet (with a delightful cowlick) and the chief girl start dancing. The cadet, with a wave of his hand, indicates that the experience isn't half bad and soon all are waltzing away.

Supervising the proceedings are the General, a doddering, bewhiskered old man, and the Head Mistress (usually, but not always, played by a man in travesty), who, despite her age, is flirtatious. During the course of the ballet, the two dance some amusing steps together and are even caught spooning on the balcony.

The *divertissement* includes a stunning dance for a Drummer Boy, a classical *pas de deux* of the romantic school, and a contest in *fouettés*, arabesque and *attitude* turns (and variations) for two girls. There is also an impromptu number for the girl whose pigtails just will not hang straight (they stick out from her head like antlers) and, of course, dance measures for the sweet little heroine, who has won the heart of the first Cadet.

There is a final dance involving everyone; then the cadets, now pleased with their discovery of girls, take their sorrowful leave. The scene, for a moment, is bare and then the first Cadet sneaks back for a final farewell with his girl; but the alert Head Mistress scares him off as the curtain falls.

Lichine and Tatiana Riabouchinska created the roles of the First Cadet and his Girl.

Grand Pas Classique

Choreography, Victor Gsovsky; music, François Auber. First performed by Yvette Chauviré and Vladimir Skouratoff, 1949. First presented by the Royal Ballet, March 12, 1963. First performance by American Ballet Theatre, July 11, 1972.

A display of technical fireworks for virtuoso performers. Rockets and Roman candles in ballet terms.

First danced by Yvette Chauviré and Vladimir Skouratoff. The first Royal Ballet cast was Nadia Nerina and David Blair. For the American Ballet Theatre the dancers were Cynthia Gregory and Ted Kivitt.

Grand Pas Espagnol

Choreography, Benjamin Harkarvy; music, Moritz Mozkowski (Spanish Dances, Op. 12, 1–5); costumes, Joop Stokvis. First produced, Netherlands Dance Theater, Sunderland, England, September 9, 1963. Added to the repertories of the Harkness Ballet (January 17, 1969) and City Center Joffrey Ballet (October 12, 1972).

A fast-paced applause-inviting showpiece for three male and three female dancers of high technical accomplishment. This *pas de six* is not only a cheerful excuse for displays of virtuosity but also a highly amusing commentary on those Spanish flavors that Petipa, and other choreographers of the past, delighted in mixing with classical ballet ingredients. In stance, in step, in gesture, a Russian-Spanish touch is almost always in evidence and the Hispanic dance style itself is introduced in terms of movements that have the rhythmic shifts in tempo, the fasts, the slows, the startings and stoppings usually associated with flamenco, but here presented with the elegance of courtly ballet. This popular aspect of Russo-Spanish ballet has been described by dancers themselves as "Spanish Minkus," in reference to the composer of the famed Petipa ballet *Don Quixote*.

Principal interpreters have included Elisabeth Carroll, Lone Isaksen, Marina Eglevsky, Helgi Tomasson, Lawrence Rhodes, Finis Jhung.

Grand Pas—Glazounov

Choreography, George Balanchine; music, Alexander Glazou-
nov (Raymonda); costumes, Karinska and Tom Lirgwood.
First performed by the American Ballet Theatre, New York,
January 28, 1961, staged by Frederic Franklin.

Grandstand

Choreography, Enid Lynn; music, compiled electronic score;
décor and costumes, Peter Max. First performed by the Hart-
ford Ballet Company, Hartford, Connecticut, May 19, 1972.

Graziana

Choreography, John Taras; music, Wolfgang Amadeus Mo-
zart; costumes, Nicolas de Molas. First produced by Ballet
Theatre (now the American Ballet Theatre), New York, Octo-
ber 25, 1945.

In this abstract ballet the principal roles were created by Alicia
Alonso, Nora Kaye, and André Eglevsky.

The Great American Goof

Choreography, Eugene Loring; music, Henry Brant; libretto,
William Saroyan; scenery and costumes, Boris Aronson. First
produced by Ballet Theatre (now the American Ballet The-
atre), New York, January 11, 1940.

This short-lived work, a sort of morality-play-fantasy, required
the dancers to speak as well as dance. The tenor of the work might
be summed up in the descriptions of some of the host of characters: The Great American Goof, the naïve white hope of the
human race; The Woman, the bright potential; The Dummy, tradition and the ordinary; Policeman, orderly idiocy; Women, sex;
Workers, misfits; A Student of Karl Marx, an opium addict, etc.

Loring created the title part, Miriam Golden was the Woman,
and Antony Tudor the Dummy.

The Green Table

Choreography, Kurt Jooss; music, Fritz Cohen; book, Kurt Jooss; costumes, Hein Heckroth. First performed by the Jooss Ballet, Théâtre des Champs-Élysées, Paris, July 3, 1932. Restaged and presented by the City Center Joffrey Ballet, New York, March 9, 1967.

Jooss's celebrated antiwar ballet grew out of an idea the young choreographer had for making a modern ballet to the theme of the medieval dance of death. This was in the process of being created when he was deeply affected by the development of demagoguery, of Hitlerism in its incipiency, of the threat of a devastating war. The ancient theme and the current trends came together, and in a brief period Jooss created his lifetime masterpiece in which the figure of Death was the key element as death came to young love, to grave heroes, to men sent off to war by a group of old men bargaining, threatening, and declaring decisions around a green diplomatic table. A profiteer seemed to win in the holocaust launched by the masked, bearded, balding diplomats, and even he was captured by inexorable death. Only a weary old mother sought the comfort of Death's arms.

Jooss himself danced Death for many years. Others have been Maxmilian Zamosa and Christian Holder.

The Guests

Choreography, Jerome Robbins; music, Marc Blitzstein. First produced by the New York City Ballet, New York, January 20, 1949.

Hamlet

Choreography, Robert Helpmann; music, Peter Ilyich Tchaikovsky; décor and costumes, Leslie Hurry. First produced by the Sadler's Wells Ballet (now the Royal Ballet), London, May 19, 1942. First presented in America by the same company,

New York, October 12, 1949. A Russian version, with chore-
ography by Konstantin Sergeyev, music by Nikolai Chervin-
sky, book by Nikolai Volkov, and décor by Sofia Yunovich,
was first performed by the Kirov Ballet, Leningrad, Decem-
ber 12, 1970.

Harbinger

Choreography, Eliot Feld; music, Serge Prokofiev (Piano
Concerto in G Major); *décor, Oliver Smith; costumes, Stanley*
Simmons; lighting, Jean Rosenthal. First performed by Amer-
ican Ballet Theatre, Miami, Florida, March 31, 1967, and in
New York, May 11, 1967. Feld's American Ballet Company first
presented the ballet at the Festival of Two Worlds, Spoleto,
Italy, May 27, 1969.

Feld's first ballet and a major one, for not only was it an instant
success with the public, it was also a work that caused critics to
suggest that Feld was the most impressive new choreographic
talent on the American scene since Jerome Robbins.

The ballet itself tells no story, but it is filled with incident.
Playfulness, loneliness, romance are present in episodes conceived
in dance terms, incorporating certain elements of ballet, much
modern-dance freeness of gesture, washes of jazz, and highly individual movement which, though skillfully wrought, have the
zest of improvisation.

The meaning of the title is mirrored on several occasions but
perhaps most powerfully when the entire ensemble, facing stage
right, sheds individuality for a compact oneness and lifts heads
slowly into an amber light, symbolizing the sun, perhaps, or heavenly warmth or a new day or, of course, the harbinger of hope.

The first cast was headed by Christine Sarry, Edward Verso,
Paula Tracy, Cynthia Gregory, Marcos Paredes, and Feld.

Harlequinade

Choreography, George Balanchine; music, Riccardo Drigo
(Les Millions d'Arlequin); *décor, costumes, and lighting,*

Rouben Ter-Arutunian (based on his settings for Rossini's La Cenerentola). First presented by the New York City Ballet, New York, February 4, 1965.

Harlequinade is a two-act recreation of the highlights of the *commedia dell'arte*. Harlequin and Columbine, Pierrot and Pierette, buffoons and fairies are all present in a rollicking ballet filled with antics, magic, transformations, romance, and broad comedy.

Edward Villella and Patricia McBride were the first to dance Harlequin and Columbine, with Deni Lamont and Suki Schorer as Pierrot and Pierette.

Harlequinade Pas de Deux

Choreography, Ben Stevenson; music, Riccardo Drigo; costumes, Rupert and Puhma. First danced by Christine Knoblauch and Kirk Peterson, Varna, Bulgaria, at the International Ballet Competition, July, 1972. The ballet has since joined the repertory of the National Ballet of Washington.

A virtuosic blockbuster.

The Harvest According

Choreography, Agnes de Mille; music, Virgil Thomson; scenery and costumes, Lemuel Ayres. First produced by Ballet Theatre (now the American Ballet Theatre), New York, October 1, 1952.

The ballet, an elaborate extension of the Civil War Ballet which de Mille originally created for the musical *Bloomer Girl*, is in three parts and depicts a cycle of life. The title is derived from Walt Whitman's, "Life, life is the tillage and death is the harvest according."

The first episode is concerned with birth and is a dance for women. Fear, pain, consuming agony, release, and joyous celebration are the shifting moods which herald a new life. In the second section, children play games, but in their display of young strength

and frolic the coming of maturity is omened. In the closing section, the young men have gone off to war, and the women, awaiting news of death, find themselves alone again, as they were at the
birth rite. Some of the soldiers return, and there is rejoicing, but
for others of the women there is only mourning.

De Mille, as in many of her ballets, has used ballet, modern
dance, and folk action, remarkably fused, to project her cycle of
life. The ancient circle form recurs from time to time as the dancers move into an orbit celebrating the miracle of birth, as they
rejoice in friendship, or as they play. In the birth sequence, the
principal figure moves with the total-body compulsiveness of modern dance, bending the torso, contracting muscles, sweeping toward mother earth. Yet the lightness and elegance of the ballet are
present where appropriate and the lilt of folk dance gives a universal and ageless touch to those moments of innocent joy.

Gemze de Lappe, Ruth Ann Koesun, Jenny Workman, and
Kelly Brown headed the cast at the première.

Haugtussa

*Choreography, Edith Roger and Barthold Halle; music, Ed-
vard Grieg Ludt. First performed by the Norwegian National
Ballet, 1972. (An earlier staging was given by a specially
formed group of dancers and actors for the Bergen International Festival.)*

A Norweigan folk epic in movement, poetry, music, acting, dancing. The theme, similar to the classical Greek myth of Persephone
—abduction, destruction, rebirth.

The Haunted Ballroom

*Choreography, Ninette de Valois; music and book, Geoffrey
Toye; scenery and costumes, Motley. First produced by the
Vic-Wells Ballet (later the Sadler's Wells Ballet and now the
Royal Ballet), London, April 3, 1934. First presented in Amer-*

ica by the Sadler's Wells Theatre Ballet, Buffalo, October 23, 1951.

The scene is a musty ballroom in a great mansion. The young Treginnis, son of the master of the house, has come into this un-used room followed by three ladies, guests at a party. They tease the boy and urge him to dance but he seems overcome by the mystery of the room. Suddenly his father enters and angrily orders the boy to leave and explains to his guests that this is a haunted room, the place in which his father and his grandfather have died.

In the second scene the master, compelled by some strange force, has returned late at night to the haunted room. A flute player and a ghostly crew of guests are there and the master, un-derstandably, asks what they are doing there. Their explanation he accepts and soon he is drawn into the dancing. Faster and faster he dances, urged on by beautiful women and the insistency of the music, and he knows that he cannot stand the pace. In desperation, he tries to escape, but the hour destined for his death in the haunted ballroom has come. In the final scene the body of the master is discovered and carried away by the servants as the young son, standing in the haunted ballroom, realizes that one day he too will meet such a destiny.

Robert Helpmann, Alicia Markova, and William Chappell headed the original cast.

The Heart of the Mountains

Choreography, Vakhtang Chabukiani; music, Andrei Balan-chivadze; book, G. Leonidze; designs, Simon Virsaladze. First performed by the Kirov Ballet, Leningrad, June 28, 1938.

A ballet with a social comment theme. Its plot has to do with an episode in Georgian history during which there was a revolt against oppressive taxation. Folk flavors as well as dramatic ele-ments are incorporated into the ballet.

Chabukiani, born in Georgia, and Tatiana Vecheslova danced the leads.

Helen of Troy

Choreography and book, David Lichine; music, Jacques Offenbach; scenery and costumes, Marcel Vertès. First produced by Ballet Theatre (now the American Ballet Theatre) Mexico City, September 10, 1942; fiirst American performance, Detroit, November 29, 1942. The ballet was revived by the American Ballet Theatre, December 3, 1967.

This ballet, in a prologue and three scenes, represents a comedy version of the famous tale of Helen of Troy. Helen is as beautiful and as desirable as legend demands, but Menelaus is a doddering fool, Paris is a flip youth, and the god Hermes is a mischievous teenager who munches apples, knits, and makes knowing grimaces as the drama unfolds.

In the prologue, the shepherd Paris is found gamboling with his sheep (they are, of course, pretty girls dressed as lambs). Hermes arrives from Olympus and tells the youth that Hera, Athena, and Aphrodite each claims to be the fairest. Paris is to make the choice. Since Aphrodite, as goddess of love, offers him the most beautiful of women as his reward for choosing her, he naturally finds her the most beautiful.

Scene One brings us to the court of Menelaus. Paris has arrived and discovered that Helen, wife of the old king, is the girl promised to him. During a series of dances and *divertissements*, Helen displays her beauty and her interest in Paris and he, naturally, reciprocates. Hermes assists by distracting the attention of the jealous old king. Eventually, Menelaus is called off to war and Hermes sees to it that Paris is given a duplicate key to Helen's bedroom.

The second scene plays like a French bedroom farce. Helen, dressed in diaphanous garb, is preparing for Paris but another lover, who also has obtained a key, confronts her. Hermes gets rid of him quickly and Paris enters. Their increasingly passionate love scene is interrupted by the arrival of the old king, but Helen manages to escape detection by donning the skin of one of Paris's devoted lambs, leaving the poor little thing shivering without its coat. Now there is a violent chase involving the king, Paris, Helen, the shorn lamb, and others and Hermes blows a blast on a policeman's whistle and assumes traffic control of the bedroom situation as the curtain falls.

In the final scene Paris and Helen set sail for Troy amid festivities, leaving poor Menelaus sorrowing on the shore.

Irina Baronova created the role of Helen, and other principals in the first peformance included André Eglevsky (Paris), Jerome Robbins (Hermes), and Simon Semenoff (Menelaus).

Las Hermanas

Choreography, Kenneth MacMillan; music, Frank Martin (Concerto for Harpsichord and Small Orchestra); libretto, Kenneth MacMillan, after Federico García Lorca's The House of Bernarda Alba; *décor and costumes, Nicholas Georgiadis. First performed by the Stuttgart Ballet, Stuttgart, Germany, July 13, 1963. First British performance by the Western Theatre Ballet, Cardiff, England, June 22, 1966. First performed by American Ballet Theatre, New York, November 29, 1967.*

Las Hermanas is MacMillan's melodramatic treatment in ballet form of Lorca's *The House of Bernarda Alba*, the story of a terrifying matriarch, her unmarried daughters, and a sensual suitor who selects for his sexual attentions the daughter (the youngest) not intended for him.

Hip and Straight

Choreography, Fernand Nault; music, Paul Duplessis; costumes, Nicole Martinet. First presented by Les Grands Ballets Canadiens, October 16, 1970.

Classical ballet pitted against jazz dancing.

L'Histoire du Soldat

Choreography, Eliot Feld; music, Igor Stravinsky; costumes, Frank Thompson; lighting, Jennifer Tipton. First performed in this version by the American Ballet Theatre, December 28, 1971.

This is a narrative-ballet not easy to place in a category. Its staging possibilities range from purely musical with a narrator through pantomimic conceptions to elaborate ballets. Often it is more drama than dance.

Briefly, it tells the story of an illiterate soldier and his cheap but beloved violin; the soldier is returning to his village after a war and meets up with the Devil in disguise who insists on trading a valuable book for the violin. Adventures follow, some sad and some pleasurable, as the magic book brings him wealth, success, and the love of a princess. The Devil, in varying disguises, keeps returning, and at the end of the work finally claims the soldier as his eternal servant.

The first production was given in Lausanne, Switzerland, September 28, 1918, choreographed by Ludmilla Pitoev. Other choreographers have been numerous, including Anna Sokolow. Eliot Feld danced the title role in the American Ballet Theatre version.

Homage au Ballet

Choreography, Frederic Franklin; music, Charles Gounod; costumes, Diane Butler. First performed by the National Ballet of Washington, Lyric Theatre, Baltimore, December, 1962.

Homage to the Queen

Choreography, Frederick Ashton; music, Malcolm Arnold; scenery and costumes, Oliver Messel. First produced by the Sadler's Wells Ballet (now the Royal Ballet), London, June 2,

1953. First presented in America by the same company, New York, September 18, 1953.

This lavish ballet was created in honor of the Coronation of England's Queen Elizabeth II. It was given its world première in the English capital on Coronation Day.

A huge company of dancers, headed by four ballerinas and six leading male dancers, was used by the choreographer in his poeticized tribute to the new monarch.

In the opening processional the Queen of the Earth, the Queen of the Waters, the Queen of Fire, and the Queen of the Air with their consorts and retinues make their appearances. Then each queen and her attendants have an episode in which the particular qualities of the element represented are projected in movement terms. Particularly memorable are the swift and swirling motions of the Spirit of Fire, the lovely intricacies of the group in the water section and, of course, the bright and wonderfully free actions in the *pas de deux* for the Queen of the Air and her consort.

The ballet ends with an apotheosis in which the queens and their entourages pay homage to the elevated figure of Queen Elizabeth I, who fades from view as a young queen, in her robes of state mounts the staircase to replace her illustrious predecessor as Elizabeth II.

Margot Fonteyn, Violetta Elvin, Nadia Nerina, and Rowena Jackson were the Queens and the six featured male artists were Michael Somes, Alexis Rassine, John Hart, John Field (the four Consorts), Alexander Grant (the Spirit of Fire), and Brian Shaw (featured in the water episode).

The Hump-Backed Horse

Choreography, Arthur Saint-Léon; music, Cesare Pugni. First produced, Russian Imperial Ballet, St. Petersburg, December 5 (Julian or Russian calendar) or December 15 (Gregorian or Western calendar), 1864. The recent Bolshoi version was choreographed by Alexander Radunsky and music by Rodion Shchedrin. The book, based on a tale by Pyotr Yershov, is by

Vasily Vainonen and Pavel Maliarevsky, and the designs by Boris Volkov. It was first performed by the Bolshoi Ballet, March 4, 1960.

This, the first classical ballet on a Russian theme, the fairy story tells of a farmer's son who saves the life of a mare who has trampled the farmer's crops. For saving her life, the mare rewards the youth with three horses, one a hunchbacked horse with magical powers who can grant wishes. Through the horse beautiful girls appear, a ring is recovered from the bottom of the ocean, and the gift of youth is granted. After several complicated plot developments, a villainous khan is destroyed and the hero and heroine are united forever.

The ballet has remained a favorite in the Soviet Union. A feature film has been made of it starring Maya Plisetskaya as the maiden desired by khan and commoner.

The Hundred Kisses

(Les Cent Baisers)

> *Choreography, Bronislava Nijinska; music, Frédéric d'Erlanger; libretto, Boris Kochno, based on a story by Hans Christian Andersen; scenery and costumes, Jean Hugo. First produced by the Ballet Russe de Monte Carlo, London, July 18, 1935. First presented in America by the same company, New York, October 18, 1935.*

Icare

> *Choreography and libretto, Serge Lifar; music, percussion arranged by J. E. Szyfer; scenery and costumes, Eugene Berman. First produced by the Paris Opera Ballet, Paris, July 9, 1935.*

This represents an early attempt to separate choreography from the formal demands of instrumental and orchestral music (mod-

ern dance had worked with percussion but not the ballet). The story is based upon the Greek myth of Daedalus and Icarus.
    Lifar created the title part.

Icarus

Choreography, Lucas Hoving; music, Chin-Ichi Matsuhita. First performed by Lucas Hoving and Company, New York, April 5, 1964. The Pennsylvania Ballet first presented the ballet, November 19, 1971.

This modern dance work, as its title suggests, was inspired by the Greek myth of Icarus who flew too close to the sun, which melted the wax holding his wings in place and causing him to hurtle to his death. This is not a literal telling of the tale, but rather an evocation of the peril of curiosity and adventure. The sun is represented by a woman resplendently dressed.
    The choreographer created the title role.

The Ice Maiden

Choreography and book, Fedor Lopukhov; music, Edvard Grieg (arranged by Boris Asafiev); designs, Alexander Golovin. First performed by the Kirov Ballet, Leningrad, April 27, 1927.

Idylle

Choreography, George Skibine; music, François Serrette; libretto, décor, and costumes, Alwyne Camble. First presented by the Grand Ballet du Marquis de Cuevas, Paris, December, 1953. The first American performance was by the Harkness Ballet, New York, 1965. The Ruth Page Ballet also performed the work. Marjorie Tallchief was featured in all three productions.

Igrouchka *or* Igrouchki

(Russian Dolls)

Choreography and libretto, Michel Fokine; music, Rimsky-Korsakoff; scenery and costumes, Nathalie Gontcharova. First produced in 1921. Added to the repertory of the Ballet Russe de Monte Carlo, New York, October 31, 1939.

This is a Russian folk ballet in which the characters move with the stiffness of wooden dolls. In it, a goose-girl spurns the wooing of a peasant boy. He tries to drown himself, she saves him and, with the rescue, falls in love with him.

Alexandra Danilova starred in the Ballet Russe de Monte Carlo production.

Illuminations

Choreography, Frederick Ashton; music, Benjamin Britten; poems (set by Britten), Arthur Rimbaud; scenery and costumes, Cecil Beaton. First produced by the New York City Ballet, New York, March 2, 1950.

The ballet, in one act and divided into a series of "danced pictures," is based upon episodes in the short and violent life of the French poet Rimbaud and upon images evoked by his poetic work, *Les Illuminations.*

The ballet opens upon a scene in which figures dressed something like traveling players of the *commedia dell'arte* period are standing or lying motionless. The Poet, in black-and-white-striped tights, a formal jacket and high collar, rises and stirs himself to intense action, turning, reaching, crashing to the floor. He attempts to rouse the limp bodies to share in the vitality, in the dreams that he experiences.

Next, he attempts to become a part of the life in which he has been born. Jauntily, he places a hat on his head, but he is no match for the whirling, dapper, pasty-faced Dandy who flashes onto the scene and he finds nothing in common with the pedestrian actions of the others who people the scene.

Alone, he proclaims, "I have hung golden chains from star to
star . . . and I dance." Stardust descends upon him and he savors
it sensually with his tongue, rubs it against his face and body.

Now two women enter his dreams. One, dressed all in white,
is the figure of Sacred Love. The other, with loose hair and dress,
one foot shod and the other bare, is the wanton, Profane Love.
He dances with both but it is Profane Love who, for the moment,
wins his passionate attention. She locks herself about him, loin to
loin, and the two move from one erotic embrace to another.

With the entrance of a procession heralding the crowning of
a king and queen, the Poet is faced with order, with a set aristoc-
racy. He watches the coronation and then, propelling himself over
the backs of the processionists, attacks the royal couple, and
crowns himself as the figures flee. The anarchy he sought now
reigns but it is empty for him. Profane Love returns but she is
now repulsive to him. She clutches his shoulders, hips, knees as he
walks away dragging her behind him. Her determination to renew
their passion is thwarted when he slaps her in dismissal.

Lying on stage, close to the footlights, with his stolen crown
upon his chest, the Poet dreams of Beauty, the Sacred Love he
once neglected. She is borne in by four handsome youths through
designs of gentle loveliness. Cool, perhaps unattainable, she moves
through turns and arabesques from boy to boy and finally, carried
aloft like a goddess, she is swept swiftly out of view.

The Poet throws away his crown, the figures which inhabited
the first scene return, and retribution begins. He is attacked by
the people, turned upside down, hurled to the ground, stripped of
half his clothes, and spat upon by Profane Love. She makes a
signal and a policeman shoots the Poet in the wrist. As the blood
spreads slowly along his arm, the Poet, holding the wound with
his other hand, removes himself bodily and mentally from the
scene of his punishment. He steps over the fallen figure of Profane Love, who has asked for forgiveness, and slowly, almost ab-
stractedly, walks through a doorway to a luminous setting where
the figure of Sacred Love has been soaring, supported by one of
her beautiful cavaliers. The people fall back into poses of inac-

tivity as the Poet, moving into a golden sunlight, pursues, perhaps hopelessly, the elusive figure of Beauty.

The ballet, employing classical ballet actions, pantomime of an emotional (rather than a stock) nature, and free dance actions, was the first production by a foreign choreographer to be commissioned by the New York City Ballet.

At the première Nicholas Magallanes danced the Poet; Tanaquil LeClercq, Sacred Love; Melissa Hayden, Profane Love; and Robert Barnett, the Dandy. The soprano soloist on this occasion was Angelene Collins. Other dancers in the New York City Ballet to dance the Poet have been John Prinz, Robert Maiorano, and Jean-Pierre Frohlich. Mimi Paul and Carol Sumner have appeared as Sacred Love, and Karin Von Aroldingen and Sara Leland have danced Profane Love.

The Illusory Fiancé

Choreography, Boris Fenster; music, Mikhail Chulaki; book, Boris Fenster and M. Kolomoitsev, based on Carlo Goldoni's comedy The Servant of Two Masters; *designs, Tatiana Bruni. First performed at the Maly Theater, Leningrad, March 22, 1946.*

In All Eternity

Choreography, Kari Blakstad; music, Antonio Vivaldi. First performed by the Norwegian National Ballet, Oslo, 1972. First performed by the same company in Brooklyn, New York, on their first American tour, March 2, 1974.

The ballet was inspired by the famous statues by Gustav Vigeland in Oslo's Sculpture Park. The four sections are concerned with the progression from childhood through youth and maturity to old age and, like the monumental sculptures, suggest through the movement flow the continuity of man.

Incubus

Choreography, Gerald Arpino; music, Anton Webern (Six Pieces for Orchestra, Op. 6); costumes, Lewis Brown. First performed by the Robert Joffrey Ballet (now the City Center Joffrey Ballet), New York, at the Fashion Institute of Technology, September 28, 1962.

Incubus is a macabre and poignant exploration of the soul of an innocent girl. A rag doll is her almost constant companion during nightmarish adventures, part real and part dream, in which she matures, fighting off bigots, attractive acrobats, lechers, and perhaps even security.

Lisa Bradley created the principal role.

Intermezzo

Choreography, Eliot Feld; music, Johanes Brahms; costumes, Stanley Simmons. First performed by the American Ballet Company, Spoleto, Italy, May 29, 1969. The City Center Joffrey Ballet first presented the ballet October 23, 1969. First presented by American Ballet Theatre, New York, July 12, 1972.

Intermezzo, a movement visualization of the sounds, phrasings, and timbres of the music, somewhat of the genre of Robbins' *Dances at a Gathering* or Balanchine's *Liebeslieder Walzer*. Characterized by a variety of highly original patterns including a series of recurring lifts as if the ladies of the ballet were sitting in air.

The first cast was Christine Sarry, Elizabeth Lee, Christina Stirling, David Coll, John Sowinski, and Alfonso Figueroa.

Interplay

Choreography, Jerome Robbins; music, Morton Gould. First presented in Billy Rose's production Concert Varieties, *New York, June 1, 1945. Added to the repertory of Ballet Theatre*

*(now the American Ballet Theatre), New York, October 17,
1945, with setting by Oliver Smith and costumes by Irene
Sharaff. Added to the repertory of the New York City Ballet,
New York, December 23, 1952. Interplay was revived by the
City Center Joffrey Ballet, and given its first performance,
October 6, 1972.*

Interplay is unmistakably an American ballet, for although it has
no folksy Americana ingredients, its pace, its flashes of jitterbug-
ging, its lusty humor, and its idioms of playful action stamp it as
American.

The first movement is "Free Play." A boy enters and dances
with great speed and exuberance. He is followed by three other
lads who join him in frolic, neither a game nor a contest, but simple
enthusiasm for the act of moving. A girl arrives and things perk
up even more when three others come on, making even partners.
They play together, move down to the orchestra pit to look at the
musicians, and respond to the calls of the music with some spurts
of jive. After some brisk and athletic antics, the episode ends, as
the four boys roll the four girls over their backs and sit on the floor
with the girls standing behind them.

The second movement is "Horseplay" and features a boy who
bounds about through difficult air turns and spins, making passing
fun at some of the balances, some of the gestures to be seen in
classical ballet. He pays formal court to the girls, gets confused
and bows to one of the boys, shrugs it off, watches one of the
lassies shake her hips, wriggles his own, and ends his solo excur-
sion with a flourish.

The third movement, "Byplay," features a *pas de deux* for a
boy and girl. To blues music, they move affectionately, easily,
pleasurably, but there is no intense romanticism here. There are
high lifts and little runs in which the girl is propelled by her partner from a crouch to an upright position, moving on *pointes* along
a diagonal line. At the close he lifts her high, she slides over his
shoulders, down his body, and the two settle, hand in hand, in a
sitting position. The others have been watching but now the music
rouses them to join in some further group fun for the finale.

The finale, "Team Play," is based on a contest. Two of the young men are the leaders and pick their crews. After a preliminary football-style huddle, they launch forth into competitive *entrechats,* multiple air turns (for the men), kicks and turns on *pointe* (for the girls), and other follow-the-leader tests. At the close of the ballet, the four girls dash to the footlights followed by the boys, who slide, bellywhoppers, between the girls' legs and grin at the audience as the curtain falls.

In the Billy Rose revue, John Kriza, Janet Reed, and Robbins headed the cast. At the Ballet Theatre première Kriza, Reed, and Harold Lang were the principals. In the revised treatment prepared by Robbins for the New York City Ballet, Janet Reed, Todd Bolender, Michael Maule, and Jacques d'Amboise had the leading roles.

In the Night

Choreography, Jerome Robbins; music, Frédéric Chopin; costumes, Joe Eula. First performed by the New York City Ballet, January 29, 1970.

A softly romantic companion piece to Robbins' *Dances at a Gathering.* The choreographer's intent is to make the audience not only hear and listen to a nocturne but "to see" a nocturne in terms of dance movements that give body shapes to the melodic lines, rhythms, textures, even "breath" of the music. Human relationships are indicated by three couples, each with its own duo-episode but concluding the ballet *en ensemble,* revealing moods that are shy or eager, reflective or rhapsodic. The lighting (by Thomas Skelton) with its shafts, softnesses, brightnesses, mottling of moonlight, are interwoven with the choreographing plan.

The first cast was composed of Violette Verdy, Peter Martins, Kay Mazzo, Anthony Blum, Patricia McBride, Francisco Moncion. (Gordon Boelzner, pianist.)

The Invitation

Choreography, Kenneth MacMillan; music, Matyas Seiber; scenery, Nicholas Georgiadis. First performed by the Royal Ballet, Oxford, England, October 11, 1960. First performance in America by the same company, May 10, 1963.

Mixed and unhappy relationships at a house party. A widow and a young man, a young girl and a married man, an unhappy married couple find that their lives cross only briefly but scars remain. The boy and the girl lose their innocence—more importantly, in spirit rather than in body.

Lynn Seymour, Christopher Gable, Desmond Doyle, and Anne Heaton headed the cast.

Irish Fantasy

Choreography, Jacques d'Amboise; music, Camille Saint-Saëns; décor and lighting, David Hays; costumes, Karinska. First performed by the New York City Ballet, Los Angeles, August 12, 1964. First New York performance, by the same company, October 8, 1964.

Ivan the Terrible

Choreography, Yuri Grigorovitch; music, Serge Prokofiev (ex-cerpts Third Symphony, Russian Overture, *Sergei Eisenstein's motion picture of the same name, arranged by Mikhail Chu-laki); scenery and costumes, Simon Virsaladze. First per-formance, Bolshoi Ballet, Moscow, February 16, 1975.*

A full-length, major dramatic creation by the Bolshoi Ballet's artistic director and principal choreographer. The ballet, almost seven years in the making, for intensive research and planning, is based upon key episodes in the life of the notorious sixteenth-century czar.

The first cast included Natalia Bessmertnovna as Queen Anastasia, Yuri Vladmirov as Ivan, and Boris Akimov as Prince Kurbsky.

Ivesiana

Choreography, George Balanchine; music, Charles Ives. First produced by the New York City Ballet, New York, September 14, 1954. Het Nationale Ballet of Holland presented Ivesiana, *June 25, 1968.*

For the great twentieth-century classicist Balanchine, *Ivesiana* is an almost violent departure from his customary form of creativity (*Opus 34* also represents a startling departure from the Balanchine norm). Taking the exceptionally difficult and strange music of Charles Ives, the unorthodox New England composer, the choreographer set out to let the unrelated compositions evoke their own images in his mind. Sometimes he works with the music; again almost against it. On occasion, he moves with its beats and phrases, and once in a while he responds mainly to its moods.

The ballet, in six episodes, has had its second movement changed three times. First, it was "Hallowe'en"; next "Arguments"; then "Barn Dance."

The first movement, "Central Park in the Dark," presents a large ensemble and two principals, a boy and a girl. The actions of the members of the corps are murky, almost aimless, sometimes frightening in their hint of evil. The girl and the boy experience a sharp romance in the midst of these unfeeling figures.

In "Barn Dance" (the third version of the second episode), the movement is light, folk-flavored, and the *pas de deux* is straightforward, classical, good-natured. The music, however, is so complex that two conductors are required to lead the orchestra.

The third and most provocative section of the ballet is "The Unanswered Question." The girl, who seems to be the image of an unattainable goddess or vision, never once touches the earth. She is carried by four men, who hold her high above them, move her like a living ribbon around their waists as they stand in a tight circle and continuously keep her out of reach of a fifth man, who struggles vainly to touch her. The movement invention in this episode is unbelievably rich, unlike anything seen before in ballet and constantly surprising, not only because of the originality of the movements but also because of the intensity of mood they evoke.

"Over the Pavements," the fourth episode, is for a girl and a boy and a quartet of men, who dance lightly as if engaged in some not very important game. The fifth section, "In the Inn," is a jazzy duet, filled with humor and touches of hijinks. The concluding episode, "In the Night," brings the huge ensemble on stage, walking on the knees, aimlessly, despairingly perhaps, as if there were no goal, no point, no future.

At the first performance, Janet Reed and Francisco Moncion were the principals in the first episode; Patricia Wilde and Jacques d'Amboise in the second (also the featured pair in "Barn Dance"); Allegra Kent and Todd Bolender in the third; Diana Adams and Herbert Bliss in the fourth; Tanaquil LeClercq and Bolender in the fifth. LeClercq later danced the role of the Girl in "The Unanswered Question."

Jardin aux Lilas

(Lilac Garden)

Choreography, Antony Tudor; music, Ernest Chausson (Poème); scenery and costumes, Hugh Stevenson. First produced by the Ballet Rambert, London, January 26, 1936. First presented in America by Ballet Theatre (now the America Ballet Theatre), New York, January 15, 1940. Added to the repertory of the New York City Ballet, with setting by Horace Armistead and costumes by Karinska, New York, November 30, 1951. The National Ballet of Canada added Lilac Garden to its repertory in its 1953–54 season, the Norwegian National Ballet in 1961. The Pennsylvania Ballet first performed the work April 11, 1967, the Royal Ballet, November 12, 1968, and the Royal Danish Ballet, December 9, 1970.

Jardin aux Lilas, one of Tudor's most popular works and considered to be one of the master pieces of contemporary ballet, is a Victorian tragedy. But it does not derive its power from melodramatic force or from heroics; rather does it find its theatrical strength in the relating of personal passion to social propriety. Beneath the good breeding of those gathered together for a Victorian party in a lilac garden we see the violent love and desperation. Passions almost break through the decorum but never quite disturb the pattern of standard behavior. We, the onlookers, know the harrowing secrets of the four principals, secrets hidden from (or ignored by) the guests and our sympathy and concern are heightened by this private knowledge.

Caroline, the heroine, is to marry a man she does not love. At this prewedding party, she meets again with her former lover and, during the course of the evening, they steal brief and tempestuous moments for their final farewells. The trysts are so fleeting that there is hardly time for more than a brush of hands, a swift embrace, last anguished appeals. The guests move on and off, and the lovers pull themselves away from each other, pretend interest in others, or run off. Two girls know of Caroline's tragedy and when they find her near the breaking point, come to her aid with sympathy and understanding.

Caroline's fiancé must also endure prewedding sorrows and difficulties, for his former mistress is present at the party in a last, desperate attempt to win him back. Their meetings are equally short and clandestine, but here anger is combined with passion. The bridegroom-to-be, though still attracted to the woman, strives to discourage her advances and pleas but her fury (a cold fury it is) matches her love and she seems determined to keep him.

The exits and entrances in *Jardin aux Lilas* are brilliantly dramatized, for they mirror surprise, fear, and emotional urgency. There are too many of them to itemize here, just as their related scenes are too numerous to describe. We witness, among many images, Caroline dancing alone, her hand pressed against her forehead in an agony of doubt, her legs kicking out into space as if she does not know in which direction to turn. Or we see her in a violent spin, almost self-destructive, which is suddenly arrested as her lover steps out and clasps her in his arms.

There is the mistress racing toward the fiancé, lunging at him, and flying up to his shoulder. There is a scene in which Caroline and her fiancé dance together, as the mistress and Caroline's lover dance with each other; over-the-shoulder glances, wordless messages, and gestures of love seen only by the two separated lovers reveal passion clothed in propriety.

At one point the music soars to a pitch of ravishing, haunting loveliness and all the guests at the party freeze in a tableau. In this picture—for Caroline has arrested time in her own mind—only Caroline moves. Her body shudders and sways, her hand stretches forth, and she comes close to fainting. Near the end of the ballet she gestures a farewell to each of her guests, but as she turns to her lover, she hesitates, her body leans forward, and it would seem that she is about to make the desperate break. But her fiancé gently pulls back the extended hand and leads her off. The party ends and the lover stands alone in the lilac garden.

At the first London performance Maude Lloyd, Hugh Laing, Peggy van Praagh, and Tudor danced the leads. At the Ballet Theater première Viola Essen, Laing, Karen Conrad, and Tudor were the principals. Later, Nora Kaye assumed the role of Caroline in almost all of the Ballet Theatre presentations. Carla Fracci and Cynthia Gregory are among later Carolines.

Jazz Calendar

Choreography, Frederick Ashton; music, Richard Rodney Bennett; décor and costumes, Derek Jarman. First presented by the Royal Ballet, London, January 9, 1968.

Ashton in a jazzy and jaunty mood as he takes the old verse "Monday's child is fair of face/ Tuesday's child is full of grace . . ." as the springboard for seven days of contrasting adventures, including an irreverent, sex-frolicking twist to "Friday's child is loving and giving" and an uproarious view of a ballet class for "Saturday's child works hard for a living."

The first Royal Ballet cast included Vergie Derman, Merle Park, Anthony Dowell, Robert Mead, Vyvyan Lorrayne, Alexander Grant, Antoinette Sibley, Desmond Doyle, Michael Coleman, and Marilyn Trounson.

Le Jazz Hot

Choreography, Ruthanna Boris; music, Paul Keuter; first presented by the Royal Winnipeg Ballet, Winnipeg, January 5, 1956.

Jeu de Cartes

(Also *Card Party, Card Game,* and *Poker Game*)

Choreography, George Balanchine; music and book, Igor Stravinsky; associate on the book, M. Malaieff; scenery and costumes, Irene Sharaff. First produced by the American Ballet, New York, April 27, 1937. Revived by the Ballet Russe de Monte Carlo (as Poker Game*), New York, October 14, 1940. Revived by the New York City Ballet, New York, February 15, 1951. A European production was staged in 1945, with choreography by Janine Charrat, by the Ballets des Champs-Élysées. Another version, with choreography by John Cranko, with designs by Dorothée Zippel, was first performed by the Stuttgart Ballet, Stuttgart, January 22, 1965. This version was first danced by the Royal Ballet, London, February 18, 1966. The Norwegian National Ballet added the work to its repertory in 1973, and the National Ballet of Washington presented it for the first time, January 11, 1974, at the Kennedy Center Opera House, Washington, D.C. The Royal Danish Ballet first presented the work October 23, 1966.*

The Balanchine ballet is divided into three "Deals," each in turn subdivided into "Hands." The dancers, costumed like a pack of playing cards, introduce each Deal with a march. They carry placards that, when exposed to the audience, define suit and number. The dance patterns culminate in specific poker hands, with the Joker causing some amusing last-minute upsets, and the winners are established. At the close of the ballet, the dancers fall into a large heap, ready for a new shuffle.

In addition to projecting the elements, suspense, and humors of a game of poker in dance terms, the choreographer has touched his figures with certain pertinent characteristics. The Joker is, of course, an unpredictable, somewhat insolent clown; the Kings, Queens, and Jacks are regal, with the Queen of Hearts being especially charming and winsome, and the Aces, dressed a bit like knights, suggest in their actions that they are all-powerful. The ironic twist in this ballet is that the high-ranking cards are not necessarily invincible. The right arrangement of supposedly inferior cards and the shenanigans of the Joker can (and do) tumble the royal ones.

At the première William Dollar headed the cast as the Joker. The Ballet Russe de Monte Carlo revival included such luminaries as Frederic Franklin (Joker), Alexandra Danilova, Nathalie Krassovska, Alicia Markova, André Eglevsky, and Igor Youskevitch. In the New York City Ballet's revival, Todd Bolender was the Joker and Janet Reed, the Queen of Hearts. In the Charrat version, Jean Babilée was the Joker. In the National Ballet of Washington production, Kirk Peterson danced the Joker. The most popular version internationally is Cranko's. It follows the basic form and continuity required by the score, but the choreography is totally different and the role of the Joker demands not only great comic skills by the performer but also a very high degree of technical prowess.

Le Jeune Homme et la Mort

(The Young Man and Death)

> *Choreography, Roland Petit; music, Johann Sebastian Bach (Passacaglia and Fugue in C Minor); book, Jean Cocteau; scenery and costumes, Georges Wakhevitch. First produced by the Ballets des Champs-Élysées, Paris, June 25, 1946. First presented in America by Ballet Theatre (now the American Ballet Theatre), New York, April 9, 1951.*

A ballet, set in a Paris attic, of violent desire, sadism, and suicide. The girl that the tempestuous youth desires is, in reality (or is it fantasy?), Death herself.

The ballet was originally rehearsed to a jazz score, but on opening night the Bach *Passacaglia and Fugue* was substituted.

This was a planned tactic on the part of the ballet's creators (the dancers did not know about it), and the result was a magnificent irony—a sordid and violent tale unfolding to the noble music of Bach, a cheap mortal love unable to attain the majestic level suggested by the music.

Jeux

(Games)

> *Choreography, Vaslav Nijinsky; music, Claude Debussy; scenery and costumes, Léon Bakst. First presented by the Diaghilev Ballets Russes, Paris, May 15, 1913. Presented in America with new choreography by William Dollar and scenery and costumes by David Ffolkes by Ballet Theatre (now the American Ballet Theatre), New York, April 23, 1950. The New York City Ballet first performed its production of* Jeux *with choreography by John Taras and décor and costumes by Raoul Pène du Bois, New York, April 28, 1966. Flemming Flindt choreographed a version for the Paris Opera Ballet, which gave its first performance in Paris, April 12, 1973.*

This ballet for a cast of three, a boy and two girls, is a dance of dalliance. A tennis ball bounds onto the stage, followed by the male tennis player. He searches for it in vain but another game appears possible as two girls enter. He dances this game of love with first one, then the other, and finally with both. He cannot decide whom he prefers. Another tennis ball bounces on, he goes to catch it, and decides to return to the game of tennis.

Nijinsky, Tamara Karsavina, and Ludmilla Shollar danced the Nijinsky choreography.

Jewels

> *Choreography, George Balanchine; music, "Emeralds": Gabriel Fauré* (Pélléas et Mélisande, Shylock); *"Rubies": Igor Stravinsky* (Capriccio for Piano and Orchestra); *"Diamonds":*

Peter Ilyich Tchaikovsky (Symphony No. 3 in D Major); *décor, Peter Harvey; costumes, Karinska. First performed by the New York City Ballet, New York, April 13, 1967.*

In *Jewels,* Balanchine has created history's first full-length three-act abstract ballet. The idea of a ballet based on gems was suggested to the choreographer by Claude Arpels of Van Cleef Arpels, jewelers. The first movement, "Emeralds," is cool as the precious stone itself, very elegant in step, almost French in its chic. The second, "Rubies," is hot and flashy, and here one finds classical ballet dissolving into a cakewalk strut, a jogging sequence, a touch of the frug, and other exuberant activities. The third, "Diamonds," glitters and shines in the manner of the Russian Imperial Ballet of the age of Petipa. A major work representing both the craft and the genius of a veteran choreographer.

The first cast was headed by Violette Verdy and Conrad Ludlow ("Emeralds"), Patricia McBride and Edward Villella ("Rubies"), Suzanne Farrell and Jacques d'Amboise ("Diamonds").

Jinx

Choreographer, Lew Christensen; music, Benjamin Britten (Variations on a Theme by Frank Bridge); *scenery, James Stewart Morcom; costumes, Felipe Fiocca. First produced by the Dance Players, New York, April 24, 1942. Restaged by the New York City Ballet, New York, November 24, 1949. It is also in the repertory of the San Francisco Ballet.*

Jinx is the story of superstition in the world of show business. Due to a series of minor accidents at which a clown is present, the other circus performers decide the clown is a jinx. Suddenly they fear him and, in their minds, invest him with an evil he does not possess.

Janet Reed (the Girl), Conrad Linden (the Boy), and Christensen (Jinx) headed the Dance Players cast. Reed, Herbert Bliss, and Francisco Moncion were the chief dancers in the New York City Ballet presentation.

Job

Choreography, Ninette de Valois; music, Ralph Vaughan Williams; scenery and costumes, Gwendolen Raverat. First produced by the Camargo Society, London, July 5, 1931. Revived by the Sadler's Wells Ballet (now the Royal Ballet) with scenery and costumes by John Piper, May 20, 1948. First presented in America by the Sadler's Wells Ballet, New York, November 2, 1949.

This masque for dancing is based upon William Blake's *Illustrations to the Book of Job.* The ballet, in eight scenes, depicts the temptation of Job by Satan.

Anton Dolin danced Satan at the première. Robert Helpmann danced the role in America.

Joseph the Beautiful

Choreography and book, Kasian Goleizovsky (based on the Biblical subject); music, Sergei Vasilenko; designs, B. Erdman. First presented by the Experimental Theater, Moscow, March 3, 1925.

Judgment of Paris

Choreography, Antony Tudor; music, Kurt Weill; costumes, Hugh Laing. First produced by the Ballet Rambert, London, June 15, 1938. First presented in America, with scenery and costumes by Lucinda Ballard, by Ballet Theatre (now the American Ballet Theatre), New York, January 20, 1940.

A satirical treatment of the ancient myth in which the shepherd Paris is to decide which of three goddesses is the most beautiful: Juno, Minerva, or Venus In this version the scene is a cheap café, Paris is a patron slowly drinking himself into a stupor, and the three goddesses are aging entertainers who are almost too tired to perform. Each tries to stir his interest with a dance. One by one they quit their card game and do a number for the guest.

One of the "goddesses" performs with a fan, trying to use it suggestively. Another dances with two hoops, and the third makes do with a ratty feather boa. Obviously their feet hurt, they are bored, the smiles are frozen, the anguish of doing a split is not worth the effort. At the end the patron is too drunk to select anyone and as he slouches down on his table, the three girls and the waiter rush to pick his pockets.

Agnes de Mille, Charlotte Bidmead, Therese Langfield, Hugh Laing, and Tudor were the dancers in the first performance. For the American production de Mille, Viola Essen, Lucia Chase, Tudor, and Laing constituted the cast.

Jungle

Choreography, Rudi van Dantzig; music, Henk Badings; décor and costumes, Toer van Schayk. First performed by the National Ballet of Washington, Kennedy Center Opera House, Washington, D.C., April 21, 1972.

Kermessen i Brügge eller De tre Gaver

(The Kermesse in Bruges, or The Three Gifts)

Choreography, August Bournonville; music, H. S. Paulli; scenography, Jacques Noël. First performed by the Royal Danish Ballet, April 4, 1851. The current Royal Danish Ballet production was mounted by Hans Brenaa and Flemming Flindt, and was performed for the first time, October 23, 1966.

Kettentanz

Choreography, Gerald Arpino; music, Johann Strauss, Sr., and Johann Mayer; costumes, Joe Eula; lighting, Thomas Skelton. First performed by the City Center Joffrey Ballet, October 20, 1971.

"*Kettentanz*" means, in German, "chain dance," and the storyless Arpino ballet, which opens and closes with a chain of dancers prancing softly across the stage, is actually a chain of dances including galops, a waltz, a polka, and the like. It is brisk, youthful, and in its course of solos, duos, trios, and ensemble numbers provides its dancers with a vast array of opportunities to display physical prowess in leaps and turns, high lifts, and daring catches.

Konservatoriet

Choreography, August Bournonville; music, Paulli. First produced as a two-act work by the Royal Danish Ballet, 1849. Revived in one-act form (without plot) at a later date and first presented in America by the Royal Danish Ballet, New York, September 29, 1956. The ballet was staged for the City Center Joffrey Ballet by Hans Brenaa, and first performed by that company, New York, September 29, 1969. Added to the repertory of the Royal Swedish Ballet, 1973.

Konservatoriet (The Conservatory) in its present staging does away with the original story line but retains intact that portion of the ballet consisting of a ballet lesson in a French dancing academy or conservatory.

The ballet represents Bournonville's tribute to his own master, Auguste Vestris, the greatest male dancer of his era, and recreates the steps and style of French ballet of a century and a half ago.

Although *Konservatoriet* is fundamentally a reproduction of a ballet class, it is shrewdly choreographed for theatrical effect. Not only does it possess humor and charm but it builds from simple steps and basic ballet positions to the most advanced actions known to the dancers of Vestris' day, and these include many steps which, by contemporary standards, remain difficult and exciting.

Labyrinth

Labyrinth, Leonide Massine; music, Franz Schubert (Symphony No. 7); book, scenery, and costumes, Salvador Dali. First produced by the Ballet Russe de Monte Carlo, New York, October 8, 1941.

Labyrinth

Choreography, John Butler; music, Harry Sommers; decor, Rudi Dorn; costumes, Stanley Simmons. First presented by the Royal Winnipeg Ballet, October 3, 1968.

Labyrinth, a world of violence, sex, desperation, and revenge. Modern dance is the technique; structure focuses upon a series of erotic sculptural lifts.

Christine Hennessey danced the lead at the Royal Winnipeg Ballet première.

Le Lac des Cygnes

See *Swan Lake*

The Lady and the Fool

Choreography, John Cranko; music, Giuseppe Verdi; scenery and costumes, Richard Beer. First produced by the Sadler's Wells Theatre Ballet, Oxford, February 25, 1954. First presented in America by the Sadler's Wells Ballet (now the Royal Ballet), New York, September 14, 1955. The Royal Danish Ballet performed the ballet for the first time, March 18, 1971.

This is the story of a beautiful coquette and two clowns, Moondog and Bootface. In the first scene the two sad clowns, one tall and one short, huddle together on the street. They are cold and hungry and weary, but a beautiful lady enters on her way to a lavish party and takes an interest in them. Hoping to get some money, they do a grotesque dance for her and she invites them to come to the ball.

In the second scene, the lady is courted by handsome and rich cavaliers but she has apparently fallen in love with Moondog and ignores their courtship. In this scene there are opportunities for the lady to display a glittering dance skill, for the clowns to perform, for the gallants to dance their measures, and for bright and gay ensemble action.

For the Sadler's Wells Theatre Ballet première, Patricia Miller was the Lady; Kenneth MacMillan, Moondog; and Johaar Mosavel, Bootface. When the senior company, the Sadler's Wells Ballet, brought the production (revised) to America, Beryl Grey was the Lady; Philip Chatfield, Moondog; and Ray Powell, Bootface.

Lady from the Sea

Choreography, Birgit Cullberg; music, Knudaage Riisager; décor and costumes, Kerstin Hedeby. First performed by the American Ballet Theatre, New York, April 20, 1960. The Royal Swedish Ballet presented the ballet for the first time, March 1, 1961. The Royal Danish Ballet added the ballet to its repertory, September 24, 1961. It has also been performed by the Norwegian National Ballet.

Based on Henrik Ibsen's play, the ballet tells the story of a girl whose first love is a sailor and whose second love is a widower whom she marries when her sailor goes to sea. In a fantasy she dreams of being reunited with the sailor at the bottom of the sea, but when he actually returns, although the husband offers the wife her freedom, she remains with the widower and his children, recognizing that her sailor is simply a symbol of youth, romance, and adventure.

Lupe Serrano, Glen Tetley, and Royes Fernandez headed the first cast.

Lady into Fox

Choreography, Andrée Howard; music, Arthur Honegger; scenery and costumes, Nadia Benois; based on the novel by David Garnett. First produced by the Ballet Rambert, London, May 15, 1939. First presented in America by Ballet Theatre (now the American Ballet Theatre), New York, January 26, 1940.

Laurencia

Choreography, Vakhtang Chabukiani; music, Alexander Krein; book, Yevgeny Mandelberg; based on a play, Fuente Ovejuna, *by Lope de Vega; designs, Simon Virsaladze. First performed by the Kirov Ballet, Leningrad, March 22, 1939. The Bolshoi production, with the same choreography and with designs by Vadim Ryndin, was first performed, Moscow, February 19, 1956.*

This ballet, with a Spanish setting, tells of a girl who leads her entire village to attack the castle of the local tyrant who oppresses them. Laurencia's betrothed kills the villain.

At the première Natalia Dudinskaya danced the title role, with Chabukiani as the hero, Frondozo. Rudolf Nureyev, dancing the lead role, staged an excerpt from the ballet, called "Laurentia" in Western Europe, for members of the Royal Ballet, London, March 24, 1965.

Legend of Love

Choreography, Yuri Grigorovich; music, Arif Melikov; book, Nazim Khikmet (based on his own play); designs, Simon Virsaldze. First performed by the Kirov Ballet, Leningrad, March 23, 1961.

Leila and Medzhnun

Choreography, Kasian Goleizovsky (assisted by Vera Vasilieva); music, Sergei Balsanian; book, Kasian Goleizovsky and S. Tsenin; designs, G. Yepishin. First performed by the Bolshoi Ballet, Moscow, December 22, 1964.

Leningrad Symphony

Choreography and book, Igor Belsky; music, Dmitri Shostakovich (Symphony No. 7); designs, Mikhail Gordon. First performed by the Kirov Ballet, Leningrad, April 14, 1961.

A ballet that pays tribute to the valor of the citizens of Leningrad in the face of the thousand-day Nazi onslaught during World War II.

The Lesson

(La Leçon, Enetime)

> *Choreography, Flemming Flindt; music, Georges Delerue; libretto, after Eugene Ionesco's play* La Leçon; *décor and costumes, Bernard Daydé. First performed, Paris, Opéra-Comique, April 6, 1964. First performed by the Royal Danish Ballet, Copenhagen, October 1, 1964. The first performance was by the same company, New York, December 7, 1965. The first performance of the ballet by the City Center Joffrey Ballet was in New York, September 27, 1968. The work was also in the repertory of the Ruth Page Chicago Opera Ballet and featured the choreographer and Josette Amiel in the leading roles.*

The scene is a half-basement studio. The ceiling-level windows permit us to see only the feet and lower legs of passers-by. There are mirrors, a piano, heavy drapes, a ballet *barre*. A grim-faced woman, the accompanist for ballet lessons, straightens up the studio, which is in disarray. She pulls the drapes. We see a pair of feet pause by the window; a bell rings, and soon a pupil enters for a private lesson (the ballet is sometimes called *The Private Lesson*). The pupil is young and shy. The ballet master enters. He seems strange and before long the viewer is certain that he is insane. The lesson progresses, the girl puts on her toe shoes, the teacher is driven to a wild emotional pitch by the *pointe* shoes and he drives the girl remorselessly. Insanity takes over. The pupil is murdered, the teacher retires after helping remove the body, and then returns to straighten the studio and restore the chairs to proper positions from their overturned states. A bell rings and another pupil arrives for a private lesson as the curtain falls.

The role of the mad ballet master has been danced by Flindt, as well as by Fredbjørn Bjørnsson and Henning Kronstam in Denmark and by other dancers in other countries.

Liebeslieder Walzer

Choreography, George Balanchine; music, Johannes Brahms (Op. 52 and Op. 65); décor, David Hays; costumes, Karinska. First performed by the New York City Ballet, November 22, 1960.

Liebeslieder Walzer's onstage cast includes, in addition to dancing couples, two pianists and four singers (soprano, mezzosoprano, tenor, bass), and is divided into two scenes. In the first scene the dancers are at a ball, and the girls wear ballgowns and high-heeled shoes. All is elegant, all is aristocratic etiquette but throughout the moods shift in shimmering kaleidoscopes from gentle reverie to coquetry, from fast to slow, from pensiveness to gaiety. Each of its many dances concludes with charming subclimaxes, some subtle, some surprising, all pertinent. In scene two, the first scene's gowned ladies give way to lightly clad girls in toe shoes and we know we have witnessed a transformation as the dancers, in their hearts, escape from the confines of a ballroom floor to the airways of the imagination and a starry night. At the close the dancers return from their flights of reverie to applaud the musicians who have led them into another world.

First cast: Diana Adams, Melissa Hayden, Jillana, Violette Verdy, Bill Carter, Conrad Ludlow, Nicholas Magallanes, Jonathan Watts.

The Limpid Brook

Choreography, Fedor Lopukhov; music, Dmitri Shostakovitch; book, Fedor Lopukhov and A. Piotrovsky; designs, Mikhail Bobyshov. First performed at the Maly Theater, Leningrad, April 4, 1935. The Bolshoi production, with the same choreography and with designs by Vladimir Dmitriev, was first performed in Moscow, November 30, 1935.

Lost Illusions

Choreography, Rostislav Zakharov; music, Boris Asafiev; book, Vladimir Dmitriev (based on Honoré de Balzac's novel); designs, Vladimir Dmitriev. First performed by the Kirov Ballet, Leningrad, December 31, 1935.

Le Loup

(The Wolf)

Choreography, Roland Petit; music, Henri Dutilleux; book, Jean Anouilh and Georges Neveux; scenery and costumes, Carzou. First produced by Roland Petit's Ballets de Paris, 1953. First presented in America by the same company, New York, January 19, 1954.

Mademoiselle Angot

(or *Mam'zelle Angot*)

Choreography and book, Leonide Massine; music, Charles LeCocq; scenery and costumes, Mstislav Doboujinsky. First produced by Ballet Theatre (now the American Ballet Theatre), New York, October 10, 1943.

The ballet, a dance version of the LeCocq opera *La Fille de Madame Angot*, is in three scenes. It is a fairly involved drama of confused loves in which Mademoiselle Angot, betrothed to a barber, falls in love with a caricaturist, who in turn gets into trouble over a cartoon involving an official and his highborn mistress. Ultimately the artist falls in love with the lady he has slandered, Mademoiselle Angot insults her publicly, and the plot continues to thicken until Mademoiselle discovers she loves the barber after all.

Nora Kaye, Massine, Rosella Hightower, and André Eglevsky headed the original cast. In a revised version prepared by Massine for the Sadler's Wells Ballet (now the Royal Ballet) and produced with new scenery and costumes by André Derain in London, November 26, 1947, Margot Fonteyn, Alexander Grant, Michael Somes, and Moira Shearer were the principals.

Madrigalesco

Choreography, Benjamin Harkarvy; music, Antonio Vivaldi; décor, Nicholas Wijnberg. First performed by the Netherlands Dans Theatre, November 4, 1963. The first American performance was presented by the Harkness Ballet, New York, January 14, 1969. The Pennsylvania Ballet first presented the ballet, February 15, 1973.

The Maids

Choreography, Herbert Ross; music, Darius Milhaud; décor, William Atkins. First performed by the Ballet Theatre (now the American Ballet Theatre), New York, May 13, 1957. Eliot Feld's American Ballet Company first presented the work, October 25, 1969. It was added to the repertory of the Royal Ballet, October 19, 1971.

Herbert Ross's *The Maids* is danced by two men in the title parts, a casting which Sartre said was recommended by its author, Jean Genet. It is a dance-drama of a homosexual relationship in which repulsion and attraction, abnegation and desire, physical union and psychic isolation are the ingredients.

Paul Olsen and Loren Hightower headed the first cast for the American Ballet Theatre Workshop presentation. Bruce Marks and John Sowinski danced it for Eliot Feld's American Ballet Company revival.

La Malinche

Choreography, José Limón; music, Norman Lloyd (La Malinche); costumes, Pauline Lawrence. First performed by José Limón and Company, New York, March 31, 1949. Edward DeSoto and Laura Glenn staged the work for the Hartford Ballet, March 3, 1972.

A modern dance work that has gone into ballet repertory. It is a dance in which three Mexican villagers reenact the old story of the Spanish conquest of the Aztecs in terms of three figures: El Indio, representing the Mexican Indian; El Conquistador, the Spanish invader; La Malinche, the Indian girl who betrayed her people to the Spaniard. The dance indicates how La Malinche is converted and the Indian doomed to peonage by her actions and how, after an era has passed, the spirit of La Malinche, divested of her Spanish finery and again in peasant dress, returns to inspire El Indio to throw off the yoke of oppression and regain his independence. Although conceived in pertinent naïveté, the ballet has great emotional poignancy and depth.

At the première Limón was El Indio; Pauline Koner, La Malinche; Lucas Hoving, Conquistador.

Manon

Choreography, Kenneth MacMillan; music, Jules Massenet (orchestrated and arranged by Leighton Lucas); scenery and costumes, Nicholas Georgiadis. First performed by the Royal Ballet, Royal Opera House, London, March 7, 1974. First New York performance, May 7, 1974.

This lavish and long three-act ballet (in seven scenes) is based upon the Abbé Prévost novel *Manon Lescaut* rather than upon Massenet's opera. Indeed, the score contains no music from the opera, but is made up of other Massenet compositions.

The story, familiar to opera followers through its several operatic manifestations, tells of a young girl so dewy and bewitching that she attracts men, young and old alike. She runs away from an old gentleman, a casual acquaintance who has money, after she meets and instantly falls in love with the young and romantic Des Grieux. Manon's brother, however, has other ideas for her and makes a financial arrangement with a wealthy Monsieur G. M. in exchange for his sister. Manon, torn between love of Des Grieux and the jewels the new liaison can provide, chooses the latter. Ultimately, of course, she tries to return to Des Grieux, who has been caught cheating at cards. Lescaut is killed, Manon is arrested for prostitution, and deported to a penal colony in

America. Des Grieux, following, kills the jailer and they escape into the swamps, but Manon dies.

The ballet, filled with street scenes and party scenes employing large groups, includes several *pas de deux* for the two young lovers, dances for Des Grieux and his mistress (a character not to be found in the operas), and *soli*, among these a drunken-party dance for Lescaut which is a brilliantly constructed fusion of virtuosic ballet technique with virtuosic lurchings, falls, and totterings in a scene which seems to call for the introduction of a new term into the ballet vocabulary: *grand pas d'ivresse.*

The first cast was headed by Antoinette Sibley (Manon), Anthony Dowell (Des Grieux), David Wall (Lescaut), Monica Mason (the Mistress), Derek Rencher (Monsieur G. M.), and David Drew (the Gaoler, or jailer).

Marguerite and Armand

Choreography, Frederick Ashton; music, Franz Liszt (arranged by Humphrey Searle); décor and costumes, Cecil Beaton. First performed by the Royal Ballet, March 12, 1963.

A ballet created especially for Margot Fonteyn and Rudolf Nureyev and identified with them and their world-famous period of partnership. The story is suggested by the *Camille* of Alexandre Dumas, fils, and is, in essence, a fantasia on the theme of the lovely courtesan, her love for Armand, her acquiescence to the pressures of Armand's father to give up his son and her final death. It is a ballet vignette in which ardor and elegance and refined tragedy are stressed rather than the customary ballet display pieces.

Michael Somes played the Elder Germont to Dame Margot's and Nureyev's doomed young lovers.

Les Matelots

(The Sailors)

Choreography, Leonide Massine; music, Georges Auric; book, Boris Kochno; scenery and costumes, Pedro Pruna. First pro-

duced by the Diaghilev Ballets Russes, Paris, June 17, 1925.
First performance in America by the Ballet Russe de Monte
Carlo, March 9, 1934. Revived by Ballet for America, 1946.

Meadowlark

Choreography, Eliot Feld; music, Franz Josef Haydn; decor,
Robert Prevost; costumes, Stanley Simmons. First performed
by the Royal Winnipeg Ballet, Winnipeg, Canada, October
3, 1968. The London Festival Ballet first performed the ballet,
with décor and costumes by Peter Farmer, Bristol, England,
December 9, 1968. Eliot Feld's American Ballet Company
first danced Meadowlark, *with new décor by Robert Mun-*
ford, in New York, October 23, 1969. It was staged for the
City Center Joffrey Ballet and first performed by that com-
pany, New York, March 2, 1972.

Meadowlark was Eliot Feld's first classical ballet, following his
first (*Harbinger*), which did not use *pointe,* and his second, *At*
Midnight, a dramatic work with strong modern dance ingredients.
Meadowlark is all balletic, all sunshine, shining with flecks of
humor. Its participants are young aristocrats of the late eighteenth
century who have nothing better to do than gambol as they flirt,
engage in amorous dalliances and coquetries, all with an easy acceptance of courtly etiquette.

At the Royal Winnipeg Ballet première the principals were
Richard Rutherford and Sheila Mackinnon.

Medea

Choreography, Birgit Cullberg; music, Béla Bartók (Pieces for
Piano, orchestrated by Herbert Sandberg). First presented by
the Royal Swedish Opera Ballet, London, February 12, 1951.
Produced in America, with costumes by Lewis Brown, by the
New York City Ballet, New York, November 26, 1958. The
Royal Swedish Ballet first performed the ballet, April 23,
1959.

Meditation

Choreography, George Balanchine; music, Peter Ilyich Tchai-kovsky (Meditation from "Souvenir d'un lieu cher," Op. 42, No. 1; *orchestrated by Alexander Glazounov); costumes, Karinska. First performed by the New York City Ballet, New York, December 10, 1963.*

Meditation finds Balanchine in a rare mood of celebrating senti-ment and dreams of elusive romance. The girl is the dream, the vision, the ideal. The boy experiences torment (poetically ex-pressed) in his lonely love-search. Schmaltz, perhaps, but of the highest grade imaginable.

Suzanne Farrell and Jacques d'Amboise created the roles.

Mendelssohn Symphony

Choreography, Dennis Nahat; music, Felix Mendelssohn (Symphony No. 4, "Italian"); *costumes, Robert O'Hearn. First performed by the American Ballet Theatre, July 1, 1971.*

An abstract ballet in which near-kaleidoscope patterns reflect the rhythms and shapes of the music.

At the first performance the ballerina was Cynthia Gregory.

The Merry Widow

Choreography, Ruth Page; music, Franz Lehár, arranged by Isaac Van Grove; décor and costumes, Rolf Gerard. First per-formed under the title Vilia, *with decor and costumes by Georges Wakhevitch, by the London Festival Ballet, Man-chester, England, April 30, 1953. First American performance, titled* The Merry Widow, *Chicago Opera Ballet, Chicago, November 16, 1955. The ballet is also performed by the Pitts-burgh Ballet Theatre.*

The Merry Wives of Windsor

Choreography, Vladimir Bourmeister and Ivan Kurilov; music, V. Oransky; book, I. Kovtunov (after Shakespeare's play); designs, Boris Volkov. First performed at the Stanislavsky and Nemirovich-Dachenko Theater in Moscow, June 10, 1942.

Messe pour le Temps Present

Choreography, Maurice Béjart; music, Pierre Henry and various texts. First performed by the Ballet of the Twentieth Century, Avignon Festival, France, August 3, 1967.

Metamorphoses

Choreography, George Balanchine; music, Paul Hindemith (Symphonic Metamorphosis on Themes of Carl Maria von Weber); *costumes, Karinska. First produced by the New York City Ballet, New York, November 25, 1952.*

Metastaseis & Pithoprakta

Choreography, George Balanchine; music, Iannis Xenakis. First performed by the New York City Ballet, New York, January 18, 1968.

Balanchine's choreographic responses to the Xenakis music reflect into two areas of action. The opening section, centered upon a group, is nonballetic, almost elemental in quality, as if being were emerging tropismatically from primeval ooze. The lighting (by Ronald Bates) is integral here as it pinpoints single bodies, duos, and masses in positions remote from the stances of ballet. In the second section, two key figures emerge. Adam and Eve? And the group becomes supportive of these key primitive figures.

Suzanne Farrell and Arthur Mitchell headed the initial cast.

A Midsummer Night's Dream

Choreography, George Balanchine; music, Felix Mendelssohn; décor and lighting, David Hays; costumes, Karinska. First performed by the New York City Ballet at City Center, New York, January 17, 1962.

This Balanchine ballet, in its two acts, incorporates not only the principal and supporting plots of the Shakespeare comedy, as does Ashton's "The Dream," but also the supplemental themes of Theseus and Hippolyta, the Pyramus and Thisbe play-within-a-play, and such figures as Mustard Seed and Peaseblossom. The choreographer has not employed traditional mime for the telling of the story; rather he has fused rhythmed acting with classical *pas or demi-caractère* actions, especially in the case of Puck whose passages combine antics with feats of ballet virtuosity. There are many major variations for solo, duo, and ensemble dancing, but these advance, and do not interrupt, the course of the telling in movement of the mixed-up romances. The ballet has been mounted as a spectacle with lavish settings, costumes, and scenic effects, and for the New York City Ballet it is usually presented at the conclusion of a repertory season on a daily performance schedule, as the company also treats its *Don Quixote* and *The Nutcracker*. The ballet has been filmed, in a special production supervised by Balanchine, as a full-length feature movie.

The first cast was headed by Melissa Hayden, Edward Villella, Arthur Mitchell, Jillana, Patricia McBride, Gloria Govrin, Violette Verdy, and Conrad Ludlow.

Mignon Pas de Deux

Choreography, Robert Rodham; music, Ambroise Thomas. First performed by the Pennsylvania Ballet, January 7, 1965.

The Miraculous Mandarin

Choreography, Todd Bolender; music, Béla Bartók; scenery and costumes, Alvin Colt; libretto, after Melchior Lengyel. First presented by the New York City Ballet, New York, September 6, 1951. Other versions, with different choreography and production, have been presented in America and abroad, among them one by the Sadler's Wells Ballet. A production with choreography by Flemming Flindt and designs by Preben Hornung was first performed by the Royal Danish Ballet, Copenhagen, January 28, 1967. A version with choreography by Ulf Gadd was first presented by the New Swedish Ballet, London, September 9, 1970. It was given its first performance in New York by the American Ballet Theatre, July 29, 1971. The Metropolitan Opera Ballet first performed a version with choreography by Joseph Lazzini, and decor and costumes by Bernard Daydé, in New York, April 11, 1965.

This macabre melodrama, filled with violence and mystery and forever spattered with the color of freshly shed blood, centers upon a prostitute whose victims are robbed and killed by her gang of associates.

The Prostitute sits atop a high platform above the dark and dingy street. An old man enters and is attracted to the woman. She handles him roughly, and as lust flares up in him, the gang strikes and he is robbed and killed. The woman now dances alone, reflecting anger with herself, passing shame, and then the lechery which is her trade. A young man is next to arrive and the Prostitute almost forgets her duties as she dances with him. But the gang's lookout sees what is happening and the young man, despite the girl's efforts to protect him, is captured and killed. The entrance of a blind woman introduces an element of mystery. She pursues the Prostitute slowly but relentlessly as if she, though blind, were the inexorable figure of fate.

Suddenly, at the top of the platform, appears the gorgeously clad Mandarin. He descends the stairs and approaches the Prostitute, who tries to avoid him but soon gives signs of succumbing. Swiftly she strikes him and the gang reappears. He is beaten, stabbed, and finally hanged; yet he refuses to die. The killers are terrified and the girl orders them to cut the noose from which the still living Mandarin is hanging. They flee and the now remorseful and frightened girl takes the Mandarin's body in her arms and gives herself to him just before he dies.

In the New York City Ballet production, Hugh Laing created the title role and Melissa Hayden the part of the Prostitute.

Les Mirages

Choreography, Serge Lifar; music, Henri Sauget; scenery and costumes, A. M. Cassandre. First produced by the Paris Opera Ballet, Paris, December 15, 1947. First presented in America by the same company, New York, September 21, 1948.

A romantic fantasy in which a moonstruck youth discovers that only the Shadow, the vision of beauty, is constant. The role of the Shadow was long identified with Yvette Chauviré.

Missa Brevis

Choreography, José Limón; music, Zóltan Kódaly; projection and scenery, Ming Cho Lee; lighting, Thomas de Gaetani. First performed by the Juilliard Dance Theatre, New York, March 11, 1958. Performed by the Royal Swedish Ballet.

This modern dance work, also performed in ballet repertory, has as its locale a bombed-out church in Poland. The dance itself mirrors the tragic past, the uneasy present, and the hope of a better future. The movement idiom is pure modern dance.

Limón danced the lead at the première.

Miss Julie

Choreography, Birgit Cullberg; music, Ture Rangstrom; scenery and costumes, Sven Erixon. First produced by the Swedish Ballet, Vasteras, Sweden, March 1, 1950. First presented in

*America by the American Ballet Theatre, New York, Septem-
ber 18, 1958. The Royal Danish Ballet first presented the ballet, December 18, 1958. Another version, with music by
Andrzej Panufnik, choreography by Kenneth MacMillan, and
decor by Barry Kay, was first performed by the Stuttgart
Ballet, Stuttgart, March 8, 1970.*

Miss Julie, based on August Strindberg's play, is a dramatic, even
melodramatic ballet that employs classical and modern dance techniques. The story is centered in the person of a beautiful, restless,
sexy, arrogant young aristocrat who drives her fiancé away by her
brutality and contemptuousness, seduces her own butler, and ultimately, plagued by her own degradation and encouraged by the
butler, kills herself.

Presented in several scenes, the ballet reproduces episodes
from the life of Julie, ranging from her vicious treatment of her
fiancé, through scenes of wild debauchery and almost abject pleading for seduction, to reproaching fantasy and final escape in death.

For the American Ballet Theatre première, Violette Verdy
(Julie) and Erik Bruhn (the Butler) headed the cast. With the
Swedish Ballet, the title part was first performed by Elsa-Marianne
von Rosen, who subsequently danced it with the Royal Swedish
Ballet.

Monotones

*Choreography, Frederick Ashton; music, Erik Satie (Mono-
tones I, Trois Gnossiennes, orchestrated by John Lanchberry,
and Monotones II, Trois Gymnopédies, orchestrated by
Claude Debussy and Roland Manuel); costumes, Frederick
Ashton. Monotones I was first performed by the Royal Ballet,
London, April 25, 1966. Monotones II was first performed by
the Royal Ballet, London, March 24, 1965. Monotones I and
II were performed together for the first time, on April 25,
1966. The two parts were presented together for the first time
in America, New York, May 3, 1967.*

Monotones, a pictorially attractive piece that sometimes suggests
a highly sophisticated version of the childhood game of "living

statues" in which pose and pattern, rather than action, are highlighted.

Antoinette Sibley, Georgina Parkinson, Brian Shaw headed
the first cast for Monotones I; Vyvyan Lorrayne, Anthony Dowell,
Robert Mead were the first in Monotone II.

Monument for a Dead Boy

*Choreography, Rudi van Dantzig; music, Jan Goerman; décor
and costumes, Toer Van Schayk. First performed by Het
Nationale Ballet, Amsterdam, Holland, June 19, 1965. The
Harkness Ballet gave the first New York performance, November 2, 1967. First performed by the American Ballet Theatre,
New York, January 11, 1973. The Royal Danish Ballet gave its
first performance of the work, April 7, 1973.*

Monument for a Dead Boy is a choreographic penetration into the
heart and mind of an adolescent boy who relives, through images
of his childhood, the crude and carnal caperings of his parents, the
love of a girl, cruelty by bullies, the evanescent comfort of a male-
male relationship, and the constant terrors of shifting environ-
ments.

In the original production Toer Van Schayk danced the title
role, and Yvonne Vendrig danced the girl. The Harkness production was headed by Lawrence Rhodes, and the American Ballet
Theatre staging featured Daniel Levins. Warren Conover danced
the image of youth in both the Harkness and American Ballet
Theatre productions.

Monumentum Pro Gesualdo

(*See also* Movements for Piano and Orchestra)

*Choreography, George Balanchine; music, Igor Stravinsky;
décor. David Hays. First performed by the New York City
Ballet, New York, November 16, 1960. Now seen as the first
part of two-part ballet with* Movements for Piano and Orchestra *given in New York City Ballet program lists as* Monu-
mentum/Movements).

Moonreindeer

Choreography, Birgit Cullberg; music, Knudager Riisager; décor and costumes, Per Faulk. First produced by the Royal Danish Ballet, Copenhagen, November 22, 1957. First performed by the American Ballet Theatre, New York, October 2, 1961. The Norwegian National Ballet has also performed the ballet.

This ballet, based on a Lapland legend, tells of a girl who, spurned by the boy she loves, succeeds in winning him through the help of a magician. In return, however, she must aid the magician in supplying human sacrifices to the demons of the underworld. Thus, on moonlight nights, she assumes the guise of a beautiful white reindeer and lures young men to their deaths over a precipice. When the young husband himself is about to become the next victim, a fight with the magician ensues, the spell is broken, and the girl resumes her natural form forever.

Mona Vangsaa (the Girl), Henning Kronstam (the Young Man), and Fredbjørn Bjørnsson (the Magician) created the leading roles.

The Moor's Pavane

Choreography, José Limón; music, Henry Purcell (arranged by Simon Sadoff); costumes, Pauline Lawrence. First performed by the José Limón Company, Connecticut College Dance Festival, August 17, 1949. First presented by the American Ballet Theatre, June 27, 1970. Added to the repertoires of the Royal Danish Ballet, December 3, 1971; the National Ballet of Canada, October 11, 1972; and the City Center Joffrey Ballet, October 13, 1973.

Mother Goose Suite

Choreography, Todd Bolender; music, Maurice Ravel. First presented by the American Concert Ballet, New York, Octo-

ber 31, 1943. Revised and presented, with costumes by André Derain, by the New York City Ballet, New York, November 1, 1948.

This ballet is not a ballet for children based upon the familiar Mother Goose tales. It is, instead, an adult fantasy inspired by the score of Ravel's *Ma Mère l'Oye*.

A woman crosses the stage, settles herself in a theater box, and looks back upon the dreams of her childhood. Her former self, a young girl, is seen first surrounded by moving clouds. She dances with four girls, then attempts to join four couples but no matter how she tries to attract their attention, they ignore her, and she is left sadly alone.

Hop o' My Thumb appears accompanied by a bird-girl but after they have danced together, the bird vanishes. The little heroine and Hop o' My Thumb play together, but the clouds return and whisk the elusive lad away, leaving the girl alone.

A Chinese prince and four girls perform a spritely dance which fascinates the dream figure, but she is even more astonished when the Prince condescends to dance with her. He too, however, disappears and is replaced by a man with a lion's head. The girl is terrified and revolted by the beast who rolls on the floor in agony when his courting is rejected. The bewildered girl runs to the spectator who gives her a ring. She returns to the beast and touches him. The clouds float in, and when they have departed, the beast has been transformed into a handsome youth. The two are lovingly united, and the youth carries her off. The spectator leaves her seat, the clouds drift by, and the dream of the past, with its anguished search for fun, friendship, romance, and love, is finished.

Mary Jane Shea and Francisco Moncion headed the original cast. Marie-Jeanne and Moncion headed the New York City Ballet restaging. Later, Janet Reed scored a success in the leading role. Nora Kaye has also danced the part.

Movements for Piano and Orchestra

(*See also* Monumentum Pro Gesualdo)

Choreography, George Balanchine; music, Igor Stravinsky; décor and lighting, David Hays and Peter Harvey. First performed by the New York City Ballet, New York, April 9, 1963. Now seen as the second part of a two-part ballet with Monumentum Pro Gesualdo, *given in New York City Ballet program lists as* Monumentum/Movements.

Moves

(A Dance in Silence)

Choreography, Jerome Robbins; lighting, Nananne Porcher. First performed at the Festival of Two Worlds, Spoleto, Italy, by Jerome Robbins' Ballets: U.S.A., July 3, 1959. First American performance by the same company, New York, October 8, 1961. The ballet was revived and first performed by the City Center Joffrey Ballet, September 19, 1967, in New York.

Moves is danced in silence—well, almost. There is no musical accompaniment, but there are the sounds that the body makes when in motion. The sounds can be as obvious as stamping, clapping, or treading and as subtle as audible breath rhythms or a curious vibration when swiftly moving bodies—turning, twisting, rushing, stopping—displace the air around them. This is a celebration of the "wholeness," perhaps the "integrity," and certainly the "independence" of dance.

Mozart Concerto

Choreography, John Cranko; music, Wolfgang Amadeus Mozart (Concerto for Flute and Harp, K. 299). *First performance by the Stuttgart Ballet, March 26, 1966.*

A lighthearted, breezy classical ballet in which two ballerinas are assisted by two attentive cavaliers.

Mozartiana

Choreography, George Balanchine; music, Wolfgang Amadeus Mozart, arranged by Peter Ilyich Tchaikovsky; scenery and costumes, Christian Berard. First produced by Les Ballets 1933, Paris. Presented in New York by the American Ballet, 1936. Revived by the Ballet Russe de Monte Carlo, New York, March 7, 1945. An adapted version was staged by Balanchine for Alexandra Danilova and her ensemble for world tours in 1956 and 1957.

Mutations

Choreography, Glen Tetley; cinechoreography, Hans van Manen; music, Karlheinz Stockhausen; film visualizations, Jean-Paul Vroom; décor, Nadine Baylis; costumes, Emmy van Leersum and Gijis Bikken. First produced by the Netherlands Dans Theatre, Holland, Scheveningen Circus Theater, July 30, 1970. First American performance by the same company, Brooklyn Academy of Music, New York, March 28, 1972.

In the ballet's sequential development the dancers slowly strip down to total nudity. They are first seen wearing white costumes with those curlicues that suggest knaves and queens in a pack of cards; next they appear in tights; the men then perform in the briefest of loinstraps, and lastly nudity is achieved. The stage and a ramp extended up the center aisle of the theatre are employed for dancing areas in the ballet, which, couched in Martha Grahamlike modern dance style, relates live figures to cinematic ones.

The Mute Wife

Choreography, Antonia Cobos; music, Niccolò Paganini (Perpetual Motion, orchestrated by Vittorio Rieti); scenery and costumes, Rico Lebrun. First produced by the Ballet International, New York, November 22, 1944. Added to the repertory of the Original Ballet Russe, New York, October 6, 1946.

Subsequently included in the repertory of the Ballet Russe de Monte Carlo, with a score comprised of music by Domenico Scarlatti (arranged by Soulima Stravinsky); costumes by Antonio Castillo.

Mythical Hunters

Choreography, Glen Tetley; music, Oedoen Partos; décor and costumes, Anthony Binstead. First performed by the Batsheva Ballet Company of Israel, December, 1965. Glen Tetley and Company first performed the ballet in New York, April 1, 1966. The Nederlands Dans Theatre first performed it, January 10, 1968. First presented by the Norwegian National Ballet, 1971.

Mythical Hunters, a modern dance work performed by ballet companies, combines physical tension with dramatic intensity. The warriors' bows, and the manipulations of these weapons, are an integral part of the choreographic design.

Napoli

(or *The Fisherman and His Bride*)

Choreography and book, August Bournonville; music, Paulli, Helsted, Gade; scenery, Christensen. First produced by the Royal Danish Ballet, Copenhagen, March 29, 1842. First presented in America by the Royal Danish Ballet, New York, September 18, 1956. A one-act divertissement version of the ballet, arranged by Harald Lander, was mounted for the London Festival Ballet, London, 1954, and presented in America during a 1954–55 tour. Hans Brenaa, of the Royal Danish Ballet, has staged the familiar last-act divertissement, adding the "Flower Festival at Genzano" pas de deux, for several major companies including the Boston Ballet (1966–67), the Norwegian National Ballet (1966), and American Ballet Theatre (1973). The Royal Winnipeg Ballet also performs this version. The Royal Ballet gave its first performance of the Third Act, London, May 8, 1962.

Act I. Teresina is courted by three young men, a seller of macaroni, a lemonade vendor, and a fisherman. Teresina has eyes only for Gennaro, the fisherman, and spurns the attentions of the other two until Gennaro returns from the sea. As he and his fellows come in with their catch, the other suitors try to convince Teresina that Gennaro is flirting with a pretty customer, but when Gennaro places a ring on her finger, her doubts leave and the two depart in a little boat to be alone together on the bay. A sudden storm comes up and Gennaro returns alone to report that Teresina was swept overboard. Teresina's widowed mother accuses the youth of drowning her daughter and the townsfolk shun Gennaro. The young man curses himself and his fate and despairingly seeks the comfort of the Madonna. A priest listens to his prayers and, giving him a likeness of the Madonna, urges him to get a boat and find Teresina.

The first act is primarily pantomimic but it does contain several lively variations, a comedy number for a street singer, and a vivid leaping sequence for a unit of six male dancers.

Act II. The scene has shifted from a street on the bay of Naples to the Blue Grotto of Capri. Two naiads bring in Teresina, whom they have rescued, and present her to their master and king, Golfo. Teresina, still carrying the guitar she was playing when the squall arose, pleads to return home, but Golfo is captivated by her beauty and determines to keep her with him. He touches her with magic and instantly her peasant dress disappears and she stands clad as a naiad.

Gennaro soon enters the Grotto in his boat, which he beaches, and steps ashore. Seeing Teresina's guitar, he knows that she must be near, and when Golfo appears, he begs the king to release her. Golfo attempts to frighten Gennaro away but he fails. Teresina is brought in by the naiads but since she is now a naiad herself, she does not recognize Gennaro nor remember their mortal love. Gennaro, however, prays to the image of the Madonna and slowly Teresina's memory returns.

Once again there is a magical flash, Teresina's naiad dress disappears and she stands in her familiar peasant garb. Golfo's fury cannot be assuaged but Teresina holds up the image of the Virgin, and Golfo, his naiads, and tritons must submit to a greater power. The lovers leave in the boat.

Act III. The scene is a square outside Naples and the townsfolk are gathered for a pilgrimage. The arrival of Teresina with her mother causes astonishment, for all had thought her dead. When she reports that Gennaro rescued her, the people fear witchcraft. However, the priest is summoned and he explains to them what the power of the Virgin has accomplished. Now come joyous dances of celebration, solo, duo, and ensemble variations, which mirror the happiness of the lovers and the gladness of their friends. As the festivities draw to a close, Teresina and Gennaro are lifted into an elaborately decorated cart from which they wave happily as they set out for marriage and a life with each other.

The ballet of *Napoli* has long been a favorite of Danish audiences and has been presented almost every season without break since its première more than a century ago. Its choreography has remained unaltered and although its long stretches of pantomime seem slow to American audiences, the lilting variations for the girls, the aerial actions of the men, the perfection of the ensemble dancing, the elaborate settings (particularly the Blue Grotto scene) and the swift dress transformations for Teresina (accomplished at such speed that the eye cannot detect how it is done) delight non-Danish audiences.

N.Y. Export, Op. Jazz

Choreography, Jerome Robbins; music, Robert Prince; décor, Ben Shahn; costumes, Florence Klotz. First produced for the Festival of Two Worlds, Spoleto, Italy, June 8, 1958, by Mr. Robbins' own company, Ballets: U.S.A. First presented in New York by the same company, September 4, 1958. Revived and first performed by the City Center Joffrey Ballet, March 21, 1974. Opus Jazz was also in the repertory of the Harkness Ballet.

N.Y. Export, Op. Jazz is not a story ballet. Rather, its purpose is to capture the rhythms, moods, and rituals of behavior of the American teenager. It in no way touches upon delinquency but it does point up the jazzy exuberance, the humor, the touches of cynicism, the pull of romance and, on occasion, the sense of lostness and aloneness which characterize the adolescent.

The choreography is a blend of ballet action, free dance steps, and movements derived and adapted from the currently popular dances. It ranges from simple affecting gesture to movements requiring virtuosic brilliance; from mood-evoking design (such as in the tender *pas de deux*) to explosive theatrical surprises. Motivating the whole work, in addition to the choreographer's concept of the teen-ager of the 1950s, is the quality of the music itself: the insistent, elusive, restless rhythm of jazz.

Patricia Dunn, James Norman, Wilma Curley, and John Jones headed the cast.

Night City

Choreography and book, Leonid Lavrovsky; music, Béla Bartók (The Miraculous Mandarin); designs, Vadim Ryndin. First performed by the Bolshoi Ballet, Moscow, May 21, 1961.

Night Song

Choreography, Norman Walker; music, Alan Hovhaness. First performed by the Harkness Ballet, New York, November 1, 1967.

A pure dance work, sculptural in outlines but pulsating in terms of kinetics, lyrical in flow but with muscular force, such as a male dancer's diagonal progression of air turns into a kneeling position.

Nightwings

Choreography, Gerald Arpino; music, John La Montaine; décor, Ming Cho Lee; costumes, Willa Kim. First performed by the City Center Joffrey Ballet, New York, September 7, 1966.

A young man fights valiantly to find himself in a wild world of fantasy. The original cast included Michael Uthoff, Lisa Bradley, and Nels Jorgensen.

Nijinsky, Clown of God

Choreography, Maurice Béjart; music, Pierre Henry and Peter Ilyich Tchaikovsky (Symphony No. 6, "Pathétique"); *text, based on Vaslav Nijinsky's diaries written during his period of madness; costumes, Joette Roustan and Roger Bernard. First performed by the Ballet of the Twentieth Century, Brussels, October 8, 1971.*

A fantasia—more of a spectacle than a ballet—based on the career of the great dancer, Vaslav Nijinsky and a psychological exploration of a tormented being who fled the protective relationship with the impresario of the Ballets Russes, Serge Diaghilev, for the love of a woman, marriage, insanity, and the end of one of the most spectacular careers in the history of ballet. This evening-long production requires a cast of ninety, giant puppets, masks, elaborate lighting effects, ramps, three Crosses for Crucifixions.

The title role was created for Jorge Donn. The woman was Suzanne Farrell. Also featured in the original production were Paolo Bortoluzzi, Daniel Lomell, Paul Mejia, and Ivan Marko.

Les Noces

(The Wedding)

Choreography, Bronislava Nijinska; music and words, Igor Stravinsky; scenery and costumes, Nathalie Gontcharova. First produced by Diaghilev's Ballets Russes, Paris, June 13, 1923. First presented in America, with choreography by Elizaveta Anderson-Ivantzova, by the League of American Composers, New York, April 25, 1929. The Nijinska original was revived by the Ballet Russe de Monte Carlo in April, 1936, and presented during that company's American tour. A completely different version, with choreography by Jerome Rob-

bins, was first performed by the American Ballet Theatre, New York, March 30, 1965.

Les Noces is a ballet-cantata in four scenes in which both dancers and singers usually appear on stage. Nijinska conceived the work as a stark, highly stylized, and almost emotionless treatment of a Russian marriage ritual. The rites include the preparation of the bride for the ceremony, the combing and binding of her hair, the advice of the women; the preparation of the bridegroom, the lamenting of the parents in losing a child, the congratulations of neighbors on the marriage; the departure for the ceremony, the arrival, the marriage rite itself; the wedding feast, the instructions to the young couple, the warming of the marriage bed by an older pair, the retiring of the newlyweds.

Felia Doubrovska created the role of the Bride. Irina Baronova danced the part in America with the Ballet Russe de Monte Carlo.

The Robbins choreography differs from the original chiefly in its substitution of a nonethnic background for Nijinska's Russian one. Robbins thus extends the horizons of the work to a universal plane so that the viewer experiences the rites of selection, betrothal, marriage, and consummation in terms of any society anywhere in the world, in any era. There are, because of the Stravinsky materials, Russian echoes, but the ballet itself is a celebration of the continuity of mankind. The movement technique employed is nonballetic, although the fruits of ballet discipline are apparent; rather is the movement idiom freely invented dance action combining the expression force of modern dance with the vigor and rough strength of primitive rhythms.

Erin Martin and William Glassman were the Bride and Groom in the American Ballet Theatre première.

Nomos Alpha

Choreography, Maurice Béjart; music, Iannis Xenakis; First performed by the Ballet of the Twentieth Century, 1969. First performed during the Ballet of the Twentieth Century's New

York appearance, Brooklyn Academy of Music, New York, January 26, 1971.

The Nutcracker

(Casse Noisette)

Choreography, Lev Ivanov, following the projected plan of Marius Petipa; music, Peter Ilyich Tchaikovsky; scenery, Botcharov. First produced by the Russian Imperial Ballet, St. Petersburg, December 5 (Julian or Russian calendar) or December 17 (Gregorian or Western calendar), 1892. First presented in Western Europe, with choreography by Nicholas Sergeyev after the Ivanov original and with costumes by Hedley Briggs, by the Sadler's Wells Ballet (now the Royal Ballet), London, January 30, 1934. First presented in America, with scenery and costumes by Alexandre Benois, by the Ballet Russe de Monte Carlo, New York, October 17, 1940. Restaged, with choreography by George Balanchine, settings by Horace Armistead, and costumes by Karinska, by the New York City Ballet, New York, February 2, 1954. Also performed by other companies in different versions. The pas de deux for the Sugar Plum Fairy and the Prince is frequently given separately from the ballet itself as a divertissement for the ballerina and a cavalier. The Nutcracker is a Christmas ballet based upon the story by E. T. A. Hoffman, The Nutcracker and the King of Mice. Some of the other major versions include Rudolf Nureyev's for the Royal Ballet, with designs by Nicholas Georgiadis, which was first performed, London, February 29, 1968. It was given its first performance in America at the Metropolitan Opera House, New York, May 10, 1968. William Christensen staged his version for Ballet West in 1955. The Boston Ballet's Nutcracker was staged by E. Virginia Williams, with decor by Horace Armistead and costumes by Linda Torto, in 1965. The Stuttgart Ballet production, with choreography by John Cranko and décor by Ralph Adron, was first performed in Stuttgart, December 4, 1966. Alexandra

Danilova staged Act I and Frederic Franklin Act II of the National Ballet of Washington production, given its first performance in Washington, D.C., December 25, 1965. The Pennsylvania Ballet used George Balanchine's second-act divertissements and Robert Rodham's "Snow Scene" for the version given its first production, November 29, 1968. Other choreographers who have staged Nutcracker include Ruth Page (Ruth Page's International Ballet), Celia Franca (National Ballet of Canada), Fernand Nault (Les Grands Ballets Canadiens), Walter Gore (Norwegian National Ballet), and Enid Lynn, Joyce Karpiej, and Michael Uthoff (Hartford Ballet).

The New York City Ballet production of *The Nutcracker* is described here.

The scene opens on a drop curtain depicting the wall of a room. Two children peer avidly through the keyhole to watch their parents and servants deck the Christmas tree. The walls become partially transparent, and through them, we of the audience can see the preparations.

Following this prologue, the drop curtain rises and we are in the large, fairly ugly but far from poor living room of Dr. Stahlbaum and his wife. The children have been joined by their many young friends and their parents, and other adult friends have come with them. The children, delighted with the Christmas tree, marvel at its size and poke around for their presents.

During the course of this scene, the children take partners and dance together, the grownups also have their stately measures. The children with their toys manage to make a racket and occasionally squabble happily. But the real highlight of the scene is the arrival of the mysterious Drosselmeyer, an old man with a patch over one eye. He brings with him three enormous boxes for Clara and Fritz, the two Stahlbaum children. From two of the boxes step two mechanical dolls, who dance together, and from the third box comes a toy soldier, who has a dashing solo. The main gift, however, is a wooden nutcracker, carved like an old man with a beard, which is given to Clara.

Fritz, a mischiefmaker, grabs the nutcracker and smashes it on the floor. Clara, in tears, is soothed by the old man, who wraps his handkerchief around the nutcracker's jaw (which is used for cracking nuts) and the little girl places her best-loved toy in a doll's bed she has found under the tree. Annoyed with Fritz, she is delighted with the gallantry of Drosselmeyer's little nephew, who behaves almost as if he were a prince.

Bedtime comes, the guests depart, and Clara is led off to bed. But after the living room has been darkened, she steals back, despite her fear of possible mice, to find her nutcracker. Suddenly, she hears a sound and the whole world seems to change. The tree grows to enormous size, beyond the confines of the ceiling, the toys come to life and the seven-headed king of the mice and his army streak onto the scene. Clara is terrified but her nutcracker, now grown to the size of a little boy, takes charge of the toy troops. Cannon shoot out colored candies and balloons, swords and guns are drawn, and eventually the battle is won as the king of the mice is killed.

Now another transformation takes place. The tree grows and rises out of sight, the windows of the room enlarge and then part and a forest covered with snow appears before the eyes. Clara's doll's bed has grown also and, propelled by no visible means, sweeps onto the stage with Clara on it. The little nutcracker now steps forth, his mask and his nutcracker uniform fall from him, and he stands revealed as a boy-prince in court attire. He approaches Clara with a tiny crown which he has taken from one of the mouse king's heads, places it on her hair, and leads her away to fairyland. The bed scurries from view and the snowflakes arrive to dance their swirling, lightfooted, leaping patterns.

Act II brings us to the Kingdom of Sweets. Here the Sugar Plum Fairy is on hand to welcome Clara and her little prince to a golden setting. Little angels play upon their instruments and turn stiffly in their formal robes as the children admire them. Then a huge table, laden with sweets, is set up on a dais and the children, with napkins tucked under their chins, settle down to eat and to watch the entertainment. The Sugar Plum Fairy has been impressed with the nutcracker's tale of his heroic adventures with the mice (a tale told in mime) and now orders the celebration to begin.

First, two soloists and a supporting ensemble offer a Spanish-flavored dance called "Hot Chocolate." Following this brisk piece, Coffee enters in the guise of an Arabian. Attended by two children, who spread a rug for him to rest upon and who pour his coffee into a tiny cup or hand him his hookah, the Arabian moves slowly and languidly through his dance. After every minor burst of energy, he sinks to his rug and rests and finally falls asleep.

Tea is a Chinese dance for a boy and two girls. This is a vivid sequence for the boy, who leaps about, does splits in air, returns to the lacquered box from which he has emerged and is rolled off by his assistants. The Candy Canes are buffoons and, led by a boy candy cane, caper about the stage with all the exuberance of youth. The music for this episode is usually employed for a rousing Russian peasant *trepak*, but in the Balanchine version (which the choreographer says is a duplicate of the Ivanov original), the boy is dressed in striped candy-cane tights and performs elaborate steps with a hoop.

The Marzipan Shepherdesses (the *mirlitons*) are dressed in the bright colors associated with marzipan and their leader guides them through a gay and dainty dance. Next comes Bonbonnière, featuring Mother Ginger and the Polichinelles. Mother (played by a man) sidles in, wearing an enormous hoop skirt. She draws a string opening the front panel of the skirt and eight children emerge to perform a formal but peppy dance. When they finish, they run back under the skirt, the curtains of the dress fall, and Mother Ginger departs.

The Waltz of the Candy Flowers follows with a Dewdrop shimmering, darting, flying among them. And the entertainment draws to a close as the Sugar Plum Fairy and her cavalier come forward to dance their classical *pas de deux*. Together, they move in soft but brilliant adagio motions with lifts and turns and balances. The Sugar Plum Fairy, alone, has an always eagerly awaited variation in which she moves with feather-lightness to soft and tinkling music.

At the close of the ballet, a walnut-shell boat appears, and with farewells from their fairyland friends, Clara and her nut-cracker prince sail away.

The Balanchine production is probably the only one in the Western world which employs Tchaikovsky's entire score, includ-ing an episode in the snow scene which calls for a singing chorus. In addition to the large adult cast, thirty-nine children take part in the ballet. The choreography is, with few exceptions, totally different from that used by other companies, although the story line and the order of the *divertissements* remain unchanged. Most companies omit the prologue, some drop the Arabian dance, others shorten the party scene. But since Petipa worked closely with Tchaikovsky on the score, telling him exactly what he wanted, measure for measure, the sequence of dances is practically un-alterable, although steps and costumes can and do vary.

At the Russian première Antoinette dell'Era was the Sugar Plum Fairy and Paul Gerdt the Cavalier. Alicia Markova and Harold Turner headed the first Sadler's Wells Ballet cast, and Markova and André Eglevsky were the first to dance the leads in America with the Ballet Russe de Monte Carlo. Maria Tallchief and Nicholas Magallanes starred in the Balanchine première, with Tanaquil LeClercq as the Dewdrop. Antoinette Sibley, Anthony Dowell, Merle Park, and Rudolf Nureyev have danced it with the Royal Ballet.

L'Oiseau de Feu

See *The Firebird*

Olympics

> *Choreography, Gerald Arpino; music, Toshiro Mayuzumi; decor, Ming Cho Lee. First presented by the Robert Joffrey Ballet (now the City Center Joffrey Ballet), New York, March 31, 1966.*

Olympics is an all-male ballet (its dance ancestor might be con-sidered to be Ted Shawn's modern dance *Olympiad* from the

1930s) that celebrates male strength, prowess, individual skills, and teamwork. The Shawn work was led by a Banner Bearer, the Joffrey work by the Torch Bearer. The older piece based its dances on a variety of different sports projected in comparatively literal adaptations; the ballet suggests various sports rather than imitates them.

At the première Luis Fuente was the Torch Bearer.

Ondine

Choreography, Frederick Ashton; music, Hans Werner Henze; libretto, Frederick Ashton (after a story by Friedrich de la Motte Fouqué); décor and costumes, Lila de Nobili. First performed by the Royal Ballet, London, October 27, 1958. First American performance, by the same company, New York, September 21, 1960.

A ballet created by Ashton especially for Margot Fonteyn. The story is the famous old tale of a creature of the sea who falls in love with a mortal and endeavors to steal him from his betrothed. She fails, but on his wedding day she comes out of the sea and gives him a kiss that places him under enchantment and causes him to return with her to live forever at the bottom of the sea. (The first *Ondine* ballet was choreographed by Jules Perrot to music of Pugni and first presented in London June 22, 1843, with Fanny Cerrito in the title role.)

In the Ashton ballet, the principals, in addition to Fonteyn, were Michael Somes (Palemon, the noble lover), Julia Farron (Berthe, his betrothed), Alexander Grant (Tirrenio, King of the Waters).

On Stage!

Choreography, Michael Kidd; music, Norman Dello Joio; scenery, Oliver Smith; costumes, Alvin Colt. First produced by Ballet Theatre (now the American Ballet Theatre), New York, October 9, 1945.

Opus Lemaître

*Choreography, Hans van Manen; music, Johann Sebastian
Bach (Toccata and Fugue in D Minor); set and costumes,
Jean-Paul Vroom. First produced by the Nederlands Dans
Theatre, January 16, 1973. Added to the repertory of the
Pennsylvania Ballet, Philadelphia, March 14, 1974.*

This ballet, dedicated to Gerard Lemaître—a principal dancer
with the Netherlands troupe and longtime colleague of the choreographer—is an abstract ballet combining free-style actions with
balletic steps. During the toccata, the principal dancer (male) is
immobile on stage while the movement is produced by an ensemble. In the second section the choreography focuses upon the
male star and provides him with highly virtuosic measures requiring both speed and force, rather in the nature of an athletic
contest in which a single contestant appears to be testing his own
potential. The fugal movements for the group are complex but
pictorially clear with respect to swiftly changing geometric designs and progressions.

In the Netherlands cast the leading role was danced by Gerard Lemaître, and the principal dancer for the Pennsylvania Ballet was Lawrence Rhodes.

Opus I

*Choreography, John Cranko; music, Anton Webern. First per-
formed by the Stuttgart Ballet, Stuttgart, November 7, 1965.
First performed by the Royal Danish Ballet, March 18, 1971.*

A ballet, closely allied to the expressiveness of modern dance,
which deals with youth, with aloneness, and with passion in the
midst of many, an exploration of that labyrinth, both inner, of the
heart, and outer, of the world, through which the individual must
find his own terribly lonely way.

Opus I was created especially for Richard Cragun.

Martha Swope

Above: Edward Villella as Oberon in New York City Ballet's A *Midsummer Night's Dream*

Left: Arthur Mitchell as Puck in New York City Ballet's A *Midsummer Night's Dream*

Below: The Harkness Ballet's *Monument for a Dead Boy*

Above: Niels Kehlet, Mette Hønningen and Eske Holm in The Royal Danish Ballet's *Moon-reindeer*

Right: Inger Johanne Rütter in The Norwegian National Ballet's *Mythical Hunters*

Below: The Royal Danish Ballet's *Napoli*

American Ballet Theatre's *Les Noces*

The bridegroom, Robert Mead, with his friends in The Royal Ballet's *Les Noces*

Anthony Crickway

Above: Kirk Peterson in The National Ballet's *The Nutcracker*

Right: Merle Park and Rudolf Nureyev in The Royal Ballet's *The Nutcracker*

Below: Television production of New York City Ballet's *The Nutcracker*

Michael Stannard

Right: Four Prima Ballerinas, Alicia Markova, Nathalie Krassovska (top), Mia Slavenska, Alexandra Danilova (bottom) in the Ballet Russe de Monte Carlo's revival of Anton Dolin's version of *Pas de Quatre*

Peter Basch

Above: Glen Tetley in *Pierrot Lunaire*

Below: Annabelle Lyon, Lucia Chase, and Nora Kaye, the original cast of The Ballet Theatre's *Pillar of Fire*

Margot Fonteyn in The Stuttgart Ballet's *Poème de l'Extase*

Margot Fonteyn and Rudolf Nureyev in The Royal Ballet's *Raymonda*

Left: Jan Holme, Henning Kronstam, and Mona Vangsaa in The Royal Danish Ballet's *Romeo and Juliet*. *Right:* Galina Ulanova and Alexander Lapauri in The Bolshoi Ballet's *Romeo and Juliet*

Michael Friedlander

Above: Frederic Franklin, Jordeen Ivanov and Alexander Filipov in The Pittsburgh Ballet Theatre's *Romeo and Juliet*

Left: Merle Park as Juliet in The Royal Ballet's *Romeo and Juliet*

Peter Smith

Above: Annette av Paul and Richard Rutherford in The Royal Winnipeg Ballet's *Rose Latulippe*

Left: Christopher Aponte in the Harkness Ballet's *Sebastian*

Below: Bonnie Alexis Wyckoff, Alfonso Figueroa, and Elaine Bauer in The Boston Ballet's *Serenade*

Bil Leidersdorf

MIRA

Left: Anthony Dowell in The Royal Ballet's *Shadowplay*. *Right:* Monica Mason and Anthony Dowell in The Royal Ballet's *The Song of the Earth*

The Russian Imperial Ballet's production of *The Sleeping Beauty* in St. Petersburg, 1890

MIRA

Left: Georgina Parkinson and Anthony Dowell in The Royal Ballet's *The Song of the Earth. Right:* Igor Youskevitch in The Ballet Theatre's *A Streetcar Named Desire*

Right: Niels Kehlet and Solveig Ostergard in The Royal Danish Ballet's *Spectre de la Rose*

Below: The Harkness Ballet's *Souvenirs*

Bil Leidersdorf

Mydtskov

Left: Nicolai Fadeyechev and Maya Plisetskaya in The Bolshoi Ballet's *Swan Lake*. *Right:* Anthony Dowell and Antoinette Sibley in The Royal Ballet's *Swan Lake*

Margot Fonteyn and Rudolf Nureyev in The Royal Ballet's *Swan Lake*

MIRA

Robert Mead, Monica Mason, David Drew, and Vyvyan Lorrayne in "The Spanish Dance" of the Royal Ballet's *Swan Lake*

Act II of The Royal Swedish Ballet's *Swan Lake*

Top: Richard Cragun in the Stuttgart Ballet's
Taming of the Shrew

Above: Antoinette Sibley in The Royal Ballet's
Triad

Right: Egon Madsen and Birgit Keil in The
Stuttgart Ballet's *The Taming of the Shrew*

City Center Joffrey Ballet's *Trinity*

Ron Protas

Right and below: The Royal Danish Ballet's *Triumph of Death*

Below: Karin von Aroldingen in New York City Ballet's *Variations Pour une Porte et un Soupir*

Martha Swope

Above: Ross Parkes (on floor), Robert Rodham and Paschal Guzman in The Pennsylvania Ballet's *Villon*

Left: Maris Liepa in The Bolshoi Ballet's *Walpurgis Night*

Below: Kay Mazzo in New York City Ballet's *Violin Concerto*

Martha Swope

Above: New York City Ballet's *Who Cares?* (with Jacques d'Amboise)

Left: Jacob Sparsø Nielsen in The Royal Danish Ballet's *The Whims of Cupid and of the Ballet Master*

Below: The Royal Winnipeg Ballet's *Les Whoops-de-doo*

John R. Johnsen

Opus 65

Choreography, Anna Sokolow; music, Teo Macero. First performed by the City Center Joffrey Ballet, September 11, 1965, and revived by that company, September 6, 1966. It has also been performed by the Royal Winnipeg Ballet.

Opus 65, Anna Sokolow's recurring theme of actions and reactions involving the angry, restless generation of the 1960s.

Opus 12

Choreography, Hans van Manen; music, Béla Bartók (Divertimento for String Orchestra); décor, Co Westerik; costumes, Jan van der Wal. First performed by the Nederlands Dans Theatre, The Hague, Holland, July 7, 1964. The first American performance was by the same company at Jacob's Pillow, Lee, Massachusetts, July 17–20, 1965. The first New York performance was April 18, 1968.

A work representing the Dutch choreographer's interest in mating free-style movement with balletic action.

Orpheus

Choreography, George Balanchine; music, Igor Stravinsky; scenery and costumes, Isamu Noguchi. First produced by the Ballet Society (now the New York City Ballet), New York, April 28, 1948. A version of the ballet with choreography by John Cranko was first performed by the Stuttgart Ballet, Stuttgart, June 6, 1970.

In the first scene Orpheus mourns at the grave of Eurydice. His lyre lies soundless at his feet as he stands, with bent back and helpless arms, longing for his lost beloved. Three figures enter, leave Eurydice's headdress on the grave, touch Orpheus gently in sympathy, move on. Orpheus now takes up his lyre and moves through a dance of lamentation. Despondency returns, for the song of the lyre fails to summon the image or the echo of Eurydice. A satyr and sprites, hearing the song, leap forth in an attempt to make Orpheus forget his sorrow. For a moment he dances with them but then returns to his lonely vigil.

But the prayers of the mourning lover have been heard, and the Angel of Death, clad in brown and with black coils looped about him, enters. He wraps the coils about Orpheus' arms and in a solo dance sequence, demonstrates his inexorable powers, his ability to lead Orpheus to Hades and to Eurydice. He frees Orpheus of the magical bonds, places a golden mask over his eyes and, placing an arm through the lyre, grasps Orpheus firmly and leads him on the long journey. A white silken curtain descends as if a mist has fallen and figures and shapes move behind it, stir it into swirling, ominous shapes as the two make their descent to Hell.

In the second scene, Orpheus and the Angel of Death have arrived in Hades. Damned figures bearing great rocks move ceaselessly and the Furies prepare to attack the invaders. The Angel moves behind the masked and unseeing Orpheus and, guiding his hand, urges him to play upon the lyre. He knows that only the magic of Orpheus' music will lull the Furies and soften the heart of Pluto, god of the underworld.

The travelers come to the throne of the god and there he stands, with Eurydice resting against him. The beauty of the music and the pleas for release have worked. Pluto delivers Eurydice to Orpheus and restores her life with the condition that Orpheus not look upon her face until the journey back to earth is complete. The Angel of Death, holding the lyre as a guide, leads and the two lovers follow. The misty curtain of white again falls and Orpheus and Eurydice commence the ascent.

At first Eurydice follows Orpheus' footsteps but her joy increases and her desire to look upon his face becomes almost unbearable. The ascent is difficult, Orpheus is blinded and the fear that he will lose her, combined with his passion to see her, torture him constantly. Their bodies touch as they move together, embraces are fused with the progressive steps of the climb, and finally Orpheus can stand it no longer. He rips the mask from his face and looks at his loved one. Instantly she falls dead at his feet. As he encircles her in his arms, the mists billow, unseen forces draw her from his embrace, and she disappears into the surging whiteness. Desperate, Orpheus reaches out for the lyre which the hand of the Dark Angel has held within view, but just as he nears it, the hand and lyre are swiftly withdrawn. Orpheus has doomed not only Eurydice but himself.

Orpheus crawls from view, the mists dissolve, and earth reappears. A scarlet-haired woman, long of limb and with weapon-like arms, enters. She is the leader of the passion-seeking Bacchantes and she is followed by a group of her corn-color-haired sisters. As Orpheus appears, they rush at him but he repulses their advances and, in a fury, they maul him, mangle him, cut off his arms, legs, and head and toss the remnants behind a hillock.

In the third scene, Apollo enters to mourn at the grave of Orpheus. Taking a golden mask of the face of Orpheus, he strokes its lips as if he would call forth again the music of the matchless singer of songs. He stands, slowly lifts an arm, and from behind the hillock appears a garland, which carries the lyre of Orpheus. It rises steadily heavenward, symbolizing the immortality of Orpheus, who has become the god of song.

The ballet, with a score especially composed for Balanchine, is not set in any period of Greek antiquity. Rather is it a primitive rite that carries with it the air of timelessness. It may be viewed as a retelling of the famous myth of Orpheus and Eurydice or as an ancient ritual in which worshipers recreate a legend they have always known. The scenery and costumes, bright, without period and almost surrealistic, suggest the magic of myth and the mystery of ancient legend. And Jean Rosenthal's lighting, which has lent historymaking distinction to all of the New York City Ballet productions, in *Orpheus* reveals not only the action of the choreography but literally illumines the drama itself. Indeed, the Rosenthal lighting is an integral part of the choreography.

The first cast was headed by Maria Tallchief (Eurydice), Nicholas Magallanes (Orpheus), Francisco Moncion (Dark Angel), Tanaquil LeClercq (the chief Bacchante), and Herbert Bliss (Apollo).

An earlier Balanchine treatment of the Orpheus myth was produced in 1936, when the choreographer staged the Gluck opera, *Orfeo ed Euridice*, in ballet form (with the singers placed in the orchestra pit) at the Metropolitan Opera House.

There have been many ballets based upon the Orpheus theme, among them works by David Lichine, Aurel Miloss, Frederick Ashton, and Ninette de Valois.

Out of Lesbos

Choreography and music, James Clouser. First performed by the Royal Winnipeg Ballet, Winnipeg, November, 24, 1966.

Out of Lesbos, a *pas de deux*, is an image of Sappho meeting her final love, a man. He is the helmsman of a ship but he is also Death.

Christine Hennessey created the role of Sappho.

Paganini

Choreography, Michel Fokine; music, Serge Rachmaninoff (Rhapsody on a Theme of Paganini); *scenery and costumes, Serge Soudeikine. First produced by the Original Ballet Russe, London, June 30, 1939. First presented in America by the same company, Los Angeles, October 12, 1940.*

Le Palais de Crystal

See *Symphony in C*

Paquita

Choreography, Mazilier; music, Deldevez. First produced in Paris (with Carlotta Grisi in the leading role), April 1, 1846. Produced in Russia by the Russian Imperial Ballet, September 26 (Julian or Russian calendar) or October 8 (Gre-

gorian or Western calendar), 1847, with music by Leon Min-
kus and Deldevez. Revised and with new choreography by
Marius Petipa, December 27, 1881 (Julian) or January 8,
1882 (Gregorian); later amended by Enrico Cecchetti. Still in
the repertories of the Russian State Ballet. Produced in a one-
act divertissement *arrangement by the Ballet Russe de Monte*
Carlo, New York, September 20, 1949, with choreography by
Alexandra Danilova after Mazilier and Petipa (and including
original material by Danilova), music of Minkus and Del-
devez, scenery by Eugene Berman and costumes by Castillo.
Other versions include one for the Festival Ballet of London,
Oxford, February 9, 1967; and extended excerpt staged by
Rudolf Nureyev for the Royal Academy of Dancing Gala,
London, November 11, 1964, and subsequently for the Amer-
ican Ballet Theatre, New York, July 6, 1971.

A fairly complicated story of a Spanish gypsy in love with a
French nobleman and prevented from union with him because of
their different social stations. In the midst of a conspiracy in which
the gypsies and the local governor attempt to rid themselves of
French rule, the Gypsy discovers she is of noble blood. All ends
happily.

At the very first performance Lucien Petipa was Grisi's partner. Lucien's brother, Marius, updated the ballet forty years later
for the Russian Imperial Ballet's increased technical accomplishments.

Paquita Pas de Deux

Choreography, Alexandra Fedorova-Fokine; music, Ludwig
Minkus. First performed by Ballet Theatre (now the Ameri-
can Ballet Theatre), New York, August 6, 1957.

Parade

Choreography, Leonide Massine; music, Erik Satie; theme,
Jean Cocteau; curtain, scenery, and costumes, Pablo Picasso.

First performed by Diaghilev's Ballets Russes, Paris, May 18, 1917. Revived for the City Center Joffrey Ballet, March 22, 1973.

Parade, now more than a half-century old, is of interest to present-day audiences, not because of its once innovative choreography, which now seems dated and thin, but because of the continuing impact of Picasso's art. Indeed, the ballet itself is rooted in Picasso's art, and the dancing is merely a very slight extension of his designs. Of chief moment today, other than Picasso, is the lively aerial dance, touched with elegant grotesqueries, for the Chinese Conjurer, and an oldtime vaudeville-style number in which two performers serve as the back and front of a frolicsome horse. The theme, upon which the ballet lightly rests, involves traveling sideshow entertainers at a Paris fair who are unable to persuade an audience to come inside the theatre once they have glanced at the free teasers outside.

Paradise Lost

Choreography, Roland Petit; music, Marius Constant; décor, Martial Raysse. First performed by the Royal Ballet, London, February 23, 1967.

The work was created for Margot Fonteyn and Rudolf Nureyev.

Pas de Dix

Choreography, George Balanchine; music, Alexander Glazounov; costumes, Esteban Frances. First produced by the New York City Ballet, New York, November 9, 1955.

In this storyless classical ballet, a Hungarian dance flavor touches the traditional steps and is prominently accented in the variation for the ballerina. Here the swiftly brushed clapping of the hands, the sudden back kick with backbend, and the hand placed behind the head give a definite *hongroise* touch to the proceedings.

The dance measures for the ensemble are mainly light and gay, and the solo for the ballerina is buoyant in spirit and exceptionally demanding in both the technical and stylistic sense. The variation for the *premier danseur* is also difficult.

Maria Tallchief and André Eglevsky were the first to dance the leading roles.

Pas de Quatre

Choreography, Jules Perrot; music, Cesare Pugni. First produced in London, July 12, 1845, the first of four performances, one a command performance for Queen Victoria. Revived, with a single change of cast (Carolina Rosati replacing Lucile Grahn) in 1847. Keith Lester recreated the Pas de Quatre *in London in 1936 for the Markova-Dolin Ballet. Anton Dolin arranged a new version of the work for Ballet Theatre (now the American Ballet Theatre), New York, February 16, 1941. Later, the Ballet Russe de Monte Carlo presented the Dolin version and Ballet Theatre presented the Lester staging. Dolin's version gained wide popularity and has been performed by the Boston Ballet, the Paris Opera Ballet, the Royal Danish Ballet, Het Nationale Ballet, the Royal Winnipeg Ballet, Les Grandes Ballets Canadiens, and the National Ballet of Washington. Alicia Alonso has staged both the Dolin version (for the Ballet Nacional de Cuba) and the Lester version (for the Pennsylvania Ballet, 1971). A very special production of* Pas de Quatre *was staged by Dolin for the Gala Benefit to save the Dance Collection of The New York Public Library at Lincoln Center. This performance featured Carla Fracci as Taglioni, Eleanor D'Antuono as Grahn, Violette Verdy as Grisi, and Patricia McBride as Cerrito, and was performed January 24, 1972, at City Center, New York.*

Pas de Quatre is certainly the most celebrated *divertissement* in ballet history, for it brought together for a limited number of performances four of the five greatest ballerinas of the Romantic Age, Marie Taglioni, Carlotta Grisi, Fanny Cerrito, and Lucile Grahn.

The fifth, who did not participate, was Fanny Elssler, Taglioni's most dangerous rival. Benjamin Lumley, manager of His Majesty's Theater, enjoyed a tremendous success when he brought Elssler and Cerrito together for a *pas de deux* in 1843. In 1845 he was determined to cap this with an incredible union of four tempestuous ballerinas. He almost failed.

Perrot, who helped in the creating of *Giselle*, was the choreographer and it was agreed that the dances would be so designed that no one ballerina would outshine her sisters and yet each would be given passages to display her special attributes. No easy task, but apparently Perrot, who was Grisi's husband, succeeded. But then came the impasse: it was settled that Taglioni should have the place of honor with the final variation, but a battle raged over who should have second place of honor. Taglioni had ushered in the Romantic Age almost singlehanded with her dancing in *La Sylphide;* Grisi, combining the earthiness of Elssler with the lightness and ethereal quality of Taglioni, had triumphed as *Giselle;* Cerrito had been hailed as one of the great artists of the era; and Grahn, the Danish ballerina, had scored a memorable success in Taglioni's own *La Sylphide*.

Perrot could not settle the dispute and it seemed that the ballet would never see the stage. Lumley had an answer. He suggested that seniority of years should prevail. Suddenly the ballerinas were modestly personified and each of the three wanted the others to have the place next to Taglioni. Remorselessly, Perrot followed instructions. Taglioni, already secure in her honored place, was the oldest; Cerrito was next; then Grisi; Grahn was the youngest.

There is, of course, no record of the choreography. Lithographs of Chalon show us a pose, the costumes, the style, and the writings of those who saw the performances provide clues to the characteristics of each dance and even to some of the steps used. Both Lester and Dolin turned to these sources and using them as guides, in addition to understanding the technique and style of the period, they recreated what they could and created the rest.

The Dolin version is described here.

The curtain rises on a duplication of the famous Chalon lithograph, which shows the four ballerinas assembled in a lovely pose. They rise and move gracefully together, dignified but apparently friendly, for they occasionally move with hands entwined. They conclude this opening dance with an equally pretty pose. Now the bounding Grahn (the Danes are still famed for their leaping skill) performs a variation that includes leaping turns, elaborate *batterie* while moving in a circle, and an extended series of *entrechats*. When she concludes and takes her bows, she gracefully directs her arms to the other side of the stage by way of graciously introducing the next ballerina.

The variation for Grisi is dainty and builds to fleetness of footwork. She moves first in a diagonal with tiny steps on *pointe,* then she turns to exquisitely mastered beats across the stage, and concludes with a series of traveling *fouettés* executed slowly. Taglioni and Grahn now return for a brief duet which leads to an introduction of the third dancer. Cerrito performs a lilting waltz which includes balances, aristocratic placements of an extended foot as the dancer slowly turns in pose, leaping turns, and a *grand jeté* in a final exit.

After her bows, Cerrito extends her arms and introduces the queen of the ballet, Taglioni. The variation celebrates the great dancer's lightness and aerial skill. Sustained poses in arabesque, with the arms somewhat retracted (Taglioni had unusually long arms) as recorded in the many lithographs of her; little jumps and an elaborate series of beats in which the dancer continuously changes direction.

All of the dancers return for a final sequence, which includes high leaps and a charming series of *échappés* in which the four, holding hands in a circle and facing outward, rise on *pointe* and descend while moving in a circle. The ballet concludes with a return to the opening pose.

In certain contemporary performances, a hint of malice and of rivalry are present as they must surely have been in the original presentations. Everything is ladylike, elegant, proper but touches of hauteur suggest that each believes herself to be unique.

The equals of the four original ballerinas have never been assembled in modern times, although one, two, or occasionally three of the finest dancers of our day have been engaged to appear in it. Needless to say, the more top ballerinas participating, the greater the power of *Pas de Quatre*, for not only is there a need for superior technique but the element of rivalry is more apparent when it is inescapably there.

At the first performance of Dolin's *Pas de Quatre*, the cast included Nana Gollner (Taglioni), Nina Stroganova (Grahn), Alicia Alonso (Grisi), and Katharine Sergava (Cerrito). Shortly thereafter, a distinguished group assumed the parts, headed by Alicia Markova, who seemed to be the reincarnation of Taglioni, with Irina Baronova (Grahn), Nora Kaye (Grisi), and Annabelle Lyon (Cerrito).

Pas des Déesses

Choreography, Robert Joffrey; music, John Field. First performed by the Robert Joffrey Ballet, New York, May 29, 1954. Staged by Joffrey for Ballet Rambert, London, June 30, 1955. First performed by Ballet Theatre (now the American Ballet Theatre), New York, May 7, 1956.

This classical ballet for a cast of four recreates four great dancers and reproduces the style of the Romantic Age of ballet. The characters, dressed as if they might have stepped from a nineteenth-century lithograph, are Marie Taglioni, Lucile Grahn, Fanny Cerrito, and Arthur Saint-Léon. Their solo variations, duets, and ensemble actions suggest the etiquette and elegance of an earlier dance era and a very delicate humorous commentary on the period is incorporated in the choreography. As in any classical showpiece, virtuosity is used to exploit the special skills of the individuals and the personal style of each is characterized by the selection of steps and gestures.

Another *Pas des Déesses*, inspired by the original of Jules Perrot and using the music of Pugni, was created for the Ballet Rambert by Keith Lester and first presented in London, November 30, 1939. It was added, more than a decade later, to the repertory of the London Festival Ballet.

The first cast of the Robert Joffrey Ballet production was Lillian Wellein (Taglioni), Barbara Gray (Grahn), Jacquetta Keith (Cerrito), and Michael Lland (Saint-Léon). The Ballet Theatre workshop performance featured Lupe Serrano (Taglioni), Sonia Arova (Grahn), Ruth Ann Koesun (Cerrito), and Erik Bruhn (Saint-Léon).

Pas de Trois

(Glinka)

> Choreography, George Balanchine; music, Mikhail Glinka; costumes, Karinska. First produced by the New York City Ballet, New York, March 1, 1955.

This *Pas de Trois*, set to music from Glinka's *Russlan and Ludmila*, is a show piece for classical dancers. Balanchine has used only the movements of the academic dance here, but he has selected those that display physical prowess and stylishness of behavior. Humor also is present in some of the passages, humor that is not always gestural but often is the result of timing and sequence.

Solo, duo, and trio passages comprise this short and brilliant work. One ballerina's variation incorporates lyrical leg swings, turns (with a slight backbend) that seem to float, and fleetly shifting foot designs. The second ballerina, though pretending to be demure, is a genuine showoff, with bursting flights into the air and on-the-ground steps accomplished at high speed and with an air of coquetry. The *premier danseur's* variation is highlighted by aerial activities which include high leaps and an array of elaborate leg-beats.

André Eglevsky, Melissa Hayden, and Patricia Wilde were the first to dance this display piece.

Pas de Trois

(Minkus)

> Choreography, George Balanchine; music, Léon Minkus; costumes, Karinska. First produced by the New York City Ballet,

February 18, 1951. An earlier presentation of this short work, set to music from the Minkus score for the full-length Don Quixote, *was presented by the Marquis de Cuevas' Grand Ballet.*

In this elegant contest, each of the three participants vies with the others (but oh, so graciously!). It is a bravura piece of smiles, virtuosity, and triumphs over technical hazards.

Maria Tallchief, Nora Kaye, and André Eglevsky were the performers at the première.

Path of Thunder

Choreography, Konstantin Sergeyev; music, Kara Karayev; book, Yuri Slonimsky (based on a novel by Peter Abrahams); designs, Valery Dorrer. First performed by the Kirov Ballet, Leningrad, January 4, 1958. First performed by the Bolshoi Ballet, Moscow, with same choreography and decor, June 27, 1959.

Les Patineurs

(The Skaters)

Choreography, Frederick Ashton; music, Giacomo Meyerbeer (themes from Meyerbeer's operas arranged by Constant Lambert); scenery and costumes, William Chappell. First produced by the Sadler's Wells Ballet (now the Royal Ballet), London, February 16, 1937. First produced in America with scenery and costumes by Cecil Beaton, by Ballet Theatre (now the American Ballet Theatre), New York, October 2, 1946. The ballet is also in the repertories of the Australian Ballet and the Royal Winnipeg Ballet.

Les Patineurs is a ballet based on the dance equivalents of skating steps, motions, and figures. It takes place in a woodland setting, prettily touched with snow, at night. Couples glide by with skatinglike steps, followed by two girls who have great difficulty staying upright. A boy in green comes on and performs a sheaf of tricks before he skates complacently away. Two lovers appear and skate romantically together before they disappear to more secluded areas.

The merriment and the skills increase, and there are ensemble dances, a vivid bit by the boy in green, whirling figures by two girls, a chain sequence for the group, and vertiginous spins by the more adept. Now the snow is falling and, as the curtain falls, the boy in green is turning like a top, ready and eager to the end to outdo everyone else.

Margot Fonteyn, Robert Helpmann, and Harold Turner headed the cast for the first Sadler's Wells Ballet presentation.

Percussion for Six—Men

Choreography, Vincente Nebrada; music, Lee Gurst. First performed by Harkness Youth Dancers, Delacorte Theatre, New York City, September, 1969.

Percussion for Six—Women

Choreography, Vincente Nebrada; music, Lee Gurst. First performed by the Harkness Ballet, Frankfurt, Germany, September, 1971.

La Péri

Choreography, Frederick Ashton; music, Paul Dukas; scenery and costumes, André Levasseur. First produced by the Sadler's Wells Ballet (now the Royal Ballet), London, February 15, 1956. First presented in America by the same company, New York, September 26, 1957. Other versions have been choreographed by Yvette Chauviré, Jean-Jacques Etcheverray, and Michel Fokine. Among the most recent stagings have been the George Skibine choreography with decor by Nicholas Cernovich, for the Paris Opera Ballet, first performed in Paris, December 14, 1966, and later by the National Ballet of Washington, New York, March 27, 1967, and the Peter

Darrel version first danced by the London Festival Ballet, London, January 9, 1973.

La Péri is an extended and elaborate *pas de deux* described as a *"poème dansé."* It tells the tale of Iskender who wanders through Iran in search of the Flower of Immortality. At last he comes upon a Péri, an Oriental fairy. She is asleep but in her hands she holds the precious flower. Iskender, moving quietly, plucks the flower from her hand. Awakening, the Péri is alarmed but she sees that Iskender has fallen in love with her, and recognizing an opportunity to regain the flower, she dances the magical dance of the péris for him. Drawing ever closer to him, the Péri stirs his passion to such a peak that he is undecided between the wish for immortality and the desire for this beautiful creature. Completely captivated, Iskender gives the Flower of Immortality back to the Péri. Aglow with happiness, the fairy disappears, leaving Iskender to face the doom of all mortals.

One of Ashton's first ballets, at the start of his choreographic career, was also a work called *La Péri.* Other ballets by the same name, but with various plots, involving these Oriental fairies, have been created by other choreographers during the last century and longer.

Margot Fonteyn and Michael Somes were the stars of the Sadler's Wells Ballet production in London and in New York.

Persephone

Choreography, Kurt Jooss; music, Igor Stravinsky; text, André Gide; decor and costumes, André Barsacq. First performed by Ballets Ida Rubinstein, Paris, April 30, 1934. Frederick Ashton choreographed another version for the Royal Ballet, with décor and costumes by Nico Ghika, which was given its first performance, London, December 12, 1961. Another version, for the Santa Fe Opera Ballet, featuring Vera Zorina, was choreographed by Thomas Andrew, with costumes by Vera Stravinsky. It was performed for the first time in Santa Fe, New Mexico, in the summer of 1961. Robert Joffrey has choreographed two ballets on the Persephone theme. The first, for Choreographer's Workshop, with music by Robert Silverman and décor and costumes by Read Arnow, was first presented at the 92nd Street YM-YWHA, New York, January 13, 1952. The second Joffrey version was choreographed to music by Antonio Vivaldi (from The Seasons: "Spring" and "Winter"), libretto after Gide, and décor and costumes by Harri Wich. It was given its first performance by Ballet Rambert, London, June 28, 1955.

Peter and the Wolf

Choreography, Adolph Bolm; music and book, Serge Prokofiev; scenery and costumes, Lucinda Ballard. First produced by Ballet Theatre (now the American Ballet Theatre), New York, January 13, 1940. Other productions include those by Ivo Cramer, for the Norwegian National Ballet; Niels Bjørn Larsen, for the Royal Danish Ballet; Samuel Kurkjian, for the Boston Ballet; and Michael Uthoff, for the Hartford Ballet. A version with members of the New York City Ballet, choreographed by Jacques d'Amboise, and with décor and costumes by Raoul Pène duBois, was given its first performance at City Center in New York, March 3, 1969.

A ballet for children with a narration that identifies the various characters by themes played on specific musical instruments. The cast includes the little boy, Peter; his rheumatic Grandfather; swift Bird; waddling slow-motion Duck (who gets eaten by the Wolf); Cat, with great spinal flexibility and cunning; the evil, snarling Wolf; the less than courageous First Hunter and his group of terrified followers.

The story concerns itself with the antics and pranks of Peter, the eating of the Duck by the Wolf, and the capture of the Wolf through Peter's strategy. A happy ending sees to it that the Duck, extricated from the Wolf's stomach (he swallowed her whole), joins her companions in good health.

At the première Eugene Loring was Peter; Viola Essen, Bird;

Nina Stroganova, Cat; Karen Conrad, Duck; Edward Caton, Grandfather; and William Dollar, Wolf.

Petrouchka

Choreography, Michel Fokine; music, Igor Stravinsky; book, Stravinsky and Alexandre Benois; scenery and costumes, Benois. First produced by Diaghilev's Ballets Russes, Paris, June 13, 1911. First presented in America by the same company, New York, January 24, 1916. First mounted (under Fokine's direction) by the Royal Danish Ballet, Copenhagen, October 14, 1925. The Ballet Russe de Monte Carlo's production was first presented in New York, January 10, 1934. Staged by Ballet Theatre (now the American Ballet Theatre), under Fokine's direction, New York, October 8, 1942. Yurek Lazowsky staged the production currently in the repertory of the City Center Joffrey Ballet, which performed it for the first time, New York, March 12, 1970. Other productions of Petrouchka are in the repertoires of the Royal Swedish Ballet, the Australian Ballet, the Royal Ballet, and the Norwegian National Ballet.

Scene One is the Shrovetide fair in the St. Petersburg, Russia, of the 1830s. Rich people and poor people in holiday attire are present to look over wares, watch street entertainers, and have a good time. It is a constantly milling, changing crowd, pausing for a moment to admire a street dancer, then her competitor, as they engage in pirouettes, kicks, and splits. But the real entertainment is about to take place, in the back of the square at a little theater with blue curtains. A Charlatan in robe and conical cap, and with an aging, pinched, and fearful face, pokes his head through the curtains. Everyone stops and watches as he steps forth and plays a melody on his flute. At his signal, the curtains open and there, supported by circular racks, are three puppets—a Ballerina with bright-red circles on her cheeks, a Blackamoor in fancy dress, and Petrouhcka, the sad-faced clown with the tragic turned-down mouth.

At the Charlatan's command they start to move, holding themselves by their supports and prancing with their legs. The crowd then draws back and the puppets run forward to the front of the real stage to perform. Through their doll-like, jointed movements it is indicated that the male puppets are in love with the Ballerina, who seems to prefer the Blackamoor. Petrouchka, though a puppet, has experienced human love and is violently jealous. He attacks the Blackamoor, but the Charlatan orders him to stop, and the puppets return to their dancing. As darkness descends, the crowds wander off, the puppets are immobilized by their master, and the scene ends.

The second scene takes place in Petrouchka's room. He is hurled through the door and locked in because of his misbehavior. All his woes come to the surface. With futile puppet gestures he tells of his hatred of the Charlatan, his love for the Ballerina, and the mortal anguish which pervades his sawdust body. He tries desperately to escape but the door is securely fastened and the walls seem impregnable. The Ballerina enters but is frightened by Petrouchka's impassioned action and flees. With a tremendous effort, the clown tries again to escape and this time succeeds in crashing through a wall.

Scene Three is the Blackamoor's exotic quarters. He is lying on a couch tossing a coconut with his feet and catching it with his hands. Bored with this, he shakes it, listens to it, and attempts to break it open with his scimitar but is unsuccessful and decides that this coconut must contain a powerful god. He places it on the floor, worships it with elaborate salaams, and falls.

The Ballerina appears, stepping lightly on *pointe* and playing a tin horn. She permits the Blackamoor to dance with her, court her, hold her in his arms. The escaped Petrouchka enters and tries to protect his beloved from the amorous advances of the other puppet, but the Blackamoor grabs his scimitar and chases Petrouchka away. The Blackamoor resumes his lovemaking, which includes some delectable nibbles of the Ballerina's waist, and the scene ends.

The fourth scene returns to the fair. Barely any time has elapsed and although dusk is approaching, the crowds are still eager for fun. Shoulder-shaking gypsy girls take part in the gaiety, a group of nursemaids dance a gentle but jolly Russian peasant dance, a trained bear displays his tricks, coachmen engage in a lusty dance featuring the famous Russian knee-bends, and masqueraders further enliven the scene. Suddenly Petrouchka comes running into the crowd chased by the Blackamoor, who is followed by the Ballerina. Although the Ballerina attempts to stop him, the Blackamoor strikes the poor Petrouchka again and again with his scimitar and the sad little clown falls. The crowd, which has drawn back, watches the last jerky trembles of the dying Petrouchka and, as he becomes still in death, surrounds him. A policeman is sent for to investigate the murder, but the Charlatan appears and picks up a limp sawdust body. It is only a puppet, he says, so how can a crime have been committed?

The crowd disperses and the Charlatan starts to drag off the grotesque figure of the doll. Suddenly there is a piercing, plaintive cry from the orchestra (Petrouchka's theme) and the horrified Charlatan looks up to see Petrouchka, or his ghost, atop the theater. The ghost of the clown shakes his fists and laments that no one realized he had a human heart, had suffered human anguish, had truly died.

Petrouchka is viewed not only as one of Fokine's masterpieces but also as a modern classic in the theater of ballet. Because of the complexity of the music, it is difficult for an orchestra (except one of top caliber) to play it accurately and for dancers to perform it. The crowd scenes, unless carefully rehearsed, seem aimless and endless and the role of Petrouchka requires a sensitive and accomplished actor-dancer. The production itself is elaborate and expensive to mount and to keep fresh. Of current productions, that of the Royal Danish Ballet is meticulous, vivid, and handsomely mounted, and appears to come closest to a realization of the choreographer's and the composer's intentions.

At the première Vaslav Nijinsky had the title role, Tamara Karsavina was the Ballerina, Alexandre Orlov was the Moor, and Enrico Cecchetti the Charlatan. At the ballet's American debut Leonide Massine, Lydia Lopokova, and Adolph Bolm were the puppets. Bolm, Yurek Lazowsky, Jerome Robbins, John Kriza,

Borge Ralov, and Alexander Grant are among the many other interpreters of Petrouchka, and the Ballerinas have included Alexandra Danilova, Alicia Markova, Tamara Toumanova, Irina Baronova, Nora Kaye, and Margot Fonteyn. David Lichine, Frederic Franklin, and André Eglevsky are a few of the Blackamoors.

Phèdre

Choreography, Serge Lifar; music, Georges Auric; libretto and décor, Jean Cocteau. First performed by the Paris Opéra Ballet, Paris Opéra, June 14, 1950.

A dance-drama, or mimed treatment, based on Racine's tragedy derived from the ancient Greek theme.

Tamara Toumanova and Lifar headed the first cast.

Picnic at Tintagel

Choreography, Frederick Ashton; music, Arnold Bax (The Garden of Fand); scenery and costumes, Cecil Beaton. First produced by the New York City Ballet, New York, February 28, 1952.

The theme of this modern ballet (set in the year 1916) is the legend of Tristram and Iseult.

The first scene takes place in the eerie ruins of the Arthurian castle of Tintagel. The Caretaker, dressed in a green which almost fuses with the gray-green of the ruins, moves mysteriously, as if he knows some secret about the love-haunted place. His actions are incantational and powerful, fast, almost acrobatic. But when he hears a party approaching, he assumes the guise of a hunchbacked old man. The picnickers, dressed in the voluminous motoring habits of the day, are a man, his wife, a male friend (in love with the wife), a maid, a chauffeur, and a footman.

Gestures and glances tell us that the wife and the second man are having a secret love affair, or are planning to, and the husband's suspicions are clearly projected. But the party is decorous and preparations are made for the picnic, with a cloth, wine, and goblets laid out. When no one is looking, the Caretaker removes the cap from the wine and makes mysterious passes over the bottle. Shortly thereafter the maid pours wine into two glasses and the illicit lovers, toasting each other and looking into each other's eyes with longing, raise the glasses to their lips. There is a crash of sound, darkness obscures the figures momentarily, and suddenly the ruins disappear, the walls and arches of a reborn Tintagel arise, and the chauffeur and footman, transformed into heralds, wave the banners of King Mark. The lovers, recreated as Tristram and Iseult, stand with glasses raised. The Caretaker (is he Merlin?) snatches the goblets from their hands and disappears. Through his magic, the modern lovers have been transported back into time to find themselves the doomed lovers of an earlier day. The husband has become King Mark and the maid Iseult's faithful Brangaene.

Tristram is knighted by his king and, kissing his hand, swears fealty. With the departure of the king, the lovers steal a moment of romance but they are watched by one of the king's knights. With the sudden return of the king, Brangaene swiftly moves to Tristram as if she had been dancing with him. Two knights, plotting to catch Tristram and Iseult in a compromising situation, suggest a hunt. The king agrees but Tristram excuses himself so that he may be alone with Iseult.

As she waits for him to come for her, Iseult performs a lovely dance which portrays her love, her eagerness, and her impatience. With the arrival of Tristram, the two dance an amorous duet and sink to the floor with limbs entwined. A spying knight rushes off, and the king (who has been warned) returns. Drawing his sword, despite Iseult's pleas, he rushes at Tristram, but Iseult steps in the way and is pierced through the body. The duel between the king and Tristram ends with the young man's death; the tragedy is over.

The castle falls away, the ruins reappear, and the two twentieth-century lovers stand with upraised glasses. Has it been a dream, a warning, a true adventure into the past? Shaken, the husband leads his wife away. The place is left to the Caretaker.

Was it a dream? He lifts the gleaming dueling swords high over his head, triumphantly. Merlin has truly made magic.

At the first performance Diana Adams played Iseult, Jacques d'Amboise was Tristram, Francisco Moncion was King Mark, and Robert Barnett was Merlin (the Caretaker).

Pictures at an Exhibition

Choreography and book, Fedor Lopukhov (assisted by Yevgeny Dmitriev); *music, Modest Moussorgsky; designs, A. Lushin. First performed at the Stanislavsky and Nemirovich-Danchenko Theater, Moscow, September 5, 1963.*

The Pied Piper

Choreography, Jerome Robbins; music, Aaron Copland (Concerto for Clarinet and String Orchestra). *First produced by the New York City Ballet, New York, December 4, 1951.*

The ballet is not a staging of the Pied Piper of Hamelin. The Pied Piper here is a clarinetist and his music hypnotizes the dancers into all kinds of activities, some romantic, some comic, some frenzied.

The initial cast was headed by Diana Adams, Nicholas Magallanes, Jillana, Roy Tobias, Janet Reed, Todd Bolender, Melissa Hayden, Herbert Bliss, Tanaquil LeClercq, and Robbins. The clarinet virtuoso was Edmund Wall.

Piège de Lumière

Choreography, John Taras; music, Jean-Michel Damase; décor, Felix Labisse; costumes, André Levasseur. First performed by the Marquis de Cuevas Ballet, at the Empire Theatre, Paris, December 23, 1952. Revived by the New York City Ballet, and first performed by that company at the New York State Theatre, New York, October 1, 1964. Festival Bal-

let revived the work and presented it for the first time April 22, 1969.

This is a theater piece which might be described as "un ballet exotique," for although it has a tropical aura, the treatment of some of the décor and costumes is "très a la couturière," juxtaposed to examples of stark realism, just as the choreography makes an analogy between butterflies and humans caught in the "snare," or "trap" of light which the title omens.

Rosella Hightower was the ballerina for the first European production and Maria Tallchief for the U.S. première.

Pierrot Lunaire

Choreography, Glen Tetley; music, Arnold Schönberg; decor, Rouben Ter-Arutunian. First performed by Glen Tetley and Company, New York, May 5, 1962. The Nederlands Dans Theatre first danced the work, The Hague, Holland, October 23, 1962. It was first presented by Ballet Rambert, Surrey, England, January 26, 1967. On October 31, 1968, the Royal Danish Ballet presented the work for the first time in Copenhagen.

A contemporary psychological extension of the familiar *commedia dell'arte* clown. The essential setting on which much of the action takes place is made up of a structure of pipes rather like a children's playground unit.

Tetley danced the premiere, and Niels Kehlet has won praise for his portrayal with the Royal Danish Ballet.

Pillar of Fire

Choreography, Anthony Tudor; music, Arnold Schönberg (Verklaerte Nacht); scenery and costumes, Jo Mielziner. First produced by Ballet Theatre (now the American Ballet Theatre), New York, April 8, 1942.

Pillar of Fire, a contemporary dramatic ballet which incorporates the technique of classical ballet, the impulsive and emotionally urgent movements of modern dance, and the walks and gestures one might see in everyday behavior, is the story of Hagar, a frustrated girl on the desperate fringe of spinsterhood.

The curtain rises on a street scene. To the left is a mysterious, dark, almost tortured-looking house and to the right is a proper Victorian home. On the steps of the neat and tidy dwelling sits Hagar, primly dressed. She is almost still but there is tension in her body, a hand strokes back a strand of hair; and we are aware of her loneliness, her feeling that she is unpretty, her grim view of the future.

Hagar's two sisters appear. One is staid, prudish-looking, already an old maid. The other is a young girl, vivacious, perhaps spoiled, mischief in her eye and coquetry in the attitudes of her newly maturing body. A young man enters and Hagar's spirits rise. She loves him, but so inhibited is she that her responses to his greeting are taut, uncertain. He returns her affection but because of her shyness, he turns his attention to the other sisters, particularly the younger, who imagines herself to be flirtatious rather than merely an exuberant girl.

Hagar watches as her younger sister works her half-innocent wiles, and when the three enter the house, she remains outside, alone in her torment. She gives vent to her fury and despair in movements which tell of her desperation, her need for escape from a barren future. Suddenly the house across the way lights up, and through its walls Hagar sees men and women in hot embraces. A feminine hand sensuously circles the bare waist of a man, the hair of the girl hangs loose and free, and the torsos of the men gleam. This experience, perhaps, is what the unsatisfied Hagar dreams she requires.

A man steps forth from the house of flesh and glowers at her. His eyes seem to strip her and appraise her, his stance is cocky, his walk is tough and suggestive. As he reenters the house, the young sister and Hagar's beloved return. Hagar makes no move to tell the man of her feelings for him and he turns his attention again upon the playful sister, whose guile has amused and delighted him though it has by no means trapped him. As he carries

off her sister, Hagar contorts her body in anguish, whirls as if she
would lose herself in the vortex of action, rushes aimlessly.

The man across the way returns and Hagar prepares to give
herself to him. They dance together, moving swiftly from a passionate embrace to an ecstatic lift; and when fire has been fully
generated, the man takes Hagar into his house. When she re-
emerges, shame and remorse rush over her. She has responded to
lust but she has not found love. Her guilt is apparent and the
oldest sister scorns her, picking up her skirts as she passes so as
not to be contaminated. Others shun her and she is alone.

The scandal has spread. Now the houses disappear, and a
light falls on the three sisters, quarantined in their homes. Soon the
young man returns to bring some comfort to Hagar, but she is
ashamed of herself and refuses his sympathy almost unwillingly.
She seeks help elsewhere, but the young innocents of the town
avoid her, the lecherous inhabitants of the house across the way
scorn her, and even the libertine who has seduced her will have
none of her. As she reaches the breaking point, the young man
returns. He refuses her potestations that she is no good, that she
does not need him, and he moves gently but firmly into her life.
Their dance together is warm and loving and wonderfully tender,
for Hagar has found the love she has so desperately sought and
unintentionally shunted off. At the conclusion of their love duet
they move away; but a few moments later they are seen walking
hand-in-hand in the luminous glow filtering down through the
trees of a forest. Together they glide slowly forward and upward
toward the light of their fulfillment.

During the course of the ballet two groups—the lovers-in-
innocence and the lovers-in-experience—serve as did the choruses
of classical Greek drama. They mirror in their actions the shifting desires of Hagar, they portend what is to come, and they
comment, through movement, upon the pure beauty of innocent
love and the harsh, bright excitement of carnal attraction.

Pillar of Fire was the first work created by Tudor in America
expressly for an American company, although ballets already produced in England formed an impressive Tudor wing in Ballet
Theatre's repertory. Many consider *Pillar of Fire* to be Tudor's

masterpiece. At its first performance, at the Metropolitan Opera House in New York, there were twenty-six curtain calls—and a new star was born, for Nora Kaye, a member of the *corps de ballet* and a junior soloist on occasion, triumphed as Hagar. On the basis of this historymaking enactment, Kaye was promoted to ballerina and began to establish herself as the greatest dramatic ballerina of our era. Although she went on to achieve enormous success in other Tudor ballets and in dramatic works by other choreographers, among them Jerome Robbins and Agnes de Mille, and although she subsequently rose to a position of international prominence as a first-rank classical ballerina, *Pillar of Fire* has remained the ballet most often identified with her special artistry.

The opening-night cast, in addition to Kaye, included Tudor as the Young man, Hugh Laing as the Man in the house across the way, Lucia Chase as the Eldest Sister, and Annabelle Lyon as the Youngest Sister. Among dancers later to become famous, who appeared in *corps de ballet* or minor soloist assignments, were Jerome Robbins, John Kriza, Rosella Hightower, Donald Sadler, and Maria Karnilova. Later Hagars have included Sallie Wilson and Natalia Makarova.

Pineapple Poll

Choreography, John Cranko; music, Arthur Sullivan; scenery and costumes, Osbert Lancaster. First produced by the Sadler's Wells Theatre Ballet, London, March 13, 1951. First presented in America by the same company during the 1951–52 American tour (New York première, March 25, 1952). The City Center Joffrey Ballet gave its first performance of the ballet, New York, February 25, 1970. It is also performed by the National Ballet of Canada.

Pineapple Poll is a Gilbert and Sullivan ballet, deriving its theme from a ballad by Gilbert and its score from compositions by Sullivan. It tells the story of a handsome captain who causes such a fluttering of hearts among a group of girls, including Poll, that they disguise themselves as sailors and board ship in order to be near their dream boy. The situation is comic and the dancing and pantomime are used to exploit the complications of multiple amours, Naval style.

David Blair and Elaine Fifield headed the first cast.

Poème de l'Exstase

Choreography, John Cranko; music, Alexander Scriabine, arranged by Wolfgang Fortner; decor, Jürgen Rose. First performed by the Stuttgart Ballet, Stuttgart, Germany, March 24, 1970. First presented by the Royal Ballet, London, February 15, 1972. The same company first presented the work in America, May 16, 1972.

This ballet, created especially for Dame Margot Fonteyn, tells the story of an aging diva who attracts the attentions of an ardent young man. Before she accepts a liaison with the youthful suitor, she dreams of four earlier lovers and the specific relationships she enjoyed with each. Her reverie ended, she dismisses the youth and stands alone with her anguished memories.

The first cast with the Stuttgart Ballet included Dame Margot, Egon Madsen as the young lover, and, as images of her earlier amours, Richard Cragun, Heinz Clauss, Bernd Berg, and Jan Stripling.

Poker Game

See *Jeu de Cartes*

Les Présages

(Destinies)

Choreography, Leonide Massine; music, Peter Ilyich Tchaikovsky (Symphony No. 5); scenery and costumes, André Masson. First produced by the Ballet Russe de Monte Carlo at Monte Carlo, April 13, 1933. Subsequently presented in New York, December 22, 1933.

This was the first of Massine's symphonic ballets that introduced a series of controversies, mainly among musicians, over the propriety of using great abstract music for choreographic purposes. The work itself was distinguished by the mass movements, the elaborate tableaux which were to characterize Massine's later efforts in the symphonic ballet field.

The ballet's theme is man's battle with destiny. The main figures are Action, Passion, Frivolity, the Hero, and, of course, Fate.

Creators of the principal parts were Nina Verchinina (Action), Irina Baronova (Passion), Tatiana Riabouchinska (Frivolity), David Lichine (Hero), and Leon Woizikowski (Fate).

Prince Igor

Choreography, Michel Fokine; music, Alexander Borodin (Polovtsian Dances *from the opera* Prince Igor); *scenery and costumes, Nicholas Roerich. First produced by Diaghilev's Ballets Russes, Paris, May 19, 1909. First presented in America by the same company, New York, January 12, 1916. Revived by the Ballet Russe de Monte Carlo, New York, January 10, 1934.*

When first presented in Paris, *Prince Igor* caused a near sensation, for its barbaric splendors, both in color and in action, introduced the people of Western Europe to the real or imagined exoticism and tribal savagery of semi-Oriental Russia.

The scene is a Polovtsian campsite at dawn. The ballet, without plot, is a sequence of dances which starts quietly and moves with cumulative intensity to a roaring finale. The action is folk-flavored rather than balletic, although there are pirouettes, *tours en l'air* and *grands jetés;* but these too are colored with a sense of violence. The work includes a lively dance for a single girl; a sensuous and gently feminine dance for an ensemble of gauzily clad women; more energetic dances for the tribal girls; rushing, running, and leaping dances for the warriors, brandishing their weapons; and interludes for the chief warrior, who outshines every-one in the vividness of his dancing, in his warlike skill.

Adolph Bolm created the role of the chief warrior. Leon Woizikowski, David Lichine, Yurek Shabelevsky, and Frederic Franklin are among others who have danced this part. The ballet, revised by Jean Yazvinsky for the Ballet Russe de Monte Carlo and starring Nina Novak in the expanded role of a girl warrior, was presented in New York, April 12, 1950.

The Prince of the Pagodas

Choreography and scenario, John Cranko; music, Benjamin Britten; scenery, John Piper; costumes, Desmond Heeley. First produced by the Sadler's Wells Ballet (now the Royal Ballet), London, January 1, 1957. First presented in America by the same company, New York, September 18, 1957.

This was the first full-length (three acts) British ballet by a British choreographer and with a specially commissioned score by a Brit-ish composer.

Svetlana Beriosova, David Blair, and Julia Farron headed the initial cast.

The Prisoner of the Caucasus

Choreography, Leonid Lavrovsky and I. Zilbershtein; music, Boris Asafiev; book, Nokolai Volkov (after a poem by Alex-ander Pushkin); designs, Valentina Khodasevich. First per-formed at the Maly Theatre, Leningrad, April 14, 1938.

This ballet is based on the story of a Russian officer taken prisoner by the Circassians who is aided in his escape by a Circassian girl who then kills herself for having played traitor to her people and to her betrothed. A later version, set to music of Aram Khacha-turian, was choreographed by George Skibine for the Grand Ballet du Marquis de Cuevas, Paris, December 4, 1951.

The Prodigal Son

(Le Fils Prodigue)

> *Choreography, George Balanchine; music, Serge Prokofiev; scenery and costumes, Georges Rouault. First produced by Diaghilev's Ballets Russes, Paris, May 21, 1929. Revived by the New York City Ballet, New York, February 23, 1950. Another version, with choreography by David Lichine, was produced by the Original Ballet Russe, Sydney, Australia, December 1, 1939; New York, November 26, 1940. The Balanchine production is in the repertories of the Boston Ballet, which first presented it in 1966, the National Ballet of Washington, November 8, 1968, and the Royal Ballet, January 25, 1973. Ivo Cramér choreographed a version to a score by Hugo Alfvén, which is a Swedish folk version of the Biblical tale. It was first performed by the Royal Swedish Ballet in 1957.*

The New York City Ballet production, in three scenes, is described here.

As the curtain opens, two boys are preparing wine jugs, assembling them for a long journey. The Prodigal and his sisters emerge from a tent and the youth becomes excited by the prospect of travel. Such is his enthusiasm that he commences a swift, powerful, and almost acrobatic dance that conveys to the two boys, his companions, something of the adventures in store for them. The sisters are frightened by their brother's determination to leave home and summon the father. For a moment the awesome presence of the bearded patriarch quiets the son and he submits briefly to a family ritual in which the father blesses his kneeling children and places their hands together, as if he would tell them never to separate. But the youth wrenches himself away and orders his companions to take his belongings. After they pass through the gate in the fence and shut it behind them, the arrogant Prodigal leaps the fence and races off.

Onto the second scene, with its backdrop showing a heavily laden festive board, comes a group of grotesque male revelers with bald heads and empty expressions. They take the fence of Scene

One and move it close to the backdrop, where they turn it upside down to form a long table. Next they play a wild and lascivious game until the Prodigal arrives. Frightened of him, they huddle into a compact mass and as he attempts to shake hands with them, their hands dart out and are withdrawn before a greeting can be achieved. The Prodigal's offer of wine, however, alters the situation and now all are friends. They dance together with bold abandon and at the end of the sequence the Prodigal is enthroned on the banquet table.

The Siren enters, wearing a high archaic headdress, a tight-fitting tunic, and a long red scarf. She moves coldly yet with erotic purpose. Her long legs step forward invitingly, she takes the scarf and twists it about her thighs or uses it to accent her bosom. Later, she tosses the scarf behind her, and facing upward, walks on her hands and the tips of her toe slippers, and finally sinks to the ground, pulling the scarf over her body.

The Prodigal, infatuated, descends from the table and rips the scarf from her. The two dance together, testing their passions, and then a group of the revelers toss the Siren high in the air, where she is caught by the upraised arms of other celebrants. The Prodigal and the Siren watch as the Prodigal's two companions engage in a playful, drunken, and sometimes lewd dance. Then the seduction begins. The Prodigal and the Siren move together in erotic proximity. Their arms, their legs become entwined, body pressures are exchanged; the youth is dragged to the table, where more wine is poured down his throat; and separate bands carry the two, pass their bodies close and permit them to dangle upside down while they embrace.

Now the table is placed on end and the drunken, helpless Prodigal is pushed against it. Hands slither over his body, robbing him of his money, his rings, his garments, even his shoes. He is left almost naked as the Siren comes up and tears a gold medallion from his neck. The Prodigal sinks to the ground and slowly, painfully crawls off. The Siren and her accomplices return, assemble their loot, take the table and move it back to its position as a fence. Then they move behind it, and with the Siren's body as a figurehead and her cape as a sail, they row away with their loot.

In the final scene, the Prodigal drags his broken body homeward, propelling himself by a staff, crawling on his knees. Exhausted, he falls by his own gate. His sisters hear the sound and run from the tent. Recognizing their lost brother, they help him through the gate and stand by him as the father comes forth. The Prodigal, fearful that his father will never forgive, turns away in anguish; but the old man holds out his arms and the Prodigal, on his knees, works his way toward him, grasps the patriarch's body and slowly drags himself up into his father's arms. The father, holding his grown son as if he were a child, wraps his robe around him protectively and lovingly.

At the première in Paris, Serge Lifar created the title role and Felia Doubrovska was the Siren. In the New York City Ballet revival Jerome Robbins was the Prodigal and Maria Tallchief the Siren. Edward Villella later danced the title role to international acclaim. The Lichine production, when presented in New York, had Lichine as the Prodigal and Sono Osato as the Siren.

The Prospect Before Us

Choreography, Ninette de Valois; music, William Boyce (arranged by Constant Lambert); scenery and costumes by Roger Furse. First produced by the Sadler's Wells Ballet (now the Royal Ballet), London, July 4, 1940. First presented in America by the Sadler's Wells Theatre Ballet, Milwaukee, November 3, 1951.

Pulcinella

Choreography, Leonide Massine; music, Igor Stravinsky after Giovanni Battista Pergolesi; curtain, décor, and costumes, Pablo Picasso. First produced by Diaghilev's Ballets Russes, Paris, May 15, 1920. Later productions have included one by George Balanchine and Jerome Robbins, with decor and costumes by Eugene Berman, first performed by the New York City Ballet, at their Stravinsky Festival, New York, June 23,

1972. Walter Strate choreographed a version for the National Ballet of Canada.

A comedy-ballet in the tradition of *commedia dell'arte* and employing its traditional characters in a variety of antics, ranging from the childlike to the macabre.

Leonide Massine headed the first cast. Edward Villella and Violette Verdy were the principals in the New York City Ballet production, which featured George Balanchine and Jerome Robbins in its première production.

Pulcinella Variations

Choreography, Michael Smuin; music, Igor Stravinsky; costumes, Stanley Simmons; décor, Jack Owen Brown. First performed by the American Ballet Theatre, New York, July 11, 1968.

Pulcinella Variations by Smuin differs from the Massine and Balanchine *Pulcinella* ballets in that it dispenses with plots and characters while retaining only the antic nature of the *commedia dell'arte*. Pretty patterns, funny actions, and bursts of virtuosity are all a part of chuckle-provoking capers. Example: a sort of human treadmill in which an ensemble of men, prone, roll across the stage and carry along a girl lying on them on her stomach posed like a giddy odalisque.

The first performance featured Michael Smuin, Diana Weber, Terry Orr, Ellen Everett, Georgina Vidal, Susan Casey, Reese Haworth, and John Sowinski.

Raggedy Ann and Raggedy Andy

Choreography, Ron Cunningham; music, John Alden Carpenter (Adventures in a Perambulator); costumes, Zoe De Jorg. First performed by the Boston Ballet, Boston, April 7, 1974.

A ballet for children based on the characters originated in stories by Johnny Gruelle.

The Rake's Progress

Choreography, Ninette de Valois; music and book, Gavin Gordon; scenery and costumes, Rex Whistler. First produced by the Sadler's Wells Ballet (now the Royal Ballet), London, May 20, 1935. First presented in America by the same company, New York, October 12, 1949.

The ballet, based on paintings by William Hogarth, follows the adventures of a young rake through romance, fun, gambling, drinking, debauchery, imprisonment, and finally, madness and death. The scene is London in the eighteenth century.

In the first scene, we are introduced to the young man who has recently inherited a great deal of money. He is besieged by merchants, peddlers, and hangers-on who want something from him. To prepare himself for his new estate, he submits to instruction in music, fencing, and dancing and also submits to blackmail, as the mother of a girl he has seduced demands recompense in cash for the violation.

The second scene is a bedchamber peopled with ladies of easy virtue and tipsy, ribald revelers. The Rake is brought in by a friend and is entertained by the women, by professional entertainers, by a striptease and bawdy song, and by drinking and dancing.

In the third scene the Rake's creditors press their suits for payment of old bills. The girl he has seduced promises to pay them for him. He is untouched by her devotion, although he is willing to let her pay, and goes off, leaving her alone to dance out her hopeless love.

The fourth scene reveals the Rake at a low ebb of fortune. Most of his money is gone and he is in a low-class gambling house, hoping to recoup something. But the cards are against him and he is wiped out.

The fifth scene returns to the girl, who prayerfully dances out her hope that the Rake will be released from debtors' prison.

In the sixth and final scene the debauched, broken, and defeated Rake is tossed into an asylum. He tries desperately to escape; the still devoted girl visits him with words of comfort, but he fails to recognize her. Rich ladies arrive to find amusement in peering at the antics of the maniacs. Finally the Rake is seized by violent hysteria and dies, still loved by the girl he had seduced and spurned.

At the London première, Walter Gore and Alicia Markova danced the principal roles. In New York, Harold Turner was the Rake and Margot Fonteyn the Girl.

Raymonda

Choreography, Marius Petipa; music, Alexander Glazounov; scenery and costumes, Allegri, Ivanov, Lambini. First produced by the Russian Imperial Ballet, January 7 (Julian or Russian calendar) or January 19 (Gregorian or Western calendar), 1898. Restaged for the Ballet Russe de Monte Carlo by Alexandra Danilova and George Balanchine, with scenery and costumes by Alexandre Benois, New York, March 12, 1946. Extracts from Raymonda *are frequently presented as a one-act* divertissement *ballet under the same title.*

To sum up a rather complicated plot, the ballet tells the story of Raymonda, betrothed to a knight, and of her difficulties with an ardent Saracen while her lover is off fighting in the Crusades. The knight returns in time to save Raymonda from the unwanted attentions by killing the Saracen and, in Act III, everyone celebrates the happy outcome.

Pierina Legnani created the title role in the Russian production. In the Ballet Russe de Monte Carlo revival, Danilova was Raymonda; Nicholas Magallanes the Crusader, and Nikita Talin the Saracen.

Raymonda Variations

Choreography, George Balanchine; music, Alexander Glazounov; scenery, Horace Armistead (backdrop for Lilac Garden); *costumes, Karinska. First presented by the New York City Ballet (as* Valses et Variations), *New York, December 7, 1961.*

Recital for Cello and Eight Dancers

Choreography, Benjamin Harkarvy; music, Johann Sebastian Bach. First presented by the Pennsylvania Ballet, Philadelphia, March 29, 1973.

The Red Detachment of Women

Staged by Chiang Ch'ing (Mme. Mao Tse-tung), and first produced by the Experimental Ballet Company of Peking, China. There is also a motion-picture version.

A ballet of social comment, focusing upon the bravery of women in the People's Republic of China. Acting is combined with ballet technique, this providing the central figure of the girl-warrior with opportunities for displays of virtuosity, chiefly in the Bolshoi Ballet style.

The Red Poppy

Choreography, Lev Laschilin and Vasily Tikhomirov; music, Reinhold Glière; book and designs, Mikhail Kurilko. First performed by the Bolshoi Ballet, Moscow, June 14, 1927. A new version, with choreography by Fedor Lopukhov (Act I), Vladimir Pomonaryov (Act II), Leonid Leontiev (Act III), and others, and with designs by B. Erbstein, was first performed by the Kirov Ballet, Leningrad, January 20, 1929. The Kirov presented another version, with choreography by Rostislav Zakharov, and designs by Yakov Stoffer, December 26, 1949. The Red Flower has, since 1957, been the title of the ballet.

This has been called the first "revolutionary" ballet to be choreographed after the Russian Revolution. It is a story of love and politics involving a Chinese dancing girl, the Soviet sea captain she falls in love with, and her employer, who, in a deal with anti-Soviet Europeans, tries to get the girl to poison the captain. She refuses, her boss attempts to shoot the captain during a peasant uprising that follows, and the dancer, flinging herself in front of the captain, dies for him, a red poppy symbolizing their love pressed against her breast.

Yekaterina Geltzer was the dancer, Tao Hoa, and Alexei Bulgakov the Captain at the première.

The Rehearsal

Choreography, Agnes de Mille; music, Morton Gould. First presented by the Royal Winnipeg Ballet, Hunter College Playhouse, New York City, October 26, 1965.

Agnes de Mille's *The Rehearsal* is a danced playlet about the labor, the frustration, the panic, the exhaustion that the dancer experiences behind the scenes, and finally the triumph on stage. It is loaded with fun and laughs as well as with poignant drama. De Mille wrote the script, which is spoken by an onstage narrator (the choreographer-author was the narrator at the première). Memorable line: "Contrary to rumor, choreography is the oldest profession."

The Relativity of Icarus

Choreography, Gerald Arpino; score, Gerhard Samuel; text, John Larson; setting and costumes, Rouben Ter-Arutunian. First performance, Lewiston, New York, August 30, 1974.

A three-character ballet based on the Greek myth. The central dance is a *pas de deux* for Icarus and Daedelus, a highly acrobatic number in minimal costumes (and bare feet), and patterns of interrelation with the figure of the Sun.

The initial cast was composed of Russell Sultzbach (Icarus), Ted Nelson (Daedelus), Anne Marie de Angelo (Sun). The soprano with the chamber orchestra was Joanne Bell.

Remembrances

Choreography, Robert Joffrey; music, Richard Wagner; decor, Rouben Ter-Arutunian; costumes, Willa Kim; lighting, Jen-

nifer Tipton. First performed by the City Center Joffrey Ballet, October 12, 1973.

The décor, the costumes, the lighting, the mood are softly iridescent. This is a ballet, as the title tells us, of memories. The memories are all romantic, but some are sad while others are wistfully gay. Meetings, partings, and arms outstretched in longing are characteristics of choreography that is classical in step but employs gesture to indicate the fleeting emotions that provide the piece with communicable warmth as well as visual beauty. The singer of the Wesendonck poems is seated downstage, extreme right (the orchestra is in the pit and the pianist is on a platform close by the orchestra), and next to her is the dreamer who mirrors her remembrances in unobtrusive but clearly defined gestures of sorrow, delight, despair and even hope, as if she would change the past. (The theatrical device is not new—it was used to pinpoint the source of memory in the person of a female dreamer in Todd Bolender's much older ballet, *Mother Goose Suite.*) Francesca Corkle and Jonathan Watts headed the first cast.

Les Rendezvous

Choreography, Frederick Ashton; music, François Auber, arranged by Constant Lambert; scenery and costumes, William Chappell. First presented by the Sadler's Wells Ballet (now the Royal Ballet), London, December 5, 1933. First presented in America by the Sadler's Wells Theatre Ballet, Minneapolis, November 7, 1951 (New York, March 25, 1952). Also in the repertory of the National Ballet of Canada.

A *divertissement* ballet with a park setting. Boys and girls, in light and bright costumes, meet by chance or by appointment in the park and dance together with playful good spirits. There are full ensemble dances; special episodes for the girls alone; bounding, whirling sequences for the males; a *pas de trois* for a man and two girls; and a *pas de deux*, with separate variations, for a romantically inclined couple. The ballerina's passages, though dainty, are filled with all manner of technical hazards, including multiple turns, hoppings on *pointe*, and allegro action of the fleetest sort; while the *premier danseur*'s variation demonstrates his virility in leaps, dynamic spins, and other examples of physical prowess.

At the London première Alicia Markova, Stanislas Idzikowski, Pearl Argyle, Robert Helpmann, and Ninette de Valois were the principals.

Revenge

Choreography, Ruth Page; music, Giuseppe Verdi (Il Trovatore); scenery and costumes, Antoni Clavé. First produced by the Ballets des Champs-Élysées, Paris, October 17, 1951. Presented in New York by the Ruth Page Ballet, December 20, 1955. The ballet's American première had been in Chicago a few weeks earlier.

A ballet that uses the story and the music of the opera *Il Trovatore* ("The Troubadour").

Reveries

Choreography, John Clifford; music, Peter Ilyich Tchaikovsky (Suite No. 1); costumes, Joe Eula; lighting, Ronald Bates. First performed by the New York City Ballet, New York, December 5, 1969.

Ricercare

Choreography, Glen Tetley; music, Mordecai Seter; décor, Rouben Ter-Arutunian. First performed by the American Ballet Theatre, New York, January 25, 1966. The Ballet Rambert presented the work for the first time, February 24, 1967.

Tetley's *Ricercare* is an extended *pas de deux* based on the principle of a return to or a search for a basic theme. The chief aspect of the staging is an arc prop that serves as a slide down which a woman (from one side) and a man (from the other) glide to a meeting. Tactile encounters and separations take place as the theme is explored.

Mary Hinkson and Scott Douglas were the first leads.

Rinaldo and Armida

Choreography, Frederick Ashton; music, Malcolm Arnold; scenery and costumes, Peter Rice. First produced by the Sadler's Wells Ballet (now the Royal Ballet), London, January 6, 1955. First presented in America by the same company, New York, September 20, 1955.

The Rite of Spring

See *Le Sacre du Printemps*

The River

Choreography, Alvin Ailey; music, Duke Ellington. First performed by the American Ballet Theatre, New York, June 25, 1970.

This work relates various aspects of water, or proximity to water, with qualities of movement: violent, flowing, caressive, separative. For example, in the duet "Two Cities" a couple seems to be separated by a barrier, which one assumes to be a barrier of water, dividing people as well as places.

Road of the Phoebe Snow

Choreography, Talley Beatty; music, Duke Ellington and Billy Strayhorn; costumes, Lew Smith. First performed in New York, November 28, 1959. The Boston Ballet performed the work for the first time, March 13, 1967.

The Road of the Phoebe Snow is a modern dance work but it has
moved into ballet repertory. It has been danced by all-black, all-
white, and multiracial casts. The ballet is about poor people who
live along the railroad tracks and its journey takes us to stopovers
with love, violence, rejection, hopelessness, hope, defiance, and
death.

Rodeo

(Subtitled *The Courting at Burnt Ranch*)

*Choreography, Agnes de Mille; music, Aaron Copland; scen-
ery, Oliver Smith; costumes, Kermit Love. First produced by
the Ballet Russe de Monte Carlo, New York, October 16, 1942.
Added to the repertory of Ballet Theatre (now the American
Ballet Theatre), Frankfurt, Germany, August 14, 1950. The
ballet entered the repertory of the Boston Ballet in 1974.*

Rodeo made dance history. It made Agnes de Mille, long a valued
dancer and gifted choreographer, famous beyond the confines of
the dance world. It led in turn to Miss de Mille's assignment as
choreographer for *Oklahoma!*, a musical that made theatrical history and introduced a new application of dance to the lyric theater.
Rodeo was received, incidentally, by twenty-two roaring curtain
calls on opening night at the Metropolitan Opera House.

The happy spirit and lusty American theme of *Rodeo* were
just right for a wartime audience. That it has endured and been
loved and cheered long beyond the war period is proof enough
that it is a wonderful ballet for any era.

Scene One. The corral at Burnt Ranch on rodeo day. Among
the cowboys assembled is a girl dressed in pants, wearing a man's
hat and, in spite of her pigtails, behaving like a rough, tough
youth. She wants to take part in the rodeo, but the cowboys will
have none of her. In the midst of their wild dance, imitative of the
prancing, bucking, galloping horses, she attempts to join them.
Especially does she hope to please the handsome head wrangler,
for underneath her tomboy actions is a girl ready and eager for
romance.

City girls from the East arrive and the young men are delighted with these elegantly groomed and well-bred young ladies. The dance in the evening should be fun! The champion roper shows off his tricks for them and the cowboys do their stuff in a rousing rodeo, which fascinates the visitors, the farm women, and the men themselves. The cowgirl, determined to get attention, returns on what appears to be a wildly bucking broncho. She is thrown, of course, much to the merriment of the ladies and the disgust of the men. The head wrangler orders her to leave and she does, tearfully. The rodeo ends, the men and the women stroll off. Now the cowgirl returns, sees her head wrangler depart with a girl of his choice, and dances her lonely measures, knowing that she is unsuccessful as a cowhand and not much better as a girl. The head wrangler, his curiosity somewhat aroused by this odd girl, returns briefly, but she is too shy to speak out. As she falls to the earth in despair, the champion roper struts by, snapping his fingers, shaking his shoulders in dreams of the fun that he expects to have at the evening's dance gathering.

A curtain, decorated with galloping horses, falls and out in front of it race four couples. A caller shouts the instructions and the couples perform a brisk and lusty square dance.

With the rise of the curtain for the second scene, we see a ranch house with the cowgirl sitting alone on a bench watching the champion roper, dressed to the teeth in striped pants and a violet shirt, click his heels to jazzy music in the company of other cowboys. Couples enter to spoon or to quarrel, running in and out of the ranch house in quest of fun. The champion roper, feeling sorry for the cowgirl, asks her to dance. He tries to clean up her face, dusts off the bottom of her pants, and introduces her to the intricacies of dancing. She is getting along nicely when the head wrangler enters. All her yearnings for him return. The roper is understandably miffed at her sudden unresponsiveness to his kindness.

In a choose-your-partner dance, the poor cowgirl is left unattached and returns to the bench, her sad haven. Again the champion roper, after a dance in which he shows off his skill as a hoofer, tries to entertain the girl but this ends disastrously when the wrangler and his beautiful girl friend arrive. The cowgirl runs off and later returns in a real dress, bright red and feminine. She is gauche at first but pretty soon forgets she doesn't have pants to hitch up and remembers she is a girl.

As the dance goes into full swing, the cowgirl and the roper dance happily together, but now the wrangler, seeing the results of the transformation, wants the cowgirl for himself. There is a fight between the two men and the girl gets tossed about. In the end she realizes it is the roper she really loves and the two look happily into each other's eyes; the wrangler goes off with the rancher's daughter, with whom he has been dancing all evening, and the curtain falls.

Rodeo, from start to finish, is filled with action. It is not classical but it is all dance and danced drama. The movements of the ensemble support, enhance, and color the activities of the principals and the lesser characters are all a part of the choreographic fabric, which captures with brilliance, humor, and touches of pathos an episode from life in the hearty, healthy, happy West.

The original cast was headed by de Mille (Cowgirl), Frederic Franklin (Champion Roper), and Casimir Kokitch (Head Wrangler). Allyn McLerie, Jenny Workman, and Christine Sarry have also danced the part of the Cowgirl, and John Kriza has often danced the Champion Roper. James Mitchell and Kelly Brown have been seen as the Head Wrangler.

Romance

Choreography, Eliot Feld; music, Johannes Brahms (Nine Piano Pieces from Op. 116, Op. 118, Op. 119, & Op. 76); costumes, Stanley Simmons; lighting, Jennifer Tipton. First performed by Eliot Feld's American Ballet Company, Brooklyn Academy of Music, New York, April 20, 1971.

Romeo and Juliet

Choreography, L. Lavrosky; music, Serge Prokofiev; scenery and costumes, Peter Williams. First produced by the Russian

State Ballet, Leningrad, 1940; first performance at the Bolshoi Theatre, Moscow, December 28, 1946. First presented in America by the Bolshoi Ballet, New York City, April 16, 1959. In three acts. Prior to the American presentation made into a full-length Russian motion picture in color, The Ballet of Romeo and Juliet. The story, in a one-act version with choreography by Antony Tudor, music by Frédéric Delius, and scenery and costumes by Eugene Berman, was first produced by Ballet Theatre (now the American Ballet Theatre), New York, April 6, 1943, in incomplete form. The finished work was presented April 10 of the same year. Still another Romeo and Juliet in three acts and eleven scenes, with choreography by Frederick Ashton, music by Prokofiev, and scenery and costumes by Peter Rice, was produced by the Royal Danish Ballet in Copenhagen, May 19, 1955, and first presented in America in New York, September 26, 1956.

John Cranko choreographed a Romeo and Juliet, which was given its first performance by La Scala Opera Ballet, Venice, July 26, 1958. A new version of his work with decor and costumes by Jürgen Rose was first performed by the Stuttgart Ballet, Stuttgart, December 2, 1962. Kenneth MacMillan created a Romeo and Juliet for the Royal Ballet, with décor and costumes by Nicholas Georgiadis, which was given its first performance in London, February 9, 1965. It was first presented in America by the same company, New York, April 21, 1965. Maurice Béjart used the Hector Berlioz score for his version with décor by Germinal Casado, which was first performed by Ballet of the Twentieth Century, Brussels, November 17, 1966. A version for Het Nationale Ballet, with choreography by Rudi van Dantzig to the Prokofiev score, was given its first performance in Amsterdam, February 22, 1967. There are still other dance stagings of the great Shakespeare play—some elaborate productions and some even in simplified pas de deux form.

The plot of this famous tragedy by William Shakespeare is familiar to everyone, and needs no repeating here.

The Soviet production is a combination of classical ballet, character dance (more Russian than Italian in character), pageantry, and a great deal of old-fashioned pantomime. The ballet actions—and there is less dancing than miming and swordplay—are traditional (of the Petipa period) and fairly limited in scope. Romeo has a few *tours en l'air*, pirouettes, and *jetés*, and Juliet's movements in the strictly balletic area are held to *bourrées, grands jetés, attitudes*, and some turns. But although the classical vocabulary is used in limited degree, the dramatic action is expansive and the street scenes are alive with rough and daring activity.

Galina Ulanova, one of the world's greatest ballerinas, created the role of Juliet in the Soviet version, danced it in the film and performed it (for the first time in the West) with the Bolshoi Ballet in London, in the fall of 1956. In her forties, she was able to give the illusion of girlishness, moving with uncommon lightness and youthful grace and investing her mimed passages with an emotional honesty, in glowing contrast to the stock overacted pantomime of some of the other characters. Among many unforgettable aspects of Ulanova's performance in the movie were the scene in which she first discovered, as her hands moved over her breast, the wonder of womanly ripening and the scene in which she raced, light as the wind, barely touching the ground, in a desperate effort to communicate with Romeo.

The stage version is far more elaborate than anything known to Western ballet companies. The crowd scenes are huge, the settings opulent, and the stage effects brilliant. The leisureliness of pace, the great quantities of mime, the bravura style of acting, and the taste in costumes and decor are not always in accord with Western standards but Ulanova's personal artistry surmounts all barriers of convention and taste. At the New York première, Ulanova and Yuri Zhdanov danced the lovers in a performance which introduced the Bolshoi Ballet to American audiences.

The Tudor one-act treatment has some pantomime but it is almost entirely danced throughout, for even the dramatic action is stylized, rhythmicized. The technical base is classical but elements of the court dance and freely expressional action are wedded with it.

The Tudor ballet is in a prologue and eight scenes. The Prologue, showing the entrance to a palace in Verona, introduces us to a sullen, intense Romeo; the girl he has loved, Rosaline; the followers of the feuding families, the Montagues and the Capulets; and the belligerent leaders of the two factions, Mercutio and Tybalt.

Scene One, "A Ball at the House of the Capulets," brings together Romeo, the Montague, in disguise, with the beautiful daughter of the Capulets, Juliet, and they fall in love. Scene Two, "Romeo Woos Juliet in the Capulet Garden." The famous balcony scene. Juliet promises to marry Romeo despite their warring families. Scene Three, "The Betrothal of Romeo and Juliet by the Friar." The lovers take vows and Friar Lawrence gives the blessing of the Church. Scene Four, "Street Scene." During this episode Mercutio, Romeo's best friend, is killed by Tybalt; and Romeo, avenging the death, slays the slayer. Juliet grieves over Tybalt's death but sends word to Romeo that her love is lasting. Scene Five, "Romeo's Farewell to Juliet," is laid in Juliet's bedchamber. As dawn comes, Juliet rises from the bed and dances in joy; the two lovers dance briefly together then part, promising they will meet as soon as possible.

Scene Six, "Preparations for the Wedding of Juliet to Paris," brings the ballet to the point of crisis. Juliet, knowing that she must not marry the man her father has chosen, appeals to Friar Lawrence and is given a sleeping potion which will simulate death. Scene Seven, "Procession to the Tomb," shows Juliet being borne through the streets while her family and friends mourn her presumed death. Scene Eight, "The Vault of the Capulets," finds Juliet lying on her bier. Romeo enters and, not having received the message telling of Juliet's plan, drinks poison just as Juliet awakes from her deep sleep. Realizing what has happened, she stabs herself, and the lovers die in each other's arms.

In the first Ballet Theatre performance the cast was headed by Alicia Markova (Juliet), Hugh Laing (Romeo), Nicholas Orloff (Mercutio), and Tudor (Tybalt). Nora Kaye, Alicia Alonso, Igor Youskevitch, and John Kriza have also starred in this production.

The Royal Danish Ballet's staging of the Ashton *Romeo and Juliet* is a magnificent production, employing many changes of scenery and extending the action over three stage levels. It is a classical romantic ballet in which there is some pantomime, with the accent on dancing and on dance treatment in the dueling scenes.

Among the many memorable features in the Danish *Romeo and Juliet*, a few may be noted: Juliet's girlish leap into the arms of her nurse; the swift and clear development of Romeo, from a carefree, curious youth to a man enraptured, daring, and willing to face death; the exciting duel between Mercutio and Tybalt, up and down staircases and along the streets; the balcony scene, as soft and rhapsodic as a dream of beauty; Mercutio's chilling dance of death; Juliet's fear-laden dance before she sips the potion; the glittering dancing of Rosaline; the bedroom love duet; the sweet death.

Henning Kronstam has danced Romeo almost exclusively, although Erik Bruhn has performed it on special occasions. Mona Vangsaa and Kirsten Petersen have alternated as Juliet. Other alternating roles have included Frank Schaufuss and Stanley Williams as Mercutio, Niels Bjorn Larsen and Fredbjørn Bjørnsson as Tybalt, and Mette Mollerup and Inge Sand as Rosaline.

An early ballet treatment (also Danish) of the Romeo and Juliet story was produced in 1811, with choreography by Vincenzo Galeotti, the first important ballet master and choreographer of the Royal Danish Ballet.

The MacMillan and Cranko productions are those most generally seen by international audiences. The story lines are, of course, identical in all versions. All key scenes—the balcony and bedroom duets and the love death, the duels, the ballroom extravaganza (often with the "cushion" dance), the marriage by Friar Lawrence, the swallowing of the sleeping potion—are present but are choreographed differently, depending on the special characteristics of their creators.

Among the great Juliets in the Lavrovsky, MacMillan, or Cranko ballets are Galina Ulanova, Margot Fonteyn, Antoinette Sibley, Marcia Haydée; among the Romeos, Rudolf Nureyev, Anthony Dowell, Richard Cragun.

Ropes

Choreography, Gerald Arpino; music, Charles Ives. First performed by Gerald Arpino and Company, New York, at the Fashion Institute of Technology, May 18, 1961. First performed by the Robert Joffrey Ballet (now the City Center Joffrey Ballet), New York, September 30, 1962.

There are seven ropes in *Ropes*, and although they provide opportunities for purely physical acrobatics in dance form, they also suggest umbilical cords that control the nurturings of yesterdays and the leashes of todays. At the end only one figure, a girl, frees herself of her rope.

A Rose for Miss Emily

Choreography, Agnes de Mille; music, Alan Hovhaness (specially commissioned score). First performed by students of the North Carolina School of the Arts, Winston-Salem, North Carolina, October 22, 1970. First presented by the American Ballet Theatre, New York, December 30, 1970, with decor and costumes by Chistinna Giannini.

A dance-drama based on William Faulkner's story. Passion, death, revenge, and macabre remembrances, focused upon a near-mad woman and her doomed lover.

Rose Latulippe

Choreography, Brian Macdonald; music, Harry Freedman; libretto, William Solly and Brian MacDonald; décor, Robert Prevost. First presented by the Royal Winnipeg Ballet, Stratford, Ontario, August 16, 1966.

Rose Latulippe, an all-Canadian full-length ballet, is based upon a Canadian legend that is curiously similar to the story of *Giselle*, for it has to do with a country girl frail to the point that her mother warns her of the dangers of dancing, her jealous village suitor, a mysterious nobleman, and even wililike creatures. Yet this French-Canadian story was published (1837) before *Giselle* (1841) was staged in Paris. The rural setting is a stockaded frontier village. There are clogs, longways, and round dances in the barn and even a comedy "tipsy" dance for Rose (the New World's Giselle).

Annette Wiedersheim danced the title role.

La Rose Malade

Choreography, Roland Petit; music, Gustave Mahler (Symphonies No. 2, 5); *Plisetskaya's costumes by Yves St. Laurent. First performance Paris Opéra, January 10, 1973.*

This ballet, inspired by the William Blake poem, was created especially for the Bolshoi Ballet's prima ballerina, Maya Plisetskaya, who danced it first as guest artist with the Paris Opera Ballet and subsequently, in excerpt, with Bolshoi Ballet units starring her. The concluding *pas de deux*, a death scene, is cast in free-style dance movements coupled with passing patterns of classical *adage*. Its form is designed to display Plisetskaya's pure balletic line, her skill as an actress-dancer, and that rippling fluidity of the arms for which she is famous in both *Swan Lake* (Acts II and IV) and in the solo, *The Dying Swan*.

Rouge et Noir

Choreography, Leonide Massine; music, Dmitri Shostakovitch (First Symphony); *scenery and costumes, Henry Matisse. First produced by the Ballet Russe de Monte Carlo at Monte Carlo, May 11, 1939. First American performance by the same company, New York, October 28, 1939.*

Although the ballet is supposed to have a dramatic theme concerning man "pursued and overtaken by brutal forces," the majority of viewers have been stirred mainly by Matisse's magnificent abstract setting and the equally abstract costumes (fleshings in several colors which reveal full body lines), and by Massine's skillfully manuvered mass movements and highly original individual dance phrases.

Alicia Markova, Frederic Franklin, Igor Youskevitch, Nathalie Krassovska, Marc Platoff, and Michael Panaiev headed the original cast.

Le Sacre du Printemps

(The Rite of Spring)

> *Choreography, Vaslav Nijinsky; music, Igor Stravinsky; book, Stravinsky and Nicholas Roerich; scenery and costumes, Roerich. First produced by Diaghilev's Ballets Russes, Paris, May 29, 1913. Rechoreographed by Leonide Massine for the same company, Paris, 1920. Revised again by Massine in collaboration with Martha Graham (as leading dancer), Philadelphia, April 11, 1930, under the auspices of the League of Composers. Restaged by Massine for the Royal Swedish Ballet, Stockholm, April 30, 1956. The ballet has also been produced by other choreographers, among them a version with choreography by Kenneth MacMillan, with scenery and costumes by Sidney Nolan, presented by the Royal Ballet, London, May 31, 1962; first presented by the same company in America, New York, May 8, 1963. A Soviet version, with choreography by Natalia Kasatkina and Vladimir Vasiliov and scenery by A. D. Goncharov, was presented for the first time in America by the Bolshoi Ballet, New York, April 26, 1966; another version, choreographed by Maurice Béjart, was first produced in Brussels, Théâtre Royale de la Monnaie, in 1959.*

The ballet is in two scenes: "Adoration of the Earth" and "The Sacrifice." In the first, primitive Russians from tribal communities gather in a stark setting near a holy place. An elder blesses the area, and girls and boys, young men and women, engage in a series of dances which suggest an ecstatic welcome to spring. They dance separately and together, in mock battle and in games of prowess, sometimes in gentle dedication and again with romantic ardor.

In the second scene a maiden is chosen for sacrifice. She

stands while the men and women of the tribes dance around her as if she were a living goddess. Then she steps forth to make her sacrifice to the gods in a frenzied dance which taps every source of energy and culminates in exhaustion and death.

The first performance of the Nijinsky choreography caused a near-riot in Paris. The audience was shocked by the strangeness of the Stravinsky score and equally outraged by the choreography, which departed entirely from traditional ballet movements in favor of angular turned-in placements of the limbs. During World War I, the Nijinsky choreography was forgotten and Massine was asked to rechoreograph it. His treatment, though equally primitive in spirit and wholly free in movement form, was perhaps not as grotesque as Nijinsky's.

At the first performance Marie Piltz was the Chosen One; Lydia Sokolova danced the part in the 1920 Massine staging; and Martha Graham was the first to dance it in America (in a production that witnessed some angry battles between Massine and Graham).

Sacred Grove on Mount Tamalpais

Choreography, Gerald Arpino; music, Alan Raph, Johann Pachelbel (Canon in D); *décor, Robert Yodice (after Ming Cho Lee); costumes, David James. First performed by the City Center Joffrey Ballet, New York, November 2, 1972.*

A modernization of ancient tribal ceremonies celebrating love, fertility, harvests, rebirth.

Saint Francis

(Noblissima Visione)

Choreography, Leonide Massine; music, Paul Hindemith; book, Massine, Hindemith; scenery and costumes, Pavel Tchelitchev. First produced by the Ballet Russe de Monte Carlo, London, July 21, 1938. First American performance, by the same company, New York, October 14, 1938.

This ballet in four scenes recounts in stylized dance action, as distinct from purely classical ballet, the mystical experiences of Saint Francis which led him from a life of idle luxury to renunciation of material possessions and the finding of spiritual peace, under the guidance of Poverty, Obedience, and Chastity. Poverty becomes his mystical bride.

Massine created the role of Saint Francis and Poverty was danced by Nini Theilade.

Salade

Choreography, John Cranko; music, Darius Milhaud; costumes, Elisabeth Dalton. First performed by the Stuttgart Ballet, June 1, 1968.

Saltarelli

Choreography, Jacques d'Amboise; music, Antonio Vivaldi (two concerti); décor and costumes, John Braden. First performed by the New York City Ballet, New York, May 30, 1974.

A ballet suggested by the little jumps and multiple figurations, or floor patterns, of the fifteenth-century Italian court dance saltarello, a relative of the more familiar galliard.

The first cast was headed by Christine Redpath, Francis Sackett, and Merrill Ashley.

Sargasso

Choreography, Glen Tetley; music, Ernst Krenek. First performed by the American Ballet Theatre, New York, March 24, 1965.

Sargasso, a ballet by the modern dance choreographer Glen Tetley, is an exploration of sex-starvation and violence. A shining ladder which climbs endlessly is a key prop, especially for the female dancer.

Sallie Wilson headed the first cast.

Scènes du Ballet

Choreography, Frederick Ashton; music, Igor Stravinsky; scenery and costumes, André Beaurepaire. First produced by the Sadler's Wells Ballet (now the Royal Ballet), London, February 11, 1948. First presented in America by the same company, New York, September 14, 1955. An earlier treatment, choreographed by Anton Dolin and featuring Dolin and Alicia Markova, was presented in the revue The Seven Lively Arts, *New York, December 7, 1944. A completely new version, with choreography by John Taras, was premièred by the New York City Ballet at the Stravinsky Festival, New York, June 22, 1972. Other versions include those by Peter Van Dyk for the Hamburg Staatsoper (1962), Nicholas Petrov for the Pittsburgh Ballet Theatre (April 7, 1972), and John Cranko for the Stuttgart Ballet (June 10, 1962).*

This is a classical ballet with romantic overtones which derives its form, pace, and intensities from the score. Using the movement vocabulary of the classical dance, Ashton creates freshly designed passages for solo, duo, and ensemble in a work which, though small in scale, is considered to be one of the finest examples of his choreographic artistry.

Margot Fonteyn and Michael Somes created the principal roles.

Scheherazade

Choreography, Michel Fokine; music, Nicholas Rimsky-Korsakoff; book, Alexandre Benois; scenery and costumes, Léon Bakst. First produced by Diaghilev's Ballets Russes, Paris, June 4, 1910. A production unauthorized by the choreographer was presented during Gertrude Hoffman's Saison Russe, New

York, June 14, 1911, in a staging by Theodore Koslov. The
Diaghilev company brought the authorized Fokine production
to America in 1916. The Ballet Russe de Monte Carlo reintro-
duced the Fokine ballet to New York, October 9, 1935. The
ballet was also in the repertory of the London Festival Ballet.

The ballet is based upon the first story in The Arabian Nights,
although the musical suite to which it is set is designed to suggest
several of the tales. (The composer wrote the opening section for
the story of Sinbad, and La Méri, in her classical Hindu dance version of Scheherazade, followed the composer's intention and introduced a Sinbad scene.)

In Fokine's conception of Scheherazade the scene is a mag-
nificently and brilliantly colored room in an Oriental palace. Here
King Shahriar, surrounded by his concubines, is petting the favorite of his harem, Zobeide. The king's brother, Shah Zeman, is also
present and shows an obvious jealousy of Zobeide and her influence
on the king. The fat Eunuch suggests entertainment and three
odalisques dance for their master a supple, provocative, semi-
Oriental dance. He has eyes for no one but Zobeide. The shah,
however, tries to tell his brother that he suspects the wives and
concubines of infidelity and the king reluctantly agrees to a test.
He orders a hunting expedition and leaves with his brother while
Zobeide angrily protests his departure. The other girls, lying allur-
ingly along his exit path, stroke him in farewell as he passes.

Once the king and his brother have left, the harem women
prepare themselves for fun. After primping, they beg, tease, and
bribe the Eunuch into opening two of three doors at the back of
the great room. Negro slaves rush out and amorously attach themselves to the girls. Zobeide now commands the Eunuch to open
the third door. He refuses her imperious commands, but a rich
bribe and her fury finally make him yield and the Favorite Slave
leaps forth.

The orgy begins. The slaves, lying on cushions and on the
floor, cover the girls with erotic caresses while the Favorite Slave
lets his lips and hands race over the beautiful form of Zobeide.
Vigorous dancing characterizes his virility, and tremendous leaps

carry him soaring through the air or from a staircase onto the cushions beside Zobeide. Food and drink are brought in and the revelers engage in a wild dance. Zobeide and the Favorite Slave bend and dip and make their sinuous progress across the room while passion mounts.

In the midst of the bacchanale the brothers return and the terrified slaves flee, chased by the soldiers, and one by one are cut down and killed. The Favorite is the last to appear and is struck by a scimitar in air. With a wild, writhing spurt of energy, his trembling legs shoot upward and he falls dead. The concubines, the slaves, the Eunuch have been killed and only Zobeide remains. She pleads for her life and Shahriar is inclined to relent when his brother boots the body of the Favorite Slave to remind the king of Zobeide's faithlessness. Zobeide realizes that all is lost, and grabbing a dagger from one of the soldiers, stabs herself to death at the foot of her master. As the curtain falls, Shahriar stands lamenting, cursing the death of his beloved.

At the première Ida Rubinstein and Vaslav Nijinsky danced the roles of Zobeide and the Favorite Slave. Nijinsky also performed his role in New York. Others who have danced the Favorite Slave include Leonide Massine, Yurek Shabelevsky, André Eglevsky, Frederic Franklin, and Istvan Rabovsky. Interpreters of Zobeide include Tamara Karsarvina, Lubov Tchernicheva, Alexandra Danilova, Mia Slavenska, and Maria Tallchief.

Scherzo à la Russe

Choreography, George Balanchine; music, Igor Stravinsky. First presented by the New York City Ballet, Stravinsky Festival, New York, June 21, 1972.

Scherzo Fantastique

Choreography, Jerome Robbins; music, Igor Stravinsky; lighting, Ronald Bates. First performed by the New York City Ballet, New York, Stravinsky Festival, June 18, 1972. Staged for the Paris Opera Ballet, March, 1974.

A light, joyous *pas de deux* with three solo male dancers, designed to appeal to the eye and to stir the beholder to thoughts of romance.

Gelsey Kirkland and Bart Cook danced the first performance.

Schubertiade

Choreography, Michael Smuin; music, Franz Schubert; costumes, Marcos Paredes; décor, William Pitkin. First performed by the American Ballet Theatre, New York, January 1, 1971.

A ballet of the genre of Balanchine's definitive (in this category) *Liebeslieder Walzer*, but with its own original patterns and a joyful air.

Schubert Variations

Choreography, Vincente Nebrada; music, Franz Schubert (orchestral arrangement by Rebekah Harkness); costumes, Stanley Simmons. First performed by the Harkness Ballet, Lausanne, Switzerland, September, 1971. First performed in America by the same company, Brooklyn College, Brooklyn, New York, October 7, 1972.

An abstract ballet designed to display a troupe's command of classical ballet technique.

Scotch Symphony

Choreography, George Balanchine; music, Felix Mendelssohn (first movement of the Mendelssohn score is omitted); scenery, Horace Armistead; costumes, Karinska and David Ffolkes. First produced by the New York City Ballet, New York, November 11, 1952. The ballet was added to the repertory of the City Center Joffrey Ballet, March 16, 1967. In Philadelphia, the Pennsylvania Ballet performed it for the first time, July 14, 1965. It was added to the repertory of the Boston Ballet in the same year.

Scotch Symphony is a storyless ballet built upon Scottish-flavored dances and including a romantic episode inspired by the first of the great romantic ballets, *La Sylphide*, which also had a Scottish background.

At the first performance, Maria Tallchief and André Eglevsky had the principal roles and the *pas de trois* of the first scene was danced by Patricia Wilde, Frank Hobi, and Michael Maule. The principal roles have also been danced by Diana Adams and Jacques d'Amboise.

Sea Shadow

Choreography, Gerald Arpino; music, Maurice Ravel; decor, Ming Cho Lee. First presented by the Robert Joffrey Ballet (now the City Center Joffrey Ballet), during the Rebekah Harkness Dance Festival, Central Park, New York, September 5, 1963. Because of difficulties with the Ravel estate, a new score was commissioned by Michael Colgrass.

Sea Shadow, a *pas de deux* ballet, captures the moonlit mysticism of the sea. In the sensuous movements of a youth and an Ondinelike girl, the viewer is aware not only of their physical responses but also of the sea itself, with its ebbs and flows and eddyings.

Lisa Bradley and Paul Sutherland were the first cast.

The Seasons

Choreography, John Cranko; music, Alexander Glazounov. First performance by the Stuttgart Ballet, June 15, 1962. An entirely new version by Cranko was given its world première, April 2, 1971.

Sebastian

Choreography, Edward Caton; music, Gian Carlo Menotti; scenery, Oliver Smith; costumes, Milena. First produced by the Ballet International, New York, October 31, 1944. Restaged with wholly new choreography by Agnes de Mille for the American Ballet Theatre, New York, May 27, 1957 (in an initial workshop production). A third version, with choreography by John Butler, was first performed by the Nederlands Dans Theatre, October 22, 1963. Butler revised his choreography for the Harkness Ballet, which gave its first performance of the work in Cannes, March 4, 1966. The Butler version is also performed by the Royal Winnipeg Ballet. Still another choreographer, Vincente Nebrada, staged his version for the Harkness Ballet which performed it for the first time in New York, April 9, 1974.

Sebastian is a melodramatic ballet set in Venice of the 1600s. Two sisters, jealous of their brother's love for a courtesan, attempt to destroy her through witchcraft. They obtain a veil belonging to the courtesan and place it over a wax replica of her figure; then, stabbing it viciously, they make a magic which causes the courtesan to experience similar wounds, bringing her close to death. However, Sebastian, the sisters' Moorish slave, thwarts the final plan, for he is secretly in love with the courtesan. Covering his own body with the veil, he is stabbed to death in her place.

Francisco Moncion created the title role in the Caton ballet and Viola Essen was the Courtesan. Lawrence Rhodes created the title role in the Butler version for the Harkness Ballet.

Secret Places

Choreography, Gerald Arpino; music, Wolfgang Amadeus Mozart (Piano Concerto No. 21 in C Major, K. 467, Second Movement); décor, Ming Cho Lee; lighting, Thomas Skelton. Dedicated in living memory of Lorraine Squadron. First performed by the City Center Joffrey Ballet, February 20, 1968, in New York.

A romantic mood-rich duet in which two figures pass each other by, seeking, but alone and lost in the twilight, until, perhaps by chance, they meet and are united in the secret places of the heart or of dreams.

The world première performance was danced by Lisa Bradley and Dermot Burke. Dennis Wayne, Donna Cowen, and Starr Danias have been featured in recent performances.

Sephardic Songs

Choreography, Eliot Feld; music, traditional (arranged by Manuel Valls); décor, Santo Loquastro; lighting, Jennifer Tipton. First produced by the Eliot Feld Ballet, New York, May 30, 1974.

A sunny, lyrical ballet, mirroring the qualities of Spanish-flavored Jewish songs. The ballet is cast in free-style movements somewhat related to Yemenite pastoral dances as theatricalized by the Inbal company of Israel. The groundcloth for the stage suggests earth scattered with bits of grain and the whole ballet thus recalls the ancient threshing-floor dances of Mediterranean countries.

Naomi Sorkin was the principal dancer in the first cast.

Serenade

Choreography, George Balanchine; music, Peter Ilyich Tchaikovsky (Serenade in C Major for String Orchestra); costumes, Jean Lurcat. First presented by students of the School of American Ballet, White Plains, New York, June 10, 1934. Later presented by the American Ballet, New York, March 1, 1935; by the Ballet Russe de Monte Carlo, New York, October 17, 1940; by the American Ballet Caravan, 1941; by the Paris Opera Ballet, Paris, April 30, 1947; by the New York City Ballet (with costumes by Karinska), New York, October 18, 1948; by the Royal Danish Ballet, Copenhagen, 1957. The ballet is also in the repertories of the Australian Ballet, the Atlanta Civic Ballet, the National Ballet of Washington, the Royal Ballet, the Boston Ballet, the National Ballet of

Canada, the Norwegian National Ballet, the Royal Swedish Ballet, the Pennsylvania Ballet, Ballet West.

Serenade, the first ballet Balanchine created in America, is without plot but threaded with emotional incidents.

The first movement presents a large ensemble of girls. They are static as the curtain opens, then slowly they move their bodies into classical stances: heads turn, the arms form their arcs in space, the limbs turn out and the preparations for classic dancing have been made before the eyes of the audience. With a kick they step forth into space and commence to move through swiftly flowing designs of great beauty and intricacy, designs which describe geometric formations on the floor and in space. A girl, separate from the ensemble, enters and weaves her own pattern through that of the group, and at the close of this first episode, as the girls stand in mass with right arms upraised, she joins them at the front in the same pose. With the withdrawal of the ensemble, a boy walks on and slowly approaches the soloist. He touches her shoulder, she responds and the two move into the second movement of the ballet, a waltz.

The boy and girl swing easily and joyously through the waltz measures and are joined by the ensemble in the lilting actions.

The third movement (the fourth movement of the musical score) introduces another male figure and romantic incident. The boy and a girl dance together with the ensemble in a bright array of fascinating patterns and are separated at the close of the movement when all rush off, leaving the girl prostrate on the floor.

In the fourth movement the man returns, guided by another girl. He comes to the fallen one, reaches for her, and they have a moment of romance together. But then the guide pulls the man gently away, and placing her hands across his eyes, leads him off. The forsaken one dances out her sorrow, the ensemble returns for final patterns of vivid action, and as the ballet closes three boys lift the deserted girl high above them while the entire corps moves slowly offstage.

The movement inventions of *Serenade* are numberless but among the images retained in the mind are those of a diagonal line of girls, peeling off from their formation one by one and rushing into the wings like a wave from the sea; a *grand jeté* by a girl into the arms of a man with a sudden reversal in midair from a forward to a backward propulsion; the quiet patterns of a kneeling ensemble of girls as they open their arms in accented pauses along the path of an arc; the traveling turns of the girls culminating in a huge spinning circle; a figure in arabesque, her leg grasped by strong male hands, pivoted slowly in two complete turns while she herself remains motionless.

In the Ballet Russe staging, there were three principals, a ballerina and two men dancers. For the New York City Ballet, Balanchine divided the principal themes among several leading women and the two men. This was the original arrangement. Balanchine himself, however, had approved and set the treatment designed for a single ballerina.

In the Ballet Russe de Monte Carlo production Alexandra Danilova, Frederic Franklin, and Igor Yousekevitch frequently headed the cast. Others who have danced the leading female passages include Maria Tallchief, Tanaquil LeClerq, and Melissa Hayden.

The Seven Deadly Sins

Choreography, George Balanchine; music, Kurt Weill; libretto, Berthold Brecht. First produced by Les Ballets 1933, Paris, June 7, 1933. First produced in America by the New York City Ballet with a new translation of the Brecht libretto by W. H. Auden and Chester Kallman and scenery and costumes by Rouben Ter-Arutunian, New York, December 4, 1958.

The Balanchine-Weill-Brecht work is a theater piece, with song, dancing, and acting, rather than a ballet. It tells the story of the lovely dancing Annie and her alter ego (the singing Annie) after they depart from their Louisiana home to find fortune in the big cities. Annie I, disciplined by the experienced and calculating Annie II, earns money through blackmail, stealing, prostitution, displaying her body in clubs and movies, accepting gifts from men later driven to suicide, and by other means. Annie II, commenting on these activities in ironic songs, sees to it that Annie I keeps her figure by dieting and exercising strenuously, that she does not make the mistake of falling in love, and that all the loot goes back to Louisiana to the family and to the building of a home.

The Paris cast for 1933 was headed by Lotte Lenya (Mrs. Kurt Weill) as the Singing Annie and Tilly Losch as the Dancing Annie. For the New York City Ballet, Miss Lenya recreated her original role and Allegra Kent was the Dancer.

Seventh Symphony

Choreography, Leonide Massine; music, Ludwig van Beethoven; scenery and costumes, Christian Bérard. First produced by the Ballet Russe de Monte Carlo, Monte Carlo, May 5, 1938. First presented in America by the same company, New York, October 15, 1938.

Seventh Symphony, the fourth of Massine's symphonic ballets, is divided into four movements: "The Creation," "The Earth," "The Sky," "The Bacchanale and the Destruction."

Heading the New York cast were Frederic Franklin, Mia Slavenska, Igor Youskevitch, Nini Theilade, and a host of distinguished soloists. Alicia Markova appeared in *Seventh Symphony* at its première in Monte Carlo and later replaced Slavenska in New York.

Shadowplay

Choreography, Antony Tudor; music, Charles Koechlin; scenery and costumes, Michael Annals. First performed by the Royal Ballet, London, January 25, 1967. First presented in America by the same company, New York, April 29, 1967.

The central figure of *Shadowplay* is a boy-lord of the jungle, an almost Kiplingesque character who must leave his semi-kneel

posture, as if he were sitting on an invisible throne, to face un-
certainties, temptations, perils. The role is both a technical and
dramatic tour de force for a young male dancer, an actor-dancer.
The part was created for and danced by Anthony Dowell.

The Shakers

*Choreography, Doris Humphrey; music, traditional; costumes,
Pauline Lawrence. First performed by the Humphrey-Weidman Group, New York, February 1, 1931. (Originally staged
for a Broadway revue* Americana.*) Revived and first performed by the National Ballet of Washington, November 8,
1968.*

A major modern dance work, one of Humphrey's most popular
creations, which has moved into ballet repertory. It is an American
folk work in that its characters and its basic ritual as well as its
music are rooted in the Shakers, a nineteenth-century religious
group who believed in and practiced sexual continence (thereby
assuring their eventual disappearance as a religious order) and, in
line with Biblical instructions, "shaking out" sin. The dance is
based on a religious service of ecstatic nature in which men and
women, separated, "shake out" their sins.

Doris Humphrey and Charles Weidman headed the cast in
their own troupe's production.

The Shining People of Leonard Cohen

*Choreography, Brian Macdonald; music, Harry Freedman; li-
bretto, spoken verses of Leonard Cohen's; costumes, Doreen
MacDonald. First presented by the Royal Winnipeg Ballet,
Chicago, February 24, 1971.*

The Shore of Hope

*Choreography, Igor Belsky; music, Andrei Petrov; book, Yuri
Slonimsky; designs, Valery Dorrer. First performed by the
Kirov Ballet, Leningrad, June 16, 1959.*

Shurale

Choreography, Leonid Zhukov and Gai Tagirov; music, Farid Yarullian; book, A. Faizi and Leonid Yakobson, based on a Tatar folk tale; designs, P. Speramsky. First performed in Kazan, March 12, 1945. The Kirov Ballet performed a new version with choreography by Leonid Yakobson, new orchestration by V. Vlasov and V. Fere, and designs by A. Ptushko, L. Milchin, and I. Vanno, on May 28, 1950. The Bolshoi Ballet performed the Yakobson version for the first time in 1955.

Sisyfos

Choreography, Birgit Akesson-Gundersen; music, Karl-Binger Blomdahl; libretto, Erik Lindgren; décor and costumes, Tor Horlin. First performed by the Royal Swedish Ballet, Stockholm, April 18, 1957.

Slaughter on Tenth Avenue

Choreography, George Balanchine; music, Richard Rodgers (arranged by Hershy Kay); décor, Jo Mielziner. First performed by the New York City Ballet, New York, May 2, 1968.

Slaughter on Tenth Avenue, the all-important dance number in the 1936 Rodgers and Hart musical comedy *On Your Toes*, became a part of ballet repertory (the New York City Ballet) in 1968. In a tough but splashy nightclub, a Hoofer, slated for shooting by mobsters, must keep dancing to avoid his promised fate. His partner is the club's sexy Strip-Tease Girl.

Tamara Geva and Ray Bolger starred in the Broadway original. For the independent ballet, Suzanne Farrell and Arthur Mitchell were the leads.

The Sleeping Beauty

(La Belle au Bois Dormant)

Choreography, Marius Petipa; music, Peter Ilyich Tchaikovsky; book by Petipa and Ivan Vsevolojsky, after tales by Charles Perrault; scenery and costumes, Vsevolojsky. First produced by the Russian Imperial Ballet, St. Petersburg, January 3 (Julian or Russian calendar) or January 15 (Gregorian or Western calendar), 1890. First presented in Western Europe by Diaghilev's Ballets Russes, staged by Nicholas Sergeyev, with additional choreography by Bronislava Nijinska and scenery and costumes by Léon Bakst, London, November 2, 1921. First presented in America by the Philadelphia Ballet, with choreography by Catherine Littlefield, Philadelphia, February 11, 1937. Staged by the Sadler's Wells Ballet (now the Royal Ballet) under the supervision of Sergeyev and with scenery and costumes by Nadia Benois, London, February 2, 1939; restaged by the same company in a new production, with additional choreography by Frederick Ashton and Ninette de Valois and with scenery and costumes by Oliver Messel, February 20, 1946; presented in America by the same company, New York, October 9, 1949. Produced by the Royal Danish Ballet, with direction by Ninette de Valois and scenery and costumes by André Delfau, Copenhagen, 1957. Frederick Ashton revised the Royal Ballet production in 1960, the new version being danced for the first time on June 10, 1960. It has recently been succeeded by Kenneth MacMillan's new production, given its first performance by the Royal Ballet, London, March 15, 1973. Other major productions include Rudolf Nureyev's for the National Ballet of Canada, with decor by Nicholas Georgiadis, first performed, September 1, 1972, and the Ben Stevenson production for the National Ballet of Washington, with decor and costumes by Peter Farmer, first performed in Pittsburgh, October 1, 1971. Current Soviet productions include Konstantin Sergeyev's for the Kirov Ballet with decor by Simon Virsaladze, given its first performance in Leningrad, March 25, 1952. First American per-

formance was New York, September 22, 1961. A Bolshoi production had choreography by Asaf Messerer and Mikhail Gabovich, décor by N. Obolenskii, and costumes by Lubov Silich. It was first performed in Moscow, April 9, 1952, later replaced by a Yuri Grigorovitch staging, December 7, 1963. Many other companies perform Sleeping Beauty, including the Royal Swedish Ballet, the Stuttgart Ballet, the Australian Ballet, and the Norwegian National Ballet, whose version was staged by Nicholas Beriosoff and first presented in its third-act version to American audiences during the Norwegian's 1973 American tour.

The Sleeping Beauty is in a Prologue and three acts, but the Prologue is long and elaborate and basically an act in itself. The time and the place are unknown, for it is a mythical kingdom ruled by Florestan XXIV, but the designs and costumes suggest the glittering court days of the sixteenth and seventeenth centuries.

For the Prologue the curtain rises on the great hall of the palace. It is Princess Aurora's christening day and guests are arriving to celebrate the happy occasion. Cattalabutte, the master of ceremonies, sees that all is in readiness. Members of the court enter and go to the crib to peek at the baby; flourishes announce the arrival of the king and queen with their attendants; the queen kisses her daughter and the king discusses the guest list with Cattalabutte, to be certain that no one has been neglected who should have been asked.

When the king and queen have been seated on their thrones, the fairy godmothers arrive. Five of them enter in a group, attended by their pages. They are the Fairy of the Crystal Fountain, the Fairy of the Enchanted Garden, the Fairy of the Woodland Glades, the Fairy of the Songbirds, and the Fairy of the Golden Vine. Then the most beautiful and powerful fairy of all, the Lilac Fairy, enters with six cavaliers as her escorts, one for each of the fairies. During this scene, the fairies dance a *pas de six*, assisted by their cavaliers, and return subsequently, each to dance a solo characteristic of her area of beauty.

The fairies have given their gifts to the child and blessed her, endowing her with special beauties and attributes when suddenly there is an ominous sound and flashes of light. A page runs in and reports to the king, who turns to his master of ceremonies, grabs the guest list and, in a rage, discovers a dreadful omission—Carabosse has not been invited. Riding in a huge black coach drawn by gigantic rats, the ugly and evil fairy speeds onto the scene. In a fury she informs the king that because of the insult, the fate of the baby is in jeopardy. Desperately the king points to the master of ceremonies as the culprit and Carabosse rips off his ceremonial wig and tears at his hair.

Carabosse, brandishing her cane, dances with her rats and then delivers, in explicit pantomime, the dreaded curse that Aurora will grow to beautiful girlhood, enjoying all the lovely qualities which the other fairies have bestowed upon her, but that on her sixteenth birthday, she will prick her finger and die. Cackling wildly, Carabosse completes her curse with a mad dance of triumph. But the Lilac Fairy steps forth and forbids Carabosse to approach the child. The infuriated witch jumps into her coach and departs amid claps of thunder. The Lilac Fairy explains to the king and queen that the curse cannot be fully removed but it can be softened; what Carabosse has said will come to pass but Aurora will not die, for she will fall into a sleep lasting for one hundred years. Gratefully the king and queen bow to the Lilac Fairy; and the courtiers and guests, relieved, turn to pay happy homage to the little princess.

Act I ("The Spell"). The scene is the garden of the palace; the occasion Aurora's sixteenth birthday. Courtiers and commoners are present and among them are three bent hags huddled over their spindles. Spindles, of course, have been banned since the curse of Carabosse. Cattalabutte, seeing the crones with the forbidden needles, grabs the spindles as the king and queen enter. The king discovers what has happened and orders death for the three offenders, but the queen pleads for their lives on this happy birthday occasion and the king consents.

Peasant girls come on to dance a lovely waltz for the king and queen. Carrying garlands, they weave patterns of floral display as they circle, bow, turn, bend. Now Aurora arrives. She runs on with all the lightness and exuberance of youth, dancing with sparkle and smiling pleasure. She greets her parents affectionately and then turns graciously to four princes from other lands who have come to seek her hand. In the famed "Rose adagio," she dances with them, moving in swift turns, darting, extending the leg high and, in two sequences, balancing on *pointe* in *attitude* as the cavaliers present her with roses and kiss her hand adoringly. Between each presentation she is left for a moment unsupported, sustaining her perilous balance with the ease of a princess, with the delighted assurance of a happy girl.

Other dances follow, including passages for Aurora filled with ecstatic leaps and swift traveling turns. An old woman, Carabosse in disguise, has slunk in and holds out a gift for the princess. Aurora takes the strange present joyously and, unfamiliar with spindles, pricks her finger with it as the court looks on in horror. Aurora falls, Carabosse reveals herself with an evil laugh of triumph, despair settles over all. The Lilac Fairy appears and orders attendants to carry the sleeping beauty up the staircase. Then she waves her magic wand, the courtiers fall asleep on the stairs, and heavy vines, great branches, greenery envelop the palace and obscure it from the rest of the land.

Act II ("The Vision"). The scene is a forest; the time a century later. A hunting party for noblemen and ladies is in progress, but the prince, Florimund, is bored with the hunt, bored with the incidental dancing and games, bored with his friends. He orders them to leave, and as night falls he is visited by the Lilac Fairy, who tells him of the hidden castle and of the sleeping princess. At first he is doubting, but an image of Aurora is seen in the trees and shortly the vision of Aurora herself dances on in the company of a band of fairies. The prince pursues the elusive vision, touches her briefly, and is enamored of her. He pleads with the Lilac Fairy to guide him to his beloved and she agrees. They step into her magical boat with its butterfly sails and skim away across a lake.

Act III, Scene One ("The Awakening"). The Lilac Fairy leads Prince Florimund into the dim castle. Guards are sleeping, courtiers are in the poses they struck a century before, great cobwebs and huge spiders obscure some of the splendor of the palace. The Lilac Fairy brings the prince to the bedroom of the princess, who lies on a vast bed. Florimund looks at the sleeping beauty, bends down to place a kiss upon her, and she awakens in his arms. The foliage, the cobwebs, the spiders, the dimness disappear, the courtiers move and light comes up to reveal restored the great hall of the palace.

Act III, Scene Two ("The Wedding"). Once again, Cattalabutte is the master of ceremonies and arranges the procedures for the entertainment. The king and queen, the guests, the performers enter, take their places and the celebration begins. The first *divertissement* is a vivacious, classcial *pas de trois*, danced by Prince Florestan (Aurora's brother) and their two sisters. Next comes a humorous, armorous, skittish, clawing dance for the White Cat and Puss-in-Boots.

The Bluebird and the Enchanted Princess appear to perform the celebrated "Bluebird pas de deux" with its swift, fluttering designs and its wonderful aerial actions (including elaborate legbeats, to front and to back) for the Bluebird.

There is a scene with Little Red Riding Hood and the wolf. Then Aurora and Florimund come on to dance their glittering *pas de deux*, which concludes with a brilliant series of *pas de poisson*, in which the ballerina turns with great speed on *pointe* and plummets headlong toward the floor where she is caught at the last perilous moment by the cavalier.

The lusty dance of the Three Ivans (created by Nijinska for the first London production) follows and introduces the only Russian folk element in this ballet. The boys, dressed in Russian peasant clothes, stomp, kick, leap, and bounce in squatting positions about the stage. Aurora and Florimund join the entire company for a shining finale, which projects the joyous spirit of Aurora's wedding day.

The Sleeping Beauty is one of the most enchanting and popular of all ballets. It has remained in the repertories of the Russian Imperial and State Ballets since it was first performed and it is one of the most distinguished and consistently popular productions in the repertory of England's Royal Ballet. The second scene of the last act has long been popular as a separate ballet, called either *Aurora's Wedding* or *Princess Aurora,* and the "Bluebird pas de deux" and also the *pas de deux* for Aurora and her prince have frequently been presented as separate *divertissements.*

At the 1890 première the cast included Carlotta Brianza (Aurora), Paul Gerdt (Florimund), Marie Petipa (Lilac Fairy), Enrico Cecchetti (Carabosse), Varvara Nikitina and Cecchetti as the Enchanted Princess and the Bluebird. In the Diaghilev production the principals (in the same order) were Olga Spessivtzeva, Pierre Vladimiroff, Lydia Lopokova, Brianza (the first Aurora, here miming Carabosse), Lopokova and Stanislas Idzikowski. The first Sadler's Wells Ballet production starred Margot Fonteyn, Robert Helpmann. The English company's first American performance was headed by Fonteyn, Helpmann, and Beryl Grey (Lilac Fairy), Ashton (Carabosse), Moira Shearer and Alexis Rassine (Enchanted Princess and the Bluebird). Succeeding decades have seen international stars as well as promising aspirants as Aurora.

Solitaire

Choreography, Kenneth MacMillan; music, Malcolm Arnold; décor and costumes, Desmond Heeley. First produced by the Sadler's Wells Theatre Ballet, London, June 7, 1956. Later added to the repertory of the Sadler's Wells Ballet (now the Royal Ballet). First presented in America by the Royal Ballet, New York, September 17, 1957.

The phrase "a kind of game for one . . ." is the only program note provided for *Solitaire.* Nothing further, however, is needed, since the ballet speaks for itself. It is a gay, bubbling, playful affair threaded with wistfulness; for the heroine, described only as "The Girl," attempts to share in the games, the frolic, the happiness of a group of young people. Somehow she never quite finds her place. Moving from episode to episode, sharing briefly the experiences of others, she returns always to her solitary path. Surrounding her are the joyful and gregarious boys and girls who have a marvelous time making danced games. And there is also another girl, of quite a different cast, whose brashness and wit win for her the attention that eludes the shy heroine.

At the London première, Margaret Hill had the leading role, with Sara Neil as the more forward lass. Anya Linden, Maryon Lane, and David Blair were the principals at the New York première.

Some Times

Choreography, Dennis Nahat; music, Claus Ogerman; décor and costumes, Rouben Ter-Arutunian; lighting, Nananne Porcher. First performed by the American Ballet Theatre, New York, July 14, 1972.

Sonata for Eight Easy Pieces

Choreography, Lar Lubovitch; music, Igor Stravinsky (Eight Easy Pieces, Sonata for Two Pianos orchestrated). First performed by the Pennsylvania Ballet, Pennsylvania State University, August 9, 1974.

This ballet for one man and seven women is a nonnarrative composition, but one in which incidents, moods, relationships vary as in the turn of a kaleidoscope.

The male lead was created by Lawrence Rhodes.

Song of the Earth

Choreography, Kenneth MacMillan; music, Gustav Mahler (Das Lied von der Erde). First performed by the Royal Ballet, London, May 19, 1966. Performed by the same company for the first time in America, New York, April 25, 1967.

Song of the Earth avoids the temptation to indulge in chinoiseries possible in songs that have their sources in Chinese poems. Instead, MacMillan has probed the heart of the music—its rhythms, its moods, its hues. Humor, sadness, solitude, love, and death are reflected in the dances while presiding is the inexorable Messenger of Death, neither fearful nor evil but inevitable.

The Messenger was created by Anthony Dowell.

La Sonnambula

(Night Shadow)

> *Choreography, George Balanchine; music, Vittorio Rieti (on themes of Vincenzo Bellini); scenery and costumes, Dorothea Tanning. First produced by the Ballet Russe de Monte Carlo, New York, February 27, 1946. Added to the repertory of the Grand Ballet du Marquis de Cuevas, London, August 26, 1948. As* La Sonnambula, *the ballet with the Balanchine choreography was produced by John Taras, with scenery and costumes by André Delfau, for the Royal Danish Ballet, Copenhagen, January 9, 1955, and presented in New York, September 21, 1956. Produced by the New York City Ballet (staged by Taras), New York, January 6, 1960. The Ballet was added to the repertory of the National Ballet of Washington, decor by David Hays and costumes by Patricia Zipprodt, November 19, 1965.*

The scene is the courtyard of a mansion. The host, a mature gentleman of aristocratic mien, greets his guests at a masked ball. He and a beautiful coquette, presumably his mistress, lead the assembly in a formal but vivacious dance. Now a handsome young poet appears and all action ceases as the guests look at him and he in turn exchanges a passionate look with the coquette. The host makes the necessary introductions and the ball continues.

A *divertissement* is presented by the host's entertainers. Two couples perform a pastoral dance, characterized by flowing yet bounding actions; a pair of blackamoors engage in a lightly humorous dance; Harlequin offers a swift number in which his joints and back appear to suffer cricks from time to time; and a group of flaxen-haired maidens make decorative patterns with hoops.

Following the entertainment, the guests depart for the sup-

per table. The poet and the coquette are left together to dance
a *pas de deux*. The host, however, interrupts, and jealously guiding the girl away, again leads the guests off, leaving the poet
alone.

Suddenly he is aware of a presence and onto the scene walks
a ghostly figure, a girl dressed in white nightclothes and carrying
a lighted candle. She moves with swift, determined steps on the
points of her toe slippers and the empty expression on her face
tells us that she is asleep.

The poet, sensing that perhaps he could become a part of
the dream which this beautiful girl is experiencing, attemps to
attract her attention. He circles her with his arms but she melts
away. He lies on the floor and holds out his hand as a barrier but
she steps lightly over it. He spins her, using the firmly held candle
as a pivot; he lowers her from *pointe* and raises her; and he tries
all manner of ways to waken her, but in vain. As she leaves the
scene, the poet rushes after her but the coquette, standing near
an entrance, has seen this strange episode and is jealous.

The host returns with his guests and the coquette whispers
to him. His fury is discernible and, in the midst of a formal dance
with his guests, he pulls out a dagger and rushes toward that part
of the building from which the sleepwalker came and to which
she returned.

The poet staggers in, bleeding and dying, and the guests
recoil in horror. As he falls dead, the sleepwalker, the wife of the
host, returns and moves forward to the body of the poet. Still
sleeping, but now mourning, she has come for the body of her
new beloved. Guests lift him and place him in her arms and, holding him as if he were a child, she carries him off. The astounded
group watches the departure and many eyes follow a light as it
creeps from window to window, higher and higher as the sleepwalker bears the poet to an unknown haven.

At the first Ballet Russe performance, Alexandra Danilova
(for whom the role was created) danced the Sleepwalker, Nicholas Magallanes was the Poet, and Maria Tallchief, the Coquette.

Souvenirs

Choreography, Todd Bolender; music, Samuel Barber; scenery and costumes, Rouben Ter-Arutunian. First produced by the New York City Ballet, New York, November 15, 1955. The ballet is currently in the repertory of the Harkness Ballet.

A comedy ballet set at a beachside hotel resort, about 1912. The cast includes an eager bride and groom, a pretty wallflower who dreams of being besieged by swains, a lothario, a jealous husband, a flirtatious wife, a gigolo, and a silent-movie-style vamp. Irene Larsson created the role of the Vamp.

Spartacus

(Spartak)

Choreography, Leonide Yacobson; music, Aram Khachaturian; book, Nicolai Volkov; decor, Valentina Khodasevich. First produced by the Kirov Ballet, Leningrad, December 27, 1956. A version by Igor Moiseyev was presented at the Bolshoi Theatre in Moscow, March 11, 1958. A revised and shortened Yacobson staging was made in 1962, and a new version was staged by Yuri Grigorovitch for the Bolshoi Ballet, April 9, 1968, with décor by Simon Virsaladze.

The story, derived from Plutarch, tells of Spartacus, a slave-gladiator, and his love, his betrayal, his fight for freedom.

Askold Makarov headed the first cast. Artists familiar to Western audiences in this ballet or in excerpts from it are Maya Plisetskaya and Marius Liepa.

Le Spectre de la Rose

(The Spirit of the Rose)

Choreography, Michel Fokine; music, Carl Maria von Weber (Invitation to the Dance); book, J. L. Vaudoyer; scenery and costumes, Léon Bakst. First produced by Diaghilev's Ballets Russes, Monte Carlo, April 19, 1911. First presented in America by the same company, New York, April 3, 1916. Added to the repertory of the Ballet Russe de Monte Carlo and other

*companies, including the Ballet Nacional de Cuba, the Pitts-
burgh Ballet Theatre, Les Grands Ballets Canadiens, American Ballet Theatre, and the Bolshoi Ballet.*

The scene is a young girl's bedroom and the girl herself has just
come in from a dance. She moves about her room, recalling the
wonders of her first ball. Taking off her cape and hat, she looks
tenderly at the rose she is carrying. Dreamily, she settles in a
chair with the rose held close to her cheek. She slumbers and the
rose slides to the floor.

Through the window comes the spirit of the rose himself.
Dressed in pink tights with stylized petals forming a cap and
decorating parts of his body, he leaps in and bends over the sleeping girl. His dance is light and buoyant and soon he sweeps the
dreaming girl into his arms and they dance together, reliving the
magic of the ball. He returns her to her chair and with a tremendous leap soars outward and upward through the open window.
The girl awakes, stirred by her dream, and retrieves the rose
which she places tenderly against her breast.

Vaslav Nijinsky, who won worldwide acclaim as the Rose
Spirit, was the first to dance the role with Tamara Karsavina as
his partner. Nijinsky also danced it in America. The first American
performance of the ballet had Alexander Gavrilov as the Spectre.
Although the ballet is most often associated with the fabulous
dancing of Nijinsky (his exit leap is now legend), the Rose Spirit
has been danced by such artists as André Eglevsky, Igor Youskevitch, Niels Kehlet, Maris Liepa, and George Zoritch.

Square Dance

*Choreography, George Balanchine; music, Arcangelo Corelli
(excerpts, Suite for Strings) and Antonio Vivaldi (excerpts,
Concerti Grossi). First presented by the New York City Ballet, New York, November 21, 1957. Revived and first performed by the City Center Joffrey Ballet, New York, March
12, 1971.*

This lively and ingenious ballet makes a series of witty parallels
between the actions of classical dance and the steps and figurations

of square dancing. Although the dancers use traditional movements of the ballet as they respond to the Corelli and Vivaldi
rhythms, they are also mirroring the instructions of a square-dance
caller, who appears on stage with a small orchestra placed on a
bandstand. The calls and the accompanying actions are intended
to be relative rather than identical. For example, while Patricia
Wilde (for whom the ballet was created) is executing *gargouil-
lades*, the caller might exclaim, "Now keep your eyes on Pat; her
feet go wicketywack." Elsewhere, closer relationships can be no-
ticed in the promenades and the formations of stars or circles. But
the point of the ballet is that the exuberance of folk dance and the
lightness of selected ballet steps find a common ground of expression, just as the Corelli and Vivaldi airs, themselves not long derived from the dance rhythms of an earlier era, find a comfortable
relationship with the folk dance calls of contemporary America.

At the première, the principal roles were danced by Patricia
Wilde and Nicholas Magallanes, with Elisha C. Keeler as the
Caller.

Stars and Stripes

*Choreography, George Balanchine; music, John Philip Sousa
(arranged and orchestrated by Hershy Kay); scenery, David
Hays; constumes, Karinska. First produced by the New York
City Ballet, New York, January 17, 1958. The Ballet was
added to the repertory of the Boston Ballet in 1969.*

Balanchine, the Russian-American choreographer, states that his
Stars and Stripes, dedicated to the late Mayor of New York City,
Fiorello H. LaGuardia, has a story and that the story is "the
United States." Actually, this ballet has no plot, but it is about
the United States in the sense that it is a tribute to and a portrayal
of American exuberance, pace, rhythm, humor, endurance, and
love of show.

Although the movements are classical, they clearly suggest
the prancings of drum majorettes, military drill, maneuvers, pa-
rades, and all manner of precision activities. Even the *grand pas*

de deux, danced by a young officer (in handsome uniform) and Liberty Bell, concludes its classical measures with a salute.

The ballet, divided into five "campaigns," is danced by three "regiments" of performers, all dressed in bright, spangled, "patriotic" costumes. At the finale a huge American flag appears as the backdrop. *Stars and Stripes,* then, may be viewed as splashy, extravagant, extrovert, and even corny, but its ebullient actions and its stunning precision teams, performing complex movements with dash and brilliance, represent a stirring balletic toast to American gusto and humor.

The first cast was headed by Allegra Kent, Robert Barnett, Diana Adams, Melissa Hayden, and Jacques d'Amboise.

The Still Point

Choreography, Todd Bolender; music, Claude Debussy (String Quartet, transcribed for orchestra by Frank Black). First presented in ballet repertory by the New York City Ballet, New York, March 13, 1956. (An earlier version, staged by Bolender for the Dance Drama Company, a modern dance group headed by Emily Frankel and Mark Ryder, had its première August 3, 1955, at the Jacob's Pillow Dance Festival at Lee, Massachusetts.) The ballet was performed for the first time by the City Center Joffrey Ballet, September 29, 1970. It is also in the repertory of the Norwegian National Ballet.

The Still Point is a dramatic ballet that is designed not to excite the viewer with physical virtuosity (although it possesses virtuosic passages) but rather to stir his senses with the revealing of human anguish, passion, and compassion. Simply but powerfully it tells the story of a girl rejected in her search for companionship with girls her own age, rejected by the boys as she seeks for friendship and romance, and finally finding peace and happiness and fulfillment in the arms of a strong but tender youth.

Through its intense movements, some balletic and many freely created, we are invited to share the longings, the secret sadness of the girl. In her wild spins we witness desperation; in terse but eloquent gestures, we see her eager (and sometimes angry) quest for comrades; and in stillness of pose we take part in her bitter defeat until the liberating lover comes to free her of loneliness.

In this ballet, recognized as one of Bolender's finest creations, Melissa Hayden and Jacques d'Amboise created the leading roles. (Frankel and Ryder headed the cast for the Dance Drama Company.)

The Stone Flower

Choreography, Yuri Grigorovich; music, Serge Prokofiev; libretto, Mirra Prokofieva (based on a story by Pavel Bazhov); scenery and costumes, Simon Virsaladze. First presented in Leningrad by the Bolshoi Ballet, July 6, 1958, and in Moscow, March 7, 1959. (An earlier version was given at the Bolshoi Theatre in Moscow, February 12, 1954.) First presented by the Bolshoi Ballet in New York, May 4, 1959.

The Stone Flower, a ballet in three acts and many scenes, tells the story of Danila, a craftsman in semiprecious stones, and his dream of creating a vase of malachite that would be as beautiful as a stone flower. As the ballet begins, he has completed one vase but is certain that the secrets of malachite have not yet been mastered. At a betrothal party which he attends with his bride-to-be, Katerina, a bailiff, Severyan, appears and tries to buy the vase; but Danila refuses to sell an imperfect object and the two quarrel. Katerina's attempt to make peace only leads Severyan into falling in love with her and behaving so obnoxiously that Danila and the guests force him to leave.

At the close of Act I, Danila breaks the imperfect vase and starts to fashion a new one. The spirit of the malachite now appears and transforms the stone into the form Danila seeks, but as the spirit disappears, the stone reverts to its unworked mass. Danila, in desperation, pursues the spirit, who is seen sometimes as a fairy and again as a lizard, until she reveals herself as the Mistress of the Copper Mountain. Ultimately, the Copper Queen leads him to her underground kingdom where her maidens are seen as the glittering spirits of gems.

In Act II, Katerina mourns the disappearance of Danila and once again, this time with a sickle, fights off the advances of Severyan. Meanwhile Danila is deep in the Copper Mountain learning the secrets of malachite and also the passionate secrets of the Mistress of the Copper Mountain, who tempts him with her beauty. Katerina, searching for Danila at a village fair, encounters Severyan again and escapes kidnaping by losing herself among the crowds. The Mistress of the Copper Mountain, however, weaves a spell around Severyan and causes the earth to open and swallow him up.

In Act III, Katerina is led by a fire fairy to the Copper Mountain where Danila has created his dreamed-of stone flower. Although the Mistress of the Copper Mountain continues to tempt him, his thoughts dwell upon Katerina and he determines to leave the mountain. But the Copper Mistress decides to keep Danila with her always by changing him into a statue. With the arrival of Katerina, Danila is subjected to a test of love. He chooses Katerina. The Mistress of the Copper Mountain, recognizing true love, releases Danila, and the two young lovers return to their village and a happy celebration.

The role of the Mistress of the Copper Mountain has been danced by Maya Plisetskaya and Nina Timofeyeva; Ekaterina Maximova has played Katerina; Vladimir Vasiliev, Danila; and Vladimir Levashev, Severyan.

Stravinsky Festival

A week-long homage to the late Igor Stravinsky by the New York City Ballet, June 18–25, 1972. Thirty-one ballets, twenty of them world premières, were created to the music of Stravinsky for the event: Scherzo Fantastique *(Jerome Robbins);* Symphony in Three Movements *(George Balanchine);* Violin Concerto *(Balanchine);* Firebird *(Balanchine/Robbins);* Symphony in E Flat *(John Clifford);* Concerto in D for

Strings (The Cage) *(Robbins);* Concerto for Piano and Winds *(John Taras);* Danses Concertantes *(Balanchine);* Octuor *(Richard Tanner);* Serenade in A *(Todd Bolender);* Divertimento from Le Baiser de la Fée *(Balanchine);* Ebony Concerto *(Taras);* Scherzo à la Russe *(Balanchine);* Circus Polka *(Robbins);* Capriccio for Piano and Orchestra *("Rubies" from* Jewels) *(Balanchine);* Duo Concertante *(Balanchine);* Song of the Nightingale *(Taras);* Scènes de Ballet *(Taras);* Concerto for Two Solo Pianos *(Tanner);* Piano-ragmusic *(Bolender);* Dumbarton Oaks *(Robbins);* Ode *(Lorca/ Massine);* Pulcinella *(Balanchine/Robbins);* Apollo *(Balanchine);* Orpheus *(Balanchine);* Agon *(Balanchine);* Choral Variations on Bach's "Vom Himmel hoch" *(Balanchine);* Monumentum Pro Gesualdo *(Balanchine);* Movements for Piano and Orchestra *(Balanchine);* Requiem Canticles *(Robbins).*

A Streetcar Named Desire

Choreography, Valerie Bettis; music, Alex North, orchestrated by Rayburn Wright; scenery, Peter Larkin; costumes, Saul Bolasni; based on the play by Tennessee Williams. First produced by the Slavenska–Franklin Ballet, Montreal, October 9, 1952. First presented in New York by the same company, December 8, 1952. Added to the repertories of the Ballet Theatre (now the American Ballet Theatre), Princeton, October 26, 1954, and the National Ballet of Washington, April 25, 1974.

The ballet follows the scenario of the play and the later motion picture. Blanche du Bois, a fading southern aristocrat, arrives penniless at her sister's apartment in New Orleans. She is dismayed by the cheapness of the place, but is warmed by the affectionate greeting of her sister, Stella. Stanley Kowalski, Stella's rough and handsome husband, fails to respond to Blanche's overly elegant manner and resents her intrusion. He shows little or no sympathy for Blanche's predicaments: the loss of her husband, of the family plantation, of money.

Blanche, rebuffed, turns to self-pity, to dreams of what she imagines her past to have been. For a time she finds companionship and the possibility of a husband in Mitch, a friend of Stanley's, but this romance is destroyed when Stanley comes upon some letters which reveal that Blanche, instead of being the pious and pure lady she pretends to be, has long been granting favors to men.

While Stella is away having her baby, Stanley comes home one night to find the terrified, near-crazy but still pathetically elegant Blanche restlessly pacing. She runs from him and he follows as she speeds through a series of shuttered doors. He catches her and ravishes her. Blanche's feeble hold on reality is destroyed. As the ballet ends a man from the asylum comes to lead her away. She departs regally, as if being escorted by a gallant to a ball.

The ballet combines ballet action with movements derived from modern dance sources and with freely invented dramatic action. A gambling session with Stanley and his friends is free, rough, and jazzy; some of Blanche's actions in her sequences of wild fantasy are primarily balletic, and the duo passages for Stella and Stanley fuse the lines of ballet with the intensities of modern dance.

At the first performance by the Slavenska–Franklin Ballet, Mia Slavenska and Frederic Franklin had the principal roles, with Lois Ellyn as Stella (the same cast was seen at the New York première). The first presentation by Ballet Theatre had Bettis as Blanche, Youskevitch as Stanley, and Christine Mayer as Stella. Nora Kaye and John Kriza later assumed the leading roles.

Street Games

> *Choreography, Walter Gore; music, Jacques Ibert; decor and costumes, Ronald Wilson. First performed in London by the New Ballet Company, November 11, 1952. Also presented, with décor and costumes by André François, by the Western Theatre Ballet. First presented by the Norwegian National Ballet in 1964.*

Suite en Blanc

Choreography, Serge Lifar; music, Édouard Lalo (from the ballet Namouna). *First performed at the Grand Théâtre, Zurich, Switzerland, June 1943, by the Paris Opéra Ballet. It was later performed by the same company at the Paris Opéra, Paris, July 23, 1943.*

An abstract ballet, performed in white practice costumes and with no scenery, for a total company of dancers, initially the entire Paris Opera Ballet.

Suite No. 3

Choreography, George Balanchine; music, Peter Ilyich Tchaikovsky; décor and costumes, Nicola Benois; lighting, Ronald Bates. First presented by the New York City Ballet, New York, December 3, 1970.

A combination of two ballets. The last movement, "Tema con Variazioni," was choreographed by Balanchine in 1947 as "Theme and Variations" for the American Ballet Theatre (see listing) and it remains a staple in that company's repertory. The 1970 *Suite No. 3* concludes with this movement but precedes it with "Elégie," "Valse Mélancholique," and "Scherzo," newly choreographed and including a section done barefoot and another echoing the qualities of Balanchine's *Serenade*. The act of running is a key motif in one portion of this enlarged ballet.

Principals in the 1970 cast included Gelsey Kirkland, Edward Villella, Anthony Blum, John Clifford.

Summerspace

Choreography, Merce Cunningham; music, Morton Feldman; décor and costumes, Robert Rauschenberg; lighting, Nicolas Cernovich. First performed by Merce Cunningham and Company, at the American Dance Festival, Connecticut College, New London, August 17, 1958. The work was staged for the

New York City Ballet and first performed by that company,
New York, April 14, 1966. The Culberg Ballet first danced the
work in Stockholm, October 22, 1967.

Summerspace, created for modern dancers (Merce Cunningham's
own company) and later becoming a part of ballet repertory, is
visually a "pointillist" dance in which dappled leotard-and-tights
costumes blend with a background that exactly duplicates them.

The Cunningham company cast consisted of Merce Cunning-
ham, Carolyn Brown, Viola Farber, Cynthia Stone, Marilyn Wood,
and Remy Charlip. The City Ballet cast was Anthony Blum, Kay
Mazzo, Patricia Neary, Sara Leland, Deni Lamont, and Carol
Sumner. The Cullberg cast featured Niklas Ek, Siv Ander, Mona
Elgh, Karin Thulin, Lena Wennergren, and Timo Salin.

Swan Lake

(Le Lac des Cygnes)

Choreography (in first staging), Julius Reisinger; music, Peter
Ilyich Tchaikovsky; book, V. P. Begitchev and Vasily Geltzer.
First produced by the Russian Imperial Ballet, Moscow, Feb-
ruary 20 (Julian or Russian calendar) or March 4 (Gregorian
or Western calendar), 1877. Reproduced by the Russian Im-
perial Ballet, with wholly new choreography by Marius Petipa
and Lev Ivanov and scenery by Botcharov and Levogt, St.
Petersburg, January 5 (Julian) or January 17 (Gregorian),
1895. First presented in America in a production staged by
Mikhail Mordkin, with scenery by James Fox and performed
by a company headed by Catherine Geltzer and Mordkin,
New York, December 19, 1911. First presented in full-length
form in England by the Sadler's Wells Ballet (now the Royal
Ballet), with the Petipa-Ivanov choreography recreated by
Nicholas Sergeyev and scenery and costumes by Hugh Stev-
enson, London, November 20, 1934; revived by the same com-
pany, with new settings and costumes by Leslie Hurry,
September 7, 1943; new productions followed, with same
designer, in 1948 and 1952; first given in America by the

same company, New York, October 20, 1949. The most recent Royal Ballet version with choreography credited to Frederick Ashton, Rudolph Nureyev, and Maria Fay, and with scenery and costumes by Carl Toms, was first presented in London, December 12, 1963; first presented in America by the same company, New York, May 6, 1965.

A recent Bolshoi Ballet's four-act production had choreography by Alexander Gorsky (Acts I, II, III) and Asaf Messerer (Act IV) with subsequent revisions by Messerer and Alexander Radunsky and scenery and costumes by Simon Virsaladze; the newest staging is by Yuri Grigorovitch, Moscow, December 25, 1969. The San Francisco Ballet also produced a full-length Swan Lake in San Francisco, 1940, with choreography by Lew Christensen.

A full-length Swan Lake was added to the repertory of the American Ballet Theatre, with choreography by David Blair (after Petipa and Ivanov), with scenery by Oliver Smith and costumes by Freddy Wittop, Chicago, February 16, 1967; the first New York performance, May 9, 1967 (Act II was presented alone in New York, January 18, 1966).

Swan Lake in one-act form (Act II of the original), was presented in St. Petersburg, February 29, 1894, with choreography by Ivanov (one year before the full Petipa-Ivanov ballet was presented). In one-act form (Act II), Swan Lake is in the repertory of the New York City Ballet and others. The New York City Ballet's Swan Lake, with choreography by George Balanchine, was first presented in New York, November 20, 1951. It was revised with designs by Rouben Ter-Arutunian, and first danced by the New York City Ballet, April 27, 1964, in New York.

John Cranko choreographed his interpretation of Swan Lake for the Stuttgart Ballet, with costumes by Jürgen Rose, which was given its first performance in Stuttgart, November 14, 1963.

Rudolf Nureyev's production (after Ivanov) was first presented by the Wiener Staatsoper, Vienna, October 15, 1964. The London Festival Ballet presented a production with

choreography by Vladimir Bourmeister (Act II) and Vaslav
Orlikowsky (Acts I, III, IV) and decor and costumes by
John Truscott, July 8, 1965. A staging by Beryl Grey replaced
the Bourmeister/Orlikowsky version on March 29, 1972. Erik
Bruhn staged his production of Swan Lake *for the National*
Ballet of Canada, with decor and costumes by Desmond
Heeley, which was given its first performance in Toronto,
Canada, March 27, 1967. Flemming Flindt's staging for the
Royal Danish Ballet, with décor and costumes by Lars Bo,
was first performed May 10, 1969. Kenneth MacMillan's ver-
sion of the ballet designed by Nicholas Georgiadis, was first
presented by the Deutsche Oper Ballet, Berlin, May 14, 1969.
The Gothenburg Ballet production, Gothenburg, Sweden, was
staged by Elsa Marianne von Rosen in 1972.

Act I (The Garden). In the garden of the palace Prince Siegfried
is celebrating his twenty-first birthday with his friend, Benno; his
old tutor, Wolfgang; young male companions; and peasant girls
and boys. The dance interludes in this mainly pantomimic act include a dance of the villagers, a bouncy solo for one of the peasant
girls, a classical *pas de trois* for a man and two girls and a little
comedy dance for the old and inebriated tutor and a village lass.
Dramatically, the act deals with the prince and his carefree attitude about life, an attitude scorned by the Princess Mother who
arrives on the scene to dampen the jolly spirits, to reprove her son
for his behavior and his somewhat rowdy companions, and to
inform him he is of age to take a wife and is to select one from a
group of beautiful and eligible maidens she will have present the
following night at a birthday ball at the palace. Dismayed at the
thought, the prince orders the revelers to resume their fun as his
mother leaves but he himself does not join in. A flock of swans
flying overhead suggests to Benno that a hunting expedition might
be a pleasant diversion for the uneasy prince. Crossbows and
torches are brought and the hunting party leaves with only old
Wolfgang, now quite drunk, remaining to enjoy his bottle in
peace.

Act II (The Lakeside). The hunters enter and are surprised

to see the swans have gathered on the lake, led by a beautiful swan wearing a crown. The prince orders his men to seek points of vantage along the lakeside and he too is about to follow when he sees something which causes him to remain and conceal himself nearby. A beautiful creature, part woman, part bird, dances into the clearing. She has the face and body of a woman, but her face is framed with a cap of white feathers, her dress is pure white, and the movements of her arms suggest the fluttering wings of a bird, while the quick motions of her head resemble preening.

The prince steps forth and the frightened Queen of the Swans attempts to escape but he reassures her of his concern for her and asks who she is. In mime she tells him the lake is made from the tears of her mother, crying for her daughter, who has fallen under the spell of an evil magician, Von Rotbart. She will never be released from the enchantment, which transforms her into a swan, except for the hours between midnight and dawn, until a man will fall in love with her, marry her, and forswear all other women.

Deeply in love, the prince promises to marry Odette, the Queen of the Swans, and at this point, Von Rotbart appears. Odette pleads with the magician while Siegfried reaches for his crossbow to slay the evil one. Odette, however, rushes toward him and, striking an arabesque over the extended bow, prevents the shooting.

The prince tells Odette of the ball and of his mother's marriage plans for him and asks her to attend. She cannot but she warns him that the infuriated Von Rotbart will try somehow to trick the prince into breaking his vow with Odette.

When the two leave the glade, the swan maidens enter in a long line and soon fill the stage with their dancing. Benno enters and is surrounded by the fluttering swans. He calls the other hunters to him and all of them take aim as the swans cower in a group. Just before the shafts fly, Siegfried runs on and tells them to halt; soon Odette follows and places herself protectively in front of her charges. She begs the hunters to spare the swans, and once they have learned that all are enchanted girls, they bow graciously to them and withdraw.

Now the swans return to their dancing, this time a charming

waltz (containing a musical theme which reminds Americans of "Sweet Rosie O'Grady"), culminating in a delicate and graceful tableau. Siegfried returns in search of Odette and orders Benno to look for her among the many swan maidens. The search is in vain and the prince is despondent when suddenly Odette appears and, to harp accompaniment, sinks slowly to the ground, her left leg doubled under her and her right leg extended to the front, with her head resting gently on her knee. With soft flutterings, she begins to arise and the prince comes forward to guide her to her feet. This is the start of the famed adagio and, to the music of the violin (Mischa Elman once played the violin solo at the performance in London starring Russia's *prima ballerina assoluta,* Mathilde Kchessinska), the prince and the swan queen move through a series of patterns which disclose their affection for each other, Odette's beauty of line, and the wonderful admixture of regality, womanliness, and birdlike qualities which characterize her. The adagio also contains some soaring lifts and difficult spins and concludes with a sequence of finger turns, the ballerina fluttering one foot rapidly in a series of *petits battements* before she is released by Siegfried and falls gently into the waiting Benno's arms.

The lovers leave with Benno, and four cygnets take over the stage for a precision dance which is light, fast, bouncy, and exciting, for the difficult ballet steps are all done in perfect unison, the girls linked closely together.

Odette returns for a lovely solo which includes *développés* to the side and into arabesque, balances and a culminating sequence of turns. The prince also has a brief solo. In the one-act Balanchine version there is a brilliant *pas de trois* for a featured swan maiden and two other swans and a gracious and exquisitely designed *pas de neuf* for an ensemble of swans.

As dawn approaches, the swans prepare to flee and Odette returns for a glittering coda composed of traveling *fouettés* and a series of *entrechats* and *relevés* executed at tremendous speed. As the transformation from girls to swans is about to take place, Odette rushes toward the kneeling Benno and leaps to his knee where she poises as if in flight. Siegfried lifts her down gently, the queen orders the swans to depart and, after the lovers have made their sad farewell, Odette disappears and the hunters see again a flight of swans passing overhead (or in some versions, gliding across the lake).

Act III (The Great Hall of the Prince's Castle). Guests are assembled to celebrate the prince's birthday. The regal and beautiful Princess Mother enters, escorted by her son, and acknowledging the presence of the bowing guests, they make a large circle around the room until they reach the dais, where the prince leads his mother to her throne.

Six lovely girls, selected by the Princess Mother, dance for Siegfried but the prince shows no interest and when he is ordered by his mother to dance with them, he moves perfunctorily with each. The Princess Mother is furious when her son states that he likes none of them but is in love with another.

The music crashes, the Queen of Swans' fate theme is introduced again (it is heard first at the close of the first act when the enchanted swans fly by and it recurs in full at the beginning and end of the second act) and in comes a knight (it is Von Rotbart) with his daughter Odile. Although she is dressed in black, her face is that of Odette. (Originally two ballerinas were to dance Odette and Odile, but with the first St. Petersburg performance, Pierina Legnani established the tradition of a single ballerina dancing both roles and the custom, with some exceptions, has been generally followed ever since.) Convinced that Odile is really Odette, Siegfried leads her off, not seeing the fluttering figure of Odette outside the palace windows.

The Princess Mother is delighted that her son has found a girl to interest him and invites the mysterious knight to sit with her for the entertainment. The *divertissements* include a Spanish-style dance, a Hungarian *czardas,* a Polish *mazurka;* and then Odile and the prince return to dance the great *pas de deux* (familiarly known as "The Black Swan"). The *entrée,* adagio, two solos, and coda are filled with all manner of virtuosity with the peak of excitement being reached in the coda, which is introduced by the prince entering on a great leap and circling the stage in soaring *grands jetés.* Soon the ballerina reappears to execute the famous sequence of thirty-two *fouettés* (introduced in 1895 by

Legnani) and the *grand pas de deux* ends after the *danseur* has performed swift turns in second position and the ballerina has hopped backwards on *pointe* in arabesque and has sped across the stage to leap into the arms of her cavalier.

During the course of this *pas de deux*, Odile moves, on occasion, to Von Rotbart's side to receive instructions and every time that Siegfried's face is turned toward the windows, where the frantic Odette is trying to capture his attention, Odile places her hand coquettishly over his eyes.

At the conclusion of the *pas de deux*, Siegfried asks for the hand of Odile (still believing that she is Odette). Von Rotbart demands an oath of fidelity. Siegfried is disturbed because he has already made his vow to Odette in the forest, but he swears again. As he does so, there is a crash of thunder in the music and the triumphant Von Rotbart and the evil Odile laugh maniacally and sweep out, leaving Siegfried to see the helpless fluttering of the true Odette beyond the window. In despair he falls to the floor.

(Act III has also been produced as an independent ballet, titled *The Magic Swan*. Staged by Alexandra Fedorova for the Ballet Russe de Monte Carlo, New York 1941.)

Act IV (The Lakeside). The swan maidens mourn the tragic outcome of their queen's romance. When she appears, they urge her to listen to Siegfried's explanation but she refuses and prepares for death. The prince, however, seeks her out where she has hidden herself among her swans. He begs her forgiveness and leads her away as the swans resume their dancing. On their return, all has been forgiven and they have restated their undying love but Odette tells Siegfried her life is forfeit, she has lost, and Von Rotbart will see that the two are never united. In a last dance, she moves sadly and tenderly, while the magician, disguised as an owl, impatiently awaits her death.

She explains to Siegfried that only in death is there escape and she rushes headlong into the lake. Siegfried, wishing never to be separated from his love, also casts himself into the lake. Von Rotbart's power is forever destroyed by a triumphant love. He dies and the swan maidens are released from their enchantment. Now dawn comes up and on the lake there glides a boat bearing

Odette and Siegfried toward a new world of happiness together.

In the first Moscow performance, Pauline Karpakova was the ballerina (discontented with her part and her music, she interpolated other music and dance variations into the ballet). This unsuccessful production lasted a few years until the scenery and costumes wore out.

At the St. Petersburg première of the new Petipa-Ivanov ballet, Legnani was the Odette-Odile (Legnani had also danced Odette in the staging of Act II the preceding year). Later interpreters in Russia included Kchessinska, Olga Preobrajenska, Anna Pavlova, Tamara Karsavina, Olga Spessivtzeva, and many others including the internationally celebrated Soviet ballerinas, Galina Ulanova and Maya Plisetskaya.

The 1934 Sadler's Wells Ballet production had Alicia Markova as Odette-Odile and Robert Helpmann as the Prince. Margot Fonteyn was the first to dance the dual role in America with the Sadler's Wells.

At the Bolshoi Ballet's first performance of its own version of the full-length *Swan Lake* in New York, Plisetskaya danced the dual role of Odette-Odile, with Nicolai Fadeyechev as the Prince.

Other ballerinas who have been seen in either the full-length or one-act versions, among an almost endless list of dancers, include Alexandra Danilova, Tamara Toumanova, Irina Baronova, Nana Gollner, Alicia Alonso, Nora Kaye, Maria Tallchief, Nina Timofeyeva, Antoinette Sibley, Cynthia Gregory, Natalia Makarova. In modern times the role of the Prince has been danced by Anton Dolin, André Eglevsky, Igor Youskevitch, John Kriza, Jacques d'Amboise, Rudolf Nureyev, Anthony Dowell, Richard Cragun, and Ivan Nagy.

La Sylphide

Choreography, Philippe Taglioni; music, Jean Schnitzhoeffer; book, Adolphe Nourrit; scenery, Pierre Ciceri; costumes, Eugène Lami. First presented in Paris, March 12, 1832. Presented in London, July 26, 1832; in St. Petersburg, September 18, 1837; Milan, May 29, 1841 (all with Marie Taglioni, who

*created the title role). An earlier St. Petersburg presentation,
with Croisette as the ballerina, took place May 28 (Julian or
Russian calendar) or June 9 (Gregorian or Western calendar),
1835. First presented in America in an adapted version, New
York, April 15, 1835. Produced by the Royal Danish Ballet,
with choreography by August Bournonville and music by
Herman Lovenskjøld and scenery by Christian Petersen,
Copenhagen, November 28, 1836 (has remained continuously
in the Danish repertory). Produced by Harald Lander (after
Bournonville) with music by Edgar Cosma (after Lovenskjøld)
and scenery and costumes by Robert O'Hearn for the American Ballet Theatre, New York, March 13, 1965.*

*The most recent production in the repertory of the Amer-
ican Ballet Theatre was staged by Erik Bruhn, and first presented in New York, July 7, 1971. Bruhn's production is also
in the repertoires of the National Ballet of Canada, which first
danced it December 31, 1964, in Toronto, and the Royal
Swedish Ballet, first performed, June 3, 1968, in Stockholm.
Elsa Marianne von Rosen has choreographed the ballet for
the Scandinavian Ballet (February 2, 1960), Ballet Rambert
(July 20, 1960), and for the National Ballet of Washington,
with décor and costumes by Robin and Christopher Ironside
(March 26, 1969).*

Act I. The scene is the huge living room of a Scottish farmhouse of
the 1830s. It is James's wedding day and the young man is dreaming as he sits in a huge wing chair by an enormous fireplace. But
is he dreaming of Effie, his betrothed? Obviously not, for an airy
creature of fantasy, a winged Sylphide, is before our eyes. She
dances with lightness and speed, bringing a breath of elusive, un-
real beauty into a staid and solid household. James stirs and
watches her. Is this darting image real? For suddenly she is frightened and running swiftly into the great hearth, disappears up the
chimney.

James shakes his head in dismay, enamored of the vision but
unsure that what he has seen really occurred. With the arrival of
Effie and the peasant girls who are to be bridesmaids, James makes

an effort to recover reality. He treats Effie tenderly but his distraction is noticeable and Gurn, a rough peasant who also loves Effie, is suspicious. Celebration, however, is in the air and after the girls have danced their happiness, they retire and Effie leaves to prepare herself for the wedding. James is again alone. Glancing toward a window high in the wall, he sees the Sylphide poised on the sill. She floats lightly down, stepping from sill to table to stool to the floor.

James and the Sylphide dance together and they fall in love. She tells him that he must not wed another and that she loves him desperately. James, tortured by his vows to Effie and his fascination with this vision, returns her ardor. But Gurn, entering from the outside, sees their embraces and scurries up the stairs to inform Effie and the others. When the Sylphide hears the sounds of someone coming down the staircase, she bounds into the deep chair and James covers her with Effie's shawl. Gurn makes his accusations, looks around the room for the girl, and then whips off the shawl. But the Sylphide has disappeared.

Effie, reassured, joins James and repels Gurn's rough protestations of affection. Boys and girls of the village arrive for pre-nuptial festivities to congratulate the two who are to be wed and to dance out their joyous feelings.

During this act, Madge, an old hag, has arrived to offer the mysterious blessings of an old seeress, but James treats her rudely and she is angered. The girls ask her to tell their fortunes and she look at their palms. One girl is delighted with her fortune, another is disappointed, one girl is violently shocked as Madge whispers something in her ear, a child is dismissed with a little push, and Effie is told by Madge that she will be married—but not to James! The young man, in a fury, drives the bent, toothless, and evil-looking old crone from the house.

In the final dances that bring the act toward its close, there are two brilliant solos for two men of the village, swift and bounding dances that suggest the aerial excursions of Highland dancers, although the technique is that of ballet. James also has his sparkling dance sequences and there is a stirring dance for the full ensemble. Realism and fantasy are fused in the concluding sequences, for as the community dance is taking place, the Sylphide reappears. So swiftly does she move that only James sees her and once more he is captivated.

Finally James can bear it no longer and races after the Sylphide as she speeds to her forest home, leaving behind him Effie, his friends, and all his promises and duties.

Act II. The scene is a woodland glade and here James pursues the elusive Sylphide. At first it would seem that now she has won him she is afraid to let him approach her. She flies in and out, appearing for a moment high in the branches of a tree, dancing with other sylphides, barely touching the ground as she flits, poises, and leaps lightly into the air.

Meanwhile Madge has brewed a magical potion in her cauldron near her cave. With incantational signs, she dips a gossamer scarf into the brew and laughs with evil delight over the plot she is hatching. As the despondent James awaits the return of his Sylphide from one of her many flights, Madge appears and tells him that the lovely scarf will solve his problems, that it will delight the delicate Sylphide, and that its charmed nature will bring her forever close to mortal man, to James.

James is delighted with the gift and pays Madge for it but the witch's payment is to be revenge for the snub she has suffered at his hands. When the Sylphide returns, James dances with her happily and the two seem to have at last found the pattern of union. Gently, in adoration, James places the magical scarf around the Sylphide. She shudders as the magic does its work. Her fragile wings fall to the earth and she sinks slowly into death as the frantic James sorrows helplessly. The ensemble of sylphides enter, and picking up the body of their dead companion, carry her in a solemn cortege off stage. In a moment they return and, bearing the fallen Sylphide in their arms, rise slowly through the branches of the trees heavenward.

As James sits forlorn and lamenting in the glade, the sound of happy music can be heard and in the distance we can see a wedding procession wending its way along a woodland path. It is the wedding of Effie and the faithful Gurn. Madge's prediction has come to pass.

   La Sylphide, created by Philippe Taglioni for his daughter,
Marie Taglioni, is one of the most important ballets of all time.
It not only catapulted the young ballerina to fame and immortality but, more important, it ushered in a new age of ballet, the
Romantic Age. Themes derived from classical mythology, popular
since the inception of ballet, fled the boards to be replaced by
European legends of fantasy and romance. Sylphides, pixies, elves,
naiads, and other improbable but alluring fauna became the elusive objects of mortal search. Artistically the period mirrored man's
higher aspirations for beauty; and the creatures of fantasy, almost
always unobtainable, symbolized the dreams and the hopes of
man.

   Although female dancers had been performing a few steps on
pointe since the end of the eighteenth century, Taglioni lifted the
new discovery to fresh artistic heights. When she rose onto the tips
of her toes, she suggested the ethereal, the nonmortal, an air-
being. Literally, she lifted the ballet into a new realm, a realm
never before exploited; and through this she guided the thoughts
of choreographers for generations to come and invited dancing
masters and creators of ballets to develop the technique of ballet
to new peaks of virtuosity and beauty.

   Unfortunately and unintentionally, her genius at the same
time transformed the male dancer into a minor figure. The ballerina, high on her toes, virginal and irresistible, became the queen
of all she surveyed. The man was merely the cavalier, the worshiper, the physical support. Almost a century was to pass before
the male dancer would reassert his position and through his own
efforts and the imagination of choreographers, find coequality
with the ballerina.

   At the first performance in Paris, Taglioni, of course, had the
title role and Mazilier (later to become a highly successful choreographer) was James. Mademoiselle Celeste was the first to offer
La Sylphide to America and Lucile Grahn appeared in the Bournonville *La Sylphide* at the Copenhagen première in 1836. Fanny
Cerrito was the first to dance the Taglioni version (adapted by
Cortesi) in Milan, January 27, 1841, four months before Taglioni
herself performed it in that city. The role was also performed by

other contemporaries of Taglioni, among them the American ballerina Augusta Maywood, but to her time and for posterity, Taglioni and La Sylphide were inseparable. In the 1946 revival by the
Ballets des Champs-Élysées, Nina Vyroubova and Roland Petit
danced the leading roles. The first American performance of the
Bournonville version was presented by the Royal Danish Ballet in
New York, September 16, 1956, with Margrethe Schanne and Henning Kronstam in the principal parts. Other Sylphides have
included Toni Lander, Carla Fracci, Kirsten Simone, Cynthia
Gregory, Margot Fonteyn. The Jameses, Erik Bruhn, Rudolf Nureyev, Ivan Nagy, Paolo Bortoluzzi, Michael Denard.

Les Sylphides

(See also Chopiniana)

Choreography, Michel Fokine; music, Frédéric Chopin; scenery and costumes, Alexandre Benois. First produced by Diaghilev's Ballets Russes, Paris, June 2, 1909. An earlier version
by Fokine, called Chopiniana and danced by members of the
Russian Imperial Ballet, was first presented in St. Petersburg,
March 21, 1908. First performed in America by the Diaghilev
company, New York, January 20, 1916 (an unauthorized version had been given by Gertrude Hoffman in New York, June
10, 1911). Added to the repertories of the following major
companies: Royal Danish Ballet, Copenhagen, October 14,
1925; Ballet Russe de Monte Carlo, January 10, 1934; Ballet
Theatre (now the American Ballet Theatre), New York, January 11, 1940; the Sadler's Wells Ballet (now the Royal Ballet),
London, March 8, 1932; the Sadler's Wells Theatre Ballet,
April 22, 1946; and other companies and ensembles. The
Royal Danish Ballet's production, staged by Fokine, is called
Chopiniana, and this title is occasionally used by other companies, among them the Bolshoi Ballet. Alexandra Danilova
staged a version for the New York City Ballet entitled Cho-
piniana in 1972. Frederic Franklin has staged several versions,
among which are the National Ballet of Washington and the
Pittsburgh Ballet Theatre productions. Other productions in-

clude those of the Stuttgart Ballet, the Pennsylvania Ballet, the Boston Ballet, the Royal Swedish Ballet, the National Ballet of Canada, and the Ballet Nacional de Cuba.

The ballet *Les Sylphides* derives its title from the famous romantic ballet, *La Sylphide,* since the dancers are costumed in the full and long-skirted white ballet dress made famous by Marie Taglioni in *La Sylphide.* The female dancers (there is only one male in this ballet) also wear little wings. *Les Sylphides* is classified as a "white ballet" (a *ballet blanc*), for it is classical in form, romantic in style, white of costume, and represents a twentieth-century tribute to or evocation of the "white ballets" that enjoyed years of popularity following the première of *La Sylphide.*

Les Sylphides, in one act, has no story to tell, for it is composed of a group of short piano pieces by Chopin (orchestrated) to which the dancers perform as an ensemble, as soloists, as duos, and as subensemble units. The setting is moonlit (usually a forest glade) and the atmosphere is one of reverie, lightness, ethereal fantasy.

The ballet opens and closes with a tableau in which the four principals (one man and three girls) are posed at the back center of the stage with the corps extending out from them in lovely, gentle design. The action between these two tableaux includes a light and flowing waltz for one of the ballerinas; a *mazurka,* an unrewarding and difficult solo for the man; a second *mazurka* for another ballerina, in which the dancer crosses the stage diagonally in a series of leaps, exits, repeats, culminating in sustained turns on *pointe;* a prelude for the third ballerina, characterized by exceptionally delicate movements, dainty steps, effortless little jumps, and a recurring gesture which suggests the act of listening; another waltz, a *pas de deux* for the ballerina and *danseur,* which contains many floating lifts, flowing arabesques for the ballerina, and tender gallantry on the part of the male; a final waltz, with ensemble action and sequences for the soloists, which include leaps for the man, swift *bourrées* (done either to the side or, more spectacularly, backward) for one of the ballerinas, turns for another ballerina, and duo passages. The ensemble, of course, has its own dance figures and from time to time melts melodically

into poses and tableaux that set off the dancing of the principals.
The Chopin selections include *Nocturne in A flat (Opus 32,
No. 2); Waltz in G flat (Opus 70, No. 1); Mazurka in C (Opus 67,
No. 3); Mazurka in D (Opus 33, No. 2); Prelude in A (Opus 28,
No. 7); Waltz in C-sharp minor (Opus 64, No. 2); Waltz in E flat
(Opus 18, No. 1).* There have been orchestrations by Glazounov,
Keller, Tcherepnine, Stravinsky, Liadov, Rieti, and Caillet.

At the Diaghilev première in Paris the principals were Anna
Pavlova, Tamara Karsavina, Maria Baldina, and Vaslav Nijinsky.
Each succeeding generation of classical dancers has lent its fea-
tured artists to fresh interpretations of this perennial favorite.

Sylvia

*Choreography, Louis Mérante; music, Léo Delibes; book, Jules
Barbier and Baron de Reinach; scenery, Chéret, Rubé, Chaperon; costumes, Lacoste. (Rita Sangalli was the first Sylvia.)
First produced by the Paris Opera, Paris, June 14, 1876. Revived by the same institution and restaged by Léo Staats,
December 19, 1919; by Serge Lifar, February 12, 1941; by
Albert Aveline, 1946. First presented in St. Petersburg by the
Russian Imperial Ballet, December 2 (Julian or Russian calendar) or December 15 (Gregorian or Western calendar),
1901, with Olga Preobrajenska in the title part. Produced by
the Sadler's Wells Ballet (now the Royal Ballet) with entirely
new choreography by Frederick Ashton and with scenery and
costumes by Robin and Christopher Ironside, London, September 3, 1952; first presented by the same company in
America, New York, September 29, 1953. Ashton revised the
work into a one-act version for the Royal Ballet which was
given its first performance in shortened form, December 18,
1967.*

This elaborate ballet (and the plot is as elaborate as the productions designed for it) is in three acts. In the first act we are introduced to the chaste and cool Sylvia, leader of the huntresses of
the equally chaste goddess Diana. Aminta, a shepherd, and Orion,

a robber khan, are secretly in love with the beautiful Sylvia. Both
are watching as Sylvia, nymphs, and sylphs dance in a sacred
grove near the temple of Eros. Aminta is discovered and the furious Sylvia, recognizing that love has caused him to watch her,
blames it on Eros and prepares to let loose an arrow against the
statue of the god. Aminta, alarmed at this sacrilege, places himself in front of the statue and is struck to the heart by Sylvia's
arrow. The god himself returns the compliment and shoots Sylvia,
who flees into the forest, wounded but alive.

At dawn Sylvia, now in love, returns to mourn over the body
of Aminta. Orion, still guarding the spot in the hope of seeing
Sylvia again, finds her unarmed and seizes her, leading her off to
his grotto. A watching shepherd sees the incident and gathers his
friends to lament the passing of Aminta. An old sorcerer appears,
and plucking a rose, places it against Aminta's lips. The youth
revives, discovers Sylvia's cloak, learns of the abduction, and turns
to pray at the temple of Eros. The old sorcerer throws off his disguise and stands revealed as the god himself. Aminta leaves in
search of Sylvia.

In the second act Sylvia is seen in Orion's grotto home. To
stave off his unwanted attentions as long as possible, she performs
a wild and sensual dance and plies him with wine. Finally, from
too much drink, he and his attendants pass out; but Sylvia can
find no way of escape. Desperately she prays to Eros, who answers
her call and causes the walls of the confining grotto to disappear.
Sylvia escapes.

In the third act villagers and even some of the gods are celebrating a festival to Bacchus on a seacoast near the temple of
Diana. The sorrowing Aminta rejoices as a ship pulls in, bearing
a veiled figure, Sylvia. The pilot has been Eros. But happiness is
short, for Orion returns to claim Sylvia. Aminta fights him but
Diana herself appears and mortally wounds the villain with an
arrow. In a rage that one of her chaste huntresses should love a
shepherd boy, Diana refuses to pardon or to release Sylvia from
her vows of purity. Eros, the god of love, is irked and causes a
vision to appear which shows Diana in amorous dalliance with the
shepherd Endymion. Embarrassed by this recollection of her own

past, Diana relents and joins with Eros in blessing the young lovers.

The title role provides the ballerina with an array of opportunities to display not only her dance skills but also a wide range of acting powers. By turns she must be cold, haughty, and athletic; gentle and amorous and sad; sensual, angry, and frightened; remorseful, pleading, and radiantly happy.

At the London première and in the first New York presentation the cast was headed by Margot Fonteyn in the title part, Michael Somes (Aminta), John Hart (Orion), and Alexander Grant (Eros).

Sylvia Pas de Deux

Choreography, George Balanchine; music, Léo Delibes; costumes, Karinska. First produced by the New York City Ballet, New York, December 1, 1950. The Sylvia Pas de Deux was added to the repertory of the National Ballet of Washington, and first performed by that company, Washington, D.C., October 10, 1963.

This classical *pas de deux* was created especially for the classical brilliance and technical daring of Maria Tallchief. Its *entrée*, adagio, *soli*, and coda contain lyric movement, deportment that is courtly and elegantly gracious, and a vast array of sparkling and exceptionally difficult actions for both the ballerina and the *premier danseur*. The ballerina, for example, is required to do *entrechatshuit*, air turns (*tours en l'air*) landing on the points of the toe slippers, rapid spins, and extended hopping on one *pointe* (while the other foot kicks out low and very fast) across the stage. The music for the ballerina's solo is the well known "Pizzicato Polka" of Léo Delibes.

Maria Tallchief and Nicholas Magallanes (replacing the indisposed Herbert Bliss, who had been scheduled to appear as the *danseur*) were the first to dance *Sylvia Pas de Deux*. Later André Eglevsky assumed the principal male role.

Symphonic Variations

Choreography, Frederick Ashton; music, César Franck; scenery and costumes, Sophie Fedorovitch. First produced by the Sadler's Wells Ballet (now the Royal Ballet) London, April 24, 1946. First presented in America by the same company, New York, October 12, 1949.

This classical ballet, without story, a long-acclaimed and perennially popular Ashton masterpiece, is motivated by the formal structure and the moods of Franck's *Symphonic Variations for Piano and Orchestra*. Certain of the dancers mirror the rhythms and qualities of the solo instrument while others observe the commands of the orchestral themes.

Margot Fonteyn and Michael Somes were the principal dancers in the London and New York premières.

Symphonie Concertante

Choreography, George Balanchine; music, Wolfgang Amadeus Mozart (Sinfonia Concertante in E-flat Major for Violin and Viola); scenery and costumes, James Stewart Morcom. First presented by the New York City Ballet, New York, November 12, 1947. (At that time, the New York City Ballet was known as the Ballet Society.)

The ballet is in three movements—"Allegro Maestoso," "Andante," "Presto"—and requires a large ensemble.

Symphonie Fantastique

Choreography, Leonide Massine; music (and story line), Hector Berlioz; scenery and costumes, Christian Bérard. First produced by the Ballet Russe de Monte Carlo, London, July 24, 1936. First presented in America by the same company, New York, October 29, 1936.

This symphonic ballet by Massine tells a romantic story in terms of a fantasy. A Young Musician, depressed and overly sensitive, has taken a large dose of opium and in his flights of fancy seeks to recapture his Beloved, a beautiful girl. In five movements, the musician's dream carries us through the tortures of his mind— memories of the inspirational powers of the Beloved; a brilliant ball during which he finds her again; a pastoral episode, partly reflective, in a happy sense, and partly foreboding in the young man's doubts about the faithfulness of his Beloved; a nightmare, which finds the man guilty of killing his loved one; and the concluding Witches' Sabbath, in which he sees his Beloved as an evil, ugly, despoiled witch.

Massine and Tamara Toumanova headed the cast in the London and New York premières.

Symphony in C

Choreography, George Balanchine; music, Georges Bizet. First produced as Le Palais de Crystal, *with scenery and costumes by Léonor Fini, by the Paris Opera Ballet, Paris, July 28, 1947. First presented in America as* Symphony in C *by the Ballet Society (now the New York City Ballet), New York, March 22, 1948. Added to the repertory of the Royal Danish Ballet, Copenhagen, October 4, 1952. In 1967 the ballet was added to the repertoires of the Boston Ballet and the Norwegian National Ballet. It has also been performed by the Royal Swedish Ballet, Het Nationale Ballet, and Ballet West.*

Symphony in C is an abstract ballet in four movements—"Allegro Vivo," "Adagio," "Allegro Vivace," "Allegro Vivace"—which requires four ballerinas and four *premiers danseurs,* a pair for each movement. In the closing section of the last movement, all four pairs participate.

This work is one of the most popular of Balanchine's non-narrative musical ballets. It makes enormous demands not only upon the principals but also upon the supporting soloists and *corps de ballet* (forty-eight dancers comprise the cast). The music, of course, governs the choreography, thus there are sections which require terrific speed and sharpness of accent, slow and sustained actions, vaulting movements, crispness, flow. Multiple turns, halted abruptly in an exact pose; gently sinking falls and slow-motion lifts for a ballerina; large leaps; patterns that fly swiftly by but never lack an almost photographic definition are but a few of the movement requirements made of the dancers.

At the Paris première the principals were Lycette Darsonval, Tamara Toumanova, Micheline Bardin, Madeleine Lafon, Alexander Kalioujny, Roger Ritz, Michel Renault, Max Bozzoni. The first New York presentation starred Maria Tallchief, Tanaquil LeClercq, Beatrice Tompkins, Elise Reiman, Nicholas Magallanes, Francisco Moncion, Herbert Bliss, Lew Christensen. The Royal Danish Ballet production was introduced by the following principals: Margrethe Schanne, Mona Pangsaa, Inge Sand, Kirsten Ralov, Frank Schaufuss, Borge Ralov, Erik Bruhn, Stanley Williams.

Symphony in Three Movements

Choreography, George Balanchine; music, Igor Stravinsky; lighting, Ronald Bates. First performed by the New York City Ballet, Stravinsky Festival, New York, June 18, 1972.

A "music visualization" style ballet for principals and *corps de ballet*, a genre of nonnarrative abstract choreography that Balanchine pursued and in which he excelled beginning in the early 1930s. *Symphony in Three Movements*, highlighting intricate and highly original patterns for dance masses, echoes some of Balanchine's earlier pieces of this type but updates them with movements introduced into ballet vocabularies in the late 1960s and 1970s. Sara Leland, Marnee Morris, Lynda Yourth, Helgi Tomasson, Edward Villella, and Robert Weiss headed the first cast.

Tales of Hoffmann

Choreography, Peter Darrell; music Jacques Offenbach (from the opera by the same name, arranged by John Lanchberry);

scenery, Alistair Livingston; costumes, Peter Docherty. First produced by the Scottish National Ballet, April 6, 1972. Added to the repertory of the American Ballet Theatre, July 12, 1973.

The ballet follows closely the story of the opera in which the poet E. T. A. Hoffmann, newly attracted to an opera star, recalls three past loves in scenes of fantasy emerging from the tales told in a tavern scene. The ballet, whose character and *demi-caractère* sequences, were conceived in classical style, provides the ballerina with a tour-de-force assignment—that is, performing four widely differing roles (the three women from Hoffmann's past, including the one who proved to be only a mechanical doll, and the new inamorata).

At the première, the role of the ballerina was shared by four dancers: Patricia Rianne (La Stella), Hiday Debden (Olympia), Marian St. Claire (Antonia), and Elaine MacDonald (Giuletta). The first performance by the American Ballet Theatre starred Cynthia Gregory in all four roles, with Jonas Kage as Hoffmann. Carla Fracci and Eleanor d'Antuono were also seen in the ballarina role with Ivan Nagy as Hoffmann. A motion picture of the Offenbach opera, *The Tales of Hoffmann*, starred Moira Shearer.

Tally-Ho!

(or *The Frail Quarry*)

Choreography, Agnes de Mille; music, Christoph Willibald Gluck, arranged by Paul Nordoff; scenery and costumes, Motley. First produced by Ballet Theatre (now the American Ballet Theatre), Los Angeles, February 25, 1944.

The "frail quarry" of *Tally-Ho!* are women, the hunters are energetic but charmingly decadent young men of a French court and the scene is out of doors near a woodland setting. The chief characters in the ballet are a studious husband, who neglects his pretty wife; the wife, who seeks amusement elsewhere, although she loves her husband and hopes to drag his nose out of his books by making him jealous; a sated but still eager young prince; an innocent from the country who is shocked by the public displays of amorousness she witnesses; a woman described as A-Lady-No-Better-Than-She-Should-Be. The ensemble is composed of richly dressed young gallants and some slickly dressed but somewhat trampish ladies.

At the New York première de Mille was the Wife; Hugh Laing the Husband; Anton Dolin the Prince; Lucia Chase the Innocent; and Muriel Bentley the Lady-No-Better-Than-She-Should-Be.

The Taming of the Shrew

Choreography, John Cranko; music, Kurt-Heinz Stolze (after Domenico Scarlatti); scenery and costumes, Elisabeth Dalton. First performed by the Stuttgart Ballet, March 16, 1969.

A full-length ballet version of Shakespeare's comedy. Cranko tells the story, stages the scenes, presents the incidents through dance action and through dance acting rather than in traditional pantomime. A lusty, bawdy, brawling, electrifying ballet that represents one of the few totally successful full-length comedy ballets—*Coppélia* and *La Fille Mal Gardée* head the limited list—in the classical repertory. The episodes concerned with Petruchio's taming of Kate are a unique mixture of slapstick and balletic virtuosity.

Marcia Haydée and Richard Cragun created the principal roles.

Tango Chikane

Choreography, Flemming Flindt; music, Per Nørgård (after Jacob Gade's "Tango Jalousie"); décor, Bernard Daydé. First performed by the Royal Danish Ballet, Copenhagen, October 15, 1967. The National Ballet of Washington first presented the ballet, October 5, 1968.

Tarantella

Choreography, George Balanchine; music, Louis Gottschalk (reconstructed and orchestrated by Hershy Kay); costumes, Karinska. First performed by the New York City Ballet, New York, January 7, 1964.

A flashing, ebullient *pas de deux*, classical and virtuosic and with Italian flavors. Humor as well as gaiety characterize this fast-paced work.

Patricia McBride and Edward Villella, for whom the dance was created, were the first to dance it, although other casting has followed in this popular piece.

Taras Bulba

Choreography, Feodor Lopokov; music, Vassily Soloviev-Sedoi; libretto, S. Kaplan (adapted from the story by Nikolai Gogol). First presented by the Kirov Ballet, the Kirov Theatre, Leningrad, in 1940. A new production, with choreography by Boris Fenster and designs by Konstantinovsky, was premièred at the Kirov Theatre in June, 1955.

Tatiana

Choreography, Vladimir Bourmeister (assisted by Tatiana Vecheslova); music, Alexander Krein; book, V. Meskheteli; designs, Valentina Khodasevich. First performed by the Kirov Ballet, Leningrad, June 12, 1947.

Tchaikovsky Pas de Deux

Choreography, George Balanchine; music, Peter Ilyich Tchaikovsky; costumes, Karinska. First performed by the New York City Ballet, New York, March 29, 1960.

A brilliant, bravura showpiece that belongs in the category which includes such enduring displays of stylish virtuosity as the oft-danced "Grand Pas de Deux" of *Don Quixote* or *Black Swan*. It is a superb example of the exploitation of the prowess of the classical dancer.

Violette Verdy and Conrad Ludlow were the first to dance it, but others have included Melissa Hayden, Patricia McBride, Jacques d'Amboise, and Edward Villella.

Tchaikovsky Suite No. 2

Choreography, Jacques d'Amboise; music, Peter Ilyich Tchaikovsky; décor, John Bradon. First performed by the New York City Ballet, January 9, 1969.

A classical ballet with pseudo-Cossack overtones, containing a romantic section, another with spates of virtuosity, and passages of antic fun suggesting kinetic, or muscle, smiles.

Allegra Kent, John Prinz, and John Clifford were among the principals at the première.

Theatre

Choreography, Eliot Feld; music, Richard Strauss; costumes, Frank Thompson. First performed by the American Ballet Theatre, January 6, 1972.

The *commedia dell'arte* is again recalled in contemporary ballet, this time by Feld, with the traditionally forlorn Pierrot as the key figure in the comedy of life.

At the first performance the choreographer played Pierrot.

Theme and Variations

Choreography, George Balanchine; music, Peter Ilyich Tchaikovsky (final movement of Suite No. 3 in G); scenery and costumes, Woodman Thompson. First produced by Ballet Theatre, New York, November 26, 1947, and by the New York City Ballet, New York, February 5, 1960. Alicia Alonso staged

*the work for the Ballet Nacional de Cuba in 1970, and it has
also been performed by Les Grands Ballets Canadiens.*

This is an abstract ballet, but the richness of its setting (a vast
palatial hall), the elegance of the costumes, and the proudness of
the movement style evoke the flavors of the Russian Imperial Ballet.

The ballerina, followed shortly by the *danseur*, introduces the
theme with simple yet beautiful steps and, as they leave the stage,
the ensemble carries on the design. As variation follows variation,
the movements become more elaborate. The ballerina is called
upon to accomplish swift turns or exquisitely sustained (she is
supported by four girls) adagio movements with high leg extensions, while the *premier danseur* moves into an extended sequence
of multiple pirouettes or soars into high leaps (with *rond de
jambe*) as he speeds diagonally across the stage. There is also a
pas de deux for the two stars and a concluding fanfare, which
brings on an augmented corps to flood the stage with full and
bright action for the finale.

Alicia Alonso and Igor Youskevitch created the principal roles.

There Is a Time

*Choreography, José Limón; music, Norman dello Joio (Med-
itations on Ecclesiastes); costumes, Pauline Lawrence. First
performed by the José Limón Dance Company, New York,
April 20, 1956. Performed by the Royal Swedish Ballet.*

This modern dance creation, suggested by "To everything there
is a season, and a time to every purpose under heaven" from the
Book of Ecclesiastes, is composed of several and richly varied sub-
themes from this Biblical source: a time to dance, a time for war,
etc.

These Three

Choreography, Eugene Loring; music, David Ward-Steinman (original score commissioned by the Ballet America Foundation); décor, William Pitkin. First performed by the City Center Joffrey Ballet, New York, September 13, 1966.

These Three is a ballet of social comment. The theme is derived from the true story of the three civil rights workers, two white and one black, who were murdered in the mid-1960s in the American South during the angry, impassioned conflicts over civil rights for blacks. The Loring treatment is not literal. Locales are not indicated nor characters named. Individuals with drives and feelings and purposes are accosted, arrested, and killed by a mob acting by instinct born of bigotry and hatred. The three of the title enter separately at first, but they clasp arms in order to march forward. Destroyed by the frenetic crowd, other individuals emerge—this time there are four—and with unified purpose also clasp arms and facing forward, step onward.

The first cast featured Richard Gain, Margo Sappington, Nels Jorgensen, John Jones, and Cleo Quitman.

This Property Is Condemned

Choreography, Donald Saddler; music, Geneviève Pitot. First performed by Ballet Theatre (now the American Ballet Theatre), New York, May 13, 1957.

A ballet with dialogue based on the play by Tennessee Williams. It is the tragic image of a girl, still wanting to play as a child would with a neighbor boy, but whose innocence is about to be condemned as was that of her older sister, a prostitute.

Ruth Ann Koesun and Ralph McWilliams were the boy and girl.

The Three-Cornered Hat

(Le Tricorne)

> *Choreography, Leonide Massine; music, Manuel de Falla; book, Martinez Sierra; scenery and costumes, Pablo Picasso. First produced by Diaghilev's Ballets Russes, London, July 22, 1919. First presented in America by the Ballet Russe de Monte Carlo, New York, March 9, 1934. The ballet is also in the repertories of the American Ballet Theatre, the Royal Ballet (Sadler's Wells). The Royal Swedish Ballet first performed the work, June 4, 1956. It was first presented by the City Center Joffrey Ballet, New York, September 25, 1969.*

The Three-Cornered Hat is not only a ballet with a Spanish setting but one that also employs the techniques of Spanish dance (adapted and somewhat simplified) instead of classical ballet. It tells the story of a miller and his wife whose married bliss (and innocent flirtations on the side) is interrupted by the doddering provincial governor (the wearer of the tricorn), who takes a fancy to the wife. The governor has the miller arrested and then pursues the wife, who eludes him, repels his advances, and finally pushes him in the river. However, she is more amused than angry and fishes him out. But at dawn the miller returns to find the governor's tricorn lying outside his home and the old man (while his clothes are drying) wearing one of his nightshirts! The miller, understandably, suspects the worst. But all ends well when the miller and his wife are reunited and the governor is first punished by his own soldiers, who do not recognize him, and then by the townsfolk, who toss him unceremoniously into the air.

Massine created the role of the Miller; Tamara Karsavina the Wife; and Leon Woizikowski the Governor. At the New York première Woizikowski was the Miller and Tamara Toumanova the Wife. Massine, however, soon resumed the role of the Miller, a part that has always been identified with his special artistry. (His *farruca* has long been considered the high point of the ballet, with the Wife's *fandango* another peak of pure dance interest.) Lubov Tchernicheva and Argentinita (a real Spanish dancer) have also danced the Wife.

The Three Musketeers

(De Tre Musketerer)

> *Choreography, Flemming Flindt; music, Georges Delarue; décor, Bernard Daydé. First performed by the Royal Danish Ballet, Copenhagen, May 11, 1966.*

Three Preludes

> *Choreography, Ben Stevenson; music, Serge Rachmaninoff. First performed by Harkness Youth Dancers, Delacorte Theatre, New York City, September, 1969. First performed by the National Ballet of Washington, Kennedy Center Opera House, Washington, D.C., December 9, 1971.*

A highlight of this highly original ballet is the opening *pas de deux*, performed by a boy and a girl standing on either side (until the last measure) of a ballet *barre* and doing their exercises, at first separately and then very much together.

Jane Miller and Robert Scevers were its first dancers.

Three Virgins and a Devil

> *Choreography, Agnes de Mille; music, Ottorino Respighi; scenario, Ramon Reed; scenery, Arne Lundborg; costumes, Motley. First produced by Ballet Theatre (now the American Ballet Theatre), New York, February 11, 1941. (An earlier version of the ballet, using different music, was seen in a London revue in 1934.) Revived by the American Ballet Theatre, 1973.*

This comedy ballet, which uses technique more closely derived from modern dance than from classical ballet, reports on how the Devil tricks three virgins into going to Hell. The action takes place in a setting which shows on one side of the stage an entrance to a cave, and on the other a church.

The virgins are the Priggish One, the Greedy One, the Lustful One, and it is the first who drags her rather reluctant companions to church, insisting en route that the Greedy One put her finery in the alms box and the Lustful One remove the decorative wreath she is wearing.

Temptation comes first in the form of a handsome youth, dressed in red, who invites the Lustful One to go off with him but the Priggish One is too strong to permit any such nonsense. Then a beggar arrives who suddenly reveals himself as the Devil. Grabbing a handy cello, he starts to play and although the virgins attempt to pray, they find that piety remains only in their clasped hands, for their bodies shudder and shake, bump and jerk in response to the satanic rhythms.

Ultimately the Youth returns, the Lustful One jumps on his back and he rushes her into the cave, the gateway to Hell. Next he tricks the Greedy One into reaching out for a bauble without looking where she is going and she also lurches headlong into the cave.

The Priggish Virgin gives the Devil more trouble and at one point she grasps the teary and terrified creature by the tail and triumphantly hauls him off toward the church. But he escapes and while chasing him at top speed the Priggish One hurls herself at him. He steps swiftly aside and she spins into the cave. The three virgins have been taken and the Devil is delighted with his day's work.

At the first performance the cast was composed of Agnes de Mille (the Priggish One), Lucia Chase (the Greedy One), Annabelle Lyon (the Lustful One), Eugene Loring (the Devil), and Jerome Robbins (the Youth). Maria Karnilova has also danced the de Mille role, Yurek Lazowsky and Robbins have also been seen as the Devil, and John Kriza has played the Youth.

Threnody

Choreography, Mary Anthony; music, Benjamin Britten. First performed in 1956 by the Bennington College Dancers and subsequently by the Mary Anthony Dance Company. First performed by the Pennsylvania Ballet, October 6, 1968.

A modern dance work, based on John Millington Synge's *Riders to the Sea*, it has now moved into ballet repertory. A mother's sad acceptance of the inevitability that the sea, by which and because of which they live, has taken the lives of all of her sons.

At the première Bette Shaler was the mother and Paul Berensohn the last son.

Til Eulenspiegel

(See also *Tyl Ulenspiegel*)

Choreography, Jean Babilée; music, Richard Strauss (Til Eulenspiegel's Merry Pranks); scenery and costumes, Tom Keogh. First produced by the Ballets des Champs-Élysées, Paris, November 9, 1949. First presented in America by Ballet Theatre (now the American Ballet Theatre), New York, September 25, 1951. (The first ballet of Tyl Eulenspiegel *was choreographed by Vaslav Nijinsky, with scenery and costumes by Robert Edmond Jones, and was given its first performance by Diaghilev's Ballets Russes, New York, October 23, 1916.)*

Time Out of Mind

Choreography, Brian Macdonald; music, Paul Creston; costumes, Rouben Ter-Arutunian. First performed by the Harkness Ballet, Cannes, France, February 19, 1965. The Alvin Ailey Dance Theatre presented the work for the first time, New York, December 8, 1971.

The wild, frenetic restlessness of contemporary youth is interwoven with sensual rituals which suggest archaic but recurrent erotic practices.

Margaret Mercier and Lawrence Rhodes headed the first cast.

Time Passed Summer

Choreography, Benjamin Harkarvy; music, Peter Ilyich Tchaikovsky (songs); costumes, Neil Bierbower. First produced, Pennsylvania Ballet, Philadelphia, February 14, 1974.

A ballet tribute to the Petipa-Tchaikovsky era of ballet set to ten songs (including "None But the Lonely Heart") and dedicated to the memory of soprano Jennie Tourel.

Tommy

Choreography, Fernand Nault; music, John Entwistle, Keith Moon, Sonny Boy Williamson; lyrics, Peter Townshend, The Who; décor, David Jenkins; costumes, François Barbeau; lighting, Nicolas Cernovitch; film sequences, Luc Michel Hannaux, Denis Morisset, Paul Vezina. First presented by Les Grands Ballets Canadiens, Montreal, Canada, October 16, 1970. The same company performed the ballet for the first time in New York, April 13, 1971.

This choreographed rock opera is totally integrated with the music of The Who. Tommy is, of course, the central character, a youth who possesses only the sense of touch following a traumatic childhood experience.

The Traitor

Choreography, José Limón; music, Gunther Schuller (Symphony for Brasses); décor, Paul Trautvetter; costumes, Pauline Lawrence. First produced for modern dance by the José Limón Dance Company, New London, Connecticut, August 19, 1954. Added to the repertory of American Ballet Theatre, June 30, 1970.

An all-male dance based upon the betrayal of Jesus by Judas. The ensemble serves as the Disciples, a crowd, onlookers, Roman soldiers, adherents, opponents. A major choreographic scene, the Last Supper.

José Limón (Judas) and Lucas Hoving (Jesus, called "The Leader" in the ballet) headed the modern dance cast. For the American Ballet Theatre the principals were Bruce Marks (Traitor) and Royes Fernandez.

Triad

Choreography, Kenneth MacMillan; music Serge Prokofiev; decor, Peter Unsworth. First performed by the Royal Ballet, January 19, 1972.

A girl invades a relationship between two brothers. Possibly there are homosexual threads present, but it is possible that the brothers' closeness is that common to twins. An element of mystique, however, pervades the work, which is balletic in its contours but also projects that inner dynamism essential to modern dance, thus relating the elegance of ballet with freely invented movements projecting intense passion and feelings almost visceral in depth. The first cast was composed of Antoinette Sibley (The Girl), Anthony Dowell (The Boy), Wayne Eagling (His Brother), and David Ashmole, Peter O'Brien, and Gary Sherwood (Companions).

Tribute

Choreography, Frederic Franklin; music, César Franck; costumes, Diane Butler; lighting, Robert Borod. First performed by the National Ballet of Washington, Lisner Auditorium, Washington, D.C., April 6, 1963.

Trinity

Choreography, Gerald Arpino; music, Alan Raph and Lee Holdridge; lighting, Jennifer Tipton. First performed by the City Center Joffrey Ballet, New York, October 9, 1970.

Trinity has proven to be one of the most popular rock ballets produced in America. Its movement style interweaves virtuosic feats from the classical ballet vocabulary with rippling torsos, pelvic thrusts, stompings, and the frenetic actions associated with responses to rock music. The opening section is especially powerful in its explosive use of the body, with leaps that hurtle the stage, front kicks and back kicks (by the males) which are forced head-high, and fast turns that cause beads of sweat to spin off wet fore-heads. This section is followed by somewhat softer passages, characterized by smooth but spectacular one-arm lifts as the boys raise the girls high in precarious diagonal lines as if the girls' bodies were garlands hanging from an upraised palm. The third and closing section focuses upon a processional pattern in which the dancers place votive candles on the floor of the stage and depart, at the close, leaving the stage populated only by flickering lights.

Triumph of Death

(Dødens Triumf)

> *Choreography, Flemming Flindt; music, Thomas Koppel; libretto, after Eugene Ionesco's* Jeux de Massacre; *scenography, Poul Arnt Thomsen; lighting, Jørgen Mydtskov. First produced for television; subsequently revised and adapted for the stage, and presented February 19, 1972, by the Royal Danish Ballet.*

The ballet deals with various reactions to the coming of death. A plague, a deadly epidemic, atomic radiation, an onslaught from outer space, an unknown terror has struck a community. A very correct funeral procession gives way to a scene in which bodies, like rubbish, are shoveled into disposal trucks; a rich man strips himself bare and uses all kinds of insecticides (some blood-red) on his body, his servants, his possessions, in his food; prisoners are unable to escape from their cells as their guards drop dead; women break department-store windows, rush in to try on expensive clothes before they die; two couples, one divided by panic, the other bound together in death. Nudity (male and female) is used not for display but as an essential act in certain terror-laden scenes.

Flindt created the role of the rich man, with Fredbjørn Bjørnsson in the alternate cast during the ballet's initial presentations.

Trois Valses Romantiques

Choreography, George Balanchine; music, Emmanuel Cha-
brier (orchestrated by Mottl); costumes, Karinska; lighting,
Ronald Bates. First performed by the New York City Ballet,
New York, April 6, 1967.

Trois Valses Romantiques, a bubbling ballet like an earlier Balanchine piece to music of Chabrier *(Bourrée Fantasque)*, it has much
humor but it is sportive rather than spoofish (as was the first
movement of *Bourrée*) and it has the carefree air of a barn dance
transported to and refined for palace pleasures.
Melissa Hayden headed the cast.

The Twelve

Choreography and book (based on Alexander Blok's poem),
Leonid Yakobson; music, Boris Tishchenko; designs, Yevgeny
Stengerb. First performed by the Kirov Ballet, Leningrad, De-
cember 31, 1964.

Two Pigeons

Choreography, Frederick Ashton; music, André Messager;
story, after La Fontaine; décor, Jacques Dupont. First pro-
duced by the Royal Ballet, London, February 14, 1961. An
earlier ballet on the same theme and with the same music was
choreographed by Louis Mérante and first produced at the
Paris Opera, October 18, 1886.

The story comes from a La Fontaine fable. The two pigeons are
a boy and a girl. The boy thinks that the gypsy life would suit him
and leaves home, but he is followed by the girl, who disguises
herself as a gypsy and wins his heart all over again. Disillusioned
by real gypsies, he returns home and all is forgiven.
Lynn Seymour and Christopher Gable headed the Ashton
cast. In the Mérante ballet, the boy, Pepio, was played *en travesti*
by Marie Sanlaville, and the girl, Gourouli, by Rosita Mauri.

Tyl Ulenspiegel

(See also *Til Eulenspiegel*)

Choreography, George Balanchine; music, Richard Strauss (Til Eulenspiegel's Merry Pranks); scenery and costumes, Esteban Frances. First produced by the New York City Ballet, New York, November 14, 1951.

Tyrolian Pas de Deux

A popular excerpt from August Bournonville's dances for Gioacchino Rossini's opera *William Tell*. The excerpt is a lively, fleet-footed, aerial dance in Bournonville's buoyant Danish style. (See *William Tell Variations*.)

Tzaddik

Choreography, Eliot Feld; music, Aaron Copland; décor, Boris Aronson. First produced by the Eliot Feld Ballet, New York, June 2, 1974.

An intensely religious dance celebrating the Jews' quest for and faith in the power of knowledge. The ballet focuses on a Hebrew scholar-teacher and his fiercely emotional guidance of two young boys into the orbit of learning within the framework of Jewish tradition. At the close the three become wrapped in a great banner bearing words from the Torah.

Feld headed the first cast.

Undertow

Choreography, Antony Tudor; music, William Schuman; libretto, Tudor, after a suggestion by John van Druten; scenery and costumes, Raymond Breinin. First produced by the Ballet Theatre (now the American Ballet Theatre), New York, April

10, 1945. The ballet was revived by the American Ballet Theatre in 1967 and 1973.

This contemporary dramatic ballet in one act, a prologue, and epilogue, tells the story of the Transgressor, a boy who, because of background, environment, and temptation, is driven to murder.

The prologue shows the goddess Cybele in labor. From between her anguished pain-racked limbs springs her son, whom she despises for the agony he has brought her and from whom she turns in quest of a young lover, Pollux. Here, the Transgressor first experiences lovelessness.

In a series of street incidents, the Transgressor finds innocent love with a young girl; is fascinated by the tawdry glitter and sexy displays of a prostitute, Volupia; is enraged when an aging libertine makes advances toward his innocent friend, Aganippe; fails to respond to the sermonizing and hymn-singing of the emptily pious Polyhymnia; spurns the invitations of the lascivious, writhing, sensually disgusting Ate; and watches, amazed and dubious, as Hymen and Hera dance joyously by, an exuberant bride and groom.

Ate returns, and the Transgressor dances with her and comes close to strangling her in a fit of vicious hatred. Momentarily he seeks escape in the superficial religious antics of Polyhymnia, but with the coming of Medusa his fate is sealed. He dances with this alluring but evil woman and, unleashing his hatred of women, murders her.

In the epilogue, the Transgressor stands alone in his guilt as people pass by, watching him as if he were an inexplicable freak. Even Aganippe, playing with a balloon, refuses him comfort and he is left alone to meet his fate.

The first cast included Hugh Laing as the Transgressor, Alicia Alonso as Ate, Nana Gollner as Medusa, Diana Adams as Cybele, Lucia Chase as Polyhymnia, Shirley Eckl as Volupia, Patricia Barker as Aganippe, and John Kriza as Pollux. The role of the Transgressor was danced by Stevan-Jan Hoff, in the 1967 revival, and Daniel Levins, in 1973.

Unfinished Symphony

Choreography, Peter van Dyk; music, Franz Schubert. First performed by the American Ballet Theatre, New York, January 18, 1972.

A romantic *pas de deux*, a vehicle for two technically accomplished and personable stars. With the American Ballet Theatre, Cynthia Gregory and Michael Denard constituted the cast.

The Unicorn, the Gorgon, and the Manticore

(or *The Three Sundays of a Poet*)

Choreography, John Butler; music and libretto, Gian Carlo Menotti. Commissioned by the Elizabeth Sprague Coolidge Foundation in the Library of Congress and first performed in Washington, October 21, 1956. Produced by the Ballet Society for the New York City Ballet, with scenery and lighting by Jean Rosenthal and costumes by Robert Fletcher, New York, January 15, 1957. Another version, with choreography by Peter Darrell, and décor and costumes by Barry Kay, was first performed in Bristol, England, June 28, 1962, by the Western Theatre Ballet. For the Cincinnati Ballet, Louis Johnson choreographed a version of the work, which was first performed in 1972.

Union Pacific

Choreography, Leonide Massine; music, Nicholas Nabokov; book, Archibald MacLeish; scenery, Albert Johnson; costumes, Irene Sharaff. First produced by the Ballet Russe de Monte Carlo, Philadelphia, April 6, 1934.

Massine's first ballet on an American theme. And very Russian it was.

Les Vainqueurs

Choreography, Maurice Béjart; music, Richard Wagner and classical Indo-Tibetan composers; décor and costumes, Yahne Le Toumelin. First performed by Ballet of the Twentieth Century, Brussels, Théâtre Royal de la Monnaie, December 10, 1968. It was given its first American performance at the Brooklyn Academy of Music, New York, January 30, 1971, by the same company.

Valentine

Choreography, Gerald Arpino; music, Jacob Druckman. First performed by the City Center Joffrey Ballet, New York, March 10, 1971.

A comedy *pas de deux* that turns into a *pas de trois* when two dancers involve an onstage contrabass player in their activities, which are in the nature of a playful sparring match.

La Valse

Choreography, George Balanchine; music, Maurice Ravel (Valses Nobles et Sentimentales and La Valse); costumes, Karinska. First produced by the New York City Ballet, New York, February 20, 1951. Another version, with entirely different choreography by Frederick Ashton, was presented by the La Scala Opera Ballet, Milan, February 1, 1958. First presented by the Royal Ballet, with costumes by André Levasseur, London, March 10, 1959. The Balanchine version was first performed by the Stuttgart Ballet, Stuttgart, January 22, 1965. The ballet has also been performed by Het Nationale Ballet, Holland, which added it to its repertory, October 4, 1967. For Ballet West, Willam Christensen choreographed a version of La Valse, with decor by Ariel Baliff.

La Valse is a ballet without plot but it is rich in mood and ominous in the implication that these are final dance pleasures before a catastrophe, especially when, at the close of the ballet, the black-clad figure of Death brings clothing and decoration of jet with which to adorn the ballerina.

The first part of the ballet, set to the *Valses Nobles et Sentimentales*, is a series of extremely elegant *divertissements* which require the polished, and sometimes mannered, dancing of several soloists. Solos, duos, and small groups, all waltzing, of course, move through a variety of designs and delicately tinted moods.

In the second part, *La Valse*, the sense of doom intrudes. Hurriedly, almost desperately, one boy and then another seeks his partner. The music and the lights brighten and eighteen dancers move swiftly into the joyous, flowing patterns of the waltz. The ballerina, dressed in dazzling white, enters with her partner and they engage in a soft and tender dance as the music lulls from its brightness to a gentle warmth. With her partner's exit, the ballerina steps forth brightly to the quickening music and executes her brilliant passages.

During a later dance with her partner, the music sends out its warnings and fear settles down upon the couple. Now, a male figure in black approaches slowly and the girl, hypnotized, accepts a necklace and looks in horror as he holds a black-glassed mirror up for her. Completely under the spell of the stranger, she puts on the long black gloves and black overdress he has provided, and accepts a bouquet of black flowers. Then he takes her in his arms and spins her around the ballroom until she sags in his arms. They stop and she falls dead. The first partner, her lover, returns to carry her off as the figure in black withdraws.

The dismayed couples turn in desperation to their dancing, mirroring in their tensions the conflicting themes and rhythms of the music. The young man returns with the girl's body, she is lifted high by a group of young men, and the ballet ends with a frenetic, eerie, whirling wheel of living bodies.

At the première, Tanaquil LeClercq was the Ballerina, Nicholas Magallanes her Partner, and Francisco Moncion, the figure of Death. Jean Rosenthal designed the lighting effects, which were woven into the phrasing of the music, the plan of the choreography, and the shifting moods of the ballet. Other New York City

Ballet ballerinas who have danced the principal role are Patricia McBride, Allegra Kent, and Sara Leland.

Valse-Fantaisie

Choreography, George Balanchine; music, Mikhail Glinka; costumes, Karinska. First produced by the New York City Ballet, New York, January 6, 1953. The first staging to this music. (See Glinkiana and also the unhyphenated Valse Fantaisie).

Valse-Fantaisie, a short ballad set to Glinka waltzes, is without story and is concerned mainly with classical movements and their sequential developments into varied patterns. The work is designed for three ballerinas and a *premier danseur.* Each of the ballerinas is given opportunities to display her special attributes in movements quick and brilliant, slow and sustained, or large and sweeping, in this graciously mannered and delightfully spirited ballet.

The first cast was composed of Tanaquil LeClercq, Melissa Hayden, Diana Adams, and Nicholas Magallanes.

Valse Fantaisie (formerly Part II of *Glinkiana*)

Choreography, George Balanchine; music, Mikhail Glinka; scenery, costumes, and lighting, Esteban Frances. First presented by the New York City Ballet, New York, June 1, 1969. (See Glinkiana.)

Variations for Four

Choreography, Anton Dolin; music, Marguerite Keogh; costumes, Tom Lingwood. First presented by the London Festival Ballet, London, September 5, 1957. First American presentation, The Ed Sullivan Show, CBS-TV, March 30, 1958; first American stage presentation, American Ballet Theatre,

September 25, 1958. The Harkness Ballet performed the work for the first time, November 9, 1967. It was added to the reppertory of the National Ballet of Washington, Washington, D.C., January 7, 1972. Les Grands Ballets Canadiens has also performed the work.

This short ballet is a tour de force in classical style. There is no story, for the purpose of the work is to exploit the technical skills of the four male dancers—the leaps, spins, balances, beats, and other standard steps and actions employed to display the prowess of the *premier danseur*. Since this ballet calls for (and requires) four *premiers danseurs*, it is, in a sense, an aristocratic contest in physical agility coupled with balletic elegance. *Variations for Four* might be viewed as the male equivalent of the Victorian *Pas de Quatre* (see *Pas de Quatre*), starring four great ballerinas of an earlier era. (Also staged by Dolin in a twentieth-century recreation of the historic piece.) The first cast was composed of John Gilpin, Flemming Flindt, Louis Godfrey, André Prokovsky.

In the first American performance the dancers were John Gilpin, Louis Godfrey, Michael Hogan, and André Prokovsky. The initial cast for the American Ballet Theatre presentation was composed of Erik Bruhn, John Kriza, Royes Fernandez, Scott Douglas. Harkness dancers to perform the work have included Finis Jhung, Helgi Tomasson, Dennis Wayne, and Lawrence Rhodes. Dennis Poole, Kirk Peterson, and Stuart Sebastian have performed it for the National Ballet of Washington, D.C. Fernando Bujones, Warren Conover, John Prinz, and Terry Orr have danced more recently for American Ballet Theatre.

Variations pour une Porte et un Soupir

Choreography, George Balanchine; music, Pierre Henry; décor, Rouben Ter-Arutunian. First performance, New York City Ballet, New York, January 17, 1974.

The *musique-concrète* score is, literally, focused upon the sounds of a creaking door and a variety of sighs. Balanchine has seen the *porte* ("door") as female and the *soupir* ("sigh" as male) and in

this *pas de deux* one might, if he so chooses, find sexual connotations in certain patterns, involving a vast cape, which suggest
penetrations and withdrawals. However, one might regard the
images simply as images which come together and part. The Ter-
Arutunian cape is an integral part of the choreography. The *Porte*,
assisted by unseen offstage hands, manipulates this costume-cur-
tain-drape which dominates the stage. It is of black silk and bil-
lows, ripples, shudders, trembles, rests, and surges in relationship
to the actions of the two principals. Their movements are not
classical but, rather, free motor responses to the sounds of the
score and to the restless drapery. The avant-garde Alwyn Nikolais
uses a similar device in his *Tent* and the late Ruth St. Denis, more
than half a century ago, manipulated stage-size materials in her
Spirit of the Sea in which her own white hair was the foam and
her silks, the ocean. The first cast of the Balanchine ballet was
Karin Von Aroldingen and John Clifford.

Variations for Tape and Choreography

Choreography, Enid Lynn; music, Josed Tal (Variations for
Tape and Choreography). *First performed by the Hartford
Ballet, April 18, 1973.*

La Ventana

*Choreography, August Bournonville; music, Hans Christian
Lumbye. First produced by the Royal Danish Ballet, Copenhagen, 1854 (an earlier and somewhat different version was
created by Bournonville for a recital performance in a casino).
Revised by the choreographer in 1856. Restaged by Frank
Schaufuss and Hans Brenaa in 1956. First presented in America, October 28, 1956, in Brooklyn, during the American tour
of the Royal Danish Ballet.*

In its present staging as a *divertissement* this lively little ballet
contains an amusing, brilliantly choreographed, and expertly performed *Mirror Dance* (requiring exactly duplicated movements

by two dancers); a vivacious *pas de trois;* a stirring number for a male soloist; a *seguidilla,* a dashing duet for a ballerina and *danseur;* and a concluding ensemble dance.

The ballet, with its Spanish flavored dance materials, exploits the technical exactitude, the bounce, and the acting skills of the Royal Danish dancers in a style of movement established by Bournonville and unique in Denmark.

Villon

Choreography, John Butler; music, Robert Starer. First danced by the Pennsylvania Ballet, Philadelphia, November 23, 1966. First presented by Les Grands Ballets Canadiens, with décor by Claude Girard, in 1970.

Villon, a rousing, roistering ballet about France's wild and wonderful fifteenth-century poet. It is not actually a narrative-biography, but rather a portrait of a brawler who was also a poet and a lecher, one who courted death while celebrating life. The key choreographic patterns are a circle, which both protects and imprisons Villon, and a lateral design, which represents his pathway to adventure.

Ross Parkes created the title role.

Violin Concerto

Choreography, George Balanchine; music, Igor Stravinsky; lighting, Ronald Bates. First presented by the New York City Ballet, Stravinsky Festival, New York, June 18, 1972.

A major ballet in the genre of "music visualization" in which Balanchine excels as he extends sound rhythms and timbres into body rhythms and movement textures. (Balanchine used the same music for a dramatic ballet, *Balustrade,* created for Tamara Toumanova in 1941.)

Heading the initial cast for *Violin Concerto* were Kay Mazzo, Peter Martins, Karin Von Aroldingen, and Jean-Pierre Bonnefous.

Viva Vivaldi!

Choreography, Gerald Arpino; music, Antonio Vivaldi (adapted from Violin Concerto, P. 151, *by Rodrigo Riera*). *First performed by the Robert Joffrey Ballet (now the City Center Joffrey Ballet), at the Rebekah Harkness Dance Festival, Central Park, New York, September 11, 1965.*

Viva Vivaldi! became, for a time, almost the trademark of the Joffrey dancers. This bright Spanish-flavored piece seemed to symbolize the youthful accent stressed by this troupe and also its desire to maintain a classical ballet base while stepping forth into new areas of movement and pattern. A highlight of the first seasons was the near-contest (in ballet technique) close to the finale of two male dancers. (In the absence of two bravura virtuosi, the passage is performed by one man.)

Robert Blankshine and Luis Fuente were the male leads at the première.

Voluntaries

Choreography, Glen Tetley; music, François Poulenc ("Concerto for Organ, Strings, and Timpani"). First performed by the Stuttgart Ballet, Stuttgart, Germany, December 22, 1973.

The first ballet created by Tetley for the Stuttgart Ballet before he assumed the directorship of that company. The work is chiefly a display piece for the dramatic and virtuosic qualities of the Stuttgart's star dancers, Marcia Haydée and Richard Cragun.

Walpurgis Night

The ballet scene, the *bacchanale*, from Charles Gounod's opera *Faust* is often given outside the opera itself as a one-act ballet. Its choreographers, over the years, are too numerous to name. Sometimes "Walpurgis" is used as an excerpt from an excerpt when a *pas de deux* is extracted from the ballet or opera ballet or is especially choreographed for a *divertissement* program.

Perhaps the most familiar "Walpurgis Night" *divertissement* is that performed by the Bolshoi Ballet with Maya Plisetskaya as the star.

Watermill

Choreography, Jerome Robbins; music, Teijo Ito; décor, Jerome Robbins and David Reppa; costumes, Patricia Zipprodt. First presented by the New York City Ballet, February 3, 1972.

A long, deliberately slow ballet in which the key figure is a youth who divests himself of the robes of a civilization and, nearly nude, contemplates the passages of time: the waxing-waning-waxing of the moon, the running steps of the young, the inching progress of an old crone, fertility, romance, quietude. The central figure, barely moving, seems to echo William Wordsworth's "emotion recollected in tranquillity," although the setting, décor, and pacing of the ballet are clearly Japanese-inspired. It is perhaps less a ballet than a theatrical experience. Some have found its slow pace and its length boring, while others have been hypnotized by the presence of an energized stillness reminiscent of Noh acting.

The central role was created by Edward Villella, and even the casting was controversial since Villella, on the international scene, had established himself as a ballet virtuoso.

Water Study

Choreography, Doris Humphrey; costumes, Pauline Lawrence. First performed by the Humphrey-Weidman Concert Group, New York, October 28, 1928. Revived and first performed by the National Ballet of Washington, January 7, 1972, at the Kennedy Center Opera House, Washington, D. C.

A modern dance work for small ensemble. Its movement characteristics and choreographic patterns do not imitate as much as they suggest qualities of water motion from stillness through waves and ripplings to turbulence.

A Wedding Bouquet

Choreography, Frederick Ashton; music, scenery, and costumes, Lord Berners; words, Gertrude Stein. First produced by the Vic-Wells Ballet (later the Sadler's Wells Ballet and now the Royal Ballet), April 27, 1937, London. First American performance by the same company, New York, October 25, 1949.

This one-act comic ballet has a French provincial setting. Everyone is determined to be quite, quite correct as the preparations for a wedding and the celebration itself take place; yet untoward incidents occur and here one finds the frothy humor of the piece. Among the characters are the Bride, who finds everything "Charming!"; the Bridegroom, who is obviously a half-reformed libertine; a lady guest given to drink; a nervous maid; Julia, a wild creature loved only by her dog (Julia is described in the Stein lines quite clearly when a voice says, "She's made no plans for the summer"); and Julia's dog.

The frequently hilarious actions, particularly those of Julia, who is obviously demented, are given extra wit by the dry, wonderfully rhythmic, and peculiarly pertinent words of Gertrude Stein.

At the première Mary Honer was the Bride; Robert Helpmann the Bridegroom; Margot Fonteyn, Julia; June Brae the Inebriated Lady; Julia Farron the Dog; and Ninette de Valois the Maid. In New York the cast (in the same order) was headed by Margaret Dale, Helpmann, Moira Shearer, Brae, Pauline Clayden, and Palma Nye.

Wednesday Class

Choreography, Kirsten Ralov, Fredbjørn Bjørnsson (based on exercises from the daily classes of August Bournonville);

music, classroom music by various composers, mainly Danish. First produced by the Royal Danish Ballet, Copenhagen, November, 1973.

This plotless ballet reproduces a class in the style of the celebrated nineteenth-century Danish dancer-choreographer-teacher, August Bournonville. Bournonville technique is still taught at the Royal School, just as extant Bournonville ballets (about ten) are still performed by the Royal Danish Ballet. The master's classes varied for each day of the week; the new ballet focuses upon a Wednesday class but incorporates exercises from other class days. The ballet, using children and adults, starts with a strict *barre*, continues with "center" adagio requiring difficult balances, and concludes with the high leaps and complex feet- and leg-beats characteristic of Bournonville technique. Principals were Flemming Ryberg and Anna Marie Dybdal.

Weewis

Choreography, Margo Sappington; music, Stanley Walden; costumes, Willa Kim; lighting, Jennifer Tipton. First performed by the City Center Joffrey Ballet, New York, October 27, 1971.

This rock ballet is performed by three pairs of dancers: two boys (perhaps lovers, perhaps just close friends); a highly romantic boy and girl who engage in near-erotic dancing; a male and female who confront each other angrily.

The first cast of Weewis was Gary Chryst and James Dunne (Two Boys), Rebecca Wright and Christian Holder (Romantic Boy and Girl), and Susan Magno and Tony Catanzaro (Angry Male and Female).

Western Symphony

Choreography, George Balanchine; music, Hershy Kay (symphony based on American folk themes); scenery by John Boyt and costumes by Karinska added February 27, 1955.

First produced, without formal scenery and costumes, by the New York City Ballet, New York, September 7, 1954.

Unlike *Billy the Kid, Rodeo,* and other examples of balletic Americana, *Western Symphony* is neither a dramtic ballet nor one that makes generous use of folk action. It is almost wholly classical and achieves its American folk flavors through a shrewd selection of ballet steps and gestures that have their equivalents in certain folk idioms, or that suggest folk rhythms and gestures. Just as the ballerina's solos in *Raymonda* (or *Pas de Dix*) are classical but touched with Hungarian colorings, so *Western Symphony* is thoroughly classical but flavored with the robustness and humor of the West.

The ballet's form follows the musical divisions of the score—"Allegro," "Adagio," "Scherzo," "Rondo"—but the classical movements capture the zip of a barndance, the showoff tactics of cowboys, the high-kicking antics of saloon girls, the teasingly elusive activities of a coquette, and the romping zest of young men and women with space to move in and with the gusto to fill that space with aerial displays, brisk steps, and intricate designs.

Stars of the first performances were Diana Adams, Herbert Bliss, Janet Reed, Nicholas Magallanes, Patricia Wilde, André Eglevsky, Tanaquil LeClercq, and Jacques d'Amboise.

The Whims of Cupid and of the Ballet Master

Choreography, Vincenzo Galeotti; music, Jens Lolle. First produced by the Royal Danish Ballet, Copenhagen, 1786. First presented in America by the Royal Danish Ballet, New York, September 22, 1956.

The Whims of Cupid is considered to be the world's oldest surviving ballet. At least, it is the oldest of untampered-with ballets, for *La Fille Mal Gardée,* which is the same age, has been changed extensively over the years. The Danes, however, have performed *The Whims of Cupid* continuously and they are known for their cherishing of tradition. If some alterations have been made, they are probably to be found in the few passages that involve dancing on *pointe,* for although toe work was introduced at approximately the same time as this ballet was created (or within a decade thereafter), it is not likely that Galeotti used it to any degree. But that is guesswork.

The slight story upon which this ballet rests has to do with lovers from many lands (what an opportunity for national dances!) who come to the Temple of Love to seek the blessing of the little god Cupid (danced by a little girl in a *tutu*). To win the approval of Love, each couple performs a dance characteristic of his land. The *divertissements* include a lively dance for a Tyrolean pair; a stiff-moving, very proper, and very funny dance for the Quakers; a *pas de deux* suggesting the poetic lyricism of classical Greece; a beautifully mimed number (the Danes are experts at pantomime) for a tottering old gentleman and his equally rickety old lady; an ensemble dance of an antic nature for six blackamoors, three girls replete with feathers and bangles, and three men dressed in what could pass for idealized plantation garb; and dances involving Norwegians, French, and, of course, Danes.

Once their danced offerings are done, Love plays a game and orders the couples to be blindfolded. In the ensuing confusion, everyone gets mixed up and the ballet reaches its comic peak when capricious Love achieves some unusual matchmaking, such as when one of the young lads finds himself paired with the feeble old lady, and the stern and forbidding Quaker woman winds up in the care of an exceptionally exuberant youth.

For the New York performance Lise La Cour-Maslev (a child dancer of the Royal Danish Ballet) was Love; Britta Cornelius-Knudsen and Ole Palle Hansen, Quakers; Elise Landsy and Arne Melchert, the Old Couple; Vivi Thorberg and Kjeld Noack, the Greeks; Lillian Jensen and Svend Erik Jensen, Norwegians; Ruth Andersen and Fredbjørn Bjørnsson, the French.

Who Cares?

Choreography, George Balanchine; music, George Gershwin. First presented by the New York City Ballet, February 5, 1970.

A ballet view of musical comedy dancing of the 1920s and Balanchine's choreographic responses to music of George Gershwin and partly to lyrics of Ira Gershwin. Highlight: *pas de deux:* "The Man I Love."

Principals in first cast included Patricia McBride, Jacques d'Amboise ("The Man I Love") Marnee Morris and Karin von Aroldingen. Gordon Boelzner, pianist. (Also included, a recording of Gershwin at piano.)

Les Whoops-de-Doo

Choreography, Brian Macdonald; music, Don Gillis; décor and costumes, Ted Korol. First presented by the Royal Winnipeg Ballet, Manitoba, Canada, October 3, 1959.

Les Whoops-de-Doo, a ballet farce, impudent and energetic, is about the lore, legends, and folk-dance measures of the Canadian wild west in which a hopelessly lost Swan Queen, a refugee from European ballet, becomes involved.

William Tell Variations

Choreography, Hans Brenaa (after August Bournonville); music, Gioacchino Rossini. Staged for the City Center Joffrey Ballet and first performed by that company, New York, March 12, 1969.

A *pas de six* from Act III of Rossini's opera *William Tell* (1829), choreographed by Bournonville. (See *Tyrolian Pas de Deux.*)

Marie Taglioni headed the first cast in the full opera ballet, with Philippe Taglioni's choreography and Bournonville's staging, in Copenhagen, 1842.

The Wind in the Mountains

(A Country Calendar)

Choreography, Agnes de Mille; music, Laurence Rosenthal (score based largely on early American songs and folk tunes); costumes, Stanley Simmons; décor and lighting, Jean Rosenthal. First performed by American Ballet Theatre, New York, March 17, 1965.

The Wind in the Mountains is a fast-paced, tender, antic, loving, and exuberant panorama of danced Americana. The ballet is a series of loosely linked scenes including a skating scene, a tapdance by a traveling salesman, and a dance symbolic of the title in the fast and free running of a man in the free air of the mountains. William Glassman was the tapdancing Traveling Salesman.

Windsong

Choreography, Michael Uthoff; music, Edward Elgar (Serenade for Strings in E Minor, Op. 20); costumes, Alan Madsen. First performed by Michael Uthoff and Lisa Bradley as guest artists with the Royal Winnipeg Ballet, Winnipeg, October 9, 1969. Added to the repertory of the Hartford Ballet.

The Young Lady and the Hooligan

Choreography, Konstantin Boyarsky; music, Dmitri Shostakovitch; book, Alexander Belinsky (after Vladimir Mayakovsky's movie script); designs, Valery Dorrer. First performed at Maly Theatre, Leningrad, December 28, 1962.

Youth

Choreography, Boris Fenster; music, Mikhail Chulaki; book, Yuri Slonimsky, after Ostrovsky's novel How To Harden Steel; *designs, Tatiana Bruni. First performed at Maly Theatre, Leningrad, December 9, 1949.*

Appendix

LONDON PREMIERES OF AMERICAN BALLETS

The Age of Anxiety—New York City Ballet, Covent Garden, July 10, 1950
Astarte—City Center Joffrey Ballet, London Coliseum, May 25, 1971
Billy the Kid—Ballet Theatre, Covent Garden, August 29, 1950
Bluebeard—Ballet Theatre, Covent Garden, July 4, 1946
Bourrée Fantasque—New York City Ballet, Covent Garden, July 13, 1950
The Cage—New York City Ballet, Covent Garden, July 7, 1952
Cakewalk—New York City Ballet, Covent Garden, July 21, 1952
Caprichos—Ballet Theatre, Covent Garden, September 5, 1950
The Concert—Ballets U.S.A., Piccadilly Theatre, September 14, 1959
Concerto Barocco—New York City Ballet, Covent Garden, August 2, 1950
Day on Earth—José Limón Company, Sadler's Wells Theatre, September 9, 1957
Designs with Strings—Metropolitan Ballet, Scala Theatre, June 2, 1948
Divertimento No. 15 (Caracole)—New York City Ballet, Covent Garden, July 14, 1952
Fall River Legend—Ballet Theatre, Covent Garden, August 28, 1950
Fancy Free—Ballet Theatre, Covent Garden, July 4, 1946
Four Temperaments—New York City Ballet, Covent Garden, August 10, 1950
Gemini (Tetley)—Australian Ballet, London Coliseum, October 8, 1973
Graduation Ball—Original Ballet Russe, Covent Garden, July 22, 1947
Helen of Troy—Ballet Theatre, Covent Garden, July 4, 1946
Interplay—Ballet Theatre, Covent Garden, July 9, 1946
Mlle. Angot—Sadler's Wells Ballet, Covent Garden, November 26, 1947
The Maids—The Royal Ballet, Wimbledon, October 19, 1971
Moor's Pavane—José Limón Company, Sadler's Wells Theatre, September 2, 1957

Moves—Ballets U.S.A., Piccadilly Theatre, September 14, 1959
N.Y. Export: Opus Jazz—Ballets U.S.A., Piccadilly Theatre, September 14, 1959
Olympics—City Center Joffrey Ballet, London Coliseum, May 20, 1971
Orpheus—New York City Ballet, Covent Garden, July 17, 1950
Pas des Déesses—Ballet Rambert, Sadler's Wells Theatre, June 30, 1955
Picnic at Tintagel—New York City Ballet, Covent Garden, August 25, 1952
Pierrot Lunaire—Nederlands Dans Theatre, Sunderland, November 7, 1963
Pillar of Fire—Ballet Theatre, Covent Garden, July 5, 1946
Pulcinella Variations—American Ballet Theatre, August 5, 1970
Ricercare—Ballet Rambert, March 15, 1967
The River—American Ballet Theatre, Covent Garden, July 31, 1970
Rodeo—Ballet Theatre, Covent Garden, August 28, 1950
Serenade—New York City Ballet, Covent Garden, July 10, 1950
Theme and Variations—Ballet Theatre, Covent Garden, August 28, 1950
There Is a Time—José Limón Company, Sadler's Wells Theatre, September 2, 1957
The Traitor—American Ballet Theatre, Covent Garden, July 31, 1970
Trinity—City Center Joffrey Ballet, London Coliseum, May 19, 1971
Undertow—Ballet Theatre, Covent Garden, July, 1946
La Valse—New York City Ballet, Covent Garden, July 7, 1952

Index

(Ballet entries appear alphabetically, and their page numbers are listed in the Contents.)

Abolimov, Pyotr, 67
Abrahams, Peter, 246
Académie Royale de la Musique et de la Danse, 5, 6
Adam, Adolphe, 99, 110, 160
Adam, Alfred, 102
Adams, Diana, 33, 93, 109, 112, 113, 125, 134, 191, 205, 225, 290, 310, 351, 355, 363
Adron, Ralph, 228
Aesop, 81
Age of Anxiety (Robbins), 14
Aiello, Salvatore, 122
Ailey, Alvin, 140, 273
Akesson-Gundersen, Birgit, 297
Akimov, Boris, 189
Albers, Anni, 72
Aldous, Lucette, 116
Alhanko, Anneli, 28
Allegri, Orest, 50, 268
Alonso, Alberto, 76, 78
Alonso, Alicia, 34, 40, 78, 134, 141, 143, 160, 166, 171, 241, 244, 279, 323, 340, 351
Altman, Nathan, 158
Alven, Hugo, 263
American Ballet, 11-12, 37, 45, 48, 91, 93, 125, 194, 221, 292
American Ballet Caravan, 292
American Ballet Company (Feld), 43, 79, 87, 94, 100, 120, 167, 173, 186, 207, 210, 276
American Ballet Theatre, 11, 28, 37, 42, 51, 56, 60, 66, 91, 104, 122, 127-28, 148, 150, 153, 158, 170, 171, 173, 177, 178, 179, 186, 202, 211, 214, 216, 217, 218, 222, 227, 239, 266, 272, 273, 281, 285, 289, 291, 304, 308, 315, 317, 324, 336, 339, 342, 343, 346, 352, 355, 356, 366
American Concert Ballet, 218
Amiel, Josette, 204
Ander, Siv, 316
Andersen, Hans Christian, 45, 181
Anderson, Ruth, 364
Andreù, Mariano, 73, 114
Andrew, Thomas, 248
Andrews, Herbert, 58
Andreyanova, Elena, 166
Andreyev, Leonid, 27
Angiolini, Pietro, 114
Anisimova, Nina, 158
Annals, Michael, 295
Anouilh, Jean, 109, 206
Ansermet, Ernest, 48
Antheil, George, 72
Anthony, Mary, 344
Arbeau, Thoinot, 4, 75
Argentinita, 63, 73, 342
Argyle, Pearl, 272
Armistead, Horace, 94, 168, 191, 228, 268, 289
Armstrong, John, 130
Arnold, Malcolm, 179, 273, 303
Arnow, Reed, 249
Aronson, Boris, 48, 171, 350
Arova, Sonia, 245
Arpino, Gerald, 81, 87, 93, 138, 186, 199, 225, 232, 270, 281, 284, 290, 291, 347, 353, 359
Asafiev, Boris, 148, 182, 206, 262
Ashbridge, Bryan, 59

Ashley, Merrill, 285
Ashmole, David, 347
Ashton, Frederick, 9, 12, 13, 40, 45, 58, 75, 76, 84, 85, 86, 105, 106, 109, 110, 114, 117, 123, 130, 141, 143, 148, 149, 160, 179, 183, 193, 209, 216, 233, 238, 246, 247, 248, 253, 271, 273, 277, 279, 286, 298, 317, 330, 349, 353, 361
Atkins, William, 207
Atlanta Civic Ballet, 292
Auber, François, 131, 170, 271
Auden, W.H., 31, 294
Auric, Georges, 93, 209, 253
Austin, Debra, 50
Australian Ballet, 48, 79, 117, 141, 159, 246, 250, 292, 299
Aveline, Albert, 330
Ayres, Lemuel, 174

Babilée, Jean, 35, 195, 345
Bach, Johann Sebastian, 27, 33, 67, 91, 101, 167, 195, 234, 269
Badings, Henk, 199
Bailey, Sally, 89
Baker, Charlene, 75
Bakst, Léon, 28, 79, 106, 167, 196, 286, 298, 307
Balanchine, George, 8, 9, 11, 12, 32, 34, 37, 45, 48, 49, 64, 66, 68, 80, 83, 87, 91, 93, 95, 100, 101, 104, 111, 112, 113, 116, 119, 124, 125, 145, 146, 151, 152, 166, 167, 168, 171, 173, 190, 194, 196, 205, 211, 212, 213, 217, 220, 221, 228, 229, 232, 235, 238, 240, 245, 263, 265, 266, 268, 288, 289, 292, 294, 297, 305, 308, 309, 312, 313, 315, 317, 332, 333, 334, 335, 338, 339, 349, 350, 353, 355, 356, 358, 362, 365
Balanchivadze, Andrei, 176
Baldina, Maria, 330
Ballard, Louis, 151
Ballard, Lucinda, 198, 249
Ballet for America, 210
Ballet Caravan, 12, 56, 143
Ballet Clasico de Mexico, 93
Ballet Comique de la Reine, 4, 13
Ballet International, 94, 221, 291
Ballet Nacional de Cuba, 37, 76, 141, 160, 241, 308, 329, 340
Ballet Rambert, 75, 107, 108, 123, 130,

191, 198, 202, 244, 249, 256, 272, 324
Ballet Society, 12, 75, 111, 112, 151, 235, 334
Ballet Theatre, 11, 12, 34, 35, 37, 56, 58, 60, 72, 73, 79, 94, 95, 107, 108, 109, 110, 118, 125, 131, 134, 141, 145, 147, 155, 160, 168, 171, 174, 177, 186, 191, 195, 196, 198, 202, 206, 207, 233, 239, 241, 244, 246, 249, 250, 256, 274, 277, 313, 328, 336, 339, 341, 343, 345, 350
Ballet of the Twentieth Century, 27, 54, 149, 212, 226, 227, 277, 353
Ballet West, 85, 88, 92, 228, 293, 334, 353
Les Ballets 1933, 125, 221, 294
Ballets des Champs-Élysées, 35, 149, 194, 195, 272, 328, 345
Ballets Ida Rubinstein, 248
Ballets Jooss, 55, 72
Ballets Russes de Monte Carlo, 9, 12, 44, 45, 48, 51, 53, 58, 63, 64, 65, 73, 79, 82, 83, 87, 88, 91, 93, 95, 98, 101, 104, 110, 114, 123, 145, 147, 153, 159, 167, 181, 183, 194, 195, 200, 210, 221, 222, 226, 228, 239, 241, 250, 260, 261, 268, 274, 282, 284, 287, 292, 295, 305, 307, 328, 333, 342, 352
Ballif, Ariel, 88, 353
Balsanian, Serge, 203
Balzac, Honoré de, 206
Banfield, Rafaello de, 118
Barbeau, François, 346
Barber, Samuel, 75, 307
Barbier, Jules, 330
Bardin, Micheline, 335
Bardon, Henry, 85, 117
Barker, Patricia, 351
Barnett, Darrell, 159
Barnett, Robert, 90, 145, 185, 255, 310
Baronova, Irina, 9, 62, 84, 99, 143, 147, 178, 227, 244, 253, 260, 323
Barsacq, André, 248
Bartók, Béla, 49, 50, 73, 210, 214, 225, 235
Baryshnikov, Mikhail, 166
Basarte, 102
Baskin, Leonard, 42
Bass, Howard, 101
Bates, Ronald, 119, 272, 288, 315, 335, 349, 358

Batsheva Ballet of Israel, 222
Bauchant, André, 37
Baudelaire, 149
Bax, Arnold, 253
Baylis, Lillian, 9
Baylis, Nadine, 123, 140, 159, 221
Bazhov, Pavel, 311
Beardsley, Aubrey, 149
Beaton, Cecil, 40, 71, 83, 209, 246, 253
Beatty, Talley, 273
Beauchamps, Pierre, 5, 7
Beaurepraire, André, 286
Beck, Hans, 95
Beecham, Sir Thomas, 167
Beer, Richard, 201
Beethoven, Ludwig von, 103, 150, 295
Begitchev, V.P., 316
Béjart, Maurice, 27, 54, 63, 146, 148,
    149, 212, 226, 227, 277, 283, 353
Bel Geddes, Edith Luytens, 87
Belinsky, Alexander, 366
Bell, Joanne, 270
Bellini, Vincenzo, 305
Belsky, Igor, 203, 296
Bennett, Richard Rodney, 193
Bennington College Dancers, 344
Benois, Alexander, 64, 82, 107, 168,
    228, 250, 268, 286, 328
Benois, Nadia, 107, 202, 298
Benois, Nicola, 315
Bentley, Muriel, 111, 134, 137, 337
Bérard, Christian, 101, 112, 123, 149,
    221, 295, 333
Berensohn, Paul, 345
Berg, Bernd, 260
Bergling, Bergen, 122
Beriosoff, Nicholas, 126, 299
Beriosova, Svetlana, 59, 148, 262
Berlin Opera Ballet, 35, 91
Berlioz, Hector, 277, 333
Berman, Eugene, 48, 64, 91, 104, 110,
    181, 239, 265, 277
Bernard, Roger, 27, 149, 226
Berners, Lord, 361
Bernstein, Leonard, 31, 119, 130, 134
Bessmertnova, Natalia, 189
Bettis, Valerie, 313, 314
Bibeyran, Mamert, 94
Bidmead, Charlotte, 199
Bierbower, Neil, 345
Bigelow, Edward, 145
Bikken, Gijis, 221
Billy the Kid (Loring), 12

Binstead, Anthony, 222
Bizet, Georges, 41, 76, 334
Bjørnsson, Fredbjørn, 44, 95, 205, 218,
    280, 348, 361, 364
Black Crook, The, 10
Blair, David, 59, 143, 170, 260, 262,
    304, 317
Blake, William, 198, 282
Blakstad, Kari, 185
Blanford, Michael, 153
Blankshine, Robert, 87, 359
Blasis, Carlo, 7
Bliss, Arthur, 81, 197
Bliss, Herbert, 64, 71, 152, 191, 237,
    255, 332, 335, 363
Blitzstein, Mark, 172
Bloc, Alexander, 349
Blomdahl, Carl-Binger, 297
Bloomer Girl (de Mille), 174
Blum, Anthony, 50, 103, 119, 139, 168,
    188, 315, 316
Blum, René, 9
Bo, Lars, 318
Bobyshov, Mikhail, 67, 205
Bodrero, James, 88
Boelzner, Gordon, 188, 365
Bolasni, Saul, 313
Bolender, Todd, 32, 33, 58, 75, 88, 138,
    144, 152, 188, 191, 195, 214, 218,
    255, 271, 307, 310, 313
Bolger, Ray, 297
Bolm, Adolph, 37, 80, 99, 145, 249,
    252, 262
Bolshoi Ballet, 37, 49, 50, 67, 76, 83,
    116, 131, 148, 150, 160, 180, 181,
    189, 203, 205, 225, 246, 269, 277,
    283, 297, 299, 307, 308, 311, 317,
    328, 360
Bonfanti, Marie, 10
Bonnefous, Jean-Pierre, 36, 51, 150,
    358
Boris, Ruthanna, 70, 86, 153, 194
Borod, Robert, 347
Borodin, Alexander, 63, 261
Bortoluzzi, Paolo, 148, 226, 328
Boston Ballet, 35, 37, 92, 118, 131, 141,
    152, 169, 228, 241, 249, 263, 266,
    273, 274, 290, 292, 309, 329, 334
Botcharov, 228
Bourmeister, Vladimir, 212, 318, 338
Bournonville, Auguste, 6, 139, 149, 199,
    200, 222, 324, 328, 350, 357, 361,
    362, 365

Boyarsky, Konstantin, 366
Boyce, William, 265
Boyt, John, 362
Bozzacchi, Giuseppina, 98
Bozzoni, Max, 335
Braden, John, 285, 339
Bradley, Lisa, 186, 226, 290, 292, 366
Brae, June, 41, 82, 361
Brahms, Johannes, 66, 67, 83, 186, 205, 276
Brant, Henry, 171
Brecht, Berthold, 294
Breinen, Raymond, 350
Brenaa, Hans, 128, 149, 199, 200, 222, 357, 365
Brianza, Carlotta, 303
Brigadoon (de Mille), 59
Briggs, Hedley, 228
Britten, Benjamin, 121, 137, 183, 197, 262, 344
Brown, Carolyn, 316
Brown, Jack Owen, 158, 266
Brown, Kelly, 175, 276
Brown, Lewis, 186, 210
Brozak, Edith, 145
Bruhn, Erik, 27, 34, 109, 160, 166, 216, 245, 280, 324, 328, 335, 356
Bruni, Tatania, 63, 84, 158, 185, 366
Bujones, Fernando, 356
Bulgakov, Alexei, 270
Burke, Dermot, 50, 292
Burr, Mary, 75
Burra, Edward, 114, 115
Butler, Diane, 179, 347
Butler, John, 28, 59, 78, 80, 201, 291, 352, 358
Byelsky, 98
Byron, George Gordon, Lord, 99

Caccialanza, Gisella, 47, 49, 152
Cadmus, Paul, 143
Camargo, Marie, 5, 6
Camargo Society, 130, 198
Camble, Alwyne, 182
Capuletti, 72
Cardin, Pierre, 37
Carpenter, John Alden, 266
Carroll, Elisabeth, 72, 110, 170
Carter, Bill, 205
Cartier, Diana, 140
Carzou, 206
Casado, Germinal, 54, 277
Casey, Susan, 266

Cassandre, A.M., 215
Castillo, Antonio, 222, 239
Catanzaro, Tony, 362
Caton, Edward, 250, 291
Cecchetti, Enrico, 66, 79, 84, 95, 147, 239, 250, 303
Celeste, Mlle., 327
Cernovich, Nicholas, 247, 315, 346
Cerrito, Fanny, 5, 166, 233, 241, 242, 327
Cervantes, Miguel de, 115
Chabrier, Emmanuel, 64, 80, 100, 101, 349
Chabukiani, Vakhtang, 168, 176, 203
Chagall, Marc, 34, 145
Chalon, Alfred, 242
Chaney, Stewart, 37
Chaperon, 330
Chapi y Lorenti, Roberto, 138
Chappell, William, 75, 76, 176, 246, 271
Charlip, Remy, 316
Charlyne, Baker, 75
Charrat, Janine, 194
Chase, Lucia, 62, 134, 199, 259, 337, 344, 351
Chatfield, Philip, 59, 202
Chausson, Ernest, 191
Chauviré, Yvette, 166, 170, 215, 247
Chavez, Carlos, 72
Chaxton, John, 106
Chéret, 330
Chervinsky, Nikolai, 173
Chesnakov, V., 168
Chief Dan George, 122
Ch'ing, Chiang, 269
Chopin, Frédéric, 82, 90, 94, 103, 127, 188, 328, 329
Choreographers' Workshop, 73, 249
Chouteau, Yvonne, 151
Christensen, Lew, 39, 58, 88, 143, 144, 152, 197, 317, 335
Christensen, William, 85, 228, 353
Chryst, Gary, 362
Chulaki, Mikhail, 185, 189, 366
Ciceri, Pierre, 160
Cimarosa, Domenico, 73
Cincinnati Ballet, 90, 126, 352
City Center Joffrey Ballet, 27, 28, 41, 42, 51, 55, 80, 87, 93, 116, 117, 129, 130, 138, 141, 170, 172, 186, 187, 199, 200, 204, 210, 218, 220, 224, 225, 235, 240, 250, 259, 271, 284,

289, 291, 308, 310, 341, 342, 347, 353, 362, 365
Clark, Christine, 108
Clauss, Heinz, 260
Clavé, Antoni, 76, 272
Clayden, Pauline, 361
Clifford, John, 50, 103, 139, 166, 272, 312, 315, 339, 357
Clouser, James, 238
Clustine, Ivan, 95
Cobos, Antonia, 221
Cocteau, Jean, 35, 195, 239, 253
Code of Terpsichore, The (Blasis), 7
Cohen, Fritz, 172
Cohen, Leonard, 296
Coleman, Michael, 193
Colgrass, Michael, 290
Coll, David, 186
Collins, Angelene, 185
Colquhoun, Robert, 113
Colt, Alvin, 214, 233
Conover, Warren, 217, 356
Conrad, Karen, 157, 193, 250
Constant, Marius, 102, 240
Cook, Bart, 36, 289
Coolidge, Elizabeth Sprague, 37
Cooper, Rex, 137
Copère, Mme., 125
Copland, Aaron, 56, 255, 274, 350
Coppelia, 7, 16
Coralli, Arcangelo, 308
Coralli, Jean, 7, 160, 165
Corkle, Francesca, 129, 271
Cornelius-Knudsen, Britta, 364
Coronado, José, 105
Cortesi, 327
Cosma, Edgar, 324
Cowen, Donna, 292
Cragun, Richard, 234, 260, 280, 323, 337, 359
Cramer, Ivo, 249, 263
Cranko, John, 52, 67, 68, 76, 95, 106, 121, 126, 128, 194, 200, 220, 228, 234, 235, 259, 260, 262, 277, 285, 286, 290, 317, 337
Creston, Paul, 345
Croisette, 324
Crome Syrcus, 41
Crum, George, 59
Cullberg, Birgit, 28, 202, 210, 215, 217
Cullberg Ballet, 315
Cunningham, Merce, 315, 316
Cunningham, Ron, 266

Curley, Wilma, 225
da Vinci, Leonardo, 3
Dale, Margaret, 361
Dali, Salvador, 44, 200
Dalton, Elisabeth, 285, 337
Damase, Jean-Michel, 101, 255
d'Amboise, Jacques, 31, 40, 66, 125, 145, 188, 189, 191, 197, 211, 249, 255, 285, 290, 310, 311, 323, 339, 363, 365
Dance Players, 58, 197
Dance Theater of Harlem, 92
Danias, Starr, 292
Danilova, Alexandra, 9, 15, 40, 47, 51, 55, 66, 73, 82, 84, 95, 98, 105, 110, 147, 155, 183, 195, 221, 229, 239, 253, 268, 288, 294, 306, 323, 328
Danieli, Fred, 145, 152
Danielian, Leon, 89, 105, 155
D'Antuono, Eleanor, 91, 241, 336
Darrel, Peter, 247, 248, 335, 352
Darsonval, Lycette, 335
Dauberval, Pierre, 7, 140
Davison, Robert, 86, 88, 94
Daydé, Bernard, 76, 128, 204, 214, 337, 343
de Angelo, Anne Marie, 270
de Basil, Colonel W., 9
de Beaujoyeulx, Balthasar, 4
de Beaumont, Comte Étienne, 51, 153
de Falla, Manuel, 342
de Gaetani, Thomas, 215
De Jorg, Zoe, 266
de Lappe, Gemze, 175
DeLavallade, Carmen, 78, 80, 151
de Medici, Catherine, 3, 4, 13
de Mille, Agnes, 12, 59, 131, 150, 174, 175, 199, 259, 270, 274, 276, 281, 291, 336, 337, 343, 344, 366
de Molas, Nicolas, 73, 171
de Mosa, Noelle, 56
de Nobili, Lila, 233
DeSoto, Edward, 207
de Valois, Ninette, 9, 12, 13, 55, 81, 115, 167, 175, 198, 238, 265, 267, 272, 298, 361
de Vega, Lope, 203
de Victoria, Tomas Luis, 114
Debden, Hiday, 336
Debussy, Claude, 28, 29, 48, 68, 84, 166, 196, 216, 310
Delarova, Eugenie, 155

Delarue, Edouard, 204, 343
Deldevez, Georges, 238, 239
Delfau, André, 27, 36, 148, 298, 305
Delibes, Léo, 94, 131, 330, 332
Delius, Frederic, 277
dell'Era, Antoinette, 232
dello Joio, Norman, 233, 340
Denard, Michael, 166, 328, 353
Denishawn Dancers, 11
Depenbrock, Jay, 126
Derain, André, 65, 93, 206, 219
d'Erlanger, Frederic, 84, 181
Derman, Vergie, 193
Derzhavin, Konstantin, 158
Deutsche Oper Ballet, 318
di Botta, Bergonzio, 2, 3
Diaghilev, Serge de, 8, 9, 37
Diaghilev Ballets Russes, 8, 11, 28, 37,
    44, 54, 65, 79, 81, 98, 106, 145, 167,
    196, 210, 226, 240, 250, 261, 263,
    265, 283, 286, 298, 307, 328, 342,
    345
Didelot, 7, 84
Dmitriev, Vladimir, 148, 205, 206
Dmitriev, Yevgeny, 255
Doboujinsky, Mstislav, 48, 169, 206
Docherty, Peter, 336
Dolin, Anton, 55, 62, 72, 73, 147, 160,
    166, 198, 241, 286, 323, 337, 355
Dollar, William, 47, 49, 93, 94, 118,
    152, 195, 196, 250
Don Quixote, 7
Donizetti, Gaetano, 105, 113
Donn, Jorge, 148, 226
Dorn, Rudi, 201
Dorrer, Valery, 84, 111, 158, 246, 296,
    366
Doubrovska, Felia, 40, 55, 227, 265
Douglas, Scott, 78, 91, 273, 356
Dowell, Anthony, 36, 117, 166, 193,
    209, 217, 232, 280, 296, 305, 323,
    347
Dowland, John, 94
Doyle, Desmond, 59, 189, 193
Drew, David, 209
Drew, John, 70
Drigo, Riccardo, 131, 173, 174
Druckman, Jacob, 353
du Pont, Paul, 58, 153
DuPuy, Edouard, 139
Dubovsky, Yevgeny, 131
Dudinskaya, Natalia, 67, 203
Dukas, Paul, 247

Dumas fils, Alexandre, 72
Dumilâtre, Adèle, 165
Duncan, Isadora, 11, 12
Dunn, Patricia, 225
Dunne, James, 129, 362
Duplessis, Paul, 58, 178
Dupont, Jacques, 76, 349
Durang, John, 10, 11
Dutilleux, Henri, 206
Dybdal, Anna Marie, 361
Dyche, Anita, 104

Eagling, Wayne, 347
Eckl, Shirley, 137, 351
Effel, Jean, 101
Egadze, O., 168
Eglevsky, André, 39, 47, 112, 166, 171,
    178, 195, 206, 232, 241, 245, 246,
    253, 288, 290, 308, 323, 332, 363
Eglevsky, Marina, 170
Eisenstein, Sergei, 189
Ek, Niklas, 316
Elgar, Edward, 123, 366
Elgh, Mona, 316
Elizabeth I, Queen of England, 5
Ellington, Duke, 273
Ellyn, Lois, 314
Eliot Feld Ballet, 292, 350
Elssler, Fanny, 5, 6, 10, 143, 165, 166,
    242
Elvin, Violette, 59, 86, 180
Entwhistle, John, 346
Erbshtein, B., 131, 269
Erdman, B., 198
Erixon, Sven, 215
Essen, Viola, 193, 199, 249, 291
Etcheverray, Jean-Jacques, 247
Eula, Joe, 103, 129, 167, 188, 199, 272
Everett, Ellen, 266
Experimental Ballet Company of Pe-
    king China, 269

Fadeyechev, Nicolai, 323
Faizi, A., 297
Falk, Per, 28, 218
Fall River Legend (de Mille), 18
Fancy Free (Robbins), 12, 13
Farber, Viola, 316
Farmer, Peter, 160, 210
Farrell, Suzanne, 40, 66, 116, 197, 211,
    212, 226, 297
Farron, Julia, 233, 262, 361
Faulkner, William, 81

Fauré, Gabriel, 196
Fay, Maria, 317
Federovitch, Sophie, 105, 333
Fedorova-Fokine, Alexandra, 239, 322
Feld, Eliot, 42, 43, 58, 94, 100, 120, 166, 173, 179, 186, 210, 276, 292, 339, 350
Feldman, Morton, 315
Fenster, Boris, 185, 338, 366
Fere, V., 297
Fernandez, Royes, 128, 202, 346, 356
Fernandez, Salvador, 76
Ffolkes, David, 196, 289
Field, John, 180, 244
Fifield, Elaine, 59, 260
Figueroa, Alfonso, 186
La Fille Mal Gardée, 7
Fini, Leonor, 109, 334
Fiocca, Felipe, 197
Firtich, G., 53
Fisher, Jules, 87, 100
Fletcher, Robert, 352
Flindt, Flemming, 196, 199, 204, 214, 318, 337, 343, 348, 356
Flindt, Vivi, 140
Fokina, Vera, 79, 107
Fokine, Michel, 8, 11, 60, 79, 82, 84, 86, 98, 106, 107, 114, 120, 123, 145, 147, 183, 238, 247, 250, 261, 286, 307, 328
Fokine Ballet, 123
Fonteyn, Margot, 1, 13, 41, 51, 59, 85, 100, 105, 107, 148, 166, 180, 206, 209, 233, 240, 247, 248, 253, 260, 268, 280, 286, 303, 323, 328, 331, 332, 333, 361
Fortner, Wolfgang, 76, 260
Fouqué, Friedrich de la Motte, 233
Fox, James, 316
Fracci, Carla, 98, 166, 193, 241, 328, 336
Franca, Celia, 85, 229
Françaix, Jean, 87, 109, 152
Frances, Esteban, 72, 75, 88, 116, 166, 240, 350, 355
Franck, César, 35, 333, 347
François, André, 314
Frandsen, Søren, 110
Frankel, Emily, 310
Franklin, Frederic, 47, 52, 82, 95, 98, 103, 110, 153, 155, 160, 166, 171, 179, 195, 229, 253, 262, 276, 283, 288, 294, 295, 314, 328, 347

Freedman, Harry, 281, 296
French, Jared, 56
Frohlich, Jean-Pierre, 185
Fuente, Luis, 139, 233, 359
Furse, Roger, 265

Gable, Christopher, 189, 349
Gabo and Pevsner, 81
Gabovich, Mikhail, 299
Gadd, Ulf, 214
Gade, Jacob, 337
Gade, Neils W., 149, 222, 337
Gain, Richard, 341
Galeotti, Vincenzo, 6, 280, 363, 364
Garnett, David, 202
Garrick, David, 202
Gassman, Remi, 58
Gautier, Theophile, 160
Gavrilov, Alexander, 308
Geltzer, Catherine, 98, 316
Geltzer, Vasily, 316
Geltzer, Yekaterina, 95, 170
Genée, Adeline, 11, 86, 95, 143
Genet, Jean, 207
Gentilucci, Catherine, 101
Georgadis, Nicholas, 32, 104, 106, 178, 189, 208, 228, 277, 298, 318
Gerard, Rolf, 128, 211
Gerdt, Paul, 232, 303
Gerhard, Robert, 115
Gershwin, George, 365
Geva, Tamara, 125, 297
Ghika, Nico, 248
Giannini, A. Christina, 81, 281
Gide, André, 248, 249
Gillis, Don, 365
Gilpin, John, 356
Ginastera, Alberto, 72, 80
Ginson, Ian, 62
Girard, Claude, 358
Giselle, 7, 10, 15
Gladke, Peter, 134
Glaeser, Joseph, 139
Glassman, William, 227, 366
Glazounov, Alexander, 49, 58, 82, 100, 171, 211, 240, 268, 290
Glenn, Laura, 207
Glière, Reinhold, 67, 269
Glinka, Mikhail, 103, 166, 245, 355
Gluck, Christoph Willibald, 7, 114, 336
Godfrey, Louis, 356
Goerman, Jan, 217
Gogol, Nikolai, 338

Golden, Miriam, 171
Goldoni, Carlo, 185
Goleizovsky, Kasian, 198, 203
Gollner, Nana, 75, 143, 157, 244, 323, 351
Golovin, Alexander, 145, 182
Goncharov, Alexander D., 53, 283
Gontcharova, Nathalie, 63, 84, 98, 103, 145, 183, 226
Goodman, Erika, 139
Gordon, Gavin, 267
Gordon, Mikhail, 203
Gore, Walter, 121, 229, 268, 314
Gorriz, Ana Maria, 122
Gorshykov, G., 63
Gorski, Alexander, 50, 115, 317
Gottschalk, Louis, 70, 139, 338
Gould, Diana, 76
Gould, Morton, 87, 131, 186, 270
Gounod, Charles, 86, 168, 179, 359
Govrin, Gloria, 213
Goya, 73
Graham, Martha, 12, 124, 125, 283, 284
Graham-Lujan, James, 88
Grahn, Lucile, 5, 166, 241, 327
Grand Ballet du Marquis de Cuevas, 36, 54, 63, 91, 93, 94, 182, 255, 305, 340
Les Grands Ballets Canadiens, 35, 80, 141, 160, 169, 229, 241, 246, 308, 346, 356, 358
Grant, Alexander, 59, 113, 117, 143, 180, 193, 206, 233, 253, 332
Gray, Barbara, 245
Gregory, Cynthia, 40, 43, 91, 127, 158, 159, 170, 173, 193, 211, 323, 328, 336, 352
Grey, Beryl, 59, 82, 113, 202, 303, 318
Grieg, Edvard, 84, 182
Grieve, William, 125
Grigoriev, Serge, 145
Grigorovitch, Yuri, 189, 203, 299, 307, 311, 317
Gris, Juan, 167
Grisi, Carlotta, 126, 165, 238, 239, 241, 242
Gruelle, Johnny, 266
Gsovsky, Victor, 170
Guimard, Mme., 5
Gurst, Lee, 247

Hadow, Ardith, 50
Haieff, Alexei, 111

Halicka, Alicia, 45
Halle, Barthold, 175
Halvorsen, Johan, 44
Handel, George Frederick, 43, 167
Hannaux, Luc Michel, 346
Hansen, Ole Palle, 364
Harkarvy, Benjamin, 110, 170, 207, 269, 345
Harkness, Rebekah, 289
Harkness Ballet, 27, 28, 49, 72, 80, 110, 140, 146, 158, 170, 182, 207, 217, 224, 225, 247, 289, 291, 307, 343, 345, 356
Harper, Yves, 110
Harrison, Lou, 157
Hart, John, 180, 332
Hartford Ballet Company, 67, 72, 93, 106, 108, 171, 207, 229, 249, 357, 366
Hartmann, J.P.E., 149
Harvey, Peter, 66, 197, 220
Hawkins, Erick, 144
Haworth, Reese, 266
Haydée, Marcia, 129, 280, 337, 359
Hayden, Melissa, 33, 40, 66, 70, 100, 112, 113, 118, 125, 166, 185, 205, 213, 215, 245, 255, 294, 310, 311, 339, 349, 355
Haydn, Franz Josef, 42, 210
Hays, David, 68, 121, 124, 189, 205, 213, 217, 220, 305, 309
Heaton, Anne, 189
Heckroth, Hein, 55, 172
Hedeby, Kerstin, 202
Heeley, Desmond, 262, 303, 318
Heine, Heinrich, 110
Helpmann, Robert, 41, 86, 105, 114, 116, 172, 176, 198, 247, 272, 303, 323, 361
Helsted, 222
Hiday, Debden, 336
Hightower, Loren, 207
Hightower, Rosella, 40, 62, 111, 151, 206, 256, 259
Hill, Margaret, 304
Hindemith, Paul, 151, 212, 284
Hinkson, Mary, 80, 273
Hinton, Paula, 121
Hoa, Tao, 270
Hobi, Frank, 71, 290
Hodes, Stuart, 27
Hoff, Stevan-Jan, 351
Hoffmann, E.T.A., 228, 336

Hoffmann, Gertrude, 328
Hogan, Michael, 356
Hogarth, William, 267
Hoiby, Lee, 28
Holden, Stanley, 143
Holder, Christian, 172, 362
Holdridge, Lee, 347
Holm, Hanya, 12
Holmgren, Bjørn, 102
Honeggar, Arthur, 202
Honer, Mary, 361
Horlin, Tor, 297
Hornung, Preben, 214
Houston, Grace, 94
Hovhaness, Alan, 225, 281
Hoving, Lucas, 182, 208, 346
Howard, Andrée, 41, 76, 108, 202
Howarth, Peter, 122
Huffman, Gregory, 129
Hugo, Jean, 181
Hugo, Victor, 105, 126
Humphrey, Doris, 12, 107, 296, 360
Humphrey-Weidman Concert Group, 360
Hurok, Sol, 9
Hurry, Leslie, 172, 316

Ibert, Jacques, 314
Ibsen, Henrik, 202
Ide, Letitia, 108, 130
Idzikowski, Stanislaus, 272, 303
Ignatiev, Alexander, 82
Imperial Ballet School, St. Petersburg, 6
International Ballet Competition, Varna, Bulgaria, 174
Ionesco, Eugene, 204, 348
Ironside, Christopher, 324, 330
Ironside, Robin, 324, 330
Isaksen, Lone, 27, 28, 170
Ito, Teijo, 360
Ivanov, Konstantin, 50, 268
Ivanov, Lev, 84, 95, 228, 316, 317
Ivanovsky, A., 168
Ives, Charles, 190, 281
Ivesiana (Balanchine), 14
Ivor, Denis Aplvor, 60

Jackson, Denise, 129
Jackson, Rowena, 59, 180
James, David, 93, 284
Jarman, Derek, 193
Jasinsky, Roman, 84, 151

Jeanmaire, Renée, 78, 102
Jenkins, David, 346
Jensen, Lillian, 364
Jensen, Svend Erik, 128, 364
Jerome Robbins' Ballets: U.S.A., 29, 88, 90, 220, 222
Jhung, Finis, 170, 356
Jillana, 205, 213, 255
Joffrey, Robert, 41, 157, 244, 248, 270
Johansen, Svend, 149
Johnson, Albert, 352
Johnson, Louis, 126, 352
Johnson, Nancy, 89
Jones, John, 225, 341
Jones, Robert Edmond, 345
Jooss, Kurt, 12, 55, 172, 248
Jorgensen, Nels, 226, 341
José Limón Dance Company, 108, 129, 130, 207, 215, 218, 340, 346
Juilliard Dance Ensemble, 45
Juilliard Dance Theatre, 215

Kage, Jonas, 159, 336
Kalioujny, Alexander, 335
Kallman, Chester, 294
Kaplan, Emanuel, 168
Kaplan, S., 338
Karayev, Kara, 246
Karinska, 48, 64, 66, 68, 112, 113, 124, 168, 171, 189, 191, 197, 205, 211, 212, 213, 228, 245, 268, 289, 292, 309, 332, 338, 349, 353, 355, 362
Karnilova, Maria, 62, 90, 259, 344
Karpakova, Pauline, 323
Karpiej, Joyce, 229
Karsavina, Tamara, 8, 79, 107, 116, 147, 166, 196, 250, 308, 323, 330, 342
Kasatkina, Natalia, 101, 283
Kauffer, E. McKnight, 81
Kavan, Albia, 111
Kay, Barry, 35, 216, 352
Kay, Hershy, 70, 87, 100, 297, 309, 338, 362
Kaye, Margaret, 53
Kaye, Nora, 34, 40, 62, 70, 108, 110, 134, 157, 171, 193, 206, 219, 244, 246, 253, 259, 279, 314, 323
Kchessinska, Mathilde, 8, 323
Keeler, Elisha C., 309
Keene, Christopher, 94
Kehlet, Niels, 98, 256, 308
Keith, Jacquetta, 245

Kent, Allegra, 31, 40, 66, 68, 70, 103, 119, 125, 168, 191, 295, 310, 339, 355
Keogh, Marguerite, 355
Keogh, Tom, 345
Kersley, Leo, 41
Keuter, Paul, 194
Khatchaturian, Aram, 158, 262, 307
Khikmet, Nazim, 203
Khodasevich, Valentina, 149, 168, 262, 307, 338
Kidd, Michael, 58, 111, 233
Kim, Willa, 66, 157, 225, 270, 362
Kirkland, Gelsey, 70, 289, 315
Kirov Ballet, 50, 51, 53, 63, 67, 84, 101, 103, 111, 148, 149, 158, 168, 173, 176, 182, 203, 206, 246, 269, 296, 297, 298, 307, 338, 349
Kirstein, Lincoln, 11, 56, 143
Kivitt, Ted, 158, 170
Klotz, Florence, 150, 224
Knoblauch, Christine, 174
Kochno, Boris, 81, 101, 149, 181, 209
Kodaly, Zoltan, 215
Koechlin, Charles, 295
Koesun, Ruth Ann, 75, 175, 245, 341
Kokitch, Casimir, 276
Kolomoitsev, M., 185
Koner, Pauline, 208
Konstantinovsky, 338
Koppel, Thomas, 348
Korol, Ted, 365
Korovin, Konstantin, 50
Koslov, Theodore, 287
Kovtunov, I., 212
Krassovska, Nathalie, 82, 120, 195, 283
Krein, Alexander, 203, 338
Krenek, Ernst, 285
Kriza, John, 34, 58, 75, 111, 118, 134, 137, 188, 252, 259, 276, 279, 314, 323, 344, 351, 356
Kronstam, Henning, 40, 205, 218, 280, 328
Krupska, Dania, 134
Kurilko, Mikhail, 269
Kurilov, Ivan, 212
Kurkjian, Samuel, 249
Kvapp, Adolf, 50
Kyasht, Lydia, 143

La Cour-Maslev, Lise, 364
La Guardia, Fiorella H., 309
La Meri, 287

La Montaine, John, 225
La Scala Opera Ballet, 48, 277
Laban, Rudolf von, 12
Labisse, Felix, 255
Lacoste, 330
Lafon, Madeleine, 335
Lafontaine, 5, 349
Laing, Hugh, 34, 62, 107, 110, 157, 193, 198, 199, 215, 259, 279, 337, 351
Lalo, Édouard, 315
Lambert, Constant, 40, 246, 265, 271
Lambert, Isabel, 60
Lambin, Piotr, 50
Lambini, 268
Lami, Eugene, 323
Lamont, Deni, 174, 316
Lancaster, Osbert, 259
Lanchberry, John, 141, 216, 335
Lander, Harald, 95, 128, 222, 324
Lander, Margot, 128
Lander, Toni, 91, 128, 328
Landsy, Elise, 364
Lane, Maryon, 304
Lanese, Lillian, 109
Lang, Harold, 137, 188
Langfield, Therese, 199
Lanner, Katti, 11
Lapiashvili, P., 168
Larkin, Moscelyne, 151
Larsen, Gerd, 157
Larsen, Niels Bjørn, 249, 280
Larson, John, 270
Larsson, Irene, 307
Laschilin, Lev, 269
Laurencin, Marie, 54
Lauret, Jeanette, 114, 155
Lavrovsky, Leonid, 131, 160, 225, 262, 276, 280
Lawrence, Pauline, 108, 129, 207, 218, 296, 340, 346, 360
Layton, Joe, 116
Lazowaky, Yurek, 250, 252, 344
Lazzini, Joseph, 214
LeClercq, Tanaquil, 31, 32, 40, 47, 64, 70, 71, 90, 112, 152, 185, 191, 232, 237, 255, 294, 335, 354, 355, 363
LeCocq, Charles, 206
LeToumelin, Yahne, 353
Lebrun, Rico, 221
Lediakh, Gennadi, 148
Lee, Elizabeth, 186
Lee, Mary Ann, 10, 11, 166

Lee, Ming Cho, 215, 225, 232, 284, 290, 291
Leeder, Sigurd, 56
Legnani, Pierina, 7, 8, 86, 268, 322, 323
Lehár, Franz, 211
Leland, Sara, 36, 50, 103, 139, 185, 316, 335, 355
Lemaître, Gerard, 234
Lengyel, Melchior, 214
Lenya, Lotte, 295
Leonidze, G., 269
Lester, Keith, 241, 244
Levashev, Vladimir, 312
Levasseur, André, 58, 247, 255, 353
Levental, Valery, 37
Levins, Daniel, 58, 217, 351
Levogt, 316
Lewis, Joseph, 88, 95
Lichine, David, 52, 84, 167, 168, 169, 177, 238, 253, 260, 262, 263
Lidolt, Mascha, 56
Liepa, Marius, 307, 308
Lifar, Serge, 29, 39, 166, 181, 182, 215, 253, 265, 315, 330
Lilac Garden (Tudor), 18
Limón, José, 108, 129, 130, 207, 208, 215, 218, 340, 346
Linden, Anya, 304
Linden, Conrad, 197
Lindgren, Erik, 297
Lipkovski, Indris, 45
Lirgwood, Tom, 171, 355
Liszt, Franz, 40, 105, 209
Littlefield, Catherine, 11, 106, 298
Livingston, Alistair, 336
Lland, Michael, 109, 245
Lloyd, Maude, 157, 193
Lloyd, Norman, 207
Loewe, Frederick, 59
Lolle, Jens, 363
Lommell, Daniel, 226
London Ballet, 155
London Festival Ballet, 126, 128, 210, 211, 221, 239, 244, 248, 255, 287, 317, 355
Lopoukhova, Lydia, 52, 66, 98, 130, 252, 303
Lopukhov, Fedor, 63, 103, 182, 205, 255, 269
Loquastro, Santo, 292
Lorca, Federico García, 178

Loring, Eugene, 56, 58, 72, 145, 171, 249, 340, 344
Lormier, Paul, 160
Lorrayne, Vyvyan, 193, 217
Los Angeles Ballet Theatre, 50
Losch, Tilly, 125, 295
Louis XIV, King of France, 5
Lourie, Eugene, 83
Love, Kermit, 274
Lovenskjøld, Herman, 324
Lubovitch, Lar, 304
Lucas, Leighton, 208
Ludlow, Conrad, 139, 197, 205, 213, 339
Ludt, Edvard Grieg, 175
Lully, Jean-Baptiste, 5, 7
Lumbye, Hans Christian, 117, 139, 357
Lumley, Benjamin, 242
Lund, Troels, 139
Lundberg, Arne, 343
Lurcat, Jean, 292
Lushin, A., 255
Lvov-Ankhin, Boris, 37
Lyadov, Anatol, 49
Lynn, Enid, 171, 229, 357
Lyon, Anabelle, 62, 244, 259, 344

Macadie, Bruce, 50
McBride, Patricia, 36, 40, 66, 70, 103, 120, 166, 168, 174, 188, 197, 213, 241, 338, 339, 355, 365
MacBryde, Robert, 113
MacClelland, Kenneth, 85
Macdonald, Brian, 33, 72, 145, 146, 281, 296, 345, 365
MacDonald, Doreen, 296
MacDonald, Elaine, 336
Mackinnon, Sheila, 210
McLain, David, 90
MacLeish, Archibald, 352
McLerie, Allyn, 276
MacMillan, Kenneth, 32, 35, 45, 91, 104, 178, 189, 202, 208, 277, 283, 298, 303, 304, 318, 347
McWilliams, Ralph, 341
Macero, Teo, 235
Maclezova, Xenia, 147
Madsen, Alan, 366
Madsen, Egon, 260
Magallanes, Nicholas, 35, 48, 49, 64, 70, 93, 112, 113, 125, 185, 205, 232, 237, 255, 268, 306, 309, 332, 335, 354, 355, 363

Magno, Susan, 139, 362
Mahler, Gustav, 42, 107, 158, 281, 304
Mahler, Roni, 104, 118
Maiorano, Robert, 103, 185
Maizel, B.S., 111
Makarov, Askold, 307
Makarova, Natalia, 1, 40, 51, 98, 120, 143, 166, 259, 323
Malaieff, M., 194
Malclès, Jean-Denis, 84
Maliarevsky, Pavel, 181
Mandelberg, Yevgeny, 203
Manuel, Roland, 216
Marchand, Colette, 118
Marie-Jeanne, 49, 58, 93, 143, 219
Marko, Ivan, 226
Markova, Alicia, 9, 34, 55, 62, 72, 120, 130, 147, 166, 176, 232, 244, 253, 268, 272, 279, 283, 286, 295, 323
Markova-Dolin Ballet, 63, 241
Marks, Bruce, 43, 87, 91, 110, 155, 207, 346
Martin, Erin, 227
Martin, Florence, 127
Martin, Frank, 178
Martin, Kathleen, 127
Martinet, Nicole, 178
Martinez, Jose, 152
Martins, Peter, 119, 168, 188, 358
Martinu, Bohuslav, 35, 122
Mary Anthony Dance Company, 344
Mason, Monica, 209
Massenet, Jules, 131, 208
Massine, Leonide, 8, 9, 12, 30, 34, 44, 51, 52, 63, 64, 66, 73, 83, 113, 147, 153, 155, 200, 206, 209, 239, 252, 260, 265, 266, 282, 283, 284, 285, 288, 295, 333, 334, 342, 352
Masson, André, 260
Mathe, Carmen, 50, 101
Mathis, Bonnie, 140
Matisse, Henri, 282
Matsuhita, Chin-Ichi, 182
Maule, Michael, 70, 145, 188, 290
Mauri, Rosita, 349
Max, Peter, 171
Maximova, Ekaterina, 116, 148, 312
May, Pamela, 15, 86
Mayakovsky, Vladimir, 53, 366
Mayer, Christine, 314
Mayer, Johann, 199
Mayuzumi, Toshiro, 68, 232
Maywood, Augusta, 5, 10, 11, 328

Mazilier, Joseph, 238, 239, 327
Mazzo, Kay, 103, 119, 139, 316, 358
Mead, Robert, 193, 217
Mejia, Paul, 166, 226
Melchert, Arne, 364
Melikov, Arif, 203
Mendelssohn, Felix, 117, 123, 211, 213, 289
Menotti, Gian Carlo, 291, 352
Mérante, Louis, 330, 347
Mercier, Margaret, 245, 345
Meskheteli, V., 338
Messager, André, 349
Messel, Oliver, 179, 298
Messerer, Asaf, 49, 299, 317
Messerer, Boris, 53, 76
Metropolitan Ballet, Edinburgh, 109
Metropolitan Opera Ballet, 95, 214
Meyerbeer, Giacomo, 246
Michell, Carl, 67, 72
Mielziner, Jo, 256, 297
Milberg, Barbara, 33, 113
Milchin, L., 297
Milena, 291
Milhaud, Darius, 53, 207, 285
Miller, Buzz, 80
Miller, Jane, 343
Miller, Patricia, 53, 202
Miloss, Aurel, 238
Minkus, Leon, 115, 239, 245
Minkus, Ludwig, 50, 115
Miskovitch, Milorad, 118
Miss Julie (Cullberg), 18
Mitchell, Arthur, 33, 212, 213, 297
Mitchell, James, 276
Mladova, Milada, 155
Mlakar, Veronika, 78
Moiseyev, Igor, 307
Molière, 64, 114
Mollerup, Mette, 280
Moncion, Francisco, 31, 32, 112, 118, 125, 147, 152, 188, 197, 219, 237, 255, 291, 335, 354
Monplaisir Ballet Company, 125
Moon, Keith, 346
Morcom, James Stewart, 112, 197, 333
Mordkin, Mikhail, 8, 11, 95, 166, 316
Mordkin Ballet, 141
Morisset, Denis, 346
Morley, Ruth, 78
Moross, Jerome, 153
Morris, Marnee, 335, 365
Mortifee, Ann, 122

Mosavel, Johaar, 202
Motley, 110, 175, 336, 343
Mottl, 349
Mounsey, Yvonne, 70, 71, 113, 138
Moussorgsky, Modest, 255
Moylan, Mary Ellen, 49, 112, 152
Mozart, Wolfgang Amadeus, 14, 112, 158, 171, 220, 221, 291, 333
Mozkowski, Moritz, 170
Mullowney, Kathryn, 47
Munford, Robert, 100, 210
Mydtskov, Jørgen, 110, 348

Nabokov, Nicholas, 116, 352
Nagy, Ivan, 40, 95, 104, 118, 127, 158, 166, 323, 328, 336
Nahat, Dennis, 66, 211, 304
National Ballet of Canada, 79, 85, 107, 114, 152, 160, 191, 218, 229, 259, 266, 271, 292, 298, 318, 324, 329
National Ballet of Washington, 50, 84, 88, 92, 95, 101, 104, 118, 121, 151, 160, 169, 179, 194, 199, 229, 241, 247, 263, 292, 296, 298, 305, 313, 324, 328, 332, 337, 343, 347, 356, 360
National Opera Company, 94
Nationale Ballet, Het, 152, 169, 190, 217, 241, 277, 334, 353
Nault, Fernand, 141, 178, 229, 346
Neary, Patricia, 316
Nebrada, Vincente, 158, 247, 289, 291
Neil, Sara, 304
Nelson, Ted, 270
Nemtchinova, Vera, 55
Nerina, Nadia, 59, 95, 143, 170, 180
Netherlands Dance Theatre, 170, 207, 221, 222, 234, 235, 256, 291
Neumeier, John, 114, 115
Neusiedler, 94
Neveux, Georges, 206
New Swedish Ballet, 214
New York City Ballet, 12, 29, 31, 32, 34, 36, 37, 45, 48, 50, 64, 66, 68, 70, 83, 87, 88, 90, 91, 93, 95, 100, 103, 104, 110, 112, 113, 116, 118, 119, 121, 124, 137, 139, 143, 145, 146, 147, 151, 152, 166, 167, 168, 172, 174, 183, 187, 188, 189, 190, 191, 194, 196, 197, 205, 210-14, 217, 219, 220, 228, 240, 245, 249, 253, 255, 263, 265, 268, 272, 285, 286, 288,

289, 292, 294, 297, 305, 307, 308, 309, 310, 312, 315, 316, 317, 328, 332, 333, 335, 338, 340, 349, 350, 352, 353, 355, 356, 358, 360, 363, 365
Nicolaides, Melisa, 108
Nijinska, Bronislava, 8, 54, 55, 79, 82, 141, 181, 226, 298
Nijinsky, Vaslav, 1, 8, 11, 28, 29, 30, 80, 82, 107, 166, 196, 226, 250, 283, 284, 288, 308, 330, 345
Nikiforov, N., 131
Nikitina, Alice, 40
Nikitina, Varvara, 303
Noack, Kjeld, 364
Noël, Jacques, 199
Noguchi, Isamu, 53, 235
Nolan, Sidney, 283
Nordgreen, Erik, 128
Nordoff, Paul, 336
Nørgard, Per, 337
Norman, James, 225
North, Alex, 313
Norwegian National Ballet, 37, 45, 107, 121, 152, 175, 185, 191, 194, 202, 218, 222, 229, 249, 250, 293, 299, 310, 314, 334
Nourrit, Adolphe, 323
Novak, Nina, 262
Novere, Jean Georges, 7, 115
Novikoff, Laurent, 115
Nuitter, Charles, 94
Nureyev, Rudolf, 1, 40, 43, 51, 100, 114, 116, 166, 203, 209, 228, 232, 239, 240, 280, 298, 317, 323, 328
Nye, Palma, 361

Obolenskii, N., 299
Oboukhoff, Anatole, 82
O'Brien, Shaun, 145
Offenbach, Jacques, 60, 153, 177, 335
O'Hearn, Robert, 139, 211, 324
Ogerman, Claus, 304
Oklahoma! (de Mille), 13
Olsen, Paul, 207
Oman, Julia Trevelyan, 123
On the Town (Robbins), 13
On Your Toes (Balanchine), 297
Opus One (Cranko), 14
Oransky, V., 212
Orchésographie (Arbeau), 4, 75
Orff, Carl, 78, 80

Original Ballet Russe, 12, 72, 84, 94, 101, 127, 145, 147, 167, 168, 221, 238, 263
Orlando, Mariane, 28
Orlikowsky, Vaslav, 318
Orloff, Nicholas, 279
Orlov, Alexandre, 252
Orpheus (Balanchine), 18
Orr, Terry, 43, 266, 356
Osato, Sono, 127, 265
Ostrovsky, 366

Pachelbel, Johann, 284
Paganini, Niccolo, 109, 221
Pagava, Ethery, 93
Page, Ruth, 11, 53, 58, 76, 148, 153, 211, 229, 272
Page-Stone Ballet, 153
Palombo, Paul Martin, 126
Panaiev, Michael, 114, 283
Pandor, Miriam, 108
Panufnik, Andrzej, 216
Paredes, Marcos, 127, 158, 173, 289
Paris Opera Ballet, 8, 29, 84, 94, 99, 128, 181, 196, 215, 241, 247, 253, 282, 288, 292, 315, 330, 335
Park, Merle, 166, 232
Parkes, Ross, 358
Parkinson, Georgina, 217
Partos, Oedoen, 222
Paul, Mimi, 155, 166, 185
Paul Taylor Dance Company, 43
Paulli, H.S., 199, 200, 222
Pavlova, Anna, 8, 9, 11, 82, 95, 98, 116, 120, 143, 166, 323, 330
Penaro, Michael, 40
Penderecki, Krzysztof, 80
Pène du Bois, Raoul, 159, 196, 249
Pennsylvania Ballet, 28, 35, 59, 80, 92, 152, 182, 191, 207, 213, 229, 234, 241, 269, 290, 293, 304, 329, 344, 345, 358
Pergolesi, Giovanni Battista, 265
Perrault, Charles, 298
Perrot, Jules, 7, 99, 125, 165, 233, 241, 242
Petersen, Christian, 324
Petersen, Kirsten, 280
Peterson, Kirk, 174, 195, 356
Petipa, Lucien, 165, 239
Petipa, Marie, 303
Petipa, Marius, 7, 8, 43, 50, 94, 95, 115, 160, 228, 232, 239, 268, 298, 316

Petit, Roland, 76, 78, 101, 102, 108, 149, 195, 206, 240, 282, 303, 328
Petroff, Paul, 84
Petrov, Andrei, 101, 296
Petrov, Nicholas, 286
Philadelphia Ballet, 63, 106, 298
Philippart, Nathalie, 35
Picasso, Pablo, 239, 265, 342
Picture of Dorian Gray, The (Wilde), 116
Pillar of Fire (Tudor), 14, 16, 18
Piltz, Marie, 284
Piotrovsky, Andrei, 205
Piper, John, 198, 262
Pitkin, William, 289, 341
Pitoev, Ludmilla, 179
Pitot, Geneviève, 341
Pittsburgh Ballet Theatre, 76, 148, 211, 286, 308
Platoff, Marc, 110, 159, 283
Plisetskaya, Maya, 37, 78, 116, 120, 150, 181, 282, 307, 312, 323, 328, 360
Poe, Edgar Allan, 36
Polunin, E., 51
Polunin, V., 51
Pomonaryov, Vladimir, 269
Pons, Helene, 73
Poole, David, 53, 356
Poole, Dennis, 356
Porcher, Nananne, 28, 220, 304
Poulenc, Francis, 54, 90, 359
Pousseur, Henri, 116
Powell, Ray, 202
Powell, Robert, 80
Preobrajenska, Olga, 8, 166, 322, 330
Prévost, Abbé, 208
Prevost, Robert, 210, 281
Prince, Robert, 224
Prinz, John, 103, 185, 339, 356
Prokofiev, Serge, 36, 84, 155, 173, 189, 249, 263, 276, 277, 311, 347
Prokofieva, Mirra, 311
Prokovsky, André, 66, 356
Prowse, Philip, 51
Pruna, Pedro, 209
Ptushko, A., 297
Pugni, Cesare, 125, 180, 233, 241, 244
Purcell, Henry, 102, 137, 218
Pushkin, Alexander, 34, 67, 98, 149, 262
Pygmalion (Salle), 6

Queneau, Raymond, 101
Quintana, Regina, 103
Quitman, Cleo, 341

Rabovsky, Istvan, 288
Rachmaninoff, Serge, 84, 238, 343
Radunsky, Alexander, 180, 317
Ralov, Borge, 253, 335
Ralov, Kirsten, 140, 149, 335, 361
Rangstrom, Ture, 215
Rapee, Erno, 34
Raph, Alan, 284, 347
Rassine, Alexis, 180, 303
Rausch, Carlos, 122
Rauschenberg, Robert, 315
Ravel, Maurice, 52, 63, 84, 106, 218,
    290, 353
Raverat, Gwendolen, 198
Raysse, Martial, 240
Read, John B., 159
Redpath, Christine, 36, 285
Reed, Janet, 64, 71, 111, 137, 145, 188,
    191, 195, 197, 219, 255, 363
Reed, Ramon, 343
Reiman, Elise, 152, 335
Reinach, Baron de, 330
Reisinger, Julius, 316
Renault, Michael, 335
Rencher, Derek, 123, 209
Reppa, David, 360
Respighi, Ottorino, 64, 343
Reyes, Rafael, 159
Rhodes, Lawrence, 28, 170, 217, 234,
    291, 304, 345, 356
Riabouchinska, Tatiana, 9, 52, 83, 86,
    99, 169, 261
Rianne, Patricia, 336
Rice, Peter, 272, 277
Richter, Marga, 27
Rickabaugh, Clive, 153
Riera, Rodrigo, 359
Rieti, Vittorio, 71, 221, 305
Riisager, Knudage, 128, 202, 217
Rimbaud, Arthur, 183
Rimsky-Korsakov, Nicolai, 73, 98, 183,
    286
Rittman, Trude, 59, 150
Ritz, Roger, 335
Robbins, Jerome, 12, 29-32, 36, 48, 62,
    64, 68, 90, 103, 112, 118, 119, 130,
    134, 137, 146, 150, 167, 172, 178,
    186, 220, 222, 226, 252, 255, 259,
    265, 266, 288, 312, 313, 344, 360

Robert Joffrey Ballet, 70, 140, 157, 186,
    232, 244, 281, 290, 359
Rodeo (de Mille), 12, 15
Roderigues, Beatrice, 129
Rodgers, Richard, 159, 297
Rodham, Robert, 213, 229
Rodrigues, Alfred, 60
Roerich, Nicholas, 261, 283
Roger, Edith, 175
Roland Petit's Ballets de Paris, 76, 102,
    109, 118, 149, 206
Romanoff, Dimitri, 62
Rosati, Carolina, 241
Rose, Jürgen, 85, 91, 128, 260, 277,
    317
Rosenberg, Hilding, 28
Rosenthal, Jean, 29, 68, 173, 237, 354,
    366
Rosenthal, Lawrence, 366
Ross, Bertram, 125
Ross, Herbert, 73, 207
Rossini, Gioacchino, 64, 88, 93, 350,
    365
Rostand, Edmond, 103
Rouault, Georges, 263
Roustan, Joelle, 27, 146, 149, 226
Royal Ballet, 13, 29, 32, 35, 37, 45, 51,
    54, 67, 85, 91, 100, 103, 117, 123,
    140, 141, 160, 170, 189, 191, 193,
    194, 207, 208, 209, 216, 222, 228,
    233, 240, 248, 250, 260, 263, 277,
    283, 292, 295, 298, 303, 304, 317,
    330, 342, 347, 349, 353
Royal Danish Ballet, 6, 29, 37, 43, 44,
    51, 60, 63, 64, 83, 94, 103, 104, 110,
    117, 128, 137, 139, 141, 149, 152,
    155, 160, 169, 191, 194, 199, 200,
    201, 202, 204, 214, 216, 217, 218,
    222, 234, 241, 249, 250, 256, 277,
    292, 298, 305, 318, 324, 328, 334,
    337, 343, 348, 357, 362, 363
Royal Swedish Ballet, 28, 35, 43, 94,
    107, 122, 130, 146, 152, 160, 200,
    202, 210, 215, 216, 250, 263, 283,
    293, 297, 299, 324, 329, 334, 340,
    342
Royal Winnipeg Ballet, 13, 33, 59, 72,
    102, 122, 194, 201, 222, 235, 238,
    241, 246, 270, 281, 291, 296, 365,
    366
Rubé, 330
Rubinstein, Ida, 63, 288
Rupert and Puhma, 174

Russian Imperial Ballet, 7, 50, 79, 82, 84, 94, 99, 115, 180, 228, 238, 268, 298, 316, 328, 330
Ruth Page Chicago Opera Ballet, 204, 211, 272
Ruth Page's International Ballet, 76, 182, 229
Rutherford, Richard, 210
Ryberg, Flemming, 362
Ryder, Mark, 310
Ryga, George, 122
Ryndin, Vadim, 203, 225
Ryzhenko, Natalia, 37

Sackett, Francis, 285
Saddler, Donald, 62, 259, 341
Sadler's Wells Ballet, 9, 13, 40, 45, 48, 58, 84, 95, 105, 106, 113, 114, 115, 130, 145, 147, 160, 167, 172, 179, 198, 201, 206, 214, 228, 246, 247, 262, 265, 266, 271, 273, 286, 298, 303, 316, 328, 330, 333
Sadler's Wells Theatre Ballet, 41, 53, 60, 75, 95, 104, 176, 201, 259, 265, 271, 303, 328
Sadoff, Simon, 218
St. Claire, Marian, 336
St. Denis, Ruth, 11
Saint-George, Vernoy de, 160
Saint Laurent, Yves, 102, 282
Saint-Léon, Arthur, 94, 95, 180
Saint-Saens, Camille, 120, 189
Salin, Timo, 316
Salle, Marie, 5, 6
Samuel, Gerhard, 270
San Francisco Ballet, 11, 37, 88, 89, 92, 197, 317
Sand, George, 131
Sand, Inge, 98, 280, 335
Sandberg, Herbert, 210
Sangalli, Rita, 10, 330
Sanjust, Filippo, 114
Sanlaville, Marie, 349
Santa Fe Opera Ballet, 248
Sappington, Margo, 341, 362
Saroyan, William, 171
Sarry, Christine, 43, 100, 173, 186, 276
Satie, Erik, 216, 239
Sauget, Henri, 81, 149, 215
La Scala Opera Ballet, 48, 353
Scandinavian Ballet, 324
Scarlatti, Domenico, 222, 337
Scevers, Robert, 343
Schanne, Margrethe, 328, 335

Schaufuss, Frank, 280, 335, 357
Schiffman, Byron, 36
Schnitzhoeffer, Jean, 323
Schönberg, Arnold, 66, 129, 256
School of American Ballet, 11, 292
Schorer, Suki, 174
Schubert, Franz, 71, 108, 125, 200, 289, 352
Schuller, Gunther, 346
Schulte, Edward, 91
Schuman, William, 350
Schumann, Robert, 79, 110, 127, 129
Schwezoff, Igor, 127
Scott, Dorothy, 109
Scottish National Ballet, 336
Scriabin, Alexander, 84, 116, 260
Searle, Humphrey, 209
Sebastian, Stuart, 356
Segerstrom, Per Arthur, 28
Seiber, Matyas, 189
Seligman, Kurt, 151
Selling, Caj, 28
Selvinskaya, T., 53
Semenov, Simon, 95, 178
Sergava, Katherine, 244
Sergeyev, Konstantin, 67, 95, 111, 173, 246, 298
Sergeyev, Nicolai, 160, 228, 298, 316
Serrano, Lupe, 202, 245
Serrette, Francois, 182
Seter, Mordecai, 272
Seymour, Lynn, 36, 189, 349
Shabelevski, Yurek, 84, 262, 288
Shahn, Ben, 224
Shakespeare, William, 117, 212, 277, 337
Shaler, Bette, 345
Sharaff, Irene, 29, 90, 109, 130, 137, 187, 194
Sharer, Hugh, 41
Shaw, Brian, 59, 180, 217
Shchedron, Rodion, 37, 180
Shea, Mary Jane, 93, 219
Shearer, Moira, 86, 130, 206, 303, 336, 361
Sherwood, Gary, 347
Shollar, Ludmilla, 79, 196
Shostakovitch, Dmitri, 49, 63, 91, 168, 203, 205, 282, 366
Sibley, Antoinette, 36, 117, 193, 209, 217, 232, 280, 323, 347
Sierra, Martinez, 342
Silich, Lubov, 299
Silverman, Robert, 249

Simmons, Stanley, 42, 87, 94, 100, 120, 150, 173, 201, 210, 266, 276, 289, 366
Simone, Kirsten, 328
Singleton, Trinette, 42
Sitwell, Edith, 130
Skeaping, Mary, 102
Skelton, Thomas, 41, 43, 188, 199, 291
Skibine, George, 34, 36, 93, 127, 151, 182, 247, 262
Skouratoff, Vladimir, 170
Slavenska, Mia, 48, 155, 288, 295, 314
Slavenska-Franklin Ballet, 313
Sleeping Beauty, The, 7, 11, 15
Slonimsky, Yuri, 246, 296, 366
Smirnov, V., 63
Smirnov-Golovanov, Vladimir, 37
Smith, George Washington, 10, 11
Smith, Lew, 273
Smith, Oliver, 31, 130, 131, 134, 173, 187, 233, 274, 291, 317
Smuin, Michael, 127, 155, 158, 266, 289
Sobeshamskaya, 116
Sobotka, Ruth, 68
Sokolova, Lydia, 284
Sokolow, Anna, 179, 235
Solly, William, 281
Soloviev-Sedoi, Vassily, 338
Soloviov, V., 131
Somes, Michael, 59, 86, 105, 107, 148, 180, 206, 209, 233, 248, 286, 332, 333
Sommers, Harry, 201
Sorkin, Naomi, 292
Sorrell, Patricia, 101
Soudekine, Serge, 141, 238
Sousa, John Philip, 309
Sovey, Raymond, 107
Sowinski, John, 186, 207, 266
Speramsky, P., 297
Spessivtzeva, Olga, 166, 303, 323
Squadron, Lorraine, 291
Staats, Leo, 330
Starer, Robert, 358
Starzhenetskaya, T., 131
Steere, James, 67
Stein, Gertrude, 361
Steinberg, Saul, 90
Steinbrenner, Wilfried, 76
Stengerb, Yevgeny, 349
Stevenson, Ben, 49, 85, 101, 174, 298, 343
Stevenson, Hugh, 155, 167, 191, 316
Stevenson, Robert, 118

Stirling, Christina, 186
Stockhausen, Karlheinz, 140, 221
Stoffer, Yakhov, 269
Stokvis, Joop, 170
Stolze, Kurt-Heinz, 128, 337
Stone, Bentley, 153
Stone, Cynthia, 316
Stowell, Kent, 66
Strahammer, Silvia, 121
Strauss, Jr., Johann, 51, 84, 148, 168
Strauss, Sr., Johann, 199
Strauss, Richard, 64, 110, 114, 120, 339, 345, 350
Stravinsky, Igor, 32, 37, 45, 68, 83, 84, 88, 104, 118, 119, 121, 145, 179, 194, 196, 217, 220, 226, 235, 248, 250, 265, 266, 283, 284, 286, 288, 304, 312, 335, 358
Stravinsky, Soulima, 222
Stravinsky, Vera, 248
Strayhorn, Billy, 273
Strindberg, August, 216
Stripling, Jan, 260
Strogonova, Nina, 244, 250
Stuttgart Ballet, 32, 35, 37, 68, 76, 95, 106, 121, 126, 129, 160, 178, 194, 216, 220, 228, 234, 235, 260, 277, 285, 286, 290, 299, 317, 329, 337, 353, 359
Subotnick, Morton, 123
Sullivan, Arthur, 259
Sultzbach, Russell, 270
Sumner, Carol, 185, 316
Surinach, Carlos, 140
Sutherland, Paul, 290
Svetlova, Marina, 127
Swan Lake, 7, 15, 18
Sylbert, Paul, 78
La Sylphide, 7
Synge, John Millington, 345
Szyfer, J.E., 181

Tagirov, Gai, 297
Taglioni, Marie, 5, 165, 241, 323, 327, 328, 329, 365
Taglioni, Philippe, 7, 116, 323, 327, 365
Tal, Josed, 357
Talin, Nikita, 268
Tallchief, Maria, 35, 40, 48, 49, 64, 93, 112, 147, 152, 155, 232, 237, 241, 246, 256, 265, 288, 290, 294, 306, 323, 332, 335
Tallchief, Marjorie, 36, 93, 151, 182
Tamiris, Helen, 12

Tanner, Richard, 313
Tanning, Dorothea, 305
Tansman, 55
Tarakanova, Nina, 155
Taras, John, 71, 109, 121, 171, 196, 255, 286, 305, 313
Taylor, Burton, 129
Taylor, Paul, 43, 125
Tchaikovsky, Peter Ilyich, 7, 34, 36, 43, 45, 48, 84, 109, 128, 172, 197, 211, 226, 228, 232, 260, 272, 292, 298, 315, 316, 338, 339, 345
Tchelitcheff, Paul, 125, 284
Tchernicheva, Lubov, 40, 55, 145, 288, 342
Ter-Arutunian, Rouben, 28, 36, 59, 80, 83, 100, 119, 145, 174, 256, 270, 272, 294, 304, 307, 317, 345, 356
Terechkovich, Constantine, 83
Terekoff, Miguel, 151
Tetley, Glen, 78, 123, 140, 159, 202, 221, 222, 256, 272, 285, 359
Tharp, Twyla, 42
Theilade, Nini, 285, 295
Thomas, Ambroise, 213
Thompson, Frank, 100, 166, 179, 339
Thompson, Woodman, 339
Thomson, Poul Arnt, 348
Thorberg, Vivi, 364
Thulin, Karin, 316
Tiger, Jerome, 151
Tikhomirov, Vasily, 50, 269
Timofeyeva, Nina, 312, 323
Tipton, Jennifer, 42, 101, 119, 167, 179, 270, 276, 292, 347, 362
Tischenko, Boris, 349
Tobias, Roy, 33, 113, 255
Tolstoy, Leo, 37
Tomasson, Helgi, 36, 72, 110, 120, 168, 170, 335, 356
Tommasini, Vincenzo, 109
Tompkins, Beatrice, 71, 152, 335
Toms, Carl, 317
Topaz, Muriel, 108
Toradze, David, 168
Torto, Linda, 228
Toumonova, Tamara, 9, 120, 127, 253, 323, 334, 335, 342, 358
Tourel, Jennie, 346
Townshend, Peter, 346
Toye, Geoffrey, 175
Tracy, Paula, 173
Trautvetter, Paul, 346

Le Triomphe de l'Amour, 5
Troll, Robert, 101
Trounson, Marilyn, 193
Truscott, John, 318
Tseitlin, A., 49
Tsenin, A., 203
Tudor, Antony, 12, 13, 62, 107, 110, 111, 122, 155, 157, 171, 191, 198, 199, 256, 277, 279, 295, 350
Turnbull, Julia, 10
Turner, Harold, 76, 232, 247, 268

Ulanova, Galina, 67, 83, 86, 120, 150, 166, 277, 280, 323
Union Pacific (Massine), 12
Unsworth, Peter, 347
Uthoff, Ernst, 56
Uthoff, Michael, 67, 72, 93, 105, 226, 229, 249, 366

Vagonova, Agrippina, 50
Vainonen, Vasily, 148, 168, 181
Valls, Manuel, 292
Van Dantzig, 199, 217, 277
van der Waal, Jan, 235
van Druten, John, 350
Van Dyk, Peter, 286, 352
Van Grove, Isaac, 76, 148, 211
Van Hamel, Martine, 159
Van Leersum, Emmy, 221
Van Manen, Hans, 221, 234, 235
van Praagh, Peggy, 157, 193
van Schayk, Toer, 199, 217
Vance, Norma, 109
Vangsaa, Mona, 218, 280, 335
Vanno, I., 297
Vasilenko, Sergei, 198
Vasilieva, Vera, 203
Vasiliev, Vladimir, 101, 283, 312
Vaudoyer, J.L., 307
Vaughn Williams, Ralph, 139, 198
Vecheslova, Tatiana, 176, 338
Vendrig, Yvonne, 217
Venza, Jac, 80, 140
Verchinina, Nina, 84, 261
Verdi, Giuseppe, 201, 272
Verdy, Violette, 103, 125, 150, 166, 188, 197, 205, 213, 214, 216, 266, 339
Verso, Edward, 173
Vertès, Marcel, 60, 77
Vesak, Norbert, 122
Vestris, Auguste, 7, 200

Vestris, Gaetan, 7
Vezina, Paul, 346
Vic-Wells Ballet, 9, 59, 81, 95, 107, 175, 361
Vidal, Georgina, 266
Vigano, Salvatore, 7
Vigeland, Gustav, 185
Villella, Edward, 66, 68, 103, 166, 174, 197, 213, 265, 266, 315, 335, 338, 339, 360
Villon, François, 358
Vilzak, Anatole, 55, 114
Virsaladze, Simon, 84, 176, 189, 203, 298, 307, 311, 317
Vivaldi, Antonio, 93, 126, 185, 207, 249, 285, 308, 359
Vladimirov, Pierre, 303
Vladimirov, Yuri, 189
Vlasov, V., 297
Volkov, Boris, 181, 212
Volkov, Nikolai, 149, 173, 262, 307
Von Aroldingen, Karin, 168, 185, 357, 358, 365
Von Rosen, Elsa-Marianne, 102, 216, 318, 324
Vroom, Jean-Paul, 221, 234
Vsevolojsky, Ivan, 298
Vyroubova, Nina, 328

Wagner, Richard, 44, 270, 353
Wakhevitch, Georges, 102, 118, 195, 211
Walbom, Emilie, 117
Walczak, Barbara, 33
Walden, Stanley, 362
Walker, David, 85
Walker, Norman, 80, 225
Wall, David, 209
Wall, Edmund, 255
Walton, William, 130
Warburg, Edward M.M., 11
Ward, Charles, 159
Ward-Steinman, David, 341
Waring, James, 88, 95
Warlock, Peter, 75
Watts, Jonathan, 33, 113, 125, 129, 205, 271
Wayne, Dennis, 58, 292, 356
Weber, Carl Maria von, 307
Weber, Diana, 266
Webern, Anton, 124, 186, 234
Weidman, Charles, 12, 296
Weill, Kurt, 198, 294

Weinberg, Chester, 42
Weiss, Robert, 335
Wellein, Lillian, 245
Wennergren, Lena, 316
Weschler, Anita, 129
Westerik, Co, 235
Western Theatre Ballet, 178, 314, 352
Weston, Alice, 126
Whistler, Rex, 267
White, Miles, 131
Whitman, Walt, 174
The Who, 346
Whyte, Ian, 113
Wich, Harri, 249
Wiedersheim, Annette, 282
Wiener Staatsoper Ballet, 37, 317
Wiinblad, Bjørn, 44
Wijnberg, Nicholas, 207
Wilcox, Virginia, 111
Wilde, Patricia, 40, 71, 93, 112, 113, 191, 245, 290, 309, 363
Williams, E. Virginia, 228
Williams, Peter, 276
Williams, S., 122
Williams, Stanley, 280, 335
Williams, Tennessee, 313, 341
Williamson, Sonny Boy, 346
Wilson, R. Marshall, 126
Wilson, Ronald, 314
Wilson, Sallie, 125, 134, 158, 259, 286
Wittop, Freddy, 317
Woizikowski, Leon, 261, 262, 342
Wood, Marilyn, 316
Workman, Jenny, 75, 175, 276
Wright, Peter, 160
Wright, Rayburn, 138
Wright, Rebecca, 362

Xenakis, Iannis, 212, 227

Yakobson, Leonid, 53, 84, 168, 297, 307, 349
Yarullian, Farid, 297
Yazvinsky, Jean, 262
Yepishin, G., 203
Yershov, Pyotr, 180
Yodice, Robert, 284
Yourth, Lynda, 335
Yunovich, Sofia, 173
Youskevitch, Igor, 30, 39, 82, 155, 166, 195, 279, 283, 294, 295, 308, 314, 323, 340

Zakharov, Rostislav, 67, 84, 149, 206, 269
Zbarsky, F., 53
Zhdanov, Yuri, 278
Zhukov, Leonid, 297
Zilbershtein, I., 262
Zippel, Dorothea, 67, 194

Zipprodt, Patricia, 118, 119, 305, 360
Zomosa, Maximilian, 42, 172
Zompakos, Stanley, 145
Zorina, Vera, 40, 84, 125, 248
Zoritch, George, 30, 110, 155, 308
Zucchi, Virginia, 7, 8
Zullig, Hans, 56